BESTSELLING
BOOK SERIES

Parenting For Dummies®

Cheat Sheet

Your age-by-age sleep guide

Age	Hours of Daytime Sleep	Hours of Night-Time Sleep
1 week	8	8.5
4 weeks	6.75	8.75
3 months	5	10
6 months	4	10
9 months	2.75	11.25
12 months	2.5	11.5
2 years	1.25	11.75
3 years	1 or 0	11 to 11.5
4 years	0	11.5
5 years	0	11
6 years	0	10.75
7 years	0	10.5
8 years	0	10.25
9 years	0	10

Adapted with thanks from Solving Children's Sleep Problems by Lyn Quine
(Beckett Karlson £12.99)

Meaningful milestones

- **First smile:** 6 to 12 weeks
- **First roll-over:** 3 to 6 months
- **First sit:** 6 to 9 months
- **First crawl:** 9 to 12 months
- **First words:** 10 to 12 months
- **First steps:** 12 to 18 months
- **First tantrum:** 18 months to 2 years
- **First pants:** 2 to 3 years
- **First bike:** 4 to 5 years
- **First lie:** 5 to 6 years
- **First 'big' teeth:** 6 to 7 years
- **First brewing of cup of tea for grateful parent:** 7 to 8 years
- **First solo road-crossing:** 8 to 9 years

Ten ways to keep your cool

- Find your deep voice
- Count to ten
- Ignore the small stuff
- Respect the clock
- Give yourself time out
- Explain what you expect
- Remember how old they are (or not)
- Say how you feel
- Say yes (sneakily)
- See the funny side

The five golden mantras great parents repeat every day

- **'Onwards and upwards':** tomorrow is another day
- **'Don't forget to laugh':** find the funny side (there usually *is* one – honest!)
- **'Once more, with feeling':** a little extra energy can make all the difference
- **'Guilt gets you nowhere':** you're doing the best you can
- **'It's a phase':** and it will pass – really

Is your child having a rough patch?

Stage	Most-Settled Phases (on average)	Most-Unsettled Phases (on average)
Baby	4, 16, 28, 40, 52 weeks	8, 20, 32, 44 weeks
Toddler	1, 2, and 3 years	18 and 21 months, 2¼ years
Preschooler	3 and 5 years	
Schoolchild	5, 7, and 9 years	

D1380147

For Dummies: Bestselling Book Series For Beginners

Parenting For Dummies®

Why me-time's not a crime

(a)

(b)

(a) Mum takes time for herself; kids looking good.
(b) Mum bent out of shape; kids in a mess.

Should you call a doctor? The 7 'yes' signs

- ✔ **High fever:** If he's under 3 months old or he's had it for 48 hours.
- ✔ **Difficulty breathing:** Especially if he is panting or rasping.
- ✔ **Vomiting:** If it's violent, blood-stained, or has continued for more than 12 hours.
- ✔ **Dehydration:** Signs include sunken eyes, dry nappies, and a dry mouth.
- ✔ **Seizures:** Especially if he's never had one before.
- ✔ **Extreme change of behaviour:** Including inconsolable crying and excessive drowsiness.
- ✔ **Rash:** Especially if it doesn't fade when pressed with a glass or is itchy and spreading.

For Dummies: Bestselling Book Series for Beginners

by Helen Brown
Senior Editor, Boots Parenting Club magazines

John Wiley & Sons, Ltd

Parenting For Dummies®

Published by
John Wiley & Sons, Ltd
The Atrium
Southern Gate
Chichester
West Sussex
PO19 8SQ
England

E-mail (for orders and customer service enquires): cs-books@wiley.co.uk

Visit our Home Page on www.wiley.com

Copyright © 2007 John Wiley & Sons, Ltd, Chichester, West Sussex, England

Published by John Wiley & Sons, Ltd, Chichester, West Sussex

For general information on our other products and services, please contact our Customer Care Department within the U.S. at 800-762-2974, outside the U.S. at 317-572-3993, or fax 317-572-4002.

For technical support, please visit www.wiley.com/techsupport.

Wiley also publishes its books in a variety of electronic formats. Some content that appears in print may not be available in electronic books.

British Library Cataloguing in Publication Data: A catalogue record for this book is available from the British Library

ISBN-13: 978-0-470-02714-1

Printed and bound in Great Britain by Bell & Bain, Ltd, Glasgow

10 9 8 7 6 5 4 3 2

WILEY

About the Author

Helen Brown is a freelance journalist, who's been writing about parenting for many years. She's been Consumer Editor of *Pregnancy & Birth*, Parenting Editor of *She*, and a judge of the Booktrust Early Years Awards. She writes regularly for *Mother & Baby* magazine and has recently helped develop and launch a series of parenting magazines for Boots. She lives in north London with her husband and their three sons, aged 8, 6 and 2.

Dedication

For Ben, Tom, and Ed, for the smiles they spread. And for Tim, who always points out the best bits.

Author's Acknowledgments

I would like to thank Alison Yates at John Wiley & Sons, Ltd, for commissioning me to write this book even though she'd originally had me in mind for something far less ambitious! Many, many thanks, too, to the whole production team at Wiley, especially Simon Bell (father of two) for his patience and humour, Tracy Barr (mother of four) for her wonderfully wise and witty editing, Kate O'Leary (mother of three) for her meticulous subbing and Eileen Hayes (mother of four) for her critical eye and expert advice.

I'd like to thank Professor Lyn Quine, author of *Solving Children's Sleep Problems* and the estate of the late Dr Louise Bates Ames, author of *Raising Good Kids*, for permission to adapt charts from their wonderful books.

Thanks also to all the parents I've admired and learnt so much from – whether I've known you for years or just watched you once with your kids in the park. And to everyone in the Brown family and the Mills family, for encouraging, supporting and goading me on, and even managing to look sympathetic when I whinged. Special mention must go to Ben, Tom, and Ed, for their ever more inventive ways of getting me to open the office door and 'do something less boring instead'.

Publisher's Acknowledgments

We're proud of this book; please send us your comments through our Dummies online registration form located at www.dummies.com/register/.

Some of the people who helped bring this book to market include the following:

Acquisitions, Editorial, and Media Development

Project Editor: Simon Bell

Commissioning Editor: Alison Yates

Copy Editors: Kate O'Leary

Technical Editor: Eileen Hayes

Executive Editor: Jason Dunne

Executive Project Editor: Martin Tribe

Cover Photo: JupiterImages/BananaStock

Cartoons: Ed McLachlan

Composition Services

Project Coordinator: Jennifer Theriot

Layout and Graphics: Carl Byers, Denny Hager, Stephanie D. Jumper, Heather Ryan

Proofreaders: Jessica Kramer, Susan Moritz, Charles Spencer

Indexer: Techbooks

Publishing and Editorial for Consumer Dummies

    Diane Graves Steele, Vice President and Publisher, Consumer Dummies

    Joyce Pepple, Acquisitions Director, Consumer Dummies

    Kristin A. Cocks, Product Development Director, Consumer Dummies

    Michael Spring, Vice President and Publisher, Travel

    Kelly Regan, Editorial Director, Travel

Publishing for Technology Dummies

    Andy Cummings, Vice President and Publisher, Dummies Technology/General User

Composition Services

    Gerry Fahey, Vice President of Production Services

    Debbie Stailey, Director of Composition Services

Contents at a Glance

Introduction 1

Part I: All About You: What Every Parent Should Know 7
Chapter 1: Help! Where Do I Start? The Basics 9
Chapter 2: You're in Charge: Setting Boundaries 17
Chapter 3: You Are Not Alone: Massing the Troops 25
Chapter 4: Other Secrets of Great Parenting 35
Chapter 5: Childminders, Nurseries, and Nannies 43

Part II: All About Babies 57
Chapter 6: Surviving, Thriving, and Diving In:
   Getting Accustomed to Having a Baby 59
Chapter 7: Mmmm, Mmmm, Good: Feeding Baby 75
Chapter 8: Moving on to Solids 93
Chapter 9: Sweet Dreams: Getting Baby to Sleep 103
Chapter 10: Playing, Learning, and Socialising 117
Chapter 11: Keeping Baby Healthy 131

Part III: All About Toddlers 145
Chapter 12: Potty-Training 147
Chapter 13: Tantrum Tactics 165
Chapter 14: Food and Sleep 173
Chapter 15: Keeping Your Toddler Safe 191
Chapter 16: Playing, Learning, and Socialising 203

Part IV: All About Preschoolers 217
Chapter 17: Behaviour and Discipline 219
Chapter 18: Food Fights and Sleep Frights..231
Chapter 19: Playing, Learning, and Socialising 243
Chapter 20: Heading to Preschool..255

Part V: All About Schoolies..265
Chapter 21: Starting School 267
Chapter 22: Eating, Sleeping, and Staying Healthy..............................281
Chapter 23: Behaviour and Responsibility 293
Chapter 24: Friends, Self, and the World Beyond.................................305

Part VI: All About Siblings 317

Chapter 25: The New Arrival 319

Chapter 26: Squabble Solutions 329

Chapter 27: Loving Them All the Same 337

Part VII: The Part of Tens 347

Chapter 28: Ten Ways to Keep Your Cool 349

Chapter 29: Ten First-Aid Must-Knows 353

Chapter 30: Ten Things You Need For Your Baby
(And Ten Things You Don't) 357

Index 367

Table of Contents

Introduction *1*

About This Book...1
What You're Not to Read 2
Foolish Assumptions 2
Conventions Used in This Book 2
How This Book Is Organised...2
    Part I: All About You: What Every Parent Should Know 3
    Part II: All About Babies...3
    Part III: All About Toddlers 3
    Part IV: All About Preschoolers 3
    Part V: All About Schoolies 4
    Part VI: All About Siblings 4
    Part VII: The Part of Tens 4
Icons Used in This Book 4
Where to Go from Here...5

Part 1: All About You: What Every Parent Should Know 7

Chapter 1: Help! Where Do I Start? The Basics 9

Knowing Your Child: Ages and Stages 10
    Baby 10
    Toddler 10
    Preschooler 11
    Schoolchild 11
    Oh, and watch for the funny bits....................................12
Knowing Yourself 12
    Your role: Parts all parents should play 13
    Your goals: Hopes all parents have.................................13
    Your fears: Worries all parents share...............................14
Don't Panic – It All Comes Together in the End!.................14

Chapter 2: You're in Charge: Setting Boundaries 17

Boundary Basics 17
    Understanding why boundaries work
        (even when they're broken) 18
    Setting boundaries wisely 18
    Strict? Easy going? What's your parenting style? 19
Toeing the Line: Making Boundaries Work 20
    Being clear, certain, and consistent................................20
    Making it cool to do the right thing 21

Spelling out the consequences 22
Following through 22
Great ways to minimise boundary-breaking...............................23
Moving on: Reshaping boundaries together................................24

Chapter 3: You Are Not Alone: Massing the Troops 25

Working with Your Partner 25
Discovering the truth about kids and relationships...................26
Sharing the load..26
'But Daddy said . . .': Presenting a united parenting front 27
Finding time to be together...28
Working with Other Parents 29
Why what they say can keep you sane.......................................30
And when you're better off not listening...................................30
A word about mothers – and mothers-in-law 31
Single but Not Solo..32
Finding back-up 32
Choosing mentors 33
Step-parenting: Raising a 'blended' family................................33

Chapter 4: Other Secrets of Great Parenting 35

Right Way? Wrong Way? Your Way...35
Big-Picture Parenting: Eight Skills That Will Serve You for Years 36
Avoiding the Common Parenting Pitfalls 38
Comparing and contrasting 38
Over-parenting..39
Setting too much store by stuff 39
Five Golden Mantras Great Parents Repeat Every Day 40
'Onwards and upwards'...40
'Don't forget to laugh' 40
'Once more, with feeling'..41
'Guilt gets you nowhere' 41
'It's a phase'..41
Horrid comments even good parents hear...42

Chapter 5: Childminders, Nurseries, and Nannies 43

Choosing the Right Option for You..43
The day nursery 44
The childminder 44
The nanny..45
The granny 46
Finding the Right People for the Job 47
Going on a nursery hunt?...47
Going on a childminder hunt? 49
Going on a nanny hunt?..50
And when they're older? 52
Separation and Settling In 53

The Wise Parent's Guide to Childcare 54
Back to Work...54
    The practicalities: Sorted! 55
    The guilt: Busted!..55

Part II: All About Babies 57

**Chapter 6: Surviving, Thriving, and Diving In:
Getting Accustomed to Having a Baby** 59
    The First Six Weeks 59
        Fasten on your L-plates 60
        Tear up the to-do list..60
        Jump at all offers of help 60
    Why Didn't Anyone Tell Me?...61
        He looks so weird! 61
        He cries such a lot..61
        It's a boy/girl thing: clinginess...63
        I can't handle this tiredness...64
        He's suddenly so hungry 64
        Heated debate: Dummies – good or bad?..........................64
    Holding Patterns...66
        Fab or fad? Attachment parenting.....................................67
    Nappy Know-how 67
        Disposables or reusables?...67
        Changing-mat rules and ruses 68
        Blotchy bottoms 69
    Settling In: Life after Six Weeks..69
        The beginnings of routine 70
        Getting out and about..70
        Eight things never to leave the house without....................71
    Looking After Yourself...71
        Making some me-time 72
        Coping? Of course I'm coping! 72
    Looking After Your Relationship 72
        Tiff triggers and how to avoid them....................................73
        The four rules of relationship rehab 74

Chapter 7: Mmmm, Mmmm, Good: Feeding Baby 75
    The Truth about Breastfeeding 75
        Why breastfeeding's great...76
        Why breastfeeding's hard..76
        Breastfeeding myths: busted 77
        Giving breastfeeding your best shot...................................78
        How to breastfeed 79
        What to do when your milk 'comes in' 81
        Why we give up – and how to avoid it 81
        Throwing up all over: reflux explained.............................83

Supplementary bottles 84
Express yourself: A guide to the breast pump 85
Doing it in public 86
Doing it and working 87
Weaning from the breast 87
The Truth about Bottlefeeding...88
Vital safety facts 89
Overfeeding and weight charts 90
The breastfed baby who won't take a bottle 90
There She Blows! The Strange New Art of Winding.......................91

Chapter 8: Moving on to Solids **93**
When to Start Solids 93
Letting the Food Fun Begin 95
Getting ready: Spoons and bowls and other essentials 95
Grub's up! Loading the spoon 96
Open wide: Here it comes! 97
Beyond First Bites: Purée and Simple 98
Baby-led weaning 100
Being a Food Whizz...100
Allergy Alert: Signs to Watch For 101
Up for the Cup?..101

Chapter 9: Sweet Dreams: Getting Baby to Sleep **103**
What's Normal? 103
Safe Sleeping..104
The family bed 105
Distinguishing Night and Day 106
A word about naps 107
And So to Bed 108
Creating the ritual: Bath, cuddle, bed.................................108
Here's the rub: Massage magic 109
Soothing ideas 110
Beware the bad bed habits 110
Sleeping bags 111
Sleeping Through: Teaching Baby to Self-Calm............................111
A room of his own 112
Wailing in the Wee Hours 113
Hungry cry? Scared cry? Hurt cry?......................................113
What to do when it happens again (1) 114
What to do when it happens again (2) 115
When enough's enough: Time to get tough 115

Chapter 10: Playing, Learning, and Socialising **117**
Big Movements for Little Babies 117
Tummy time 118
And . . . sit! 119
Doing the locomotion 119

Shake, Rattle, and Roll: The Truth about Baby Toys 121
Baby Talk, Buddy Talk: Developing Early Language and Social Skills ...123
  Coochy-coo: Why baby chat works 123
  Baby signing..124
  Do I know you? Becoming aware of self and others 125
  It's a boy/girl thing: girls talk; boys walk..........................126
Six Cool Things New Mums Should Do (Eventually) 127
Over-stimulating (and How to Avoid It) 128
On or Off? Babies and TV 129

Chapter 11: Keeping Baby Healthy **131**
Newborn Niggles and Teething Twinges 131
  Cradle cap 131
  Oral thrush 132
  Nappy rash 132
  Teething pains...132
Vaccinations: What You Need to Know 133
  The vaccination programme 133
  The heated debate: To jab or not to jab? 134
  Making jabs less of a pain..135
  Seven ways to boost your baby's health...........................135
What to Do When Your Baby is Ill 136
  Fever...136
  Vomiting and diarrhoea 137
  Coughs and colds 137
  Spots and rashes 138
  Common infectious illnesses 139
  Meningitis: The need-to-know facts 141
Allergies, Asthma, and Eczema 141
  Allergies 142
  Eczema...142
  Asthma...143
  Protecting your child in the sun.....................................144

Part III: All About Toddlers **145**

Chapter 12: Potty-Training **147**
Why Potty-Training's Easier Than You Think –
And How We Make It Harder 147
Realistic Expectations 148
  When to try for dry days...149
  When to try for dry nights 149
  Natural infant hygiene 150
Potty Preparations 150
  The warm-up 150
  Is your child ready?...151
  Are you ready?...152

Got the props? 153
Pick a method, any method 153
Okay, Let's Go! Potty-Training Boot Camp, Day One 154
How to make it easy pees-y for her.....................155
How to make it easy pees-y for you 155
Nappies and naps 156
Accidents will happen 156
Now wash your hands 157
So, how did it go? 157
The ups and downs of pull-ups 157
You're Almost There: Beyond Day One 158
Venturing outside 158
Letting her take the lead......................................159
Using the big toilet 160
'I can wipe my own bottom' 160
'I want to stand up like Dad' 160
Dealing with Setbacks...161
Poo refusal 161
Regression 162
The tough nut 162
Nappyless Nights: Worth the Wait 163

Chapter 13: Tantrum Tactics 165
What Lies Beneath: The Toddler Tantrum Explained............165
The beginner-level tantrum 166
The intermediate-level tantrum 166
Reacting with a Bomb, er, Aplomb....................................166
Staying cool: Chill skills you need to know 166
Being firm: It's what he wants (really) 167
Your Anti-scream Action Plan..168
Spotting the tantrum triggers (and why you're
probably one of them) 168
Heading off the meltdown 169
Oh no! Stopping the strop 169
Calming after the storm.....................................170
Special Tantrums, Special Measures 171
Ssh, everyone's looking! The public strop 171
Pushing, biting, and other nasty habits..............171
Smacking (why it won't get you anywhere)........172

Chapter 14: Food and Sleep 173
Toddler Eating: The Need-to-Know Facts..........................173
Good eats, good treats.......................................174
Manners maketh matters worse?.......................176
Little porkers: The truth about tubby tots 176
Food and teeth: Surprising stuff........................177
What We Worry About: Common Parent Complaints............178
She won't eat vegetables 179
She won't drink (cow's) milk 179

Giving up the bottle 180
She won't eat meat 181
She won't let me feed her 181
She won't try anything new 182
She just won't eat 182
Five ways to fox fussy eaters 183
Sleeping Patterns: What's Normal, What's Not 183
A word about naps 184
What Keeps Us Awake At Night – and What To Do About It 185
She still won't sleep through 185
She suddenly won't sleep through 186
She won't go to bed..187
She comes into our bed 188
She gets up too early 188
Time for a 'big' bed?..189

Chapter 15: Keeping Your Toddler Safe **191**
Toddlerproofing Your Home: The Hands and Knees Tour.....................191
Danger zone one: The kitchen 193
Danger zone two: The bathroom....................................194
Danger zone three: The stairs......................................194
Danger zone four: The garden 195
What about other people's houses? 195
Houseproofing Your Toddler 196
Staying Safe on the Road...197
Buckling up in the car 197
Kerbside rules 198
Playing Safe...199
Danger! Don't lose your perspective 200
At the park..200
At the pool..201

Chapter 16: Playing, Learning, and Socialising **203**
Word Up! Encouraging Language Skills 203
The art of conversation 204
The sway of song..206
The power of books 206
Saying Daddy before she says Mummy – it's not personal..........207
Why dogs are cats – and other mysteries 207
Watching TV: The good and the bad..............................208
Ready, Steady, Go! Winning Play for Active Bodies 208
Upwardly mobile: From toddling to trikes 209
Fun at her fingertips: Little hands at work.......................211
The Art of Play: With You, With Others.................................213
Friends over? Time to parallel play 213
In adult company? Time for reflective play 214
Going solo? Time for independent play...........................214
Playtime over? Time to tidy up!....................................215
Making the most of toddler groups...............................215

Part IV: All About Preschoolers 217

Chapter 17: Behaviour and Discipline 219
Warning! Tough Times Ahead! 219
    Why little darlings act like little demons...................................220
    Great expectations? Lower them now! 221
Managing Behaviour 221
    Tactics that work..221
    Watch your language...224
    Tactics that can backfire – and why..225
    Five patented parent wind-ups – and
        how not to let them get to you....................................226
Teaching Please, Thank You, and Other Good Manners 228
Instilling Values: Five to Teach Your Child by the Age of 5...................229

Chapter 18: Food Fights and Sleep Frights 231
The Picky Eaters' Club..231
    Getting the nutritional facts straight 231
    Eat up! Feeding fads that drive you mad 232
    Food mistakes even good parents make 235
    Ten ace appetite-boosting ideas..236
    But what if she's a big eater? 237
Sleep and Not-So-Sweet Dreams..238
    What's normal, what's not...238
    What keeps her up – and how to get her back down 239

Chapter 19: Playing, Learning, and Socialising 243
Mind Games and Make-believe..243
    Imaginary powers...244
    It's a boy/girl thing: The car/doll divide 245
    Curiouser and curiouser 246
    'Where do babies come from, Mummy?' 247
    A word about TV 247
Look Who's Talking! Language Skills 248
Let's Get Physical! Revving Up Those Motor Skills...........................249
    Active bodies 249
    Busy fingers..250
Fun with Friends...251
    Mine! All mine! Oh, okay, your turn...251
    It's playtime!...252

Chapter 20: Heading to Preschool 255
Choosing the Best Preschool for You Both..255
    What matters most?..256
    What to look for 257
    Ten questions not to leave without asking 257

Getting Ready for the First Day 258
Preparing your child 259
Settling in and saying goodbye.................................259
And when she comes home 260
Thinking Ahead to Big School 260
Making the right choice...261
What your child needs to know before she starts –
and what she doesn't 263
What if we don't get the place we want?................264

Part V: All About Schoolies 265

Chapter 21: Starting School 267

School's Cool: Creating the Right Attitude 267
Taking the First Year (Reception, P1) in Your Stride 269
The first day..269
Ten little things that'll make a big difference.............270
Strange faces, tricky places.......................................271
It's a boy/girl thing: The great gender divide.............271
Bouncy boys and summer-borns 273
Things that may take you by surprise: Part one 273
The Lowdown on Moving on Up: From Infants to Juniors 275
The 'small' years (Years 1 and 2) 275
The 'big' years (Years 3 and 4) 276
Things that may take you by surprise: Part two 276
The Secrets of Good Parent-Teacher Communication 278
Be the kind of parent teachers appreciate................279
Listen and learn at parents' evening........................279

Chapter 22: Eating, Sleeping, and Staying Healthy 281

Smart Food Tactics for Smart Kids 281
Good choices, bad choices 282
Tackling weighty issues 283
Want to try this? Widening tastes 284
School lunch or lunch box?..285
Time for Bed! Sleep for Schoolies 285
Into bed..286
Out of bed...287
Wet beds 288
Keeping Your Older Child Healthy....................................288
Wobbling teeth...288
Accidents will happen 289
Growing up and puberty..289
Bringing home more than homework 290
Keeping Your Older Child Safe 291

Chapter 23: Behaviour and Responsibility 293

What to Expect: The Good and the Bad 293
Refining Your Tactics One: Encouraging Good Behaviour..................294
    Spend some time alone with him 294
    Set clear rules 295
    Dish out the praise.......................................295
    Give rewards 295
    Seek co-operation cleverly 296
    Make sure that he's heard you.............................296
    Be open to negotiation 297
    Hold family meetings 297
Refining Your Tactics Two: Handling Bad Behaviour 298
    Have a code word 298
    Act as cool as a cucumber 298
    Acknowledge his feelings and share yours 299
    Withdraw your attention 299
    Make him take a break 299
    Offer a choice: Way out or consequence?...................300
    Impose consequences 300
    Forgive and forget 301
    The five patented parent wind-ups – and how
      not to let them get to you 301
Done Your Chores? Fostering a Sense of Responsibility 302
Plugging Away at Good Manners..303

Chapter 24: Friends, Self, and the World Beyond 305

Fostering Friendships..305
    Making friends: The need-to-know facts....................306
    Friendship smoothers and fixers 306
Nurturing a Sense of Self..307
    Boosting self-respect.....................................308
    Accepting your child for who she is 309
    Giving her space 309
    It's a boy/girl thing: Different ways to praise...........309
    Letting her be bored 310
    Doing stuff after school 310
    'Oh, the things they say!' 311
    Nine things to have done by age 9 312
Nurturing Values and Respect for Others.................................312
    The rites of passage 313
Understanding Big People's Upheavals and
  Small People's Feelings 314
    Death...314
    Divorce...315

Bombs and bad news 315
The truth about TV and computer games 316

Part VI: All About Siblings *317*

Chapter 25: The New Arrival **319**

Don't Mind the Gap! 319
Setting the Scene 320
    Preparing Child One for Child Two 320
    Thinking about the practicalities 321
Hello, Baby! Making Introductions 322
Reactions To Be Ready For 323
    What your child may do 323
    The sibling doll 325
    How you may feel 326
Five Ideas to Keep Your Head Above Water 328

Chapter 26: Squabble Solutions **329**

Born to Fight: Why Squabbling's Normal 329
Diversionary Tactics 330
Oi, Referee! Knowing When and How to Get Involved 331
    When to stay out of it 331
    When to step in – and how 331
    'No, mine!' Fights over property rights 333
Fixing It So They Squabble Less 334
    'But it's not fair!' 335

Chapter 27: Loving Them All the Same **337**

Am I Your Favourite, Mummy? 337
    Making each child feel special 338
    When one child needs more attention 339
    What if you really do have a favourite? 339
He's Sporty, She's Clever: Not Letting Those Labels Stick 340
    Beware of labels that limit 340
    Give a dog a bad name 341
Born To Be Different? The Truth About Birth Order 341
    'I never get to muck about': Understanding
        your oldest child 342
    'No one ever listens to me!': Understanding your
        middle child(ren) 343
    'No one takes me seriously': Understanding your
        youngest child 344
    But I've only got one child 345

Part VII: The Part of Tens.................................**347**

Chapter 28: Ten Ways to Keep Your Cool **349**

Find your deep voice 349
Count to ten 349
Ignore the small stuff 350
Respect the clock 350
Give yourself time out..350
Explain what you expect 350
Remember how old they are (or not) 351
Say how you feel 351
Say yes (sneakily)..351
See the funny side 351

Chapter 29: Ten First-Aid Must-Knows **353**

She's had a bump 353
She's got a huge cut 354
She's been scalded 354
She's got such a high fever...354
She's having a fit 355
She's swallowed poison 355
She's choking 355
She's been bitten or stung 356
She's got a nosebleed...356
She's just not right 356

**Chapter 30: Ten Things You Need For Your Baby
(And Ten Things You Don't)** **357**

Shopping on a tight budget...358
The Moses basket...358
The cot (and bedding)..358
The changing mat and bag..359
The nappies..359
The travel cot..360
The car seat..360
The wheels 361
The baby seat 363
The sling 363
The clothes 364
Ten Don't-needs (Whatever the Ads Say) 364

Index...**367**

Introduction

*T*his is the book I wish I'd been able to read when I first gave birth: a straight-talking, practical guide to parenting. Not a baby manual ('101 ways to top and tail a newborn'), not a child-development textbook ('By month seven, your baby may crawl'), and certainly not some rigid, do-it-this-way-or-fail month-by-month parenting programme. Just a treasure-trove of tips and techniques that other parents had tried and tested – and found to be pretty darn useful – before me.

It's also a book that acknowledges that there's still a fair old bit of parenting to do after your child's learned to walk and talk. So many parenting books cover infancy and, maybe, toddlerhood – and then stop. And all of us sporting our post-toddler parenting credentials know that there's still quite a lot of new stuff to figure out once your kids have turned 3.

Now, I'm not some parenting guru. I'm not a child psychologist (or even a parent psychologist, come to that). And I haven't got a money-back-guarantee raising-kids miracle plan to peddle. What I have got – from years of writing about parenting, researching parenting techniques, talking to parenting experts and parenting a few kids of my own – is a whole wodge of clever insights into what floats a child's boat and a whole load of clever ideas that can help us navigate those (often choppy) parenting waters more smoothly. So that's what I'm sharing with you.

And there you have it. Think of *Parenting For Dummies* as your trusty little companion on your journey with your child from birth to 9. You can turn to it for advice, plumb it for ideas, ask it to explain what on earth's going on but, in the end, it's going to be you at the helm, steering your family in the right direction and marvelling at all the wonderful sights along the way. And that, of course, is exactly how it should be.

About This Book

You don't have to start this book at the beginning and read it all through to the end (although I'd be rather thrilled if you did). Each chapter is self-contained, so there's no need to have read the ones before it to understand what's going on; just find the chapter or section that relates to the age or stage of childhood you're interested in – and off you go.

What You're Not to Read

The sidebars (grey shaded boxes) dotted throughout the book contain 'bonus' bits of info. I think that they're very interesting (obviously), but they're not essential and they aren't crucial to your understanding of the rest of the chapter they're in. Read them if you like, ignore them if you want – I really don't mind (too much).

Foolish Assumptions

Because you've picked up this book, I'm assuming:

- ✔ **You have a child (or several) or are about to have one.** And want to be the best parent you can be.
- ✔ **You want to know what the first nine years of parenting have in store for you – and your child.**
- ✔ **You want some down-to-earth tips from someone who knows what it's like to have kids (and is still trying to follow her own advice).**

I've also assumed you don't have a child with special needs – not because I'm trying to ignore parents of children with special needs but because I don't have enough experience or expertise in caring for a special-needs child to offer you any worthwhile advice. And I'm sure that you've had your bellyful of worthless advice already.

Conventions Used in This Book

Is your child a 'he' or a 'she'? Or do you have one (or more) of each? To avoid confusing or upsetting any of you, I've used 'he' and 'she' in alternate chapters. Please do not read anything into the fact that, in this book, tantrumming toddlers turn out to be 'he's and food-fussy preschoolers turn out to be 'she's; that's just practicalities, not a prediction!

How This Book Is Organised

You'll see this book has seven parts and 30 chapters. Each part deals with a different age and stage of your child's first nine years of life, and each chapter deals with an issue that's specific to that age and stage. Here's a little run-down of the parts and what's in them.

Part I: All About You: What Every Parent Should Know

The first part of this book looks at parenting in the big picture. It takes you through the kid-raising basics, from getting your head round how much becoming a parent may change you to setting boundaries, getting back-up, and finding great childcare. It also outlines the parenting secrets: 'golden' techniques that work – and keep on working as your child matures and grows.

Part II: All About Babies (The First Year)

This is your guide to the first 12 months of parenting. There's a chapter all about coping in the early weeks, plus special advice about breastfeeding and bottlefeeding, and when – and how – to move on to solid food. There are also chapters on health, sleep (how you can both get more of it), and encouraging your baby's efforts to sit, crawl, walk, babble, and play.

Part III: All About Toddlers (1 to 3 Years)

Things get a little different when your baby's up and toddling, so this part's all about revising your food and sleep tactics for 1-to-3-year-olds, plus some essential advice on dealing with the inevitable arrival of the toddler tantrum. There are also plenty of tips on boosting his language skills, having fun indoors and out, and keeping him safe while you're at it. Plus, a chapter on the strange – and soggy – art of potty-training.

Part IV: All About Preschoolers (3 to 5 Years)

In this part, you'll find out how to choose the right preschool and how to settle your child into it happily. There are also chapters on dealing with stroppy behaviour, fussy eating (both particular preschooler specialities), and broken sleep (this is the age of scary dreams and monsters under the bed). Plus, there are tips on keeping him active, feeding his imagination, and encouraging his first forays into the world of playdates and friendship.

Part V: All About Schoolies (5 to 9 Years)

Starting school's a pretty scary stage in your parenting life – which is why this part has a whole chapter on how to help your child breeze through it. Plus, there's some no-holds-barred advice on keeping him fit and healthy, and getting him to help out around the house. There's a special chapter on school-age friendships (more complicated than you'd think) and self-image (more wobbly than you'd imagine). And loads of tips on fine-tuning your discipline skills to teach him more about choices, responsibility, and self-control.

Part VI: All About Siblings (Through The Ages)

These are the chapters to read when (or before) one child becomes two (or more). You'll find out how to prepare your first child for the new arrival and how to deal with his (understandably) jealous reactions. There are also plenty of tips on dealing with sibling squabbles and on giving each child the attention he deserves (without collapsing in a parental heap of exhaustion).

Part VII: The Part of Tens

This is a handy little collection of clever tips and need-to-know facts that every parent could do with reading, learning, and inwardly digesting. They cover essential first-aid skills, baby-kit must-(and-mustn't) buys, and that perennial parental essential: keeping your cool.

Icons Used in This Book

In every chapter, you'll see certain paragraphs have icons next to them. This means that the paragraph contains information of special importance. You can tell exactly how important it's going to be to you by looking at the kind of icon used – each one signals something different. Here's how to tell what:

This is the stuff you'll find extra useful – little golden nuggets of advice from one parent to another.

This is the stuff you really need to hang on to – even if you forget everything else in the book.

This is the stuff to be extra careful about. Or things could go seriously wrong.

This is the stuff to take special notice of if you have twins.

This is the stuff that's funky and new on the parenting scene. You'll either think that it's wonderfully innovative or you'll think that it's just plain silly.

Where to Go from Here

Now all the introductions are over with, you're free to start rifling those pages. Where you start reading it is up to you but, if you've just had a baby, I suggest you leap straight in at Chapter 6. If you already have kids, you can dip into the bits that relate to their ages and stages right now. And, if your parenting life has yet to begin, it probably makes sense to go all chronological and start at Chapter 1.

Part I
All About You: What Every Parent Should Know

"She just _won't_ eat – I just don't know what she's living on."

In this part . . .

*P*arenting's a skill and, like any other skill, it needs takes lots of learning and plenty of practice. But there are a few basics it's worth boning up on right from the start. And you'll find them all in this part. From understanding how much becoming a parent may change you, to finding great back-up and brilliant childcare. From realising it's up to you to set boundaries, to accepting that parental perfection doesn't exist (and is not what your kids really want, anyway). Best of all, you'll discover the parenting secrets that'll work for you, and your children, for many years to come.

Chapter 1

Help! Where Do I Start? The Basics

In This Chapter

▶ Doing the parenting reality check

▶ Understanding what makes a child tick at different ages

▶ Realising what being a parent means

*T*ake off those rose-tinted spectacles right now: You need to get the picture nice and clearly. Parenting is tough. Yes, it's rewarding, enjoyable, and absolutely brilliant at times, but it is tough. And that's because life changes when you have children. In all sorts of ways. And adjusting to change (however nice) isn't easy.

Now, at this point, I have to tell you that anyone who'd told a pregnant me that life was going to get tough when my baby arrived would've been given shrift so short you'd need a microscope to see it. I mean, I wasn't naive. I *knew* things were going to be different. But I didn't know *how* different. Which is why I'm sticking my older, wiser neck on the line and telling you now.

Having children forces you to plumb parts of yourself you never knew existed, to dredge up superhuman levels of patience, to be firm and consistent even if you're wobbly inside, to be bouncy and enthusiastic when all you really want to do is crawl into bed and catch up on a few thousand hours of lost sleep. And that is all good stuff, when you think about it; it just doesn't come very naturally. So, this chapter's here to ease you in gently, with a little snapshot of what to expect – from your child and yourself – in the parenting years to come. Enjoy the ride!

Knowing Your Child: Ages and Stages

Between birth and 9, your child goes through four distinct developmental stages (baby, toddler, preschooler, schoolchild) and each one has its own particular delights – and challenges. You'll find loads of specific tips to help you deal with each of these stages in Parts II to V of this book but, here, as a kind of taster, is a brief overview of how it all pans out, parenting-wise.

Baby

The Baby stage runs from your child's actual birth day to her first birthday. It's the shortest stage but probably the one with the steepest, most stunning learning curve – for both of you!

What she's like

She's getting bigger by the day – sometimes quite literally. In just 12 months, she's going to grow from a helpless teeny babe-in-arms to a moving, babbling tot. Until then, you must do everything for her and be everything to her; you are the centre of her universe.

What she needs from you

This is the *holding* year. Your baby needs you to cuddle her, soothe her, and cradle her close. And this situation is, of course, the most wonderful thing – except when you're desperate to eat or sleep. Later, as she becomes more mobile, she needs you to hold her steady and catch her when she falls.

Toddler

The Toddler stage covers ages 1 to 3. These are the vivacious, vocal, – and, sometimes, volatile! – years. Your child will test your patience one minute, melt your heart the next.

What she's like

She's a little ball of energy, scooting at lightning speed from pillar to post (except when you need to get anywhere fast, when she immediately slows to sub-funereal pace). She's starting to talk and is developing a theatrically strong urge to do things her own way.

What she needs from you

These are the *shadowing* years. Your toddler needs you to follow her closely, allowing her some chance to explore on her own but staying near enough to keep her from harm. She also needs you to keep a close eye on her behaviour – and teach her that throwing a tantrum isn't the best way to express feelings and doesn't get her what she wants.

Preschooler

The Preschooler stage takes your child from 3 to 5 years old. It's a time of fun and first friendships, and of finding her feet at playgroup or preschool.

What she's like

She's an inquisitive, imaginative, often cheeky little thing, full of enthusiasm for life and bursting with endless (often gobsmacking) questions about how the world works. She likes being busy and active and doing things for herself, and is taking a growing delight in playing (but not necessarily always sharing) with friends her own age.

What she needs from you

These are the *shepherding* years. Your preschooler needs you to show her the path and then let her make her own way down it, safe in the knowledge that you're watching and won't let her go astray. She also needs you to set clear boundaries, and show her how to take turns and mix nicely with her peers.

Schoolchild

The Schoolchild stage covers the first five primary-school years, from age 5 to 9. It's a time of emotional growth and social jostling, as friends start to assume a more central part of her life.

What she's like

She's calmer and quieter, eager to please you and to fit in with her friends. She's starting to compare herself to others – and often find herself wanting. She's very independent and often quite happy to amuse herself. And she's becoming much more aware of the (sometimes scary) realities of the grown-up world.

What she needs from you

These are the *steering years*. Your schoolchild's at the beginning of the long journey towards adolescence and she needs you to start her off in the right direction by boosting her belief in herself, her abilities, and her own strength of character. She needs your trust and guidance as she learns how to show respect for others and to take responsibility for her own behaviour.

Oh, and watch for the funny bits

During each of these four big developmental stages, your child will probably have a series of 'settled' and 'unsettled' patches (for a rough idea of when each of these may occur, see Table 1-1). This can be really quite disconcerting for us parents (in a 'hey, what did I do to suddenly make her like this?' kind of way), but it's actually perfectly normal (and almost certainly nothing to do with you at all).

You see, children grow – emotionally, mentally, and physically – in little spurts. Between spurts (when everything's nice and stable), they're settled: Calm, happy, easy in their skin. In the middle of a spurt (when everything's changing rapidly), they're unsettled: Anxious, sensitive, less able to cope. Of course, not all children react to unsettled patches in the same way – some kids can become much more difficult; others, blessed with a more naturally serene temperament, may take everything more or less in their stride. Either way, it helps us, as parents, to know that these patches happen – and that they pass – and that all we probably need do to get through them is continue doing what we're doing the best way we can.

Table 1-1	Your Age-by-Age Guide to Settled/Unsettled Phases	
Stage	**Settled phases (often but not always)**	**Unsettled phases (often but not always)**
Baby	4, 16, 28, 40, 52 weeks	8, 20, 32, 44 weeks
Toddler	1, 2 and 3 years	18 and 21 months, 2 1/2 years
Preschooler	3 and 5 years	3 1/2 and 4 years
Schoolchild	5, 7 and 9 years	5 1/2, 6 and 8 years

Adapted with thanks from Raising Good Kids *by Louise Bates Ames*

Table 1-1 is just a guide and the ages on it are only very approximate. If your child does not seem particularly settled or unsettled at any of the ages mentioned or goes through settled or unsettled patches at another age, don't take it as a sign that something is wrong.

Knowing Yourself

Once you're a parent, you can't be the same person you used to be. Because things have changed: You've got new responsibilities and, with them, new perspectives and a new set of priorities.

Now this doesn't mean you have to morph into some totally different person (that would be *weird*), but you do need to carry out the odd modification, and build on a lot of extra bits and pieces. Some of these changes you'll make quite instinctively, without even really noticing. Others may not come quite so naturally – so here's your handy little heads-up.

Your role: Parts all parents should play

We all have various roles to play in life – partner, colleague, son, daughter, sister, brother, boss, friend. And parent is just another one of those – albeit a bit scarier because you're not so familiar with the script. But you'll slip into – and fill out – your new role just fine if you remember your child sees you as

- ✔ **The person to copy:** Your child will model herself on you. From the moment she's born, she'll watch what you do and how you behave – and learn that that's the way to do things. So, if you talk with your mouth full, swear like a trooper, tell fibs to your friends, and break the speed limit on motorways, she'll think that's okay. Quite a scary thought, isn't it? Except when you know that what matters is not being a perfect role model in every way but trying hard to do what is right – and apologising or explaining when you get it wrong.

- ✔ **The person in charge:** Your child's not going to *know* how to behave nicely. You have to teach her. Partly by leading by example and partly by making rules and setting limits. And then enforcing them, when you need to. You don't need to enforce rules heavy-handedly, but you do need to do it consistently. You'll find more about boundaries in Chapter 2 and then, in a more specifically age-related way, in Chapters 13, 17, and 23.

Your goals: Hopes all parents have

You want to do your best by your child, give her things you never had and opportunities you were never able to take. You want to give her the tools to make a real success of her life. But in the end, what really matters is that you

- ✔ **Raise a happy, confident child.** Who is strong, self-reliant, and resilient enough to take on whatever adolescence and adult life happens to throw at her. To do this, you need to give her a safe, healthy, loving, and pre-dictable home life, and the certainty that she is valued, understood, and approved of. You'll find lots of tips on doing this throughout the rest of this book.

- ✔ **Make growing-up fun.** Which means rediscovering the little child in you. You need to find time to spend with your child, giving her your whole attention and sharing her interests and games and flights of fancy. You need to get back in touch with the joys of tickling and giggling and playing rough-and-tumble. You need to pull silly faces, fly kites, kick a ball, finger-paint, and splash through puddles. You need to let go and live in the moment, just like she does.

Your fears: Worries all parents share

On top of all the stuff you want to get right, there's all this other stuff you don't want to get wrong. Having a child comes with so many doubts and fears, you should be issued with a free set of worry beads the moment the umbilical cord is cut. But the worries that will probably obsess you most are

- **Keeping her safe:** From illness, injury, and all sorts of other harm. Which is entirely natural but important to keep in perspective. In survey after survey, parents say that their biggest fear is of their child being abducted and hurt by a stranger when, in fact, our children are at far, far greater risk of being hurt in an accident at home. You'll find specific advice on health in Chapters 11, 22, and 29, and on safety in Chapters 15 and 22.

- **Keeping up to scratch:** We all do it: Measure other parents' ways against our own and find ours rather rubbish by comparison. But what we forget is that there are loads of different ways to parcel up your life as a parent, and each has its own particular ups and its own particular downs – no better, no worse, just different. As in all other walks of life, there will always be those you think are doing it better than you, just as there'll be those you think are doing it worse. And the truth? Even that mum who effortlessly copes with four children under 5, never shouts, and bakes all her own (organic) bread is comparing herself to someone else and feeling bad. And that's just such a waste of energy.

 Being a parent's a funny old job. You don't get proper hours, you don't get promotions, you don't get pay rises – and you never get to resign. But you do get great bonuses: Children who love you to bits, make you laugh, and never cease to astonish you with the wonderful things they do and say.

Don't Panic – It All Comes Together in the End!

There's a lot to learn about being a parent but the great thing is, you don't need to know it all from the start. Every day, week, month, and year that you look after your child, you're building experience upon experience, like the layers of coils in one of those Slinky toys that 'walks' down the stairs.

And that collected coil of experience gives you confidence to stretch yourself further as your child gets older. Yes, you may get it wrong and 'ping' back a few times but, slowly and surely, the coils keep on stacking up until you're suddenly the most experienced parent on the block.

Parenting's a funny old game but, with the right attitude (and maybe the odd tactics talk now and then), we can all pick it up and play it well.

Chapter 2

You're in Charge: Setting Boundaries

In This Chapter

▶ Understanding why rules are important

▶ Setting the right rules at the right times

▶ Teaching that actions have consequences

*Y*our child needs to know what's expected of him. And since he can't read your mind, you need to tell him – or show him by drawing boundaries between the kind of behaviour that's okay and the kind of behaviour that is absolutely not. And then consistently enforcing those boundaries. Which isn't always as easy as it looks (or as severe as it sounds).

So, pay attention now: I expect you to read this chapter about setting boundaries properly (no line-skimming, no page-flipping, no daydreaming) and then put what you've found out into practice. Or else!

Boundary Basics

Every parent has to set boundaries: This is part of our job description. Because we are responsible for teaching our children the rules that shape our society. The tricky part is knowing exactly what boundaries to set – and where to set them.

Understanding why boundaries work (even when they're broken)

You're not being a big old meanie making all these rules. Quite the opposite, in fact. Your child actually *wants* you to mark out clear boundaries for his behaviour, because

- **They make him feel secure:** When you set a boundary and consistently maintain it, he's absolutely clear about how you want him to behave.

- **They keep him safe:** Some of the boundaries you set are lifesavers in the most literal sense – such as staying on the pavement and not running into the road.

- **They help him out:** When your child's learning to walk, you move furniture close together so he's got something firm and stable to cling to. And, when your child's learning how to behave, you give him guidance and rules, so he has something firm and stable to cling to.

- **They teach cause and effect:** If his behaviour is out of bounds, it has consequences – for him and for others.

- **They give him something to push against:** Testing your parents' limits – to see how far you can go before an adult yells 'Stop!' – is a natural part of growing up. But if you have no limits to test, you have no expectations to live up to, and feel no sense of responsibility for your own behaviour.

- **They teach him right from wrong:** All the right stuff lies within your boundaries, all the wrong stuff's outside. Simple.

Little babies don't need boundaries. Because they don't misbehave. And they can't understand rules. Some babies are more tricky to look after than others but that doesn't mean they're 'testing' you; they wouldn't know how. Never draw a boundary until your child has the brainpower to grasp what it's all about. For more about this, see Chapter 6.

Setting boundaries wisely

Okay, so you set boundaries to draw a clear dividing line between acceptable and unacceptable behaviour. But pinpointing that dividing line can actually be quite hard. And not every parent draws the line in the same place.

Take swearing, for example: Most parents quickly assign the 'f-word' to the 'unacceptable' side of the line but I'm betting not nearly so many do the same with 'Oh, God' or 'damn' and even fewer with 'bum'. Setting your child's boundaries takes some careful thinking about your own boundaries and personal choices. You also need to

- **Make them age-appropriate:** Having rules about table manners when your child's 4 or 5 is fine but you really can't expect a toddler not to get crumbs down his front and yoghurt in his hair.

- **Be a role model:** Setting boundaries is pointless if you don't stick to them yourself.

- **Be selective:** Having too many rules and regulations is dispiriting for kids (they feel they can never put a foot right) and a policing nightmare for you. Save your boundaries for the things that really matter.

- ✔ **Tell him why they're there:** Once your child's old enough to understand, spend time explaining why you've set that particular boundary. Talk about why behaviour outside that boundary is unacceptable to you. And give him an example of the kind of behaviour inside that boundary that pleases you. This is really important when you're drawing boundaries where other parents may choose not to.

- ✔ **Be adaptable:** As your child grows and matures, you'll need to shift (or even lift) many of your boundaries. Or you'll end up stifling him. And his ability to make decisions for himself.

- ✔ **Remember he's a kid:** And kids are allowed to run around and be noisy and make a mess and generally behave like kids. Setting boundaries is not about forcing them to behave like adults.

You and your partner – and other significant carers in your child's life – need to be working to the same rules. Which means you need to discuss them before setting them. And then again before changing or adapting them. For more on parenting as a team, see Chapter 3.

Strict? Easy going? What's your parenting style?

Every parent has a different idea about discipline and about how many rules and regulations a child should be expected to respect and obey. But experts tend to categorise us either as:

Strict. This is the old-fashioned, do-as-you're-told-without-question approach to parenting. It is adult-centred and involves lots of rules, rigid routines, and severe sanctions for misbehaviour.

- ✔ Pros? Your child knows where he stands. His structured routine makes him feel secure.

- ✔ Cons? It's very confrontational. Your child is never given a choice. Lots of rules can mean lots of failure.

Or easy going. This is a more modern, loose, and liberal approach. It is child-centred and involves few clear rules, little routine, and lots of discussion about, but few sanctions for, misbehaviour.

- ✔ Pros? You have a close and loving relationship with your child, with almost no confrontation. Your child has enormous choice.

- ✔ Cons? Your child never knows where he stands. He becomes used to getting his own way and may cause havoc until he does. Lack of routine can make it difficult for him to fit into the structured environment of school.

Not thrilled with either choice? Don't worry: There is a third way – one that cherry-picks the best aspects of the other two approaches and ignores the worst. I like to call it:

Firm but fair. This is a more democratic approach to parenting. The adult is in charge but the child has some say in what he can and cannot do. It involves some clearly stated rules and a basic routine with some room for flexibility. There are appropriate sanctions for misbehaviour.

- ✔ Pros? Your child knows where he stands. He feels accepted for who he is. He has space to be himself and to make mistakes, within clear boundaries. You have a close and loving relationship with him.

- ✔ Cons? Constantly steering the middle path between strict and easy going can be something of a challenge.

Toeing the Line: Making Boundaries Work

It's no good just setting boundaries: You need to enforce them, too. After all, there's no point drawing a line in the sand and telling your child how important it is not to step over it if you then don't react in any way when he does.

Of course, you don't have to patrol those boundary lines with a big fat stick (Heaven forbid). Your child simply needs to know that overstepping the mark always elicits a predictable and measured parental response. The following sections show you how to get that message across – and how to follow it through.

Being clear, certain, and consistent

Don't take it for granted that your child understands what you're after. You're the one setting the boundaries, so you need to spell out what they are all about.

- **State clearly what you want:** Just yelling 'Behave!' is no good. You need to be really clear and specific about the rules you're laying down: 'No sticking tongues out at the vicar!'

- **Look confident:** Your body language and tone of voice need to reinforce your words. So barely lifting your head from your magazine to mumble, 'Oh, sweetheart, please don't hit' isn't going to cut it; moving over to the miscreant in question, looking him right in the eyes and saying firmly, 'No hitting!' is. It's not about being mean; it's about meaning business.

- **Be fair:** Your toddler's tipped washing powder all over the floor. But who left the washing powder within his reach in the first place? Both of you have strayed over the mark. Being fair also means keeping things in proportion: Don't make your child suffer for your bad mood.

- **Be consistent:** Every time a boundary is breached, you need to respond. Firmly and decisively and in the same way. Even if your child's being cute. Even if you're dog-tired. The repetition of your reaction is what drives home the message that his behaviour is wrong.

Making it cool to do the right thing

All this talk of boundary-enforcing and firm responses sounds such negative stuff but, done the right way, it isn't at all, especially if you're also making a serious effort to show your child the positive benefits of behaving well. The cleverest way to get your child to stay within your boundaries is to make the idea so attractive to him, it's the obvious option. So

- ✔ **Heap on the praise:** When he behaves well. What better way to make him want to do so again?

- ✔ **Offer rewards:** For a toddler, nothing is more rewarding than being given a huge round of applause and then being scooped up for a lovely cuddle. With an older (and, maybe, cuddle-allergic) child, let him know you've noticed a sustained improvement in behaviour by buying him a present or taking him on a special trip. Or use the promise of a reward to change behaviour for the better – by setting specific goals or pinning up a star chart (one star for every good day; ten stars wins a reward, for example).

- ✔ **Act surprised when he starts to behave badly:** So demonstrating to your child that your expectation always is that he'll behave well.

- ✔ **Offer a way out:** At the merest whiff of misbehaviour, suggest (or demonstrate) a more positive alternative.

Spelling out the consequences

Oh dear, despite your valiant efforts to promote the general wonderfulness of good behaviour, everything is heading in a distinctly boundary-breaking direction. Time to make it really clear what such behaviour's going to mean. So

- ✔ **Say what needs to change**. Very clearly and *very calmly*. As in, 'I want you to stop throwing the ball in the sitting room – right now!' You're not asking, you're telling.

- ✔ **State exactly what will happen if the behaviour doesn't stop**. As in, 'If you continue to throw the ball, I will take it away for the rest of the day.'

- ✔ **Make the consequence fit the crime**. Always take a deep breath and engage your brain before outlining any consequences. Otherwise you end up saying, 'If you continue to throw the ball, I'll never let you play football again.' Not only a mite out of proportion as consequences go but also rather tricky to follow through.

- ✔ **Keep the consequence age-appropriate**. For a small child, that usually means his physical removal from the scene of the crime; for an older child, it may mean a removal of privileges. You'll find more about age-appropriate consequences in Chapters 13 (toddlers), 17 (preschoolers) and 23 (schoolies).

- ✔ **Have a warning system**. Children often need a minute or two to put the brakes on their bad behaviour. Give them that brief period of grace with a clear countdown: 'I'm going to count to three (or five or ten) and then I expect you to stop.'

- ✔ **Praise him if he stops**. He deserves it.

For older children (particularly football-crazy ones) a yellow and red-card warning system can work well: Yellow card (make one or just say 'Yellow card!') means a final warning; red card means an immediate consequence.

Try to be fair. Don't dish out a heavier consequence than the behaviour deserves just because your child's got you particularly wound up.

Following through

Right, this is the tough bit but sticking with it is crucial. You said there'd be a consequence if the boundary-breaking behaviour didn't stop, so, if it hasn't, you need to follow through. Or your child won't think twice about breaking that boundary again – and, like as not, every other boundary you've set as well. So

- ✔ **Get a move on:** Children have short memories, so you need to make the consequence happen pretty smartly after the event. The longer the period of time between action and consequence, the weaker the link between those two events will be in your child's mind.

- ✔ **Explain what's going on:** Never assume your child will just understand. Even if you've spelled it out award-winningly clearly before, you need to do it again. 'Right, you decided to keep throwing the ball, so I'm taking it away for the rest of the day.'

- ✔ **Stay calm:** Yes, you may be a seething volcano inside but you need to be as chilled as an iceberg on top. Keep reminding yourself you're angry at your child's behaviour, not your child.

- ✔ **Be focused:** This is not the time to pile in with other complaints about your child's behaviour. They're irrelevant to what he's up to now and will only muddy the actions-have-consequences waters.

- ✔ **Be prepared to be the bad guy:** Nobody likes upsetting or annoying their child. Nobody likes provoking wailing and tears. But you have to do this. Because you said you would and your child needs to know you can be relied upon to mean what you say. Remember, he had a choice and, by not stopping, he chose this consequence.

- ✔ **Forgive and forget:** Once it's over, it's over. Give him a cuddle to reassure him of your love. And move on.

The more consistent you are in following through, the less you'll actually need to. Your child will quickly realise that changing his behaviour is the only way to avoid the consequence.

Great ways to minimise boundary-breaking

Sometimes, a child breaks boundaries because he's upset or wound-up or looking for limits. And you can't do much to change that – his behaviour's just a natural part of growing up. But, sometimes, he breaks boundaries because he's bored or ignored or feeling over-controlled. And there are things you can do to change that. For a start, you can

✔ Keep him busy. Small, idle hands tend to get up to big amounts of mischief. Now, no one's suggesting you devote your every waking hour to staging a one-parent stream of stimulating child entertainment but it does pay to have some ideas up your sleeve for those moments when it's bucketing with rain and you really need to do the washing, peel the potatoes, or call the plumber. Keep a basket of 'treasure' (child-safe bits and bobs, such as cotton reels and yoghurt pots) for a toddler to rifle through; encourage older children to draw birthday cards (one's always coming up), construct Lego masterpieces, make camps, hold teddy-bear tea parties, read books, or even (gasp!) help you with your chores. Make

time to keep commenting on and praising your child's efforts as you get on.

✔ Notice the good. Your attention is one of the biggest rewards you can give your child. And he can learn amazingly quickly that behaving badly gets your attention double-quick. Which can make bad behaviour a rather tempting means to an end. Unless you make a positive effort to give him masses of attention when he's behaving well. And to spend time with him, listening, talking, playing games, and showing an interest in his life.

✔ Have fun. Being concerned about your child's behaviour is good. But not if it takes over so much of your time as a parent that you forget what great fun a child can be. And how much laughter and stress-busting silliness he can bring into your life. If you feel you're doing nothing all day but barking orders, maybe you need to loosen up a little and think of ways to encourage good behaviour with a smile on your face and a twinkle in your eye.

Moving on: Reshaping boundaries together

As your child matures, you can start to take a more democratic approach to boundary-setting. Which means including him in the process. Not putting him in charge, mind, just allowing him a voice. This idea tends to work better when done in a structured way at a 'family meeting', where everyone gets to sit down and discuss ways to address the problem behaviours of the moment. You may think it all sounds very airy-fairy but I bet you'll be surprised by how sensible and respectful your child's suggestions turn out to be – and how tough the consequences he chooses for breaking the new boundaries! Be warned, though: To be truly democratic, parents have to accept that they may need some new boundaries, too! (For more about family meetings, see Chapter 23.)

Chapter 3

You Are Not Alone: Massing the Troops

In This Chapter

▶ Seeing parenting as a team game

▶ Leaning on other parents for support and advice

▶ Making a great job of single parenting

*E*very parent needs back-up. Not of the round-the-clock cook, bottle washer, and nappy-warmer variety (although that does has its obvious attractions) but of the you're-not-in-this-alone one. Because, without back-up, the day-to-day (to-night-to-day) parenting grind is a million times more, well, grinding than it needs to be.

Unlike other jobs, looking after your own children doesn't come with colleagues eager to shoot the (posset-fragranced) breeze or people in Human Resources who want to develop your potential. (And let's not even get started on the pay and conditions.) So, it's really down to you to find the support, advice, and hearty pats on the back you need – and so richly deserve. But how on earth do you manage that when you've got so much else on your plate? Read on to find out.

Working with Your Partner

Time was when women did the baby thing and men did the work thing. But times have moved on and so have we – but only a little. In truth, however thrustingly egalitarian your relationship is when there are just the two of you, things do tend to slide back to a more traditional set-up – at least for a while – once you are three. And that's fine, as long as each of you is still pulling together in a way that works for you both. Because raising a child together is all about teamwork – and the tricky bit is not so much working out who's doing what as making sure that you're both playing on the same field.

If you're a single parent, you're playing in a different, tougher league but that doesn't mean you can't rustle up some teammates of your own: You can find some more specific tips for you nearer the end of this chapter.

Discovering the truth about kids and relationships

You're probably not going to like me for saying this (and, to be honest, if someone had said it to me as I cradled my newborn, I wouldn't have liked them much, either) but it needs saying because it's true: Becoming a parent puts a big strain on the relationship between you and your partner. And that's because

- ✔ **The dynamic changes.** Obviously. Before, all you had to think about was each other. Now, not only is there someone else to think about, but you're having to change the whole rhythm of your life to fit around her.

- ✔ **One of you is at home all day.** While the other goes out to work. Even if this is only a temporary arrangement, it's a big change for both of you. And it can take some adjusting to.

- ✔ **The realities of parenthood may take you by surprise.** You may like being a parent more than you thought. You may find it much harder than you were expecting. You may each find it challenging in very different ways.

- ✔ **You've got less time for each other.** Because looking after your child soaks up so much of the time you used to spend together.

- ✔ **You've got less money.** And (at least for the moment) one of you is having to bring home all the bacon.

- ✔ **You're both exhausted.** Especially in the first few months, when you've got so much stuff to learn and so little time to sleep.

Sharing the load

If you're going to be a team, you're going to need a game plan. And a bit of a team talk about tactics. Before you pull on your positional shirts (stay-at-home parent, working parent, or some clever combination of the two), you need to be absolutely sure that you and your partner have a clear idea of how your separate efforts are going to combine to reach your common goal: a happy and rewarding family life. To do this, you need to

✔ **Have a housework debate.** Being a stay-at-home parent isn't the same as being a stay-at-home cleaner, cook, and laundry maid. Being a working parent doesn't automatically exclude you from all household chores. Sit down together and divvy up the domestic duties – you don't have to be exact equals in the dusting department but you do have to be willing to do your bit.

✔ **Share time with your baby.** It's all too easy for the parent who's taking on the lion's share of the caring to get a little territorial about things. But if Mum (and it is usually Mum in the early days) is doing all the feeding, changing, cuddling, and settling, Dad's never going to cut it as a hands-on parent, is he? Give each other time to get to know your baby from the start, and you'll be setting up patterns of shared involvement and responsibility that will last for years – and will benefit you all.

✔ **Pick up stuff.** Babies and children mean all sorts of extra bits and bobs cluttering up your house. Don't assume the de-clutter monitor will be along in a minute – if you see something lying around, put it away.

✔ **Give each other a break.** Looking after kids all day is hard work; slogging away in an office all day is hard work, too. So there's no point having a 'Who's had it hardest?' contest. Try to find ways to give each other a few moments' peace instead. Maybe the at-home parent would like some child-free time in the morning to shower and dress. Maybe the working parent would love a lie-in on a Sunday. Figure out what each of you would appreciate most – and make that your regular treat to each other.

✔ **Enjoy your children together.** Don't always parent in shifts. Make sure that you also spend time together as a family, just taking pleasure in each other's company.

Family life is different to couple life. Expect things to change – some for the better, some for the worse – and then it won't all be such a shock.

'But Daddy said...': Presenting a united parenting front

You probably talked quite a bit about bringing up kids before you had any. You probably agreed about most things. You probably watched other parents in the cafe, at the park, and in the supermarket and told each other, 'We'd never allow a child of ours to do anything like that!'

And then you have your child and discover that there are, actually, quite a lot of parenting-related things you disagree about – and plenty you didn't even think to discuss in the first place. Don't panic: We've all been there! To stand united once more, what you need to do is

- ✔ **Respect each other's point of view.** Listen to your partner's opinions. Be open to his or her suggestions. Especially if you're the main carer: You don't always automatically know what's best.

- ✔ **Keep talking.** Your views on parenting will evolve as you gain more experience at the 'bringing up baby' coalface, and as your child develops and grows. So it's important to keep discussing the things that really matter, from day-to-day discipline to choice of schools.

- ✔ **Reassess your lifestyle priorities.** Are you putting extra pressure on yourselves – and each other – to maintain your pre-children standard of living? Look at what you want and compare it to what you actually need. Sometimes, sacrificing a few lifestyle expectations for the sake of family life and security is worth it.

- ✔ **Keep your parenting arguments private.** It's okay for children to hear their parents disagreeing (respectfully) about other stuff (and then making up), but it's not so great for them to hear you having a right old ding-dong about them.

- ✔ **Back each other up.** Once you've agreed on a discipline or behaviour issue, you need to stick fast to the parental party line. Or your children will quickly work out what Mummy will let them get away with that Daddy wouldn't (or vice versa). And try never to criticise or take over from your partner when he or she is handling a situation (however badly). Bite your tongue firmly and resolve to discuss your parenting differences later – when you're well out of kiddie earshot.

Finding time to be together

Being a parent absorbs masses of your time and energy, and lots of your attention gets diverted away from your relationship towards your children. But don't just assume your relationship will take care of itself while you're doing the parenting thing. You need to find ways to protect it and nurture it and keep it special – or you may look round one day and wonder how much of it you have left.

Now, of course, you're going to ask where on earth you can find the time to do all that on top of everything else, but the good news is, you don't have spend hours at it – a few snatched moments of closeness every day is often all it takes to keep those lovelights glowing. You can

✔ **Get virtual.** Send each other e-mails and texts – just as a way of touching base and injecting a little loving fun into the day.

✔ **Stay in touch.** Literally. You may both be more shattered than you ever thought possible, but you can still dredge up enough energy to hold hands, have a cuddle, snuggle up together on the sofa, can't you?

✔ **Make dates.** To have time together without children. Write the date on the calendar, so you really do commit to it. You don't have to go out (although that's always a bonus); you can just turn off the telly, ignore the chores, eat dinner, and talk. Do this often.

✔ **Tell each other honestly how you feel.** Particularly in the first few weeks. There's no point pretending everything's absolutely wonderful if it's not. And your partner can't help make things better if he or she doesn't know what the problem is. You started this baby thing off together; you owe it to each other – and your baby – to tackle the tough bits together.

✔ **Lose the guilt.** It's easy to believe that the kids need your affection more than your partner does. But, actually, that's not true. Your kids need you to stay a loving, committed couple for their sakes, as well as your own. Be in no doubt: If you're looking after your relationship, you're looking after your children, too.

There ain't much room for spontaneity in your relationship now. Get used to the idea of 'planned romance' – organising your love life isn't worse, it's just different.

Working with Other Parents

In your common-or-garden office job, you have colleagues to talk to, find motivation from, and share stresses and triumphs with. These people may not be your bestest bestest friends but you find ways to rub along with them just fine – and their presence makes your working life so much less lonely and dull. And that's just how it should be when your job is parenting. Except your 'colleagues' don't come ready-supplied; you have to get out there and find them.

And how do you do that? Well, it's really not that tricky. Other parents hang out where you hang out: at mother-and-baby groups, at toddler softplay sessions, in playgrounds, at library story times, at the playgroup door, at the school gates, at the side of the pitch or the pool. And whether you just have the odd chat or form a friendship for life, what you gain from spending time with them is often worth its weight in parenting gold.

Why what they say can keep you sane

Going from independent, free-wheeling, working person to can't-even-go-to-the-loo-on-your-own parent is a strange transition. And it can be an isolating one, too. So it really helps to know that you're not alone, that other people are dealing with the same changes and challenges and feeling just as weirdly triumphant, tentative, and tearful as you. And the real beauty of sharing your experiences with other parents is that

- ✔ **You can swap tricks, tactics, and traumas.** There's nothing like talking to someone who has a child the same age as yours for boosting your morale and calming your anxieties ('So, you're going through that, too?'). You can trade tips, dissect techniques, and laugh over your mutual ineptitude. Whatever your current parenting obsession – sleep, toddler tantrums, school admission policies – there's nothing like a bit of bonding with another (similarly obsessed) parent to put it all into perspective.

- ✔ **You can find strength in common values.** Inevitably, you'll gravitate towards parents whose parenting style most closely fits yours. And their support and encouragement will be invaluable as you try to bring your kids up the way you think is right.

- ✔ **You can tap the been-there-done-that wisdom.** Although you may have to work at it a bit first. There are lots of older, wiser mums and dads out there who are positively brimming with pearls of parenting wisdom. But because they're wise and don't want to seem like pushy Mr or Mrs Know-it-alls, they tend not to give advice until they're asked. So, ask – often.

And when you're better off not listening

Sadly, there are a few breeds of other parent with whom bonding closely is not wise. Their intentions probably aren't suspect, but their advice is – for all sorts of reasons. Keep your eyes open for – and your ears well muffled from – advice-dispensing approaches from

✔ **The evangelist:** She's read some highly structured, don't-deviate-from-this-for-a-second parenting bible and found it's worked for her child. And she's convinced it will work for yours, too. Well, it may – but it may not. Don't let anyone bully or guilt-trip you into adopting a rigid routine or method of discipline if it makes you feel uncomfortable or unhappy. Parenting really isn't a one-size-fits-all kind of thing.

✔ **The competitive mum:** She's not really giving you any tips, she's just parading her own parenting prowess – or her offspring's precocious talents. She often doesn't realise quite how competitive she's being – underneath that show-offy exterior, she's probably desperately insecure – but spending too much time discussing children with her will do you no favours at all. Back away slowly, smile politely, and leave her to her own insecure devices.

✔ **The parent from another planet:** She's not (necessarily) spacey or scary, just light years away from you in terms of parenting style. She may have the same views as you on all other aspects of life but she has a completely different idea of what being a parent is all about. Taking advice from her is about as useful as buying a chocolate teapot.

A word about mothers – and mothers-in-law

Have a child, and two major things happen to your relationship with your mother: One good; the other, frankly, a bit iffy. First, you appreciate just how much your mum did for you when you were little. But, second, you get streams of your mum's advice on How Things Should Be Done. And, well, things have moved on a bit since she last burped a baby or made toddlers eat their greens.

And much the same can be said by your mother-in-law – only her advice, however well meant, seems somehow more critical because she's your partner's mum, not yours. So how do you ignore their words of 'wisdom' without starting some giant family rift? Take your pick from the following tactics:

✔ **Acknowledge her point of view:** 'You could be right.'

✔ **Deflect her:** 'Having your support means a lot to me.'

✔ **Inform her:** 'Actually, I've looked into this. Shall I tell you what I've found out?'

✔ **Value her opinion:** 'I'd like to try it this way for now, but what you say is really interesting.'

✔ **Wheel in the big guns:** 'Well, my doctor/health visitor/child's teacher says. . . .'

And remember, these people are your children's grandparents – it may drive you nuts that they stuff your kids with sweets at every visit or tut at your 'lax' attempts to discipline, but maintaining as good a relationship with them as you can is important to your children (and, also, let's face it, your future babysitting needs).

Single but Not Solo

Few people choose to bring up their children alone; most stumble into single parenthood by default. And there's no pretending it's easy: Parenting on your own is relentlessly challenging because it's up to you – and you alone – to be the stable centre point from which your family draws its strength.

But many single women (and yes, nine out of ten single-parent households are headed by women) do manage to raise their kids amazingly successfully, often on very limited resources. Their secret? They do their damnedest not to feel sorry for themselves, and they're not ashamed to ask for help.

Finding back-up

The old jigsaw that made up your family life may have been broken up when two parents became one (or two in separate houses), but you can reassemble it. You'll make a different picture – with different pieces in different places – but the jigsaw can fit together just as well as before. To re-build, seek help and support from

- ✔ **Your family**: Ask your mum, your brother, your cousins, and your aunts to spend time with your children and help you create a strong and loving family environment for them to grow up in. If your family live far away, creating time together may not be easy – or even possible – but do all you can to keep the connection alive with letters, e-mails, texts, and phone calls.

- ✔ **Other single parents:** People in the same position as you are always better at understanding your concerns and passing on crucial getting-by tips. If you don't know any single parents in your area, find some through Gingerbread (www.gingerbread.org.uk) or get some virtual support on parenting Web sites such as Mumsnet (www.mumsnet.com).

- ✔ **Your ex**: If he or she's still in your children's lives. Try to come to a civil agreement about access – find a mediator to help you if things get tricky – and be prepared to become more flexible as your children grow and their lives become more complicated. Resist the urge to get petty: Your children's relationship with both their parents must always come first.

✔ **Your community:** Are you friendly with your neighbours? Can you call on their friendship for help with babysitting? Are there groups or friendly churches in your area that welcome families of all shapes and sizes? Can you set up an 'exchange' scheme with local friends, where you take it in turns to care for each other's children while the 'free' parent has some time on her own?

✔ **Your kids:** As soon as they can toddle, they can help around the house – putting away toys or collecting the washing. Make sure that they grow up understanding that housework is a family effort – and everyone has to pull their weight.

It's fine to encourage your children to give you practical support but never let them become your emotional support. Dumping your adult worries on your kids isn't fair. Find someone else to talk to or let all your feelings out onto the pages of your diary.

Choosing mentors

The only thing a single parent can't do is be two people – which is where mentors come in. You bring them on at appropriate stages to do the being-the-extra-person bit. What you're looking for is someone who's the same sex as your child and who can be a great role model. For a boy, for example, that person may be a sports coach – someone who can, for example, show him how to channel aggression constructively, for the benefit of those around him. Mentoring works for girls because they get to learn from someone who isn't their mother; it works for boys because they get to learn what it is to be a man.

You don't have to march on your mentors with a great announcement and a trumpet fanfare; in fact, they don't even have to know that they've been chosen (although they'd probably be very touched). What matters is that you make sure that your child has regular (but sensible, safe, and appropriate) contact with that person for a while, and senses your approval.

Step-parenting: Raising a 'blended' family

Being a step-parent is tough – you're building a whole new family from the remnants of other ones and taking on responsibilities for children other people have raised. But tough doesn't have to mean terrible: You and your partner have every chance of helping your new family work together well as long as you

✔ **Agree on your roles and rules.** Before you move in together. Work through all the big issues – how you're going to discipline the kids, when and where you're all going to eat, sleep, do chores, and spend time together. And then be consistent about what you decide, so the children know where they stand (even if things are different in their other parent's house).

✔ **Accept your feelings – and your partner's.** It's impossible to love your stepchild as your own from the moment you first meet. You need to let loving feelings develop in their own time, without feeling anxious or guilty.

You also need to try not to be jealous of your partner's special bond with his or her own child.

✔ **Understand your separate challenges.** You're each having to make big adjustments but they're not necessarily the same ones.

✔ **Don't take children's negative reactions too personally.** They're kicking against the situation, not you. All they're looking for is reassurance that all these changes won't also change their parents' love for them.

✔ **Make time for each other.** Life as a 'step-couple' is busy and complex, and all sorts of practical 'who's meant to be where?' stuff can get in the way of your closeness as a couple. Don't let it. Set aside a special time every week to be alone together and have a laugh – your relationship needs some serious emotional investment for the whole stepfamily's sake.

Chapter 4

Other Secrets of Great Parenting

In This Chapter

▶ Believing in your own abilities

▶ Working out what really matters

▶ Discovering how to be strong, warm and positive

*L*ots of things make you a good parent. Being loving and cuddly and kind. Being clued-up about growth and development. Being sensible about behaviour and discipline. Being able to conjure up a healthy, kid-friendly meal from two scraggy onions and a tin of lentils. But there's really only one thing that makes you a *great* parent: Doing all of that – and more – with *attitude*.

And that's because, in the end, what influences your child most is not so much what you do as a parent as the way you do it. Great parenting's about staying positive, energetic, and strong; about trusting in your own abilities and learning from your mistakes; about not being afraid to stand back and let your children find their own feet; about hanging in there when things get tricky or sticky; and about keeping your sense of humour and remembering to have fun. Easy-peasy? Not always. But this chapter should certainly help.

Right Way? Wrong Way? Your Way

The first thing you need to accept is that you can't be a perfect parent. Perfect parents don't exist. There is no formula you can follow, no book you can read (even this one!), no course you can take that will stop you messing up or getting cross on a pretty regular basis. And there's no blueprint for parenting that fits every child: What works for one may be quite useless for another.

So, stop looking round for someone to show you the 'right' way to raise your kids; the right way is trusting yourself to do it 'your' way. Watching other parents – and reading this book – will give you vital insights, helpful hints, and crucial tips, but, in the end, it's up to you to discover what works best for you and your family. And to make that discovery, you need to

✔ **Believe in yourself.** You know your kids better than anyone else. Which means you are better equipped to bring them up than anyone else. Sure, you may need some help or guidance with the details every now and then, but, if it's all working well without you shouting the odds and without your kids being troublesome or unhappy, you're getting the essentials right.

✔ **Know what's important.** Which is that your children grow up feeling secure, loved, and understood – and able to treat other people with respect. Next to that, what time they have a bath or how old they are when they stop wearing nappies really doesn't matter one little bit.

✔ **Keep questioning yourself.** When you see other parents doing things differently, ask yourself whether there's anything you could learn from them. Are you being too rigid? Too laid-back? Are you stuck in a parenting rut? Great parents are always open to new ideas and not afraid to adapt what they do to suit their children's changing needs.

✔ **Be honest with your kids.** We all lose the plot at times, and we all make mistakes. When you do, admit it, apologise, and put it right. As long as your children know you love them, you've always got room to mess up – and make amends.

✔ **Remember you have a life, too.** Your children may be the focus of your day, but that doesn't mean being a parent has to define you completely. It's healthy for you to have things to do, people to see, and interests to explore outside your life with your kids. And it's healthy for your kids to see that you do, too.

Parenting's not about being perfect – but about being good enough. Sometimes what you do works; sometimes, it doesn't. What matters is that you keep doing your best in the most loving and committed way you can.

Big-Picture Parenting: Eight Skills That Will Serve You for Years

In the rest of this book, you'll find plenty of detail about the particular parenting skills you need during the four distinct phases of your child's first nine years (baby, toddler, preschooler, schoolchild). But there are some parenting dos and don'ts that are so useful and so fundamental that you'll need them whatever age and stage your child is at. So, never lose sight of the need to

✔ **Have great expectations:** Set high (but not impossibly high) standards and create clear, comprehensible rules. Explain them clearly and age-appropriately. And show belief in your children's ability to live up to them. As one very wise mum once told me, 'Treat your kids not as they are but as you'd like them to become.'

✔ **Build structure into the day:** Kids thrive on routine – they like their days to follow a pattern, and they like to know what they're going to be doing when. You don't have to timetable every minute of their day or give up on being spontaneous. But you do have to make your children feel safe by framing their daily life in a familiar and reliable way.

✔ **Notice when they're great:** Always comment on the things your children do that you like, admire, appreciate, or approve of. Especially if it's something they've struggled to do right or well before. You'll know how worth it this is when you see their faces light up at your words.

✔ **Listen and acknowledge:** Show your children you care about their feelings by listening properly to what they've got to say and then 'reflecting' back the essence of what you've heard (even if you don't agree with it or condone it): 'You sound really cross.'

✔ **Be consistent:** Do what you said you'd do. Every time. Your children need to know they can rely on you to mean what you say (even if they don't like it). For more on being consistent, see Chapter 2.

✔ **Keep them healthy:** Feed them well, exercise them often, and make sure they get enough sleep. They'll feel better and behave better for it – and prompt you to live more healthily, too!

✔ **Slow down:** Children don't operate at the same pace we do. They walk slower, think slower, do everything slower. You could spend your life getting cross and yelling at them to hurry up, but it's much, much nicer for everyone if you just take a deep breath, summon up bucketloads of patience, and settle for taking life at a more snail-y pace.

✔ **De-prioritise the housework:** Which would you rather be saying in 20 years' time: 'I wish I'd spent more time having fun with my kids' or 'I wish I'd spent more time scrubbing the skirting boards'? When your children are young, a sparkly, spick-and-span house is really not your top priority (even if it was, they'd only mess it up again in ten minutes). Do the stuff that matters (clean the loo, tidy the kitchen, unclutter the living-room floor); the skirting boards will keep for now.

✔ **Remember what it's like to be a child:** And cut them some slack now and again. There's no point going on and on at them to behave like grown-ups when, er, they're not actually grown-ups at all.

Your children actually *want* to behave well. They love you and want to please you. It's just that, sometimes, you need to show – or remind – them how.

Avoiding the Common Parenting Pitfalls

So, there you are, trying to get this parenting thing licked. You think you're doing okay – and then you notice that, all around you, other people are doing it very differently indeed. And you wonder whether you should be following suit.

Well, there are lots of brilliant parents out there who can certainly teach you a thing or two about raising great kids – and you can spot them because they're just quietly (and brilliantly) going about their parenting business. The ones you have to be careful of are the ones who parent 'in your face'. Because these people are often too busy flaunting their parenting superiority to realise they're making one (or all) of the three most common parenting mistakes. Read on to find out what they are – and how to avoid them.

Comparing and contrasting

There is absolutely nothing to be gained – and quite a lot to be lost – from constantly measuring your child against others. It's not good for you and it's certainly not good for your child because

- ✔ **Comparing is mean.** Yes, it *is* wonderful that your baby's sleeping through the night, but it's really not very nice of you to keep bragging about it to your friend whose baby's up from dusk to dawn. Besides, you shouldn't be taking all the credit: Your parenting skills aren't the main reason for your baby's sleeping prowess. Babies (and older children) only reach developmental milestones when their bodies are good and ready – great parenting skills can help but only so much. You'll find more about developmental stuff for the different ages in Chapters 10, 16, 19, and 24.

- ✔ **Things change.** So, Smug Mum's child can read at 3, and your child barely knows his letters? Well, fast-forward four years and, what do you know, Smug Mum's child's still reading well, but your child's the class bookworm, devouring stories so fast your library card's giving off sparks. Children rarely progress in a ploddy, gradual way; they tend to go through a series of super-speedy spurts. And there's no telling who's going to spurt when – or how far. Never get smug; it often leads to egg on the face.

- ✔ **Labels stick.** Your first baby crawls early: He's the sporty one. Your second baby talks early: She's the clever one. Your third baby's rather quiet: He's the shy one. See what you're doing? By giving your children labels, you're restricting what they can grow to be. Every child has a whole range of qualities and talents, and, as parents, we need to stand back and let them all emerge and develop in their own sweet time. Comparing and contrasting stops us doing that.

Over-parenting

Yes, it's our job to love and protect our children, but it's not our job to take it too far and smother them. They need space to think for themselves, try things themselves, do it all wrong themselves. Allowing this to happen is all rather counter-intuitive (you don't want them to botch *anything* up), but you need to stop yourself being

- **The do-it-all parent:** Running round after your kids, clearing up their mess, and picking out their clothes doesn't do them any favours at all. All it does is make your kids hopelessly dependent on you. As soon as your child can pick up and drop toys, he can put them back in the box; as soon as he can dress himself, he can find clean clothes to wear. Try to never do anything for your child that he could do – with a little how-to session from you – quite easily for himself.

- **The hover parent:** Babies and small toddlers need constant supervision, but they don't need constant hovering. As long as you've made your house reasonably childproof (for more on this, see Chapter 15), you can let your child crawl or toddle off and explore – not far, mind, but you don't need to be actually breathing down his neck. And older children should be allowed even further off the parental leash: Let them disappear up to their bedroom to make a den with a friend; encourage them to play on their own while you potter around nearby; sit on the bench in the playground and let them scramble up the climbing frame without you lurking nervously underneath. They'll be so much more confident for it.

Setting too much store by stuff

You wouldn't believe the amount of stuff some kids have. We're talking vast playrooms, shelves, and cupboards a-bulge with toys and games of all descriptions. And you also wouldn't believe how fervently – and regularly – some parents rush out to add the latest, grooviest, most developmentally stimulating children's toy to those already-bulging shelves.

Now, there are some truly great toys out there, and I'd hate us to return to the days when all children had to play with was a gnarled stick and a mouldy old orange, but I do think we parents have to guard against overdoing it on the buying-stuff front. And not just because it's flipping expensive (and heavy on the shelves). But also because

- **You can give your kids 'toy overload'.** Yes, they *can* have too much of a good thing. A child with zillions of toys to choose from simply gets over-whelmed and loses interest in them all.

- **You could be starting something you'll come to regret.** The child who's given every toy, gadget, DVD, and computer game going is a child who comes to expect them. Which means he never learns about waiting, working, and saving for something. He also never appreciates the value of things ('Got that, what's next?'). And he may also start to associate getting material goods with getting your affection and love – which could be as damaging to his emotional health as it is to your wallet.

✔ **It's not actually big, plastic, shiny things they want to play with.** It's you. A parent's time and undivided attention is worth so much more than shelves full of toys.

Five Golden Mantras Great Parents Repeat Every Day

Of course, knowing what you should – and shouldn't – be doing is all very well but, when you're in charge of a real live child (or three), your best parenting intentions can go out of the window amazingly fast. What matters at this point – when things are going rapidly to pot – is not what you've just done but what you're going to do next. Because most parenting slip-ups (and we all have them on a regular basis) can be rescued by reminding yourself of one (or maybe several) of the following five sanity-saving sayings.

'Onwards and upwards'

Your baby screamed all round the supermarket. Your toddler threw spaghetti all over the restaurant floor. And you're plummeting into the depths of parenting despair. This, you think, is the beginning of the end: You'll clearly never be able to shop or eat out in peace again. Whoa! Stop right there! Things didn't go that well today, that's true, but you have no reason to think that's how life's always going to be. There could be all sorts of reasons why everything kicked off – and maybe none of them had anything to do with your (lack of) parenting skills. Perhaps your baby was tired or your toddler had to wait too long for his food. You've had a bad experience. Learn from it if you can. Then let it go. Tomorrow will be so much better if you come at it with an optimistic and positive attitude.

'Don't forget to laugh'

Kids do really stupid things. Things that would crack you up – if you weren't already cracking up in a different kind of way. A bad day with the kids can test anybody's sense of humour, but try not to let it dent yours. Laughing at the stuff your children get up to is part of the joy of being a parent – even if you can only wind down enough to see the funny side once they're all tucked up in bed.

'Once more, with feeling'

Sometimes, all it takes to turn a parenting situation from grim to good is a little spurt of energy. That's not always so easy to muster when you're tired, but it really can make all the difference. Be enthusiastic about what your child's going to do, get excited about what he does do, be creative about the way you do things together. The more energetic and sparky you can be, the more your child will blossom in your company – and the easier you'll find it to be a better parent in his.

'Guilt gets you nowhere'

There will always be occasions when you're too stressed or too busy or too tired to give your children the kind of attention you'd like. And, okay, that's not something to be particularly proud of, but you do need to keep it in proportion: It's not like you do it all the time. We all have a tendency to filter out all the good things we do as parents and only remember the bad. So make a conscious effort always to come at your parenting the other way: Stop beating yourself up about what you haven't done, and start smiling about what you have. Every evening, think of three positive things you've done that day as a parent. And pat yourself on the back for that. It's a great way to sign off each day – feeling good, not guilty.

'It's a phase'

Every stage of childhood has its sticky patches: the non-sleeping-baby sticky patch; the tantrummy-toddler sticky patch; the picky-preschooler sticky patch; the smart-aleck-schoolchild sticky patch – to name but a few. And, when you're in the middle of one of these, you do begin to wonder if you'll ever find a way out. But you will. As long as you're patient, firm, and consistent (and this book is full of clever ways to be all three), the stickiness will pass. And you'll look back and laugh. Honest.

If you're having the parenting day from hell, get everyone outside. A little bit of exercise, a lot of fresh air, and a serious change of scene is just the thing to blow bad feelings away.

Horrid comments even good parents hear

Most people are nice to you when you have kids. They beam at you in the street, coo over your baby in the shops, smile sympathetically when your older kids badger you for sweets at the checkout. But there are always the exceptions, of course.

One sort specialises in new-mum confidence-undermining. Their favourite comments include 'He needs a feed' and 'That baby will catch his death without a hat'.

Others can be guaranteed to turn up just when your children, having behaved beautifully all day, decide to (shock!) be a bit noisy, run on ahead of you, or forget to say, 'Excuse me' as they pass by them on the pavement. Their well-rehearsed repertoire of bad-tempered phrases includes 'That child needs a good slap', 'Some children have no manners', and the particularly withering 'Can't you keep your children under control?'

Trouble is, these people's comments hurt. Nobody likes being told they're a bad parent, especially if their child is having a less-than-cherubic moment at the time. I had the 'catch his death without a hat' comment on a bus once and burst into tears on the spot.

So, how do you handle the comments? Remind yourself that you know nothing about these people – how bad a day they're having, how much their joints are aching, how long it's been since they had any sort of meaningful contact with anyone under the age of 10. And they don't know anything about you or your children, either – they've no more right to criticise your parenting skills than you have to criticise their fashion sense. Just smile ever so politely, say, 'Yes I am *wicked*, aren't I?' and trip merrily off into pleasanter public pastures.

Chapter 5

Childminders, Nurseries, and Nannies

In This Chapter
▶ Finding the best childcare
▶ Making it work as a working parent

*P*arenthood is full of big, scary stuff. But perhaps nothing is so big and scary as the prospect of handing over your baby to someone else for the day while you go off to work. What seemed so wonderfully simple before you became a parent suddenly seems incredibly difficult now that you are.

Childcare comes in so many shapes and guises that it can be hard to think straight and choose wisely. So this chapter's all about sorting out the right set-up and getting the best out of it – for you and your child. After all, whether you're going back to work full-time or part-time, because you want to or because you need to, what matters more than anything is knowing that you're leaving your child in the most loving and capable of hands.

Choosing the Right Option for You

First, you need to have a good old think about the kind of care you're after. Here are your four main options, with a rundown of the pros and cons of each.

Just because a particular childcare option is right for your best friend, it doesn't necessarily mean it's right for you. Your friend probably doesn't have the same working hours or the same income – and she certainly doesn't have the same child.

The day nursery

A day nursery – whether workplace, community, council, or private – is the number-one childcare choice for most working parents. And they plump for a nursery because

- ✔ **It's regularly inspected.** By Social Services, by Ofsted (the Office For Standards in Education; read the reports at www.ofsted.gov.uk), and by environmental health officers.
- ✔ **It's full of children the same age.** So your baby will have others to interact with.
- ✔ **It's (usually) open all year.** So you're not left in the lurch if someone's ill or on holiday. And its hours (8 a.m. to 6/6.30 p.m.) wrap well around the working day.
- ✔ **It has dedicated staff.** With no other demands on their time. And at least half of them must be qualified in early-years education.
- ✔ **It must have 'an appropriate and structured learning programme'.** Or Ofsted will be down on it like a ton of bricks.

But, before you shout, 'Hallelujah!' and flip the phone book to N for nursery, do get your head around these potential drawbacks:

- ✔ **It doesn't offer one-to-one care.** Although, with babies under 2, the adult/child ratio should never be less than 1:3.
- ✔ **It won't take your child if she's ill**. You'll have to arrange other care if your child's under the weather and you can't stay home.
- ✔ **It's probably got a long waiting list.** Which may present a problem for those who need childcare now.
- ✔ **It could be very expensive.** Although you may be able to get help with fees through the Working Families Tax Credit.
- ✔ **Its hours may not be flexible enough.** Especially if you work shifts or only want part-time or part-day childcare.
- ✔ **It's not your home.** And you may have to travel some way to get there.

The childminder

A childminder is a self-employed carer who looks after children in her (and it is, almost always, her) own home. Parents who rate the childminder option tend to do so because

✔ **She is regularly inspected.** As is her home. She may well have other childcare qualifications and, in many parts of the country, she'll have to have completed a basic registration course, including first-aid training.

✔ **She's likely to be a parent herself.** It'll help that she has experience of how children behave.

✔ **She lives locally.** Which can make the commute more manageable.

✔ **She may be able to offer flexible hours**. A good thing if your work schedule isn't of the every-day-from-9-to-5 variety.

✔ **She provides care in a home environment.** With a small group of other children for your child to play with.

✔ **She doesn't have an age limit.** Childminders can look after children of all ages, from babies to teenagers. Which means you won't need to scrabble for after-school care in a few years' time: She could do it for you.

But despite all the good stuff she has to offer, a childminder may not be right for you because

✔ **She may not take your child if she's ill.** Or if your child's ill.

✔ **She probably can't offer one-to-one care.** But childminders can only care for one child under 1 and no more than three children under 5.

✔ **She will have a set pattern to her day.** And other children to take/collect from school. Your child will have to fall in with this routine.

✔ **She may be caring for other children who are a lot older than yours.** Which may not be what you want.

The nanny

A nanny is a carer employed by you to look after your child in your own home. She (or, occasionally, he) may live with you in your house or live somewhere else and come to you every day. Sometimes, you can 'share' a nanny with another family – with the nanny either working different days for each family or looking after both sets of children every day.

The advantages of having a nanny are pretty clear-cut:

✔ **She can provide one-to-one care.** And your darling will reap the benefits.

✔ **She's caring for your child in your house.** Getting used to a new environment is one less thing your child will have to handle in the transition from mummy- (or daddy-) care to childcare.

✔ **She can follow your routines and methods.** Which can make the transition a bit easier for both you and your child.

✔ **She works the hours/days you need.** You can set up the schedule in your contract.

✔ **She can babysit.** If she's 'live in', it may even be part of her contract.

But you do need to ponder if you can live with these very real drawbacks:

✔ **She may not be trained.** Although many nannies are.

✔ **She's your employee.** So you're responsible for sorting out her tax and national insurance contributions.

✔ **She may be expensive.** Experienced nannies often are.

✔ **She's harder to check up on**. There is no central 'nanny register', so it's up to you to check her references very thoroughly indeed.

✔ **She'll have a very personal relationship with you.** Especially if she's 'living in'. You may find this uncomfortable or difficult to manage. And, if you're employing her as a nanny share, you'll also have to work at building a good relationship with the other family.

The granny

If Granny (or any other relative) is up for the responsibility, you may see this as the most obvious – not to say the most economical – childcare solution. But it's definitely worth taking the time to think this idea through properly first.

Obviously, Granny scores major points on the childcare front because

✔ **She's a family member.** And so probably loves your child almost as much as you do. Giving her the opportunity to strengthen her bond with your child can only be a good thing for everyone.

✔ **She'll probably be flexible about hours and days.** But beware of abusing her generosity on this point.

✔ **She's a mother herself.** Obviously.

✔ **She'll probably be able to look after your child even if she's ill.** And few things are better than Granny cuddles when you're feeling poorly.

✔ **She'll care for your child in her home or yours.** Both of which are familiar environments.

But don't assume granny-care's a done deal without considering that

- ✔ **She may find it too much.** Caring for a small child can be exhausting, particularly if you're not in the first flush of youth.

- ✔ **She may have a different parenting style.** And it can be trickier to get her to do things your way if she's your relative, not your employee.

- ✔ **She may not have a very child-friendly home.** If that's where she's caring for your child.

- ✔ **She may not 'mix'.** An older relative may not feel comfortable at toddler groups and baby-singing classes, which means your child may not meet many other children her own age.

- ✔ **She may feel taken for granted.** Informal childcare arrangements, particularly ones where no money changes hands, are tricky to sustain in the long term. You may feel it's not worth the risk of falling out with a much-loved member of your family.

Finding the Right People for the Job

Once you've a clear idea of the kind of childcare you're after, you need to start researching what's on offer near you. (Unless, of course, you're going for the granny option – see preceding section – in which case you can just feel smug and put your feet up.)

Going on a nursery hunt?

There are good nurseries and bad nurseries, and there's really no way of telling one from the other unless you have a real nose around. So find a list of local nurseries in your phone book, call them to find out which have fees and hours that suit you, and then get out there visiting the contenders.

What to look for

Bear in mind that some nurseries have very good 'patter-merchants' doing their parent tours. But much more important than the spiel you're being fed are the things you see around you on the way. Good signs include:

- ✔ **A welcoming feel:** Big, cheerful, informative noticeboards. Children's artwork on the wall. Staff who smile when they see you.

- ✔ **Bright, clean, child-friendly rooms:** And a separate quiet room where babies can nap in peace. Depending on the age of your child, you may also feel that having some outside space is important.

✔ **Calm, happy children:** Who are interacting well with their carers.

✔ **Happy, busy staff:** Who look cuddly, capable, and interested in what their little charges are up to.

✔ **A good routine:** With time for play, music, cuddles, sleep, and healthy food. And a willingness to accommodate any special requirements.

✔ **A great feedback system:** How do you find out what your child's been up to all day? And how detailed a report will you get?

What to ask

Don't feel embarrassed to ask as many questions as you like. Take a list with you, so that nothing slips your mind on the day. Good questions include:

✔ **How many children do you look after here?** How many of them are babies? Do you have specific carers to look after the babies? What is the ratio of carers to babies ? And what are their qualifications? Will my baby have a *keyworker* (a main-contact carer)?

✔ **How long have most of your carers been here?** A rapid staff turnover is not a good sign. A good nursery should be able to retain its staff.

✔ **Can I see your most recent Ofsted report?** Ask this even if you've already read it. Because then you can ask: What improvements have you made in response to their recommendations?

✔ **Talk me through an average day.** When will my baby eat/sleep/play? Will my baby have to fit into your routine or will you fit round hers? Where do you change nappies? Do you take the children outside?

✔ **What's your policy on discipline and bad behaviour?** Make sure the answers are age appropriate and agree with your own feelings about suitable discipline practices.

✔ **How do you keep in touch with parents?** How do parents contact you?

✔ **Can I stay for a while and watch?** A good nursery shouldn't have a problem with you doing this.

Don't sign on the dotted line until . . .

There may be dozens of other parents beating down the door for a place, but never let yourself be pressurised into signing your child up before

✔ **You've been back at least once and spent time there with your child.** You may love the place, but if it's not a good fit with your child, all bets are off.

✔ **You're sure you can afford the fees.** And you're clear about their 'sick child' policy and late pick-up penalties.

- ✔ **You've talked to other parents who send/sent their children there.** And are comfortable with their opinions.

- ✔ **You feel you can trust the carers.** And they understand what really matters to you.

Think overall picture, rather than picky details. And be prepared to 'give' a little. However much you'd like your child to have organic food, say, is it really worth passing on the friendly, good-quality nursery that ticks all your other boxes for the organic-food one that doesn't quite 'feel' so right?

Going on a childminder hunt?

The best way to find a childminder is through word-of-mouth recommendation. But, even if every parent you meet recommends the same one, try to visit some other childminders in your area, too, so you compare and contrast their methods and personalities. Your local authority should have a list of childminders in your area. Or you can visit www.childcarelink.gov.uk (not available in Northern Ireland; try www.nicma.org instead).

What to look for

Childminders can't compete with nurseries on the purpose-built, flashy-equipment front. But that's not important. What *is* important to see is

- ✔ **A clean, safe, and welcoming home.** With suitable toys and books. And a quiet space for babies to nap in.

- ✔ **Some outside space to play in.** Or at least a park nearby.

- ✔ **A registration certificate, Ofsted report, and course certificates.** Don't forget references from other parents you can follow up.

What to ask

Don't hold back with the questions – forget social niceties and get nosey. You need to find out as much as you can about the childminder and the way she likes to work. And always remember to ask:

- ✔ **How many children do you look after?** And what are their ages? Will your own children be around when my child is here? How old are they?

- ✔ **Who else lives in your house?** Do any of them smoke? Do you have pets?

- ✔ **How long have you been childminding?** What do you like about it? Have you done any extra training? Do you have a first-aid qualification?

✔ **Talk me through an average day.** When will my baby eat/sleep/play? Will my baby have to fit into your routine or will you fit round hers? What food do you serve? Where do you change nappies? How much TV do the children watch? Do you take them outside? Or to other activities?

✔ **How will I find out what my child's been doing all day?** Do you keep a record book?

✔ **How do you discipline and encourage good behaviour?** Again, make sure you're comfortable with her answers.

✔ **What's your 'sick child' policy?** Do you charge for late pick-ups? How much holiday do you take every year?

Don't sign on the dotted line until . . .

Think you've found the right childminder for you? Never book a place with her before

✔ **You've been back at least once and seen the childminder interact with your child.** You may even be able to organise a trial session.

✔ **You've got a proper contract.** That details everything from fees and contracted hours of care to holiday and sick pay and late pick-up charges.

✔ **You've talked to other parents who send/sent their children to her.** And found out what they like about her and how she deals with parents.

✔ **You feel you can trust her.** And she understands what matters to you.

The best child carers aren't necessarily the best at getting on with parents. Watch how your child responds to the childminder before making your mind up.

Going on a nanny hunt?

Nannies aren't listed on a central register, so you need to put out feelers in several directions. You can ask other parents for recommendations; look in the local paper or on noticeboards at toddler groups or in child-friendly shops; or take out an ad in *The Lady* (be warned: You'll get *a lot* of replies, some of them laughably unsuitable) or, if you live within the M25 area, in *Simply Childcare* (a kind of *Exchange & Mart* for nannies; for details, visit www.simplychildcare.com). You can also phone a nanny agency but, if they find you a nanny, you'll have to pay a hefty fee.

Once you've got a list of possibles, give them all a call and weed out the ones who clearly don't have the experience/non-smoking habits/driving qualifications (or whatever) you're looking for. Then arrange interviews with the rest.

What to look for

First impressions count. You'll probably know within minutes if this nanny is your sort of nanny – but make sure she also ticks the boxes for:

- ✔ **The right attitude:** A bright, friendly, can-do attitude will do nicely, thanks.

- ✔ **An obvious and immediate interest in your child.** You can tell quite a bit by how this nanny interacts, however briefly, with your child.

- ✔ **Relevant certificates.** Including, preferably, an NNEB or NVQ level 3 qualification and a first-aid certificate.

- ✔ **References.** Many nannies come with a folder of testimonials from previous employers. Make sure you follow these up.

What to ask

Be thorough with your questions: Because nannies aren't regulated as tightly as nurseries and childminders, you really can't afford to take anything for granted. Don't forget to ask:

- ✔ **What was your last job like?** Why did you leave it? Why do you want this one? What do you enjoy about nannying? What do you think is the most important part of your job?

- ✔ **How will you organise my child's day?** What sort of things do you like to cook? What activities do you like to do? How would you let me know what my child's been doing/eating each day?

- ✔ **Have you ever had to deal with a medical emergency while a child was in your care**? What did you do?

- ✔ **How would you encourage good behaviour in my child?** How would you discipline a child of this age?

- ✔ **What type of household chores would you be prepared to do?** Make sure her expectations and yours are compatible.

- ✔ **Do you have any friends working as nannies nearby?** If so, they're likely to visit your house in the day, so you may want to meet them, too.

- ✔ **How long would you stay in this job?** Even Mary Poppins didn't stay forever. Find out when this nanny plans to fly.

Don't sign on the dotted line until . . .

You may think she's just the nanny you're looking for, but it's still not wise to employ any nanny before

- ✔ **She's had a second interview.** And preferably a trial day. And you're both clear exactly what the job entails, what the salary is, and what the live-in arrangements (if any) are.

- ✔ **You've got a proper contract.** That details everything from the job description and hours of work to holiday and sick pay and notice periods.

✔ **You've talked to previous employers.** As many of them as possible. Bear in mind that good nannies don't just get good references, they get gushing ones – of the 'we'd have her back tomorrow'/'she'll always be part of our family' type.

✔ **You feel you can trust her.** And she understands what matters to you.

If you feel daunted by the paperwork involved with sorting out your nanny's tax and national insurance, think about getting a specialist firm, such as Nannytax (www.nannytax.co.uk), to do it for you. They'll charge you a small fee but save you a lot of hassle.

And when they're older?

'Oh, this whole childcare thing will be so much easier when they're at school.' Or so you think – until you come to it. Childcare for preschoolers or school-age children is generally less expensive (fewer hours to pay for) but can be trickier to organise. That's because, most of the time, you only need a couple of hours of care a day but, in the school holidays, you need full days. And it can be hard to find takers for that sort of arrangement. Most parents opt for one of the following, often combining it with some sort of activity club or camp in the school holidays:

✔ **Wrap-around care:** More and more schools and preschools are offering breakfast clubs and after-school sessions to meet working parents' childcare needs. Advantage? Your child doesn't have to schlep off to someone else's house. Disadvantage? If you use wrap-around care every day, your child's spending an awfully long time in the same place.

✔ **A childminder:** Many childminders will drop off and pick up from school and preschool. Advantage? Your child gets to chill after school with a small group of children in a loving and stimulating home environment. Disadvantage? Not all childminders will be able to look after older children full-time during the school holidays.

✔ **An au pair:** Au pairs are young foreign nationals who come to the UK to study English and offer help in the house in exchange for board, lodging, and a small wage. Advantage? Your child gets to come home at the end of the school day. Disadvantage? Your au pair may have no childcare experience and, as English is not her mother tongue, you can't expect her to oversee homework. She also lives in your house and her welfare is your responsibility.

✔ **Friends:** If both you and your friend work part-time, you could arrange to look after each other's children on your days off. Advantage? The childcare's free and your children get great playdates out of it. Disadvantage? Unless you work very hard at keeping it fair and worthwhile for both of you, this kind of arrangement can break down very easily.

Separation and Settling In

When you've done the hard-headedly practical research-and-question bit, you're ready for the heart-breakingly emotional hand-over-and-reassure bit. You're probably anticipating floods of tears at this point, but don't be surprised if you're doing just as much – if not more – blubbing as your baby. Lay in extra supplies of tissues and make sure you

✔ **Do some groundwork.** Get her used to being in the company of other adults and children by taking her to baby groups and friends' houses (if you don't already).

✔ **Talk to her.** About the lovely nursery she's going to or the lovely childminder/nanny she's going to meet. Okay, so there's no knowing how much she'll understand but hearing you say 'nursery/childminder/nanny' in such a calm and happy way will set up good associations – and you'll definitely feel better for saying it!

✔ **Give yourselves lots of time.** You'll feel better about going back to work if your child's already in a settled routine with her new carer and that can take longer than you think – three weeks is probably about average. To begin with, you'll need to stay with your child for a while, then leave for a while, gradually extending the length of time you're away from her. Assume that, for much of the first week at least, you'll be hanging out in the local coffee shop, clutching your mobile phone, and counting the minutes till you're due back.

✔ **Be guided by your carer.** Let her set the pace of the settling-in process – she's the one with the experience here.

✔ **Hold your nerve.** Your child will be much less likely to wobble if you look completely happy and positive about what's happening (even if you're really a nervous wreck underneath).

✔ **Have a transitional object.** If your baby's not being cared for in your own home, take a (cheap and replaceable) toy or blanket with you. This object's a part of home to hang on to – and taking it is a ritual that helps your baby understand what's coming up today.

✔ **Leave quickly.** When it's time to go, go. But don't sneak out. Say goodbye with a kiss and a big smile. You can sob all you like once you're out of earshot.

Tears are not a sign that your child hates her nursery/nanny/childminder. They're a sign that she's sad to see you go.

The Wise Parent's Guide to Childcare

What matters as much as choosing the right carers for your child? Keeping them, of course! And making sure they continue to provide your child with loving and nurturing care as she develops and grows. To do both, you need to

✔ **Be considerate.** The parent-carer relationship is a two-way street. You can't expect Mary Poppins-like perfection from your carer if you don't pick up on time or at least phone ahead when you're delayed.

✔ **Communicate well.** Your relationship with your childminder/nanny/ nursery carers will work much better if you make an effort to get to know them and point out all the things you appreciate. Always be clear about your concerns and ready to listen to theirs. Try to approach bigger challenges, such as potty training and behaviour issues, as a team, instead of simply issuing orders.

✔ **Anticipate relapses.** Even if she settles well at first, your child will probably have the odd 'crying patch' every now and then. This behaviour is normal and not a sign that her care is poor. Be more worried about consistently unsettled behaviour.

✔ **Check up.** Every now and then. Ask friends/neighbours who see your childminder/nanny out and about how your child seems with her. Does she look happy? Are they interacting well? If your child's at a nursery, drop in unannounced one day just to see if all's as it should be.

✔ **Organise back-up.** Try to enlist relatives/friends as emergency carers, should your carer fall ill or your child fall ill at nursery when you're stuck in a meeting. Make an agreement with your partner to share days off when your child is ill.

✔ **Try not to nitpick.** If your nanny's wonderful with your child, is it worth criticising her less-than-perfect tidying at the end of the day? If your nursery's great but you don't like the way the staff always put on a video at pick-up time, is it really worth making a fuss?

✔ **Keep reviewing things.** It would be nice to stick with the same carers till your child starts school, but sometimes that's just not possible. Maybe you want your child to go to preschool and can't afford to pay a nanny as well. Maybe the cosy little nursery that suited your baby so well is too small for the restless toddler she's become. Change isn't a bad thing, if you're doing it for the right reasons.

Back to Work

Returning to the 9-to-5 after maternity leave is a breeze for some and a challenge for others, but one thing's a certainty for all of us: Going to work is never as simple as it used to be. Now you need to organise all this extra stuff before you set off and then deal with lots of emotional stuff once you're there.

The practicalities: Sorted!

Annoying fact of back-to-work life: You've got less time than ever for all those little chores but, because you've got a baby, you've more chores than ever to do. To minimise the daily faff factor as much as possible

- ✔ **Cut down on shopping.** Try ordering your groceries online.

- ✔ **Get ready the night before.** Put out your baby's clothes for the next day (and her bag of spare clothes and nappies) before you go to bed. Ditto your own work outfit. Wear an old T-shirt at breakfast time if your child plays fast and loose with the Weetabix.

- ✔ **Get filing.** Have a folder for all your childcare contracts and documents. And a calendar for marking down parents' evenings, fundraisers, childminder's holidays, and so on.

- ✔ **Plan ahead.** Be that annoying person in the office who's booked all her annual leave days by the first week in January. You don't want to go to all the trouble of co-ordinating your carer's holiday with yours only to find one of your co-workers has booked that week off before you.

You can't be a working parent and a domestic goddess without turning into a pleasure-starved drudge. Cut culinary corners, get a cleaner, and spend your time at home with your child, not your duster.

If you're breastfeeding, you may decide to give up when you return to work, but doing so certainly isn't compulsory. For more on breastfeeding and working, see Chapter 7.

The guilt: Busted!

Inside every working mother's head (and I'm not being sexist here – it really is only mothers who hear it), a nasty, nagging little voice is telling you you're just not up to motherhood scratch. You're blighting your child's chances in life, it says, by leaving her at nursery and tripping off to work instead of staying home and hothousing her with home-made flashcards. Shut that voice up nice and firmly by reminding yourself that

- ✔ **It's wrong:** Yes, there have been plenty of scary studies about the damaging effects of poor-quality childcare (from mothers, as well as other carers). But no one has ever shown that loving and high-quality childcare disadvantages a child in any significant way.

✔ **Your child's happy:** And thriving and learning in a loving environment. Which is what matters most, after all.

✔ **Good childcare has lasting benefits:** Children who go to nursery or have a childminder are generally more sociable. They make friends easily and quickly learn to take turns and behave considerately towards others. They also get to experience another slice of life: Maybe you're not very sporty, for example, but your nanny's an active, outdoor type, or maybe you're not very good at arts and crafts, but the staff in your nursery are wizards with tissue paper and a pot of PVA glue.

✔ **You're doing your best:** Maybe you have to work to make ends meet; maybe you need to work to get some balance in your life. Either way, you're striving to keep everyone in your family healthy and happy.

✔ **You're still her mother:** And, when the chips are down, the most important person in her life. Nothing's going to change that.

If you're finding working full-time too much, you have a right to ask your employer to consider a request for part-time or flexible hours.

Don't rush the switch from worker to parent at the end of the day. Go for a short walk or sit in the car for a few minutes. Shake off your office mood and re-focus on that huge cuddle you're about to share.

Part II
All About Babies

"For God's sake, Martha, not here!"

In this part . . .

Babies look sweet, smell gorgeous, and snuggle heart-meltingly into your arms. They also dribble, cry, poo and throw up down your best jumper. The first 12 months of parenthood are packed with joy and challenge and this part's all about helping you through. In it, you'll find practical tips for the blurry-eyed early days, honest advice on breast- and bottle-feeding, and straight-talking guides to sleep, health and weaning onto solids.

Chapter 6

Surviving, Thriving, and Diving In: Getting Accustomed to Having a Baby

In This Chapter

▶ Finding your feet in the first six weeks

▶ Getting your head round the stuff nobody told you

▶ Taking care of yourself and your relationship

Congratulations! Your bump has landed – welcome to Planet Parent! Your mission (no choosing; you have to accept it) is to find a way through the strange, alien landscape that is early parenthood and emerge, a little wearier and a lot wiser, a year later. I'm not going to pretend it'll be a walk in the park (you've a steep learning curve to climb) but, with this chapter to guide you, you'll find it easier to skip round the most common pitfalls and even find time to marvel at your wonderful new world view.

The First Six Weeks

Right, let's cut to the chase: The first six weeks of a new parent's life are amazing, exhausting, and bewildering in pretty much equal measure. You may have attended every antenatal class going, but nothing, absolutely nothing, prepares you for the shocking realisation that this tiny bundle of life in your arms is now your responsibility – and yours alone. And, dammit, you haven't a clue what to do.

Fasten on your L-plates

So it takes you fifteen minutes to put on a nappy? Half an hour to fix the rain-cover on the pram? Don't beat yourself up: Your baby's not going to trade you in for someone with quicker fingers.

Accept that, however talented and experienced you are at other things in life, as a parent you're a stumbling, nervous trainee. Your lack of experience is nothing to be ashamed of: As with any new job, it's going to take a while for you to get the hang of things but, the more hours you put in, the more confident you'll become – and the faster those fingers will move.

Tear up the to-do list

In the days Before Baby, you could get up, get dressed, have breakfast, wash up, vacuum the living room, pop out for a paper, pick up the dry cleaning, and still have a couple of hours to kill before lunch. In the days After Baby, you're doing well if you've got up and got dressed before lunch.

While your body's getting over the birth and your mind's getting used to this whole being-a-parent thing, doing the household chores should not even figure on your list of priorities. Just for now, forget the ironing, eat ready meals, get the papers delivered, pay for a cleaner (if you can), and stamp firmly on any guilty feelings by reminding yourself that anyone can vacuum but no one else can be your baby's parent.

Jump at all offers of help

A new baby in the house will have people beating a path to your door, bearing gifts and goodies and offering help. Make it your policy never to turn them down.

Whether these people are up for pushing your baby round the park for half an hour, tackling that ironing mountain, rustling up lunch, or simply making you a cup of tea, say yes straight away and gratefully let them get on with it while you read a magazine, take a long bath, or veg out on the sofa. Why? Partly because making people feel useful is nice but mainly because, take it from me, the offers will dry up in a few weeks' time when the novelty of your new-parent status starts to wear off. This is your being-helped window of opportunity: Don't let it pass you by.

Why Didn't Anyone Tell Me?

However prepared you think you are for this whole parenthood lark, there are some things about your newborn that will come as a bit of a shock. Here are some of the postnatal realities that took me by surprise (so they won't scare the pants off you). . . .

He looks so weird!

Babies rarely enter this world looking as cute and cuddly as you'd imagined. Your average newborn has an enormous head, chicken legs, and, often, a bit of a bashed-up face (the temporary result of being squeezed through somebody else's pelvis). Other things not to panic over include:

- ✔ **A pointy head:** Getting down that birth canal can mould a baby's head into a positively Martian state of pointiness, especially if he's helped out with a ventouse (a vacuum suction cup). All should return to Earthly roundness in a couple of weeks.

- ✔ **A throbbing patch on the top of his head:** This is the *fontanelle,* a soft spot where the skull bones have not yet fused together. Being able to see a pulse beating beneath the skin is quite normal. (If the fontanelle ever looks sunken, though, that's not normal and can be a sign your baby's dehydrated.)

- ✔ **Squinty eyes**: Another short-lived newborn quirk, thought to be caused by post-delivery swelling.

- ✔ **Spots on the face:** These can either be white (and known as milia or 'milk spots') or red with yellow centres. Don't squeeze or put cream on either. They'll disappear on their own.

- ✔ **Body hair:** This is *lanugo,* a downy prenatal fuzz that won't linger long after the birth.

- ✔ **Swollen breasts and/or genitals:** Common (and temporary) in both girls and boys and caused by maternal oestrogen passing into their blood during birth. Sometimes, there can be a little bleeding from a baby girl's vagina and/or a little leaking of milk from either a boy's or a girl's breasts. Weird but normal.

He cries such a lot

All small babies cry. Sometimes they cry a bit, sometimes they cry a lot, and sometimes they never seem to stop. And babies cry because doing so is the only way they have of letting you know they want something. Sadly, exactly what that something is isn't always obvious (even to second- or third-time-around parents).

Decoding his cries

Unless your baby is ill (showing a temperature, being sick), start by assuming he's after one of the following five things:

- Milk
- Sleep
- A clean nappy
- A good burp
- A cuddle

Work your way through the list (and the wails) until you hit the jackpot. If nothing on the list works (and this is certainly not unknown), try checking his clothes for itchy labels or snagged socks. If that doesn't work, try some of these comforting tricks:

- **The swaddle:** Many newborns find it really comforting to be bundled up in a blanket and held close.

- **The pram push:** Put him in the pram and wheel it back and forth over your living room floor. The rhythmic motion can soothe his cries.

- **The sshh:** Hold your baby and, with your lips about 10 centimetres from his ear, murmur 'Sshhh', slowly getting louder until you're as loud as his cries. Keep sshhing till he stops.

- **The change of scene:** Fresh air can stop wailing in an instant. Put your baby in the pram or sling and get outside.

As your baby gets older, you may find you can hear the variations in his cries – a tired baby, for example, usually has a very different cry to a hungry one. Listen carefully to the pauses between wails and the changes in their volume and pitch and, soon, you should be able to figure out what he's after pretty much as soon as he opens his mouth.

Coping with colic

Colic is a kind of uber-crying some babies do that breaks your heart, tries your patience, and shreds your nerves. It kicks off at specific times of day (often the late afternoon or early evening) and lasts for at least two hours. A colicky baby will pull up his knees, clench his fists, and scream and scream and scream. Nobody's yet discovered exactly what causes colic (though

there are plenty of theories around) but everyone agrees that this screaming's a shocker to handle. If your baby has colic, it may help to:

- ✔ **Get in the car:** The combination of a change of scene and the vibration
  of the engine often delivers a lovely, sleep-inducing double-whammy.

- ✔ **Offer a finger:** Or a dummy. Sucking for comfort, rather than food, can
  be very soothing.

- ✔ **Put him over your knees:** Most babies love lying on their tummies in
  your lap, and colicky babies often quieten when you combine this with
  some gentle, rhythmic back-patting.

- ✔ **Feed upright:** Colic does sometimes seem to be associated with wind:
  Your baby will swallow less air as he feeds if you prop him up a little.
  Make sure you wind him frequently, too (for more on winding, see
  Chapter 7).

- ✔ **Offer a new pair of arms:** Struggling to calm a colicky babe is incredibly
  stressful and what does a baby do when he senses your stress? Cries
  more. As soon as you start tensing up, hand him over to someone else, if
  you can.

- ✔ **Take time out:** If you've reached breaking point, put your baby down
  somewhere safe and leave him for a few minutes. Use these minutes to
  take deep breaths, have a cup of tea – anything that helps you regain
  your calm and perspective.

- ✔ **Know it will end:** Almost all babies grow out of colic before they're 3
  months old, and even the diehard screamers have calmed down by 5.
  Hold fast to the knowledge that this awfulness won't last forever and
  colic has never been shown to damage babies in any way.

Not all babies who cry a lot have colic. Some babies just cry a lot, full stop. If
you're unlucky enough to have an all-hours crier, don't waste your energy
looking for special colic cures; just hang in there, doing the best you can, and
it will pass – honest.

Your baby is crying because he needs you to make something happen. And if
you don't turn up and try to make it happen, he'll only cry louder. Only now
he'll be crying because he's feeling abandoned and confused, too. Picking up
your baby quickly is not spoiling him; it's self-preservation: The sooner you
respond to your baby's cries, the easier you'll find it to calm him.

It's a boy/girl thing: clinginess

Boys are the weaker sex. No, really. From the moment of conception, boys are more fragile, and, after they're born, although they may look more muscular, they are, developmentally, about a month behind the girls.

Why does this matter? Because this extra vulnerability makes newborn boys much needier than newborn girls, so they tend to demand more attention and take longer to calm after crying. If you have a cranky, clingy baby boy, don't try to 'toughen him up' by denying him cuddles; he needs your comforting touch more than you think.

I can't handle this tiredness

No matter how many all-night benders you clocked up before you became a parent, nothing, but nothing, prepares you for the bone-achingly deep numbness that is new-mum tiredness. Adrenaline and excitement may carry you through the first couple of weeks but then the sleep deprivation hits you like a sledgehammer and you stumble through life in a bleary-eyed daze.

Take comfort from the fact that everyone else with a tiny baby is in the same bleary-eyed boat as you (even if they swear their child sleeps from dusk to dawn). Don't be ashamed to grab daytime naps whenever you can – if your baby's sleeping, you should be, too. And above all, trust that this sleep deprivation will pass – the very worst is usually over in six to eight weeks, the worst by fifteen weeks, and, boy, is it wonderful when it is!

He's suddenly so hungry

This baby behaviour's a real killer. There you are, exhausted but happy, congratulating yourself on finally getting some sort of handle on this baby-feeding thing when your sweet little once-every-three-hours feeder suddenly starts rooting around for milk at all hours of the day and night.

Don't panic; you're just having a growth spurt (or, rather, your baby is). Growth spurts can happen at any time but tend to be most common at 3 weeks, 6 weeks, and 3 months. The good news is, growth spurts rarely last longer than a week so surviving is simply a question of (are you detecting a theme yet?) hanging in there till it passes. (For more about growth spurts, see Chapter 7.)

Heated debate: Dummies – good or bad?

If you haven't found out already, you soon will: Dummies are controversial. Parents either love them or hate them. It's amazing, really, how much emotion a small piece of plastic can stir up. So, before you throw in your lot with the dummy-lovers or the dummy-haters, allow me to present the case for both sides of the dummy divide – and sort out the dummy truths from the myths.

The dummy-lovers' case is short and sweet: Dummies are great because they soothe your baby's cries when nothing else seems to be working. And, for many babies, that's indisputably true: Not for nothing are dummies called pacifiers in the US. Regularly giving your baby a dummy while he sleeps has also been linked with a lower risk of cot death. For more on cot death and precautions you can take to try to avoid it, see Chapter 9.

The dummy-haters' case is longer and slightly less watertight:

- They are ugly and make babies look stupid. Granted, they're no thing of beauty but maybe you can live with that.

- They make breastfeeding harder. Certainly possible. Giving a very small baby a dummy can cause 'nipple confusion' (sucking on a dummy is quite different to sucking on a human nipple), making it harder for you to establish breastfeeding.

- They can give your child wonky teeth. True, but only if your child still has a dummy at age 5 or 6 when his permanent teeth are coming through. Also, sucking a thumb can cause just as much tooth-wonkiness as sucking a dummy but at least you can throw a dummy away.

- They can delay language development. Possibly, but only if your child's plugged in to it morning, noon, and night.

- They become such a source of comfort to your child, you'll have a battle getting him to give it up when he's older. Very possible.

- They can cause night-time waking when they fall out of your sleeping baby's mouth. Often true but at least the back-to-sleep solution is close at (your) hand.

- They are used by lazy mums who can't be bothered to find out what their baby's really upset about. I wouldn't put it quite like that but I would say that, if you use a dummy a lot during the day, questioning your motives every now and then is worthwhile: Does your baby really need a comforting suck or are you just buying his silence for a while? While there's often nothing wrong with taking the quick route to peace (when you need to take an important phone call, for example), be aware that a dummy is essentially your baby's route to peace, not yours.

As long as you have your dummy facts straight, I don't think it much matters whether you use one or not – and I mean that in the nicest possible way. For some 'sucky' babies, having one makes all the difference in the world and, if that's the case with yours, fine. You know best what works for your baby and you shouldn't have to justify your decision to anyone.

Once your baby's over six months old, though, and generally seems more settled, I would try limiting dummy-use to night-time or nap-time or even try taking it away altogether. Removing the dummy may not work but, if it does, you may well have saved yourself a giving-up struggle with a dummy-dependent toddler.

Holding Patterns

A newborn's head and body flop all over the place, so he needs to be picked up, held, and carried with care. While he still has no control of his neck muscles, you need to support his neck and head for him but that doesn't mean you're doomed always to adopt the two-armed Madonna-and-child-style cradle; with a bit of practice, you'll find you can

- ✔ **Cradle on one arm:** Hold his bottom in your hand and let his head and neck rest along your forearm.

- ✔ **Cradle on your chest:** Put his chest to your chest, with one hand on his bottom, and the other at the back of his head.

- ✔ **Carry in a sling:** The straps and buckles can take a bit of getting used to but doing so is worth it to be able to carry hands-free. Take extra care when bending down, though, or your baby may come shooting out.

Bend over and get your body close to your newborn as you put him down and pick him up. The less distance your baby has to travel 'unaccompanied' through space, the less likely he is to be spooked when you move him.

When your baby's neck muscles are strong enough to hold his head up, offer him a parent's eye view of the world and

- ✔ **Carry facing out in your arms:** Hold his back to your chest, one hand supporting his bottom, the other pressing his chest gently back against your own.

- ✔ **Do the 'Tiger in a Tree':** Rest him, belly down, along your forearm, with your hand under his chest. Accompany with plane noises (optional).

- ✔ **Reverse-carry in a sling:** But, as your baby gets heavier, do watch your back.

- ✔ **Carry on your hip:** You'll find one side feels more natural to you than the other but alternate sides if you can – doing so is easier on your spine and pelvis.

- ✔ **Carry on your back:** In a special framed-rucksack-style carrier. Great if you're itching for a hike in the countryside.

Beware the baby head-butt. A baby who's on the verge of full neck control will often hold his head up strongly for a minute or two, then all of a sudden get tired and 'let go', slamming his head down on your jaw/nose/forehead with breathtaking force. Always keep a steadying hand at the ready or you'll both regret it.

FAB OR FAD?

Attachment parenting

There is a doughty, dedicated breed of mother out there who believes that the only way to raise a happy, settled baby is to wear him. All day long, she carries her baby (in her arms or in a sling), allowing him to feed and doze whenever the fancy takes him.

Attachment parenting, as this method's known, is, of course, accepted practice in many parts of the world and there's a lot going for it in terms of mother–child closeness and baby content-

ment. But this practice is not for every mother (or indeed every baby). Having your baby dangling from you all the hours of the day can be emotionally suffocating and physically exhausting, and some quite young babies quickly grow to resent being strapped in and unable to move. You'll instinctively know what you think about attachment parenting: Go with your feelings, but try not to judge those whose instincts are different to yours.

Nappy Know-how

Let's talk about poo. I know you want to. For one of the most secret obsessions of new parenthood is the myriad variation of baby evacuations. From the black-and-tarry just-born meconium to the loose-and-yellowy newborn poo to the brown-and-pongy baby-on-solids job (with all sorts of surprises in between), the contents of your baby's nappy will hold a weird, if whiffy, fascination for months to come. And you know, you're not completely mad: Peering at poo (and wee) is actually good parental practice because it can tell you an awful lot about your baby's current state of health.

Disposables or reusables?

Before you even get round to changing a nappy, you need to decide what kind of nappy you'd rather be changing: disposable or reusable (cloth). Here, to help you make your mind up, is a quick run-down of the pros and cons of each:

- ✔ **Disposables:** They're quick to get on and off, and they're very absorbent. But, they're pricey, and because they're not degradable, they create lots of waste.

- ✔ **Reusables:** They're 'greener' and made of more natural materials, and they're cheaper (in the long run). But they're not as absorbent as disposables, and they're fiddlier to deal with (so other carers may not like using them).

Reusables have got much funkier-looking and more user-friendly in recent years (Velcro straps rather than nappy pins; nappy-laundering services that will whisk away your dirty ones and deliver lovely clean ones), but they do still require that little extra bit of parental commitment. Good for you if you go for this option but please don't feel guilt-ridden if you don't (instead, look out for 'biodegradable disposables' and make that nappy waste mountain a little less permanent).

Save money by using budget-brand disposables in the day – when you're changing nappies all the time – and a more expensive but more absorbent brand at night.

Changing-mat rules and ruses

To save yourself hassle at the changing mat (and leave you more time to peruse the poo), here are some essential tips:

✔ **Must-dos for girls:**

  • Turn the mat round, so there's a raised edge at her feet, rather than her head. This way, if she wees mid-change, the wee collects on the mat, rather than pooling at your knees.

  • Wipe from front to back to avoid getting poo and germs into her vagina.

✔ **Must-dos for boys:.**

  • Undo the nappy but don't pull the front half down straight away. Little boys almost always wee as soon as the nappy's undone and you don't want to be sprayed in the face.

  • Point his willy down as you fasten on the new nappy. Otherwise, next time he wees, it'll all go up his vest.

✔ **Dealing with a dirty one:**

  • Change it now! Not only does leaving poo in contact with your baby's bottom increase the risk of him getting nappy rash (see the 'Blotchy bottoms' section later in this chapter), wiping up a 'squashed' poo is so much worse than whisking away a fresh one.

  • Once you've undone the straps, lift your baby's bottom up and fold the front half of the nappy on top of the dirty back half. Wipe your baby's bottom in mid-air or place it down on the clean top of the nappy's front half first: Either way, he won't be able to accidentally dip his heels in poo.

✔ **Provide entertainment:** Cut down on unhelpful wriggles and squirms by hanging a mobile over the changing station or, for an older baby, keeping a special toy for changing time.

Nappy wipes don't just clean baby bottoms. They're also jolly good at cleaning shoes, wiping crayon scribbles off walls, sponging baby sick off clothes, and getting sticky finger marks off just about everything.

Blotchy bottoms

Nappy rash (red or raw skin on the bottom or in the groin) happens for three reasons:

> ✔ You're leaving nappies on for too long. So change them more often.
>
> ✔ Your baby's got a tummy upset or a food sensitivity. So see a doctor if it continues.
>
> ✔ Your baby's skin is irritated by your nappy wipes. So switch to a hypoallergenic brand or use water and cotton wool.

Treat nappy rash by using lots of zinc-oxide barrier cream at every change and letting your baby go nappy-free as much as you (and your carpets) can stand.

If the nappy rash lasts longer than a week, looks really sore, and/or you can see yellow spots, take your baby to the doctor. He may need special ointment or other treatment.

Settling In: Life after Six Weeks

After you're over the six-week hump, life with a newborn starts getting easier. Gradually, your baby will become more settled and smiley and (hurray!) sleep for longer stretches at night. And, gradually, you will get the hang of his little needs and quirks and start finding a parenting confidence you never dreamt you'd have.

The beginnings of routine

Babies (and older children) like the rhythms of a daily routine: In this crazy, chaotic world, it's comforting to have some idea of what's likely to happen next. How strict a routine you build into your day really depends on how much of a stickler for structure you are – and only you will know how much set-in-stone timetabling you can handle. But even if you tend to go more with the flow than most, consider:

✔ **An afternoon walk in the park:** A dose of fresh air and daylight towards the end of the day does clever things to a baby's biological clock and sets him up for a better night's sleep. For more sleep tricks, see Chapter 8.

✔ **The three-hour/two-hour rule:** Before 3 months, babies generally need a feed roughly every three hours and need a snooze after being awake for two hours on the trot.

✔ **Proper naps:** After 4 or 5 months, babies tend to start having two longish sleeps in the day: One in the morning and one in the early afternoon. If you notice this pattern, encourage it. Being able to count on this time to yourself every day is wonderful.

Getting out and about

In the early days of parenthood, it's instinctive to cocoon yourself indoors, taking private time to recover from the birth and getting to know your way around your new baby. But once you've got more into your stride, venturing out in public a little bit more is good for the soul (yours and your baby's).

Go for lunch

While your baby's nice and portable (and not yet up to rampaging round restaurants), meet your friends or your partner for a midday munch. In those bewildering early weeks, lunching is a great way to add focus to your day (got to get out of the house; got to wear babysick-free clothes) and you get to eat nice food while everyone else, waiters included, coos over the baby. Savour these moments: Once your baby's mobile, long lazy lunches out will be off your list of options for a good while to come.

Go to a mother-and-baby group (even if you're a dad)

Simply having a cup of tea and a chat with others on the same new-baby journey as you can lift your spirits and often forge friendships that last for years. Many groups are run either by local health visitors, by the NCT (www.nct.org.uk) or by churches (you don't have to be religious to go). If you can't find a group near you, go virtual: Parenting sites such as www.mumsnet.com run great, we're-all-in-this-together discussions on their message boards.

Eight things never to leave the house without

Why are those changing bags they sell in baby-care shops so cavernous? Because the smaller your baby, the bigger the amount of stuff you're going to have to cart around with him. You may think this list sounds blindingly obvious but I found that, particularly when in the grip of major sleep-deprivation, it often helps to have the obvious spelt out.

✔ **Nappies**: Lots of them. At least one more than you think you'll need.

✔ **Wipes**: Even more.

✔ **A change of baby clothes:** Unless you fancy sitting in the child health clinic holding a baby with fetching streaks of sick down his front.

✔ **Nappy bags:** For bagging up those sicky clothes as well as the dirty nappies (though obviously separately).

✔ **A muslin:** For mopping up sick. Also useful as a kind of shrug-cum-scarf to make public breastfeeding more discreet.

✔ **Food:** As in bottles (if you use them) or little snacks (if your baby's on solids). Breastfeeders obviously come ready-pre-pared but do pack a couple of breastpads (public leaks are never very elegant).

✔ **Raincover:** It always rains the day you leave it at home.

✔ **A rattle/toy:** Yes, you're only popping to the post office but what if there's a big queue and your baby's bottom lip starts to wobble?

Oh, and always get ready to leave the house way, way, way before you're actually expected anywhere: Babies have a delightful habit of pro-ducing a super-explosive, clothes-ruining poo just as you open the front door.

Looking After Yourself

You're probably working so hard at looking after your baby, you think you haven't a moment to look after yourself. But you must. And here's why: If you're subsuming your own needs to your baby's, you won't have much posi-tive energy to share with him but, if you're healthy and happy and enjoying life, you'll be parenting with verve and joy.

Not convinced? Picture yourself, then, as a wire coathanger (bear with me on this one) with your child (and any subsequent children) hanging off you. Everything's fine with everyone in this picture to begin with but what hap-pens if the coathanger gets bent out of shape? Yup, your kids feel the conse-quences, too.

Making some me-time

You won't be consigned to bad-mother (or bad-father) hell if you occasionally put your own needs first and reclaim some time to yourself. So, start thinking about how you can achieve this dream. Can you negotiate with your partner for some time off one night a week or a half day at weekends so you can see friends or go to the gym? Will friends or family members babysit while you have your hair cut or go shopping? Often, all it takes is a new top or an excuse to put make-up on to help you reclaim a big slice of the old you.

Coping? Of course I'm coping!

When my first baby was born, I would never have admitted to anyone just how hard it was getting through the day sometimes. I would look at other new mums breezing through the park and think I was just making heavy weather of this whole new-baby situation. If only I'd been more honest and less proud, I'd have found out that most of them were finding things just as hard as me. (How can I be so sure? Because some of them are now my best friends and we've shared many a nightmare new-parent confidence together.)

If you feel overwhelmed at times, don't keep it to yourself like I did; trust me, you don't win any prizes for struggling on in silence. Instead, tell your partner, your mother, your friends how you feel and you'll probably be amazed at how sympathetic they'll be and how willingly they'll offer to share some of your load. Most people are usually delighted to help out – once you've let them know they're needed.

If you find you're feeling negative, numb, empty, and low pretty much all the time, you may have postnatal depression. It's nothing to be ashamed of – postnatal depression is a proper illness that affects one in ten new mums (and occasionally dads, too) – but it's important to get help and treatment from your GP.

Looking After Your Relationship

Babies are supposed to bring you together but, the truth is, they can sometimes drive you apart. The sudden infusion of new emotions and scary responsibilities into your life together can create all sorts of little wobbles in your relationship. And these wobbles need sorting out before they get serious.

Tiff triggers and how to avoid them

Here, in no particular order, are some of the most common new-parent relationship flashpoints. Don't feel too bad if they all sound familiar: I honestly don't think it's possible to make it through your baby's first year without saying or hearing at least one of these several times over.

- **'I'm more tired than you are.'** A classic one, this, usually uttered in the middle of the night to a background of baby howls. How to head off the row? Remember that new parenthood is equally exhausting for both of you but perhaps in different ways. It may be more intense and more relentless for whoever is the main baby carer but that person probably doesn't have to split his or her energy focus between baby and work (yet).

- **'You're doing it all wrong.'** Usually hissed by Mum, as Dad fumbles his way through a nappy change or tries to strap Junior into the car seat. How to head off the row? Take a deep breath and remind yourself how much of a butterfingers you were at first. He'll only get it right if you let him get enough practice. And remember, too, that, as long as you agree on the big things, it won't hurt your baby if you each do the little things in your own different way.

- **'We never go out any more.'** Going out together requires so much more planning than it used to, it's easier to give up and settle for supper in front of the telly – again. How to head off the row? Get out your diaries and book time with each other every week, even if only for a walk in the park while Granny babysits. Even five minutes chatting alone without the distraction of your baby (or the telly) can bring you closer together.

- **'We never have sex any more.'** Their bits may all be back in working order six weeks after the birth but some women take considerably longer to reconnect with their libido. How to head off the row? It never hurts to tell your partner how much you still fancy him/her, whatever's not happening between the sheets. And if it's been a long time, it's sometimes just worth giving it a go: Often you'll find all you needed to do was to jog your sexual memory.

- **'I hate asking you for money.'** When the balance of earning power changes between partners, it often causes tension – and the one who's bringing in less (or nothing) can suddenly feel vulnerable. How to head off the row? Sit down and talk about how you can share responsibility for your finances – no one should be in sole charge of the family purse strings.

- **'What's for dinner, love?'** When one partner's at home caring for the baby and the other's out at work, your roles within the household shift and, before you know it, the worker's expecting to come home every night to a three-course meal and a spick-and-span house. How to head off the row? Someone needs a crash course in what an average day with a small baby is like: Only then can he (or she) understand why being a stay-at-home carer is not the same as being a slob-about-the-house.

The four rules of relationship rehab

Three's a crowd in any relationship but that doesn't mean the little one has to come between you. For couple-preserving crowd-control:

- ✔ **Talk all the time.** Never try to second-guess what your partner is thinking – or expect him or her to know what you're thinking.

- ✔ **Make time to be together.** Without the baby.

- ✔ **Get your priorities straight**. Being a good partner is as important as being a good parent. It's important to your baby that his mum and dad have a strong relationship

- ✔ **Share the highs of parenting.** Try not to parent in shifts. Cuddle, tickle, and play with your baby together. It will reinforce your bond as the couple who created him.

Chapter 7

Mmmm, Mmmm, Good: Feeding Baby

In This Chapter

▶ Understanding the pros, cons, and how-tos of breastfeeding

▶ Deciding when (or if) to bottlefeed

▶ Getting to (backpatting) grips with winding

*Y*our baby needs to eat and, in her first year, that means breastmilk or formula (not cow's milk) – just on its own, to begin with, and then accompanied with, and gradually replaced by, mushed or chopped-up versions of what we grown-ups eat. Simple, huh? Er, no!

The complicated bit's all about the kind of milk you feed your baby. Health experts are in no doubt that breastmilk is the best choice, but not everyone can – or wants to – breastfeed. And even those who can *and* want to can find breastfeeding really quite tricky at first. Mix into all this other people's very varied and rigid (and, often, mistaken) views about breast or bottlefeeding, and it's easy to get ever so confused and emotional about what you should do.

So this chapter is all about giving you the feeding facts honestly and clearly. I'm not going to tell you what to do, but I am going to tell you like it is, so you can reach your own decision as wisely and confidently as possible.

The Truth about Breastfeeding

There's no doubt that nature intended us to breastfeed (or women wouldn't come ready equipped for it), but that doesn't mean we're all going to find it easy. Or pleasant. Or even possible.

For every mother who lactates like a fountain and waxes lyrical about the joys of nursing a child at the breast (and, trust me, you'll meet a few), there's another who winces at the mere thought of unhooking her nursing bra and letting a small mouth clamp down on her nipple. But whichever woman you think (or know) you're going to relate to most, it's still worth genning up on the realities of breastfeeding – the good and the bad – so you get some idea of what you're letting yourself in for (or not).

Why breastfeeding's great

Breastfeeding is good for you and your baby because

- ✔ **It's free and low-maintenance.** No equipment to sterilise; no formula to mix and warm; no bottles to carry around.

- ✔ **It's tailor-made for your baby.** The nutrient make-up of breast milk changes day by day to suit your baby's growing needs. (It even becomes more watery on a hot day.)

- ✔ **It boosts your baby's immunity and protects her gut.** Breast milk contains white blood cells and antibodies (courtesy of Mum) that help fight off bacteria and other nasty germs. It also makes it less likely she'll get constipation, wind, or nasty bouts of diarrhoea; it can also prevent her getting asthma and allergies – or delay how soon or how badly she gets them.

- ✔ **It lowers *your* disease risk.** Breastfeeding reduces your risk of breast cancer. Not by masses, but every little helps.

- ✔ **It brings you closer together, literally.** As well as involving lots of cuddly skin-to-skin contact, breastfeeding releases hormones that promote bonding.

- ✔ **It can help you get your figure back faster.** Breastfeeding super-stimulates your uterus to contract back to its pre-pregnancy size – and, as your body has to burn extra calories to produce milk, it can make it easier for you to shed your baby weight.

Why breastfeeding's hard

Breastfeeding can be difficult for you and your baby because

- ✔ **It can hurt**. You may feel a brief tingling pain at the beginning of a feed, and you may get sore (or even cracked) nipples, particularly if your baby's not 'latching on' properly. For more on latching on, see the section 'Giving breastfeeding your best shot', later in this chapter.

- ✔ **It's tricky at first.** Breastfeeding's rarely just a question of plug-your-baby-in-and-go. It can take a while for both of you to get the hang of it.

✔ **It's a one-woman job.** No one else can do it for you – which, in the early weeks, can leave you feeling like an exhausted dairy cow and your partner feeling like a spare part.

✔ **Others may disapprove.** Either because they think that it's indecent in some way or because they think that you're making a rod for your own back.

✔ **It's not predictable.** Breastfed babies don't really 'do' strict feeding schedules (if schedules are your thing) – and they usually need to feed more often than bottlefed babies (breast milk's more easily digested than formula).

✔ **It's hard to combine with work.** Particularly if you're going back before your baby's 6 months old. For advice on how it can be done, see 'Express yourself: A guide to the breast pump'.

✔ **Your body's just not made that way.** Some people's eyes don't work properly; some people's breasts (or nipples) don't work properly. And just as no one thinks less of you for wearing glasses so you can see, no one should think less of you for bottlefeeding so your baby can thrive.

Breastfeeding myths: busted

A whole lot of nonsense is talked about breastfeeding (particularly from those who've never even tried it), and being able to sift the truth from the old wives' tales is important. Here are some of the most commonly heard breastfeeding myths:

✔ **The smaller your breasts, the less milk you'll have.** Wrong! Whether you're a 32A or a 42DD, the size of your breasts has absolutely no impact whatsoever on the amount of milk they can produce. Unless you've had breast surgery, that is – in which case, you may not be able to breastfeed at all.

✔ **Breastfeeding gives you saggy/shrunken breasts.** Nope, it's pregnancy, not breastfeeding, that can alter the size and shape of your breasts. In fact, breastfeeding can actually delay postnatal boob-droop because a milk-filled breast looks lovely and big and full and round.

✔ **You have to cut out certain foods.** Listen to enough old wives and you'd never again eat tomatoes, chilli, garlic, strawberries, or curry (the list goes on and on) for fear your baby will either refuse to feed or writhe for hours with colic. True, some babies don't seem to go a bundle on breast milk flavoured with essence of something Mum doesn't often eat, but it's rare for them to react badly to foods that are part of your normal diet (unless your baby has a specific allergy). By all means, go easy on the curry if you notice your baby not enjoying the results, but don't give it up just because your next-door neighbour said that you should.

✔ **You can't get pregnant when you're breastfeeding.** Allow me to introduce you to my second son, Tom, conceived when his breastfed brother was 8 months old. Breastfeeding only works as a contraceptive when you're doing it every three hours or so, round the clock. You have been warned.

Some medicines can pass into breast milk and affect your baby. If you are taking medication for an ongoing health condition, ask your GP if breastfeeding's an option for you. And, before you buy any over-the-counter medicine, ask the pharmacist if it is safe to take while breastfeeding.

Giving breastfeeding your best shot

If you want to give breastfeeding a go, there are several ways to make those first nipper-to-nipple encounters go as smoothly as possible:

- ✔ **Start as soon as you can.** Try to put your baby to your breast within an hour of her birth. Babies are born with an incredibly strong 'rooting' reflex – left alone on your tummy, a healthy baby will 'crawl' up your body, search for your breast, and begin suckling of her own accord. Responding to this reflex by putting your baby to your breast mere moments into her life helps establish the feeding connection and kick starts your own body's milk supply. If you can't manage this (perhaps because you had a Caesarean) or if your baby's too sleepy to feed, a skin-to-skin cuddle is the next best thing.

- ✔ **Get comfortable.** Breastfeeding a newborn can take up to an hour (thankfully, they get quicker at it as they get older), so make sure that you find a comfy chair (avoid ones with baby-head-bashing arms) and place everything you may need (phone, drink, TV remote) within easy reach. You may need to put cushions behind your back to prop yourself into a more upright position. And you may find it helps to raise your baby up a little by resting her on a pillow or cushion in your arms.

- ✔ **Make sure that your baby's latched on properly.** This is really important: If you don't get your baby 'plugged in' right, she'll have trouble getting the nourishment she needs, and you'll have nipples that hurt or crack – and you'll both end up in tears. For more about latching on, see the section 'How to breastfeed', later in this chapter.

- ✔ **Forget schedules:** Babies digest breast milk more easily – and, therefore, more quickly – than formula milk, so a breastfeeding baby may want to eat again sooner than a bottlefed one. Watch your baby, not the clock, for signs that feeding time's arrived again. Good clues include finger-sucking, yawning, rooting for an imaginary nipple – oh, and crying! Try not to fret if your baby wants to feed a lot in the first few weeks; she'll settle into a more predictable pattern soon.

Feeding on demand is not the same as feeding every time your baby cries. Crying is not always a sign of hunger; your baby may want a nappy change, a sleep, or just a cuddle instead.

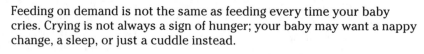

✔ **Ask for help:** If you really can't get the hang of breastfeeding or think you've got it but could do with some reassurance, ask for help – and keep asking till you're happy. There are loads of people out there who are can offer advice and support. Find out if there's a breastfeeding counsellor at your maternity unit; if not, call the La Leche League Support Line on 0845 1202918 or the Association of Breastfeeding Mothers on 0870 4017711.

Breastfeeding twins (or triplets) is possible but requires stacks of determination and a lot of support from others. If you'd like to give it a go, call the La Leche League Support Line (see number above) or The Twins and Multiple Births Association helpline on 0800 138 0509.

How to breastfeed

There is a definite knack to breastfeeding – and, like all knacks, it's easy when you know how and endlessly frustrating when you don't. Your midwife should be able to help you get it right – and tell you when you've got it wrong – but, essentially, it all boils down to getting your baby to latch on to your breast in the correct way and making sure that she stays on long enough once she's there.

Step 1: Latching on

The key here is getting your baby to open her mouth wide enough to get a big enough mouthful of breast (stop wincing at the back – this is the only way to prevent lots of excruciatingly frantic nipple-tugging).

In theory, you achieve latching on by bringing your baby's chest close to your chest, lining her nose up to your nipple, and then gently brushing her lips against your nipple. This should make her tilt her head back, turn her face in, open her mouth wide and then, as you move her in towards your breast and aim your nipple towards the roof of her mouth, latch on perfectly. (For a more detailed explanation of latching on, with pictures, visit www. kellymom.com.)

In practice, it may take you (and her) several tries to get this manoeuvre right. Your baby may miss her target altogether and need re-positioning; she may not open her mouth wide enough and need to start again (slip a fingertip into the corner of her mouth to break the suction); she may even need you to lift up your breast in your cupped hand and kind of mould it into an easier shape to latch on to. Stay as calm as you can and persevere. You'll know you've got it right when

✔ **You can see she's got more than your nipple in her mouth.** Some of the dark area around your nipple (your areola) should be in there, too.

✔ **Her lower lip is curled back towards her chin.** Someone else will have to check this for you!

✔ **Her chin is touching your breast.** You'll be able to feel this.

✔ **Your baby is relaxed and you can see her jaw moving.** You shouldn't hear any clicking or lip-smacking sounds.

✔ **It doesn't hurt.** Although you may feel a tingle or even a short stab of pain as her first sucks trigger the flow of milk through your breasts.

✔ **She finishes of her own accord, looking full up and spaced out.**

Don't worry if your baby doesn't start sucking the moment she latches on – she's learning, too. Some tiny babies do seem to spend a little while licking your nipple before remembering to turn the suction on.

Step 2: Drinking up

Once your milk 'comes in' ('What to do when your milk comes in'), let your baby empty one breast before offering the other.

Breast milk is a two-course meal: A starter of light, thirst-quenching *foremilk,* followed, several minutes later, by a main course of creamier, tummy-filling *hindmilk.* If your baby doesn't get both courses, she'll stay hungry – and you could get a blocked milk duct or a related breast infection called mastitis.

Always let your baby stay at the breast she started off on long enough to empty it completely (hindmilk is naturally sleep-inducing, so droopy eyes are a sign of success). You can then offer her the other breast if you like – but she may well not be that interested. Always offer this other breast first at the next feed (even if she did feed from it a little last time).

Use a bracelet to help you remember which breast to 'serve up' next: After each feed, slip the bracelet onto the wrist that's nearest the breast you didn't use (or only used a little). When the next feed comes round, one look at your wrists will tell you which side is 'on'.

What to do when your milk 'comes in'

In the first few days after the birth, your breasts make small amounts of a super-nutritious, anti-body-packed kind of pre-milk called *colostrum*. Then, sometime between the second and the fifth day, the colostrum gives way to bigger doses of your 'regular' milk – and, boy, do you know it! Your breasts swell up to a gargantuan size, they may throb or leak, and they'll feel as red-hot and rock hard as a couple of boulders on Mars.

Fortunately, the rock-hard bosoms stage only lasts a day or two; the not-so-good news is that, during that day or two, breastfeeding may become a bit of a pain – literally for you and logistically for your baby.

Let's take your baby first: The way her meals are served up has suddenly changed and you can't blame her for being a bit bothered by that. Her main problems are likely to be

- **Getting started**: Your breasts are now so hard and huge, she may have trouble latching on. So, express off a little milk with your hands or put a warm flannel on your breast before a feed to soften things up for her. If doing so doesn't work, try feeding (carefully) in the bath.

- **Going with the flow**: Your breasts are now so full, the milk may well shoot out much faster than before. So, keep a towel to hand (that flannel will do) and, if she starts gasping or gurgling or pulling away, take her off, and wait for a few seconds for the flow to slow.

And now for you. Minimise that exploding-breast feeling by

- **Cooling them down**: With a frozen bag of peas (wrap it in a tea towel and stuff it down your bra). A chilled cabbage leaf also works brilliantly (yes, really).

- **Taking a painkiller**: An ibuprofen-based one. But always check with your midwife what medication's suitable for you.

- **Breathing deeply**: Your nipples may feel even more sensitive than usual at the moment. Take a big breath in just before your baby latches on and breathe out slowly as the deed is done. Doesn't sound like much but deep breathing really helps.

- **Continuing to breastfeed**: Don't skip feeds or you'll swell up even more.

Why we give up – and how to avoid it

Seven in ten British mums give breastfeeding a try when their baby's born; six weeks later, half of them have given up. Which is a shame because, if you can get through the first six weeks, breastfeeding almost always becomes a breeze. Here are the main reasons we decide to hang up our nursing bras – along with some little tips that just may make us reconsider:

✔ **'It hurts too much'.** Check you've got the latching-on thing sorted (see the earlier section 'Step 1: Latching on') and, at each feed, try slightly altering the position you hold your baby in, so the same part of your nipple doesn't always feel the most pressure. If your nipples are cracked, try using nipple shields (from chemists) just until they heal, and change your breastpads frequently. If you get itchy nipples, become suddenly sore after a period of problem-free breastfeeding, or feel pain deep within the breast (especially with a fever), see your GP: You may have thrush or mastitis.

✔ **'It takes too long'.** A newborn does take forever to feed but, give her a few weeks, and she'll be slurping it all down in no time. Average feed time for a 12-weeker? Five to seven minutes flat!

✔ **'I haven't got enough milk'.** Is your baby gaining weight? Do your breasts leak a little milk into your breastpads during the day? If so, you've got enough milk. If not, make sure that you're eating properly, your baby's latching on properly (yes, that again), and ask your health visitor for advice.

✔ **'My baby's not gaining enough weight'.** Breastfed babies are, generally, leaner than bottlefed babies, and grow more slowly. This doesn't mean they're less healthy; quite the reverse, in fact. Recent studies suggest that breastfed babies not only weigh less when they're tiny, they also weigh less when they're tiddlers, toddlers, and teenagers – which is actually good news in this flabby new world of rising childhood obesity. The trouble is, some of the more old-fashioned baby height/weight charts are based on the growth patterns of bottlefed babies, which means some breastfed babies can come up as underweight when they're not. If you – or anyone else – have concerns about your breastfed baby's weight, talk to your health visitor or a breastfeeding counsellor; it could well be nothing to worry about.

✔ **'I've got too much milk'.** It is rather embarrassing when your T-shirt's wetter than a Club 18–30 rep's, and your breasts squirt milk in all directions the moment a baby cries (even if it's not yours). And it can be frustrating for your baby, too, when everything's gushing into her mouth quicker than she can swallow it. So, never leave home without a vast supply of breastpads and always spread a towel on top of your sheet at night. And, if your baby's gasping or gurgling as she feeds, take her off the breast for a few moments and wait for the spurt to slow down a little.

✔ **'My baby wants to feed all the time'.** Let me tell you about growth spurts: Your baby's appetite doesn't grow steadily but in funny little jumps. So, one day, she'll seem calm and settled; the next, she'll be desperate for loads more milk than usual. This milk frenzy will continue for a few days, and then settle down – only to kick off all over again in a few weeks' time. Growth spurts can happen at any time but are (anecdotally) most common at 3 weeks, 6 weeks, and 3 months.

✔ **'I'm ill'.** You can breastfeed through most common-or-garden illnesses, including a cold, a sore throat, and even a stomach bug. And, no, doing so isn't more likely to make your baby ill: Chances are that, if you've got a virus, she's been exposed to it already. Besides, your milk will now be so full of virus-fighting antibodies, continuing to breastfeed can actually help her fight off the illness more quickly or even stop her getting it altogether. Do make sure, though, that you drink lots of water (so you don't get too dehydrated to produce enough milk) and check that any medicine you take is compatible with breastfeeding.

✔ **'I've got to go back to work'.** If your baby is over 6 months and on solids, combining work and breastfeeding (see the 'Doing it and working' section, later in this chapter) is actually quite possible. But, if you're heading back to the office while your baby's still quite little, it's an awful lot to ask of your body (and your breast pump) to provide all the milk your baby needs while you're away. Before you switch to bottles altogether, though, you may want to consider continuing to breastfeed first thing in the morning and last thing at night – which is perfectly do-able (unless you take lots of business trips) and can be a powerful way to reconnect with your baby when you get home.

✔ **'My baby's 6 months old now'.** Yes, the baby-health powers-that-be recommend we breastfeed our babies exclusively for six months, but that doesn't mean passing the half-year mark has to be your cue to get the bottles out. In fact, you may just be creating more work (and expense) for yourself. Once your baby's 6 months old and on solids, the bulk of your breastfeeding work is done: now's the time to gradually start cutting down the number of feeds you offer in a day (see the 'Weaning from the breast' section, later in this chapter). If you've got this far by breastfeeding alone, carrying on could well be your least-hassle option.

Throwing up all over: reflux explained

All babies sick up a bit of milk (usually right down your new black jumper) and some babies sick up more than others. But there are babies who sick up *all the time* – and, often, cry all the time while they're at it. If your baby's hard to feed and impossible to comfort, and barely a surface in your house is unsplattered by baby sick, she could well have reflux (gastro-oesophageal reflux disease). This condition is caused when the muscle ring that closes off the top of your baby's stomach doesn't work properly and so lets milk and stomach acid leak back into your baby's windpipe, causing vomiting and pain. Most babies do grow out of reflux, but it's heartbreaking – and exhausting – to deal with alone. If you suspect your baby has reflux, see your GP as soon as you can; there are treatments that can help.

If breastfeeding's no longer for you (for whatever reason), don't waste time feeling guilty. Be proud of the effort you've made up to now: Giving breast-feeding a go – even for one day – makes a difference to your baby's health.

Supplementary bottles

Okay, let's get real: Even if you find breastfeeding as easy as falling off a log, being the sole provider of your baby's milk kind of ties you down. Maybe, just maybe, you may want to go out to dinner/go back to work/let someone else do the honours at some point before the candle's out on your baby's first birthday cake and she's old enough to drink cow's milk.

To get off duty, you need to get out a bottle. Easy enough – or is it? Before you so much as touch a teat, ask yourself the following questions:

- ✔ **What's going in the bottle: Breast milk or formula?** Formula's quicker (breast milk needs pumping out; see 'Express yourself: A guide to the breast pump') but second-best nutritionally.

- ✔ **Is your baby under 4 weeks old?** Offering regular bottles (of breast or formula milk) this early in your baby's life can lead to 'nipple confusion'. Milk flows out of a bottle faster and more steadily than it does out of the breast, meaning your baby doesn't need to work so hard to get it. So, when your little L-plate breastfeeder goes back to Mum's milk dispenser, you may find she's either lost the knack or lost the will to suck harder. Try to avoid bottles for the first few weeks, if you can.

- ✔ **Is this a one-off?** Your breasts are wondrously efficient things but they're not psychic. They can't tell that you were out all day today but will be at home to breastfeed 24/7 tomorrow. The amount of milk they produce tomorrow depends solely on the amount of milk that got used today: If you skip one feed, fine (it'll sort itself out) but, if you skip a few in a row, you're likely to diminish your milk supply for good.

Breast milk works on a use-it-or-lose-it basis: Skip a breastfeed one day (and don't express the milk you would have used), and you'll produce less milk the next. To keep your milk supply going strong, it makes sense to express every time you skip.

There's a difference between waiting a few weeks before introducing a bottle and waiting a few months. Older breastfed babies do sometimes flat-out refuse to take a bottle if they've never seen one before. If you know that you're going to be going back to work while your baby still needs regular milk feeds, make sure that you get her used to having the odd bottlefeed by the end of her second month. If you find doing so tricky, see the sidebar 'The breastfed baby who won't take a bottle', later in this chapter.

Express yourself: A guide to the breast pump

Of all the particular 'un-delights' of new parenthood, using a breast pump to express your milk ranks right up with having the midwife inspect your stitches. Hunching half-naked in a chair with one breast squeezed down a plastic funnel is *not* a sexy look – even before the schlurp-schlurp-drip sound of breast milk hitting the collecting bottle kicks in. But, for all its hideousness, you may actually come to love your breast pump: It can be your passport to a peaceful night, your ticket to a dinner out, or your licence to return to work without giving up breastfeeding.

Here's your six-point guide to taking the distressing out of expressing:

✔ **Find the right pump for you.** Breast pumps come in all shapes and sizes, from the really quite dinky to the frankly uber-industrial – and it's not always easy to tell which one will work best for you. Generally, electric pumps extract more milk more quickly but tend to be expensive, bulky, and noisy (not the ideal choice for discreet pumping in your office lunch hour!); manual pumps are cheaper, smaller, and quieter but fiddlier to operate and, in some cases, make mincemeat of your nipples (if you're going the manual route, look for a pump with a silicone insert that's gentler on your breast).

✔ **Wait six weeks before starting.** Breastfeeding in the first weeks is exhausting and time-consuming enough; don't wear yourself out even more by trying to express, too.

(Obviously, if you're expressing *instead of* breastfeeding – because your newborn's in special care, for example – that's a completely different story.)

✔ **Pump in the morning.** Expressing when your breasts are fullest is best, which, for most women, is first thing in the morning (milk production does tail off towards the end of the day, especially if you're tired) or after you've skipped a feed.

✔ **Don't expect too much too soon.** Getting to grips with a breast pump can take a while. My first attempt produced precisely six drops of milk! Pumping does get easier with practice.

✔ **Use props.** The hardest part of expressing is that you haven't got your baby there: The pump can mimic your baby's sucking action but it can't provide the emotional trigger that helps get your milk flowing. Try thinking about your baby as you start to pump, or looking at her picture. One friend of mine used to sniff her daughter's hat! And some (extremely co-ordinated) women resort to feeding their baby on one breast and expressing on the other.

✔ **Stockpile in the freezer.** You can store expressed milk (in bottles or in special bags that come with your pump) in the fridge for five days or for four months in the freezer. Date the milk and freeze it in small batches to avoid waste.

Doing it in public

Unless you're planning to skulk in your house till your baby's weaned, the day will come when you have to breastfeed in front of other people. And that idea's bound to make you feel a bit uncomfortable – after all, you've never undone your bra and whipped out a breast in public before (or, if you have, I bet you'd probably sooner forget it). Let me offer you a little pre-public-debut comfort, then, with these four vital tips:

- ✔ **Dress clever.** Always wear a top that can be 'accessed' discreetly. Jumpers or T-shirts are good (you just hitch them up a little on one side); button-up blouses or cardies are bad (undo the buttons and you expose both breasts and a large expanse of midriff).

- ✔ **Survey the scene.** Is there somewhere where you can feed in partial privacy? Some department stores and most baby stores, for example, do have special mum-and-baby areas just for this purpose. Whatever you do, though, don't retreat to a toilet: Would you want to eat dinner there?

- ✔ **Use a muslin.** Before you start, tuck a muslin cloth under your baby's chin and open it out over her front. Once she's latched on, pull the muslin over to cover your modesty, too.

- ✔ **Ignore the ignorant.** Turn a deaf ear to anyone uneducated enough to object to what you're doing. Breastfeeding's not illegal and it's not immoral and, in many countries, it is now a mother's legal right to do it in public.

Doing it and working

It is possible to carry on breastfeeding once you've gone back to work. But, in all honesty, if your baby's over 6 months, it's a challenge; and, if your baby's under 6 months, it's a *real* challenge. Here are your options:

- ✔ **Leave expressed breast milk for your baby while you're at work.** And breastfeed morning and evening. This plan can work well if your baby's on solids and only needs one or two other milk feeds during the day – trying to express more than two bottles'-worth a day is asking a lot of yourself when you're adjusting back to working life.

- ✔ **Switch to formula while you're at work.** And breastfeed morning and evening. This is probably the only sustainable option if your baby's under 6 months and needs frequent feeds in the day. Remember that, if you do use this method, your milk supply will diminish, so you'll have to use formula 9-to-5 at weekends, too.

If you go for the first (expressing-milk) option, think carefully about where you're going to express and when. To keep your milk supply up, you'll probably have to express at work during your lunch break – employers are now required to provide somewhere suitable for a breastfeeding mother to express (and, no, the ladies loo won't do). Take in your sterilised breast pump and a cooler bag for bringing the milk home in. Always store your expressed milk in a fridge until the end of the working day.

A few weeks before you return to work, pump like crazy and build up a store of breast milk in the freezer. This way, you've always got an emergency supply if you're not able to express at work or you have to stay late one day. Stop the extra pumping a week before your return or your breasts will leak everywhere on your first day back.

Always make sure that your baby's carer understands how important it is to you that your baby's fed on breast milk – and how much effort you've gone to to express the milk for her. A friend of mine came home early from the office one day to find her childminder giving her baby a bottle of formula. Her tortuously expressed breast milk had been chucked down the sink for days because 'it just looked so thin and weedy'.

Weaning from the breast

However much you love (or loathe) breastfeeding, someday it has to end. And, whether that day comes after a year or more (as the baby-health experts recommend) or after a week (for whatever reason), you can expect some degree of physical and emotional fallout. But it definitely helps if you

- ✔ **Take it slow.** Gradually weaning over several weeks is easier on your baby and on your breasts (stopping abruptly can be very painful). Drop the feeds one by one, starting with the one your baby seems least interested in – if your baby's on solids, for example, this will probably be the feed after her biggest meal of the day.

- ✔ **Have your alternatives ready.** If your baby's under 6 months and hasn't started on solids yet, she'll need to have formula feeds to replace the breastfeeds you're dropping, so make sure that she's happy to take a bottle first (for more on this, see The breastfed baby who won't take a bottle'). If your baby's well established on solids, and eating dairy foods, you don't need to introduce formula at all: Plan the gradual weaning to take you slowly up to her first birthday, dropping the last breastfeed just as she's old enough to have cow's milk.

- ✔ **Expect to shed a tear when it's over.** Giving up breastfeeding can send your hormones and your emotions into a bit of a nosedive. You may find yourself feeling sad; you may find yourself feeling guilty (either because you gave up sooner than you think you ought to have or because you're secretly delighted to have given up – or both!). Remind yourself that breastfeeding is only one stage of a lifetime of parenting – and plenty more close, cuddly, vitally nurturing stages are still to come.

If your breasts feel sore and full, try the old chilled-cabbage-leaf-down-the-bra cure again. Make sure that bra is really supportive, too. Whatever you do, though, don't pump: it will only get your breasts to make even more milk.

The Truth about Bottlefeeding

Maybe you always intended to bottlefeed, maybe you didn't: Whatever your reasons for ending up with a bottle, a teat, and a tin of formula in your hands, don't waste even one moment feeling bad about it. You've taken your decision (or had it made for you by circumstances you could never have predicted) and, whatever anybody else may say, you're now providing your baby with a perfectly healthy and acceptable source of nourishment in a way that gives her all the love and contact she needs. Your success as a parent depends not a jot on the kind of milk you serve up right now: Being a great parent is so much bigger than that.

Oh, and if anyone (including that nagging old conscience of yours) utters a word of criticism in your presence, you may care to remind them that bottle-feeding does actually have a few definite advantages over breastfeeding:

✔ **Your partner gets to have a go.** Which means he has more chance to bond with your baby – and you have more chance to sleep.

✔ **It won't make you cry.** Bottlefeeding is rarely the struggle breastfeeding can be – and it doesn't hurt your nipples.

✔ **You can wear nice underwear.** Don't underestimate the pleasure of putting on a bra that's designed to make you look good, rather than to flip out your nipple with maximum efficiency.

✔ **It may even let you get more sleep.** Bottlefeeding babies do, generally, start sleeping through the night earlier than breastfeeding ones.

Vital safety facts

Getting the formula milk out of the bottle into your baby may be a cinch, but you do have to make a big effort to make sure that you're putting the formula into the bottle properly in the first place. Never cut corners on this one: If you do, your baby could get very ill. For safe bottlefeeding

✔ **Sterilise everything first.** The teat, the bottle, the ring, the cap, even the tongs that help you put everything together. And wash your hands thoroughly before you touch them.

✔ **Make up each feed as you need it.** You may be tempted to save time by making up all the day's feeds at once, but it's safer not to (bacteria can breed in made-up formula).

✔ **Always mix the formula with cooled, boiled water.** Not mineral water. Not filtered water. Not softened water. And not water that's been boiled before or has been left to cool for more than half an hour. If you want to keep some just-boiled water for your next feed, you must store it in a sealed flask.

✔ **Throw away leftover formula.** Never keep it for another feed.

✔ **Don't warm formula up.** If you're using just-boiled, there is no need to. In fact, you may actually need to cool it down by holding the bottle under cold running water. You can test the temperature of the milk by dripping a little onto the inside of your wrist: It should feel just a little warmer than blood temperature.

✔ **Don't use 'follow-on' milk for a baby under 6 months old, however big she is.** Her digestive system won't be able to cope with it yet.

✔ **Never leave your small baby alone with a bottle propped up**. She could choke. And, anyway, she could do with a cuddle as she feeds.

✔ **Try not to let your older baby go to bed with a bottle.** The formula will pool in her mouth, providing ideal conditions for bacteria to grow and start causing tooth decay.

If your baby swallows a lot of air during a feed, she'll get a pain in her tummy and cry. To prevent this, try to position her in your arms so that her head's higher than her stomach. And tilt the bottle as you hold it, so that the teat fills with milk, not air. For more about air bubbles and winding, see the section 'There she blows! The Strange New Art of Winding', later in this chapter.

Overfeeding and weight charts

Bottlefed babies tend to be little chubsters compared to their breastfed friends. There are many reasons for this but the three real biggies are:

✔ **Formula is calorie-constant.** Every millilitre of formula contains exactly the same number of calories – unlike breast milk, which automatically adjusts to your baby's degree of hunger.

✔ **You can see how much milk she's had (or not).** And it's tempting to get her to finish up the bottle.

✔ **Some height/weight charts are out of date.** The World Health Organisation is concerned about some charts that are based on the growth patterns of babies who were bottlefed years ago, when 'feeding up' was common and solids were started very early. It is now issuing new charts with a less generous 'normal' weight range. Ask your health visitor about them.

The breastfed baby who won't take a bottle

Earlier in this chapter, I said that bottlefeeding was easy. Well, here is the exception that proves the rule: Some babies who've got used to feeding at the breast can put up a bit of a struggle when you bring out a bottle – *even if it's full of breast milk.* If you've got a little bottle-fighter on your hands, your top taming tactics are

✔ **Try a different teat and/or bottle.** The short, stubby teats that fit wider-necked bottles look more like a real breast but only the long, silicone teats deliver milk far back in your baby's mouth, in the same way breast-feeding does. Your baby may hate one but like the other.

✔ **Check the flow.** Teats come with slow-flow, medium-flow, and fast-flow holes at the tip. Many breastfed babies prefer a slow-flow teat (because it means they have to suck hard, just like they do at the breast), but an older baby may turn out to prefer a faster-flow one.

✔ **Get the bottle out before her tummy rumbles.** A very hungry, fretful baby won't take to change nearly so well.

✔ **Make those breasts scarce.** Your baby's less likely to take a bottle if she can see a familiar alternative nearby. Time for breast-feeding Mum to leave the room – maybe even the house – and let someone else serve up the milk.

✔ **Turn the light off.** Sometimes, it's the look of the bottle, rather than the feeling of sucking at it, that freaks your baby out. Feeding in the (almost) dark could be all that it takes.

✔ **Warm the teat.** In your (clean) hand. And rub it against her lip before you plunge it in.

✔ **Give up, then try again.** Don't dig in for a long bottle battle. If she's really fighting the idea, down tools, regroup for half an hour, then have another go. Be patient: Cracking this may take a while.

✔ **Try a cup.** If your baby's over 4 months, she make take to a baby cup with a soft spout much more readily than to a bottle with a teat.

So, is it really that bad to have a roly-poly baby? All babies do go through chubby stages but it certainly seems clear that heavy babies tend to turn into heavy children who turn into heavy adults – and that pattern isn't good for anyone's health. Fear of excess weight doesn't mean you need to start cutting down your baby's bottles but it can help to

- ✔ **Make sure you level that measuring scoop.** Follow the instructions for mixing your formula precisely: Adding more than the recommended dose can make your baby overweight and could endanger her health.

- ✔ **Watch for signs that she's full.** A baby who's had enough milk will often cry or turn her head or even hit the bottle with her hands. Don't encourage her to keep on sucking when she doesn't actually need to.

- ✔ **Don't 'feed up' your low-birth-weight baby.** If your baby was tiny at birth, your desire to have her gain weight fast is only natural. But experts have identified the low-birth-weight baby who catches up quickly as being the most at risk of childhood obesity.

There She Blows! The Strange New Art of Winding

Burping is good (for babies, that is). Forget grown-up good manners and after-dinner etiquette (you'll have plenty of time to insist on those later); there's nothing your baby needs more after a feed than a good, long, noisy burp. You see, babies tend to gulp down a fair bit of air with their milk (whether it comes from the bottle or the breast), and if that air doesn't come back out of their tummy pretty smartly, it can cause them discomfort and pain.

Trouble is, small babies don't really know how to produce a burp by themselves, which is where you – and your winding technique – come in. Good baby-burping is more about perseverance than style. Here's your four-step guide to getting the wind up:

1. **Find a muslin.**

   Or some other cloth that will protect your clothes (and the carpet) from any milk that comes up with the burp.

2. **Position your baby for optimum burping.**

   You're looking for a way to hold her with one hand that lets you get at her back with the other. Top positions to try include propping her against your shoulder, lying her face down across your lap, and sitting her on your leg with your hand supporting her chest.

3. **Pat her back.**

   Or gently rub it with the palm of your hand.

4. **Keep going till you hear the sound of success.**

   Acknowledge your baby's achievement with proud words and cuddles.

Always wind your baby at the end of a feed – even if she's fallen asleep. (Better to have to cuddle her back to sleep for a couple of minutes post-burp than to have her wake five minutes later and scream in pain for hours.) If she's a real air-gulper or was crying a lot when you started the feed, you may find you need to wind her mid-feed, too.

Chapter 8

Moving on to Solids

● ●

In This Chapter

▶ Knowing when it's time to start

▶ Understanding what to feed and when

▶ Recognising food allergies and intolerances

● ●

Here's the thing with parenting: Just as you've mastered one big scary new skill (getting your baby to drink milk), along comes another big scary new skill (getting your baby to eat 'solid' food) for you to master – and you're sure that you're going to make a mess of it.

Well, I'm afraid you *are* going to make a mess of moving on to solids – but not at all in the way you think. The mess I'm talking about will be in your baby's hair, down your front, on your floor, even up your walls: Believe me, the only thing that's scary about this new venture is how long it's going to take you to clear up afterwards.

When to Start Solids

Once upon a time, everyone knew when to get going with the solids: Your baby turned 4 months old and out came the feeding spoons. Then the World Health Organisation (WHO) came up with a recommendation that babies should be breastfed exclusively for their first 6 months (and, therefore, not given any solids until they're 6 months, either).

Trouble is, while most babies are quite happy to tootle on for six months on a milk-only diet, there are some babies who quite clearly aren't: At some point after 4 months but before 6, they're suddenly no longer satisfied after a large breast- or bottlefeed and start chewing their fists in hunger pretty much all the time.

So, what's the right thing to do if your baby is under 6 months and hungry as hell? Struggle on for weeks (and it may well be a struggle, especially if you're breastfeeding) or ignore the WHO advice and move on to solids early?

I'm afraid there's no one answer that's right for every baby, and the right answer for your baby depends largely on how she's developing. If, as well as being hungry, your baby's showing other signs of being ready for solids, discuss your next move with your health visitor. These 'ready signs' include:

✔ She's doubled her birthweight.

✔ She has four or five good, regular milk feeds a day and used to go about four hours between them, but now she gets hungry again much sooner.

✔ After a big feed, she's often still hungry.

✔ She watches with fascination when you eat and may start imitating your chewing movements or even trying to grab your food.

✔ She can sit well by herself or when lightly propped.

✔ She's started waking with hunger earlier in the morning – or even in middle of the night.

✔ She's lost her tongue-thrusting reflex. Small babies instinctively use their tongue to push objects out of their mouth; until this reflex fades, you're not going to have much luck getting a spoonful of food in there.

Don't forget about growth spurts! Some babies do suddenly have a ravenous patch round about the 4-month mark. This is not a 'ready sign' unless it continues for more than a few days.

Before you make a decision on solids, however, here are some things you must know:

✔ **Starting solids before 17 weeks is dangerous.** And it's better to wait till 20 weeks at least. Your baby's kidneys and digestive system simply won't be ready to cope with solids before then – and she could become ill.

If your baby was born prematurely, the 17-week minimum age for starting solids counts from the day she was due, not the day she was born. Many experts also advise waiting the full six months before putting a premature baby on solids.

✔ **Be cautious of allergies.** There is some evidence that starting solids early can trigger allergies, asthma, and eczema in susceptible babies. So, if you've a history of any of these conditions in your family (or your baby already has symptoms), waiting until 6 months may be wise.

✔ **Starting early means going slowly.** There are quite a number of foods you can't give your baby till she's 6 months old (see the section 'Letting the Food Fun Begin', later in this chapter). And she's unlikely to be able to manage finger foods before 6 months, either. So, if you introduce solids before then, you'll have to stick to simple fruit and veg purees for a fair few weeks.

✔ **Starting solids early is better than giving up breastfeeding.** If your 5-month-old has suddenly started screaming for milk 24/7 and both your breasts and your energy levels are running on empty, switching to formula milk can seem like the ideal solution – but it's not. Your baby's main source of nutrients is still breast milk – and will continue to be so for weeks after she's started solids. If you have to switch to formula for other reasons (going back to work, for example), fine; otherwise, remember that breast milk still has the nutritional and illness-protecting edge.

✔ **You shouldn't delay introducing solids beyond 6 months.** Particularly if you're breastfeeding. After 6 months, your baby needs more iron than breast milk (or infant formula) can provide. There is also some evidence that babies who start solids much later than 6 months can go on to become fussy eaters.

The most important thing about starting solids is to take your lead from your baby, not from what other parents with babies the same age are doing. Your baby may be bigger or smaller than theirs and will almost certainly be developing at a slightly different rate. Just because your friend's baby is lapping up mashed carrots at 20 weeks, it doesn't necessarily mean yours needs to be – or vice versa.

You may well find one of your twins is ready for solids before the other. This is nothing to worry about – you'll find the other one soon catches up.

Letting the Food Fun Begin

Okay, so your baby's ready for solids, but are you? Before you start, you need a few extra bits and pieces to serve things up in, some idea of what to serve up – and the low-down on how to serve it like a pro.

Getting ready: Spoons and bowls and other essentials

Don't panic at the length of this list: Some of the stuff you've probably got already, and most of the rest is very cheap. The highchair is the only big buy, but you'll be using it for a good couple of years – longer if you go on to have more children. So, here's what you need:

- ✔ **Something for your baby to sit in:** A car seat or bouncy chair is fine if your baby's under 6 months. She should only move on to a highchair when she can sit for long periods without slumping. Make sure that you can clean the chair easily and that it has a five-point harness.

  Buying a highchair? Make sure you've thought through your choice. Freestanding ones come with a tray, so your baby (and her mess) are (slightly) more self-contained; wooden ones don't fold away and don't have trays, so your baby needs to eat at (and make a mess on) the table. Wooden ones usually convert into toddler seats; freestanding ones need replacing with a booster seat at the table once your baby's about 2.

- ✔ **A hand blender:** Your baby's first foods need to be very smooth purées. You can manage with a sieve, but a blender's a lot less hassle.

- ✔ **Weaning spoons:** These are softer and smaller than regular teaspoons.

- ✔ **A plastic bowl:** It needn't be fancy, but it does need to be dishwasher-safe and hurl-at-the-floor-proof.

- ✔ **A beaker:** Once your baby's 6 months, getting her used to the idea that milk and water can come in a beaker as well as a bottle is a good idea. Start with a lidded beaker with handles and a soft spout (see the later section 'Up for the cup' for more details).

- ✔ **Mess mat (or newspaper) and bibs:** For protecting your floor and your baby's clothes from freewheeling purée. Choose fabric bibs with long sleeves for maximum coverage (the plastic 'pelican' ones are fine for later but young babies tend not to go a bundle on them).

All the spoons and bowls and beakers you use must be sterile if your baby's under 6 months. If you haven't got a steriliser, put them through the hot cycle of your dishwasher.

Grub's up! Loading the spoon

The best first foods to offer your baby – and the only foods you can offer if she's under 6 months – are baby rice, cooked puréed vegetables, and cooked puréed fruit. (For more on what you can feed your baby and when, see Table 8-1.)

Many parents find baby rice the best choice for the very first spoonful because this food's easy to prepare and easy for a baby to digest. Also, mixed with lukewarm breast or formula milk (cooled boiled water is okay, as well), it tastes reassuringly familiar, and in the days to come, will combine well with fruit and vegetable purées as you start to introduce your baby to new flavours. Make sure that the baby rice (or purée) is very smooth and really quite runny, to begin with.

Table 8-1	What Can My Baby Have When?
Age	*Food*
From 6 months (and, if necessary, before*)	Baby rice, apple, pear, papaya, banana (uncooked), carrot, cauliflower, potato, courgette, squash, green beans, swede, sweet potato, dried fruit, peach, kiwi, plum, apricot, melon, avocado (uncooked), peas, tomato, spinach, celery, leek, parsnip, sweet pepper
From 6 months (but not before)	Bread, pasta, flour, cereals, eggs, fish, chicken, red meat, dairy products (including cow's milk but only in cooking), citrus fruits, raw fruits, berries, sweetcorn, mushrooms
From 8 months	Lentils, split peas, butter beans
After 12 months (but not before)	Honey, unpasteurised cheese, shellfish, salt, cow's milk (as a drink), peanut spreads (wait till 3 years), whole nuts (wait till at least 5 years)

*Note: If your baby's under 6 months, always seek advice before starting solids. Never start solids before 17 weeks.

Open wide: Here it comes!

Okay, bibs at the ready – let the solids show begin! To increase the chance of rave reviews from your baby, you can

- ✔ **Time it right.** Pick a moment when your baby's hungry but not frantically hungry, and when you're feeling calm and collected.

- ✔ **Pick a tactic.** You have three choices: Bring out the baby rice at the start and finish off with her regular breast/formula feed; feed her the milk first, then get the baby rice out; or 'sandwich' her first solids between two halves of a milk feed. All can work equally well, but each has its own potential pitfall (solids first could freak her out, feeding first could fill her up, and the sandwich could wear you out). It's really all down to what feels easiest for you.

- ✔ **Think small.** A spoonful or two is all you're aiming for. Even half a spoonful is fine at first.

✔ **Raise the spoon gently as you take it out.** This will help her upper gums take the food off the spoon.

✔ **Smile**. A lot. Talk to her enthusiastically about the lovely, tasty new food she's eating.

✔ **Don't be put off by funny faces.** Babies pull the most amazing grimaces when they taste new textures and flavours – but they do that when they like what they're tasting as well as when they don't. And spitting food out doesn't mean they hate it, either.

✔ **Know when to stop.** If your baby turns her head away from your advancing spoon, it's time to call it a day.

Milk is still a key part of your baby's diet. If your baby's under 6 months old, do not cut back on her milk feeds when you introduce solids. Once she's past 6 months and eating protein, you can gradually start cutting back, dropping one feed at a time. By about 12 months, your baby should only need about 600ml/1 pint breast or formula milk a day (including the milk on her cereal and any cow's milk used in cooking) or the equivalent in dairy products, such as yoghurt or cheese.

Beyond First Bites: Purée and Simple

Once those first few servings of baby rice or fruit/veg purée are down the hatch, you can think about moving on to different, stronger tastes and thicker textures. Obviously, how quickly you can do so depends on how old your baby is – if she's under 6 months, some foods will be off limits to begin with (see Table 8-1, earlier in this chapter) – but offering as wide a variety of tastes as you can is crucial. By introducing your baby to lots of interesting flavours from the word go, you're educating her palate to accept all sorts of tastes, and that means she's less likely to become a fussy eater later on (although I'm not promising miracles!).

Start by varying the purées: pear one day, for example, then sweet potato the next. When your baby's had a selection of single-flavour purées, try mixing two flavours together. (I'm not going to give you any recipes here because there are lots of excellent baby cookbooks out there that do the job much better than I could.) Gradually increase the amount you offer, the thickness of the mixture, and the number of times you serve up solids in a day (for more on this, see Table 8-2).

By the time your baby's 7 months, she should be eating three servings of solids a day (including meat and fish) – and you should be starting to get lumpy. Over the next few weeks, you need to introduce her very gradually to the idea of chewing. Keep the purées soft at first but don't whizz them quite so smooth, and offer her melt-in-the-mouth finger foods, such as breadsticks, toast soldiers, chunks of cheese or cooked potato, steamed carrot sticks, and sliced banana.

At about 9 months, start chopping, pulsing, or lightly mashing her food, rather than puréeing it. By now, she'll be able to eat small portions of the same food you're eating, as long as you don't put salt in it.

Bananas are a brilliant anytime-anywhere baby food and most babies do go, er, bananas about them. But there are two important things you should know: First, bananas can bung them up (avoid them if your baby's already constipated); second, mashed banana stains like the deuce (that's why older babies have those weird brown patches on their bibs).

Watch out for foods that are hard, sticky, or small and round: They're all easy for a baby to choke on. For now, avoid raw carrots, whole cherry tomatoes, and whole grapes (cut them into quarters), unmashed sweetcorn and peas, chunks of meat, slices of apple (offer a whole one, peeled), and hard boiled sweets. Never leave your child alone while she's eating.

Table 8-2 Your At-a-Glance Solids Timetable

Stage of Starting Solids	*What to Dish Up Each Day*
Week 1	1 small serving of baby rice
Week 2 (weeks 2 to 4, if under 5 months)	2 servings fruit/veg purée
Week 3 (and following weeks,) if under 6 months	2–3 servings fruit/veg purée
Week 4 (but not before 6 months)	2–3 servings fruit/veg purée, plus small amounts of natural yoghurt, fromage frais, cheese
Weeks 5 to 6 (but not before 6 months)	3 servings fruit/veg/meat/fish purée, plus bread, cereals, and dairy products
From 7 months	3 lumpier servings fruit/veg/meat/fish purée, plus dairy products
From 9 months	3 servings chopped/mashed food

Raising a mini-vegetarian? Keep your veggie baby healthy by making sure that she has enough high-protein beans, lentils, eggs, and cheese (once she's old enough to eat them), as well as plenty of iron-rich dried fruit and green veg.

One last need-to-know fact: A baby on solids produces a whole different kind of poo – much more solid and much more smelly. Now you know why nappy bags are scented.

Baby-led weaning

There is a new trend on the introducing-solids front – or, rather, a very old one revisited. And there's not a weaning spoon in sight! Baby-led weaning is all about putting a selection of soft-ish, baby-fist-sized chunks of food in front of your baby and letting her get on with it – much as babies would've done centuries ago when hand blenders (not to mention electricity) simply didn't exist.

And those who've gone for this self-feeding approach over the spoon-feeding one swear babies love being able to pick and choose what they eat in this way, turn out to be less fussy eaters later, and often develop fine-finger control much quicker than their spoon-fed peers. They also chuckle slightly smugly at the hours the rest of us put in on the puréeing frontline.

A word of warning, though: Baby-led weaning is slightly hippy and seriously splatty. It's definitely not for the love-a-schedule, can't-abide-a-mess kind of parent. It also seems to suit breastfed babies better than bottle-fed ones (probably because breastfeeding tends to be a baby-led kind of process, too). If you fancy giving it a whirl, wait till your baby's 6 months old, talk to your health visitor, offer a good variety of foods (starter ideas include steamed broccoli florets, chunks of ripe pear, rice cakes), and make sure that your baby's sitting (or propped) nicely upright as she tucks in. As soon as she can bring her thumb and first finger together in a pincer motion, you can offer her smaller-sized foods, such as peas, raisins and tiny sandwiches.

Being a Food Whizz

There's no getting round the fact that puréeing and mashing is a bit of a faff. And completing the bowl-to-baby purée transfer is all rather hit and miss. But you can cut right down on the stress and the mess if you follow these four golden baby food rules:

- **Prepare food in batches.** It's a huge waste of time and effort (not to mention money) peeling, cooking, and puréeing a whole sweet potato, only for your baby to eat two spoonfuls of it – or worse, chuck it all on the floor. So, get all *Good Housekeeping* and do it in batches: Cook up a whole load of sweet potatoes at once and freeze the purée in an ice cube tray. Then do the same with a few other fruits and veg, and you'll have several days'-worth of meals, in handy three-spoon portions, all ready to defrost when you need them. Licence to feel smug or what?

- **Give your baby a spoon to hold.** Some older babies will try to snatch your spoon off you just at the crucial moment; give her a spoon of her own to wave about, and you should have fewer purée-in-hair incidents.

✔ **Let your baby feed herself.** Some babies are desperate to feed them-selves right from the start. If yours is, resign yourself to the mess and let her have a go – or mealtimes will start becoming a power struggle between the two of you. Either give her a spoon (and pop in the odd spoonful yourself every now and then) or cut the food into soft lumps or slivers so she can pick it up herself.

✔ **Junk the jar guilt (but don't go mad).** Ready-made baby food can be a lifesaver when you're away from home or you're just too pooped to purée. As well as the traditional jars of baby food, you can now buy frozen cubes of organic purée to stockpile in your freezer for when your home-made stash runs out. But do try not to get into the habit of reach-ing for a jar every day. Ready-made baby foods tend to be very bland, very smooth, and often very high in sugar. Handy though they are from time to time, jars are really no match for home-made food in terms of flavour, texture – and, of course, cost.

Allergy Alert: Signs to Watch For

There are no end of scare stories about the rise of food allergies but, the truth is, they're still pretty rare. But it pays to be watchful, especially if there are people with food allergies in your family already.

Always introduce new foods to your baby one at a time, preferably over a couple of days, so you can see if anything causes a reaction. The most common 'trigger' foods are eggs, nuts, shellfish, and wheat-based products. If you notice any of the following symptoms within an hour of your baby eating a new food, call your GP (or dial 999 if the symptoms are severe):

✔ Wheezing or breathing problems

✔ A rash

✔ Swelling of her lips and tongue

You may notice that your baby nearly always gets diarrhoea, constipation, tummy ache, or is sick after eating a certain food. This reaction could be a sign of a food intolerance and is worth checking out with your GP.

Up for the Cup?

Allow me to let you in on a secret: The earlier you start getting your baby used to drinking from a cup, the easier your life is going to be later on. Remember, at some point you're going to have to wean your baby off the breast or bottle and, if she's already a dab hand with a cup by then, you've something else to put the milk in and one less thing to worry about.

Bring out the cup when you start solids. Choose one with a soft-spouted lid and handles and fill it with just a little cooled boiled water. Sit your baby in her bouncy chair (or highchair) and, keeping your hand on the bottom of the cup, tip it up gently so a few drops drip into her mouth. Then take the cup away so she has a chance to splutter and swallow. To begin with, offer just a few sips at every solid meal. Your baby will soon start grabbing at the cup and trying to drink by herself – grit your teeth and let her, even if you both get soaked!

Later on, your baby may enjoy drinking from a leak-proof (hurray!) cup with a harder plastic spout or from one of those sports bottles with an inbuilt straw. For the sake of her teeth, sticking to milk or water is best, but fruit juice is okay (after 6 months) as long as you dilute it well.

Chapter 9

Sweet Dreams: Getting Baby to Sleep

. . . .

In This Chapter

▶ Getting your sleep expectations right

▶ Creating the right conditions to help your baby to sleep through

▶ Coping when the going gets tough

. . . .

'To sleep, perchance to dream . . .' Sorry, but Hamlet didn't know the half of it! He may have had a few things on his mind when he was trying to get a bit of shut-eye, but he never had to withstand anything like the level of sleep deprivation that is routinely suffered by all new parents.

This chapter is all about coming to terms with sleep – how much your baby's getting and how little you are. It's about understanding your baby's sleeping patterns and accepting how they are going to impact on yours. It's also about giving you the tools and techniques to teach your baby to know the difference between night and day, and to settle himself back to sleep on his own. The result? Ever-longer (night-time) journeys to the land of Nod – for all of you.

What's Normal?

The average newborn sleeps for 16 to 20 hours out of every 24 (but not all at once and, sadly, not all at night); the average 1-year-old sleeps for 11 and-a-half hours at night and two-and-a-half in the day.

The journey from the newborn's random, round-the-clock waking and dozing to the 1-year-old's (fairly) predictable day-time naps and night-time sleeps is slow, often bumpy, and not very parent-friendly. There are lots of clever ways to make the journey easier (and this chapter's full of them) but it's still unde-niably long-haul.

So, it helps, right at the outset, for me to be blunt and for you to be realistic: Expect to be a sleep-deprived zombie for a good while yet. This way, you won't be disappointed every night – and, you never know, soon you may find you're pleasantly surprised in the morning.

It also helps to ignore other parents who tell you their 4-week-old's sleeping through (either they're lying or they're sneakily only counting the hours from midnight to 5 a.m.). To help you put your baby's current sleep tally in proper context, use Table 9-1 as a guide to what's normal now and what's normal (most of the time) at various different stages in his first year.

Table 9-1	Your Month-by-Month Baby-Sleep Guide	
Age	*Hours of day-time sleep*	*Hours of night-time sleep*
1 week	8	8.5
4 weeks	6.75	8.75
3 months	5	10
6 months	4	10
9 months	2.75	11.25
12 months	2.5	11.5

Adapted with thanks from Solving Children's Sleep Problemsby Lyn Quine (Beckett Karlson, £12.99).

This chart is only a guide, not a timetable that your baby must adhere to. Some babies, like some adults, do seem to need less or more sleep than most. If your baby is getting more or less sleep than the chart indicates but seems perfectly content in every other way, then he's doing fine.

Safe Sleeping

Before you even begin to work on your baby's sleeping patterns, focus your attention on his sleeping arrangements. And I'm not talking about which cute baby-chick pattern his cot sheet should be. This issue is far more serious than that. For where your baby sleeps, what he sleeps on, and even what position he sleeps in could well be a matter of life and death.

The family bed

Sharing your bed with your baby seems a lovely, cuddly idea (unless you're blessed with constant little wrigglers like me), and the idea's held up by a fair number of midwives and parents as a brilliant way to promote bonding and breast-feeding. But there are others (many of them SIDS experts) who say that co-sleeping is so dangerous, it puts your baby's life at risk.

Let's take the bed-sharing bashers first. These people say that, if you let a small baby sleep in your bed, he could fall out, get trapped between the bed and the headboard or wall, or get scarily overheated under a duvet next to two hot adult bodies. They also suggest that, as your child gets older, he'll find he is unable to sleep without you – which means either you're doomed to being three (or four or five) in a bed for years to come or you're going to have some serious bedtime battles in the future.

Co-sleeping champions counter by saying that your baby will feel safer and sleep better next to you, that you'll feel more connected to your child, and that, if you're breastfeeding, your baby can latch on without even waking you up.

They also say that weaning an older child off the family bed is a cinch: He'll probably decide for himself that he wants his own bed once he's about 2.

If you like the idea of co-sleeping, it's crucial to make sure that your partner does, too. There's no getting round the fact that a family bed does reduce your opportunities for intimacy as a couple and you'll have to get used to anywhere-but-bed sex if your love life isn't to disappear altogether. Be honest with each other about how this makes you feel: There's no point co-sleeping to bring your family together if it actually drives the two of you apart.

Still think co-sleeping's for you? Make sure that your mattress is firm, and that your bedcovers are light (ditch the duvet) and don't fall over your baby's head. Don't bed-share when you're really tired or you've been drinking or taking drugs or medication that make you drowsy. Don't even think about co-sleeping if either of you smoke (even if neither of you smoke in the bedroom).

Cot death (or SIDS – for *sudden infant death syndrome* – as the scientists call it) is the leading cause of death among infants between the ages of 1 month and 1 year. No one knows exactly what causes it, but it is thought that a baby is more at risk if

- ✔ He is a boy.
- ✔ He was born prematurely.
- ✔ His birth-weight was below average.

But, even if your baby is a late-for-dates, roly-poly girl, it still makes good parenting sense to follow the safe-sleeping guidelines. This means you should

- ✔ **Check out his bed.** Make sure that his mattress is firm (second-hand is fine as long as it's not saggy) and fits right up to the edge of the Moses basket or cot without any gaps. Choose a Moses basket with a thin lining and a cot with bars no more than 6.5 cm apart.

- ✔ **Put him to sleep on his back.** Stomach-sleeping is known to be more risky. Once your baby's strong enough to roll over onto his stomach, you can safely leave him sleeping like that.

- ✔ **Think feet to foot.** Your baby's feet should be right down at the foot of his bed, so he can't accidentally wriggle down and get smothered by the covers in the night.

- ✔ **Consider using a dummy.** Recent studies do suggest that settling your baby to sleep with a dummy for the first six months can lower his risk of cot death. If you're breastfeeding, you should wait till your baby's a month old before introducing the dummy (to avoid nipple confusion – between a human nipple that dispenses milk and a plastic one that doesn't). If your baby clearly doesn't want a dummy, don't force it. But if you and he are both happy with it, you should use it every time you put him down to sleep (or settle him back). You don't need to keep popping it back in if it falls out while he's asleep, though.

- ✔ **Keep bedding simple.** Small babies can get tangled up or overheated in lots of extra covers. Stick to a bottom sheet, a top sheet, and a thin cotton blanket. No baby under 1 should sleep on a pillow or under a duvet.

- ✔ **Watch the room temperature.** Your baby's room should be no hotter than 16 to 20°C (don't guess; buy a room thermometer – you can get one for under £3 from most babycare shops). To check that your baby's not too cold or too hot, feel the back of his neck; cold hands and feet are nothing to worry about.

- ✔ **Keep his cot in your room for the first six months**. You'll feel better having your baby close.

- ✔ **Don't smoke.** Anywhere in your house. (And preferably not anywhere else either.) Ask visitors to smoke outside.

Distinguishing Night and Day

Most newborns take a while to get the day/night thing sussed. In fact, a fair few seem to be born with a distinctly precocious 'Hey, it's dark: let's party!' attitude to nightfall. This behaviour isn't really very surprising when you think that your little one's just spent nine months in 24/7 darkness – but that's not much comfort when you're still pacing the floor at 3 a.m. with a wideawake babe in your arms.

Your baby's biological clock will eventually adjust to outside-the-womb time all on its own, but you can wind up the pace by

✔ **Taking an afternoon walk:** Studies show that good little sleepers are generally exposed to twice as much daylight between noon and 4 p.m. as poor sleepers.

✔ **Being noisy in the day:** When your baby takes a day-time snooze, don't disconnect your phone and start creeping round on tip-toe. Walk, talk, natter, and clatter around as usual: You need your baby to get used to the idea that day-time sleep happens with the hum of everyday life in the background. When he wakes, greet him with a bright smile and a warm, energetic voice.

✔ **Being boring at night:** When your baby wakes for a night-time feed, pick him up quietly and calmly. Don't talk, don't put the light on, and don't change his nappy unless you absolutely have to. You're aiming for body language that tells your baby, 'I'm here when you need me but no way is this playtime!'

✔ **Making day-time sleeps different:** Let him nap in his pram or, if you do put him in his cot, don't draw the curtains as you would do at night. Tell him he's having a 'nap-nap' or 'sleepy-time' – it doesn't matter what word you use as long as it's different to the one you use for night-time sleep. And give him a special toy or use a special blanket that only comes out for day-time naps.

✔ **Getting the jim-jams out for bed:** Well, okay, a babygro is fine as long as it's different from the one your baby's been wearing all day. Changing clothes is a small but crafty signal that bedtime is different to nap-time. (For other bedtime signals, see the section 'And So to Bed', later in this chapter.)

Don't think your baby will sleep longer at night if you keep him awake all day. One of parenting life's little ironies is that babies sleep even less well when they're over-tired. By all means, limit naps if you've a diehard day-time dozer on your hands, but always use the month-by-month baby sleep guide in Table 9-1 (see earlier in this chapter) to make sure that you're not denying him the day-time sleep he really needs.

A word about naps

Once your baby's about 6 months old (often well before), he'll stop dozing off after every feed and will pool (or can be persuaded to pool by judicious depositings in the cot or being taken once round the block in the buggy) all his day-time sleeps into two decent-length naps: one in the morning and one in the afternoon.

But from about 9 or 10 months (sometimes a little later), he won't need as much sleep and will have to give up one of these day-time naps (usually the morning one), if you want him to snooze for a good stretch at night. You'll know when the time is right: Either he'll fight sleep at nap-time or he'll start waking from his night-time sleep, bright-eyed and bushy-tailed, at 5 a.m.

When he gives up that nap, expect him to take a few weeks to adjust: You'll probably find you have to make his lunch (or supper) earlier for a while or he'll fall asleep in his mashed carrots.

And So to Bed

First, a word from the (weary) wise: You can't control how many times your baby wakes up in the night, but you can control how easy he finds it to go to bed in the first place.

You do this by setting the stage for sleep at the end of the day in a calm, simple, consistent routine that *you only ever use at bedtime*. Basically, you're giving him a clear but gentle countdown to sleep, rather than whisking him from sitting room to bedroom and expecting instant shut-eye. Get this process right, and the start of the routine soon becomes your baby's cue that bedtime's on its way – and is actually something to look forward to.

Creating the ritual: Bath, cuddle, bed

With any bed-bound babe, your main aim is to get him feeling all nice and warm and sleepy before you tuck him in. To do this, you need to help him relax and wind down and give him some quiet, cuddly time with you.

And it's really not rocket science to work out that the best way to achieve both of these is to give your baby a good meal, a warm bath, and a big hug – after all, it works pretty well for us grown-ups, too! Here's a simple routine to get you started:

1. **Bathe him.**

   Time this for about half an hour before his next feed (or, for an older baby, the last milk feed of the day). Never leave bathing till he's frantically hungry. Feel free to start off fun and splashy but, as the warmth of the water relaxes his little limbs, change down into an altogether calmer gear.

2. **Cuddle him.**

   Once he's dry and dressed for bed, take him to his bedroom (or somewhere equally quiet). When he's older, this part of the routine will develop into story-time but, for now, just hold him close. Give him an extra-peaceful breast- or bottlefeed and let him suckle himself into a really calm, dreamy state.

3. **Put him to bed.**

   Carefully lower him into bed, make sure that he's warm and comfy, give him a goodnight kiss – and leave.

Of course, you don't have to follow this routine to the letter – you can play around with the order (some parents prefer to feed before the bath, for example) or add in little variations of your own. Bear in mind that a good routine must be structured clearly enough to become a familiar ritual but remain flexible enough to grow and accommodate new ideas as your child gets older.

Whatever you do, remember that the best bedtime routines are short and sweet: sweet because you want your baby to associate going to bed with all sorts of loveliness for now and evermore, and short because you deserve a decent dose of adult-only time once it's over.

Here's the rub: Massage magic

The idea of giving a little baby a massage used to be thought a bit 'out there' but now everyone's at it – and for good reason.

Experts say that massage can improve your baby's digestion and bowel function, encourage his muscle and joint development, and help him become more aware of his body and how it moves. But the icing on the massage cake, for us non-expert parents at least, is that it makes a baby calm, content – and wonderfully sleepy. Slip a spot of post-bath massage into your bedtime routine and your baby will be beautifully blissed out before it's even time to hit the sheets.

You can go to classes to learn a 'proper' baby-massage routine (ask your health visitor where to find a class near you or log on to www.iaim.co.uk), but the basic idea's simple enough to pick up on your own – and babies really don't give you extra points for fancy technique. To be a great soothe operator, all you need to do is

✔ **Make sure that your baby's comfy.** The ideal baby 'massage couch' is a changing mat on the floor, covered with a warm towel.

✔ **Keep eye contact.** Look and smile at your baby throughout the massage – he'll enjoy it more if you look like you're having fun, too.

✔ **Use the right oil.** Sweet almond or grapeseed oil (from healthfood shops) are both lovely, but plain old sunflower oil (yes, the one you cook with) is just as good. Steer clear of mineral-based oils and don't add essential oils unless you know what you're doing.

✔ **Get the pressure right.** To get an idea of how hard you can press (probably a little harder than you think), close your eyes and press your eyelids with your fingers; the right pressure feels firm but not uncomfortable.

✔ **Stroke and knead.** Stroke down his back with your palms either side of his spine; gently knead his arms and legs with your fingers and thumbs.

✔ **Keep it short.** Or your baby will get cold and restless (which kind of defeats the whole purpose, doesn't it?). Five minutes is fine; ten, if you know all the fancy fingerwork.

Soothing ideas

It's not only your baby who needs filling with calm at bedtime, but also the place where you're putting him to sleep. There's no point working so hard to wind him down if you're then going to rev him back up again by sticking him in a brightly lit room with the telly on full-blast. Put his cot or Moses basket somewhere quiet and dark, and think about powering up the peace by

✔ **Singing a song:** If you sing the same quiet lullaby just before you leave the room every night, it soon becomes an accepted sign-off signal between the two of you: Song ends; sleep starts.

✔ **Getting a clock:** Nothing beats the eyelid-drooping rhythm of a nice, steady tick-tock. 'You are feeling very sleepy . . .'

✔ **Declaring a blackout:** Back your curtains with blackout lining (or buy special blinds) that won't let through a chink of light. Now you're guaranteed a clear visual signal that night's arrived, even on bright summer evenings, or hasn't yet stopped, even when it's dawn outside.

✔ **Plugging in a lava lamp:** Some babies can't settle in pitch darkness – and, if you're still night-feeding, it helps to be able to see which end of your baby's pointing where. The lava lamp's slow floaty bubble show is more soothing than the conventional night-light.

✔ **Dreamfeeding:** With a small baby who still needs one (or more) feeds in the night, picking him up for a feed before he actually wakes and demands it can work well. The idea is that he gets the milk he needs without ever waking fully, and therefore has no problem sleeping on when the feed's over. I have to confess I never had the nerve to try this myself, but I have friends who swear it works like, well, a dream.

Beware the bad bed habits

Of course, you may find you come up with some soothing ideas of your own and that's great. But before you and your baby get too used to them, please pause and fast-forward a few months. Will what you're doing now still be pleasurable – or even possible – then?

Trust me, this is an important question. You really don't want to end up like the (lovely) mother I know who used to dance her newborn to sleep – and then ricked her back trying to pirouette with a 20-pounder. Or the woman I met in a hotel last year whose baby will only nod off to the sound of a vacuum cleaner: She had to pay a chambermaid double-overtime to Hoover up and down the hall every night. Consider yourself well and truly warned!

 If your baby has a special toy or comfort blanket for bedtime, buy an identical spare – now. And keep the spare in the car boot. Every parent has at least one, 'Oh no, we left Blankie at home!' moment when they're halfway up the motorway. This is your chance to save yourself several hundred miles of grief.

Sleeping Through: Teaching Baby to Self-Calm

Face the facts time: You cannot expect your baby to shut his eyes at bedtime and not open them again till morning. Sleep just doesn't work like that, particularly in the first year.

For a start, very small babies need to wake frequently in the night to feed – and they don't stop needing to do so until they weigh at least 10–15 lb and, often, are well into their third month. (Even then, it'll probably be at least another three months before your baby can reliably last more than ten hours without waking from hunger.)

What's more, babies' sleep cycles are different to ours. Throughout the night, we all alternate periods of deep sleep with periods of lighter sleep, and in this lighter-sleep phase we often come close to waking or even actually wake momentarily (you may not notice it but you do, honest). But, for babies, each deep-sleep and each light-sleep period is shorter than an adult's, so they go through way more cycles every night than we do – and have way more wakening moments.

Sleeping bags

The baby sleeping bag could be your passport to calmer nights. It looks a little like a zip-up sleeveless dress with the bottom hem sewn together and you pop your baby in it at night, instead of covering him up with the traditional sheet-and-blanket combo. And the sleeping bag's clever little secret is that it stops your baby getting chilly. So what? Well, so a lot. All babies wriggle and squirm in their sleep and many wriggle so much, they shake off their blankets, and then wake because they're cold. But even the wriggliest of little wrigglers can't wriggle out of a sleeping bag. Result: fewer midnight cold calls and happier, more rested parents.

The only trouble is, the baby sleeping bag does come as a buy now, pay later kind of deal. For, at some point in the future, your child is going to have to sleep under conventional covers – unless you want to be woken every morning by the sound of your 3-year-old jumping (literally) out of his bed. And, while he gets used to the change, you're probably going to have to deal with a nasty spell of post-midnight sorties to recover chilly toddler legs with errant duvets.

So, do you bag 'em up now or not? It's your call (although if you travel a lot, I'd say yes: Your baby will cope more easily with a strange sleeping place if he's snuggled up in his familiar bag). If you do go for it, make sure that you get the right bag for your child's age and the right tog rating for the weather. Precisely because your baby can't shrug the bag off, you really do have to be extra-sure that he won't get overheated in the night.

So, if you want your baby to sleep through, you need to do more than make sure that he's dozy when you tuck him in at bedtime; you also need to teach him to settle himself back to sleep when he wakes in the night. To do this

- ✔ **Stay put when he stirs.** Resist the impulse to leap up at every murmur and snuffle. Unless your baby's actually crying, wait a few seconds before you react – he may well drift back to sleep on his own.

- ✔ **Rein in the cotside rituals.** If you stay with your baby till he's nodded off or stroke, pat, or sing him to sleep, odds are he soon won't be able to get to sleep any other way – and that includes the times when he wakes in the night. Once your baby's in bed, leave the room.

- ✔ **Put him down awake.** Many small babies simply conk out towards the end of their bedtime feed (and most other feeds, come to that) and slumber on as they're put into their cot. And that's jolly handy. But, as your baby approaches the 6-month mark and is generally less likely to doze off as he feeds, try to put him to bed drowsy but awake, so he can get used to drifting off on his own. It may help to talk to him quietly before you put him down or to feed him in another room and use the motion of your walk to the bedroom to keep him just this side of serious slumber.

A room of his own

At some point, your child's going to need to sleep in his own room – and, unless you're a diehard family-bed fan – there's something to be said for making the move sooner, rather than later.

Having your baby's cot or Moses basket at arm's length from your own bed can be a godsend when your nights are broken and your body is weary but, once your baby's sleeping for longer stretches at night, this handy little set-up can seem suddenly less attractive. If you're anything like me, you'll wake up with a start every time your baby so much as stirs in his sleep – so, even if he gets a great night's kip, you still look (and feel) like a zombie in the morning. And then there's the tip-toeing-to-bed-in-the-dark scenario: You can't read, you can't talk, you can't even plump a pillow when it's your bedtime for fear of waking your little dreamer. And let's not get started on how hard it is to have totally silent sex.

You can make the move anytime from 6 months (when your baby's SIDS risk decreases). And, since 6 months is often the age at which your baby outgrows his Moses basket, it makes sense to combine the room move with the crib-to-cot move and get both changes over with at once.

As long as your baby is familiar with his new room (I made a point of changing nappies there for precisely this reason) and has a familiar bedtime routine, there's no reason why he shouldn't adjust to the change very easily. If his bedroom is some distance from yours, though, do make sure (using monitors, if you need to) that you'll be able to hear if he wakes and cries.

Wailing in the Wee Hours

Face the facts time: Even if you're a whizz at bedtime routines and a master of getting-baby-to-settle-himself technique, there'll still be some nights when your baby wakes and cries himself silly. It's not your fault, and it's almost certainly not his; it just happens. But there are ways to handle it that make it a whole lot more bearable – for all of you.

Hungry cry? Scared cry? Hurt cry?

First, you need to establish the cause of all the wailing. With under-1s, you can be fairly sure that the crying's kicked off because

- **He's hungry.** If he's under 6 months and not yet on solids, feed him. He may not be big enough to make it through the night yet or he could be going through a growth spurt. It's also quite common for a big baby of 4 or 5 months who's not yet on solids to suddenly get hungry in the night (for more on this, see Chapter 8). If he's over 6 months and on solids, he doesn't need a feed in the night; he's just not kicked the habit of waking to snack. Try giving him a beaker or bottle of water instead; he may well decide that's not worth waking up for tomorrow.

✔ **He's uncomfortable.** Maybe his nappy's dirty or his clothes are itchy. Or maybe he's tossed off his covers and got cold. Change or tuck in firmly, as appropriate.

✔ **He's in pain.** He could be teething. Or he could have a cold, a temperature, or an ear infection. Give him a cuddle and get out the Calpol. (If his fever's very high or he seems very unwell, call your doctor's emergency service for advice or call NHS Direct on 0845 4647; for more on teething and illness, see Chapter 11.)

✔ **He's just not tired.** This can happen with an older baby who's had a daytime nap (or two) but really no longer needs one (or two). The telltale sign is waking (and crying) much earlier than usual each morning.

✔ **He's all at sea.** Perhaps his routine has changed or he's in a strange house. Whatever it is, the change is new and confusing and your baby wants some reassurance. Give it to him.

What to do when it happens again (1)

After one night of wailing, your baby may well sleep like an angel the next. Then again, he may not. Which will it be? Well, if the cause of the wailing (those troublesome teeth, that strange bedroom) is still at large, I wouldn't hold out much hope for the sleep-angel option.

If the wails do strike again, there's not much you can do – for the moment – except be a loving shoulder to cry on. Odds are, you're stuck in a situation that will only resolve itself in time (when the teeth come through, when you get back home) and, until then, you'll just have to soldier on and suffer in anything but silence. You may find it helps to

✔ **Take turns with your partner.** A broken night shared is not exactly a broken night halved but it helps. Alternatively, if you're both at home the next day, let the up-all-nighter grab a catch-up nap or two.

✔ **Go to bed early.** A post-midnight baby-comforting marathon is always easier to handle with a few hours' kip in the parental sleep bank.

✔ **Sleep with him.** Either take him into your bed (following the co-sleeping precautions in 'The family bed') or bed down on a mattress in his room. You'll probably both get more sleep doing this than if you keep trying to settle him back on his own – but you may pay for it in the days to come (see the next section, 'What to do when it happens again (2)').

✔ **Repeat, 'It's just a phase.'** As often as possible. Because it is.

What to do when it happens again (2)

This is the bit that drives you spare. The ear infection's cleared up, the teeth are through (or whatever), but your baby's still howling from dusk to dawn. What's going on?

What's going on is what experts call 'incorrect sleep association' and what I call 'I'll-have-some-more-of-that-nice-hugging-in-the-night-please syndrome'. Unfortunately, your baby's had a succession of nights when you've comforted him every time he woke and wailed (because he needed it) and now he'd like the arrangement to continue (even though he doesn't need it any more).

So what do you do? You have two options (try the first before the second):

- ✔ **Treat it as a (another) phase.** And offer cuddles or reassuring pats but much more briefly and boringly than before.
- ✔ **Get tough**. Withdraw all middle-of-the-night cuddling privileges (for how to do this, see the next section).

When enough's enough: Time to get tough

If your baby has been waking and crying for nights on end, you'll be beside yourself with exhaustion. You'll do anything to stop the crying and get some sleep. Well, there is something you can do, but you have to be prepared to get tough – and stay tough – because it'll probably get worse before it gets better and it won't work at all if you don't do it right.

What we're talking about here is often called sleep training, or *controlled crying*, and what it involves is either ignoring your child when he cries – or responding ever more slowly and briefly. Basically, it's a crash course in self-comforting: Dad and Mum aren't going to settle you back any more, so you'll have to do it on your own.

This really is a 'tough love' solution for ending the sleepless nights. And you shouldn't even think about using it unless

- ✔ Your child is over 6 months.
- ✔ You're sure that he isn't ill or adjusting to a change in his life or routine.
- ✔ You and your partner are equally determined to see it through. By far the most common reason for this sort of sleep training not working is one or other parent 'cracking' before their child does.

Whether it's best for you to try the hardcore ignoring-the-cries approach or the gentler responding-more-slowly one really boils down to your ability to tolerate your baby's wails and to your level of desperation. Table 9-2 can help you decide.

Table 9-2	Which Sleep-Training Method Is for You?
Hardcore	*Gentler*
It works in two or three days	It can take a week to ten days
You'll have to listen to your baby crying – maybe for over an hour	You don't have to leave your baby crying f or long
Almost always works if you can stick it out	May not work with a very stubborn baby

The hardcore method is pretty self-explanatory: Do nothing when your baby wakes and cries, and steel yourself for a lot of wailing. Your baby will probably cry for a very long time the first night, a shorter time the next, and will generally sleep through by the third or fourth night.

The gentler method involves some clock-watching. When your baby wakes and cries, wait two minutes, then go in and gently but firmly settle him back down. Don't cuddle or sit with him (although it's fine to give him a few reassuring pats on the back). Talk only briefly and matter-of-factly: 'Back to sleep now.' Leave while he's still awake (this step is crucial!). If he continues to cry, wait ten minutes before going back in. Repeat as long as he keeps crying, lengthening the wait by five minutes each time. The following nights, repeat the whole process, as necessary, but wait five minutes longer each night before you respond for the first time.

Your child will still love you in the morning if you've been tough at night.

If your baby cries incessantly despite your best efforts and you feel you're at the end of your tether, call the Cry-sis helpline on 08451 228669 (9 a.m. to 10 p.m., seven days a week).

Chapter 10

Playing, Learning, and Socialising

In This Chapter

▶ Boosting your baby's physical development

▶ Encouraging her first words

▶ Discovering when to play and learn – and when enough's enough

*Y*our baby's first year is a whirlwind of physical, mental, and emotional change. And your baby changes quite a lot, too! A mere 12 months from now, that tiny babe with her lolling head and curled-up toes will have morphed into a sitting, crawling – maybe even walking – proto-toddler who can babble, giggle, play peekaboo, and smear yoghurt through your hair in a trice.

Some of these changes happen slowly and surely; some seem to happen overnight. They may happen in the same order and at the same time as they happen to your friends' babies; they may not. At times, they may even happen, un-happen, and then happen again (usually just when you've given up hope).

This chapter is not about charting these changes but about making the most of them. And that means tips and tricks to help you encourage your baby through the key developmental changes of the first year, as well as some wise words and hard facts that'll help keep things in perspective when it seems everyone else's child is (literally) leaps and bounds ahead of your own.

Big Movements for Little Babies

Your baby will end her first year a lot more mobile than she started it. And, to manage that, she's not only going to have to get bigger and stronger, she's going to have to work on her gross motor skills.

Or at least that's what your doctor will call them. A rather more helpful way of putting it (with fewer confusing garage-mechanic overtones) is to say your baby's going to have to work out how to move and co-ordinate her body's main muscles. And, as she gradually manages that, she'll learn to hold up her head, to roll, to sit, to crawl, to stand, and, eventually, to walk – with a whole lot of other clever stuff in between.

The wonder of this process is, your baby's already pre-programmed to do it all on her own. Which doesn't mean we parents are only fit to sit and cheer from the sidelines (although that helps a lot) but does mean we need to follow her lead. We can't make her reach any of these physical milestones before her body's ready but we can make it easier for her to get there once it is.

Tummy time

Small babies spend a lot of time lying on their backs – either because they're asleep in a cot (putting a baby to sleep on its back is known to reduce the risk of cot death; for more on this, see Chapter 8) or because they'd look pretty silly strapped into a car seat or bouncy chair the other way round.

Trouble is, lying on her back all the time gives your average babe a bit of a flat head. Or, to be more precise, a flat patch at the back of the head (where the still-soft bones of the skull are being pressed against all those flat surfaces). This condition usually rights itself in time but it's not a terribly becoming look – and it makes it pretty hard to find a baby hat that fits.

So, once your baby has enough control over her neck muscles to stop her head wobbling about all over the place (usually, by about 2 months), let her spend a few minutes every day lying on her tummy on the carpet or a soft playmat.

Get down there with her and keep tummy time short to start with. Your baby may grizzle when she's first put down the other way up – many babies do – but, if you keep your nerve and persevere you'll see her confidence grow. Soon, not only will she soon be sporting a nice round skull, she'll also be getting loads of chances to practise raising her head right up and to strengthen her chest, neck, and arm muscles – vital prep for mastering the art of rolling over and, eventually, pushing up to crawl.

Never leave your small baby alone while she's lying on her stomach. There's always a danger that her neck muscles could suddenly tire and let her head drop into a position in which she cannot breathe properly.

And . . . sit!

Nearly all babies learn to sit sometime in their first nine months or so but, sadly for the most eager-beaver of parents, they cannot be schooled to plonk themselves posterior-wards on command, like little puppy dogs. How soon (or not so soon) your baby achieves sitting status depends very largely on the genes she's inherited – and very little on parental pressure to perform.

But, even if you can't make her sit when you want, you can employ a few tricks to make those bottom-depositing manoeuvres easier when she's up to it:

- ✔ **Limit time in the sling:** It stands to reason that a baby who spends a lot of her day strapped into a baby carrier isn't going to have much chance to practise sitting.

- ✔ **Prop her up in the pram:** When your baby's about 3 months, you can try raising the back of the pram's seat unit up at a gentle incline. If she's not ready to sit up like this (or grows tired of it), she'll soon tell you, either by slumping down, sliding sideways, or raising merry hell. If she is ready, she'll love getting a new perspective on life – and you'll be giving her back muscles a little taster of what they'll be expected to do all on their own in a few months' time.

- ✔ **Sit her between your legs on the floor:** This is a lovely, cuddly way to give her a preview of 'sitting world'. She can look around, reach for her toys, feel her postural muscles supporting her – and still have a nice, comfy body to fall back against when everything goes a bit pear-shaped.

- ✔ **Make a cushion circle:** It's one thing to be able to sit on your own; quite another to be able to stay there. To stop your wobbly sitter losing her confidence, surround her with cushions, so that whichever way she topples, she'll always have a soft landing.

Doing the locomotion

If knowing when your baby's going to sit is hard, predicting when she's going to crawl is nigh on impossible – and it's pretty much anybody's guess when she's going to walk. Crawling, in particular, is such a haphazardly-programmed part of every child's developmental timeline, it's routinely left off most paediatric assessment charts.

All of which is pretty unsatisfactory news for all us anxious parents – especially if our own offspring remains unmoved (literally) by the acres of carpet suddenly being covered by little Johnny-same-age from next door.

It's hard not to compare your baby with others and easy to assume you've got the cleverest/slowest/sportiest/laziest one just because she does or doesn't get from A to B before everyone else. But take it from one who's been there and compared and assumed – and despaired – before you: Comparing babies is a huge waste of time.

I've fretted over a child who walked late, a child who crawled late, and a child who did both before any of us were ready, and I wish I'd saved myself the stress. I know now that my two late movers were actually busy working on other stuff at the time (one talked early; the other had a major obsession with building Lego towers). I also know that early movers present something of a gymnastic challenge to parents on the safety front – the younger they crawl, the less natural caution they have and the more often you'll be leaping up and rushing across to retrieve them from impending disaster.

But, above all, I know that all babies get there in the end, each in their own sweet, distinctive way, and all you can do is offer them the odd helping hand – and cheer like crazy when they finally make it.

Here are a few tips to help a 'nearly-there' crawler:

- **Get down and dirty:** Your floor doesn't need to be scrubbed, washed, and sterilised before your baby makes contact with it. Sweep away anything truly awful, then get her down there. The more floor-time you give her, the sooner she'll be up and off.

- **Dangle a carrot:** Try putting a favourite toy – or a fascinating new one – just a couple of centimetres beyond her reach.

- **Forget about style:** When it comes to crawling, anything goes, from the traditional hands-and-knees and the more cheeky bottom-in-the-air to the commando-style stomach-slither, the deceptively quick knee-scoot and the gloriously comical bottom shuffle. Does it really matter which method she picks if it gets her where she wants to go?

And to help a 'nearly-there' walker:

- **Ditch the shoes.** And slippery socks. As they take their first tentative steps, babies use their toes for gripping, so bare feet are best.

- **Re-arrange the furniture.** If your baby likes pulling herself up and 'cruising' along the edge of the sofa, position an armchair at the end of her route, so she can transfer over to it. When she can manage that, move the armchair just a little farther away, so she has to make a small unsupported step.

- **Get some wheels.** Pushing a trolley or a toy pram is a great way to practise walking when you still need something to hang on to (and Mummy's arms are in use elsewhere). Keep the trolley/pram away from stairs and make sure it's solid enough not to run away on its own or topple over if she wobbles.

Once your child is mobile, you'll need to remove, rearrange, or lock up stuff in your house that can hurt her or that she can reach and break. (For more on childproofing your home, see Chapter 14.)

Buying that first pair of shoes? Resist the temptation to get those scaled-down designer trainers: They're cute but not the right cut for just-walking feet. Instead, choose a light, low-top shoe, with a flexible, non-skid sole – something that doesn't interfere too much with the foot's natural motion. Get your child's feet properly measured (length *and* width) before you buy – and re-check her shoe size every couple of months.

Shake, Rattle, and Roll: The Truth about Baby Toys

Enter the world of parenthood and you enter the wallet-shrinking world of toys. There are more toys out there than you can shake, well, a rattle at. Cuddly toys, wooden toys, plastic toys, electronic toys, all-singing-all-dancing toys, seriously educational toys, wild and wacky fun toys, organically made and ethically-sourced toys – the choice is endless and, frankly, completely bewildering.

Allow me then to un-bewilder you a little. Children love toys but, to be honest, they're not really that into them in their first year. Yes, babies need plenty of opportunities to practise seeing, reaching, grasping, and generally honing their hand–eye co-ordination (otherwise known as fine motor skills) but, for the first six months, they'd rather just look around a lot or use bits of you (your hair, your nose, your necklace, your glasses) as toys.

After that, babies love fiddling and twisting and pushing and banging pretty much anything they can get their chubby little hands on – but whether that's a couple of saucepan lids or a custom-made, hand-crafted, interactive baby-entertainment centre from Harrods really doesn't bother them much.

And the speed of your baby's fine-motor-skill development does not depend on the fullness of her toy box; at this stage in her life, she'll get great pleasure and huge stimulation from just four or five familiar things (see the suggestions below). So, save yourself money and stress and rein in those toy-buying impulses for now (believe me, you'll be down that toy shop so often in the years to come, you'll be grateful for this short reprieve).

Table 10-1	Great toys for the first six months	
The Toy	*Why Experts Rate It*	*Why Your Baby Rates It*
Cot mobile	It stimulates vision	She loves cooing at the colourful shapes dancing through the air above her
Activity mat	It stimulates hand–eye co-ordination	When she swipes with her arms and legs, the dangling toys move and jingle
Rattle	It teaches cause and effect	It makes a great noise
Mirror	It helps her eyes to focus, and reinforces her inborn response to the human face	The friendly face makes her smile – even if she doesn't yet know it's her own

Table 10-2	Great toys from 6 to 12 months	
The Toy	*Why Experts Rate It*	*Why Your Baby Rates It*
Books	They stimulate physical skills, such as pointing and turning pages, and mental skills, such as memory, concentration, and word recognition	She gets to snuggle into your lap, listen to your voice, look at lovely, bright pictures, and grab at the pages
Bricks and blocks	They teach touch, grip, and stacking skills	They're good to bang together – and to knock back down when they're stacked up
Ball	It encourages hand–eye co-ordination, timing, aim, and shape recognition	It's exciting to watch the ball roll up – and fun to push it back to Mum or Dad
Kitchen utensils	They can stimulate hand control and strength, grasp, creativity, and listening skills	Nothing beats a nice, noisy percussion session with a saucepan and a wooden spoon
Treasure basket (filled with socks, empty cotton reels, rattles, and other small but safe delights)	It promotes curiosity, concentration, manipulation, and sorting skills	She loves the thrill of finding, extracting, and examining each new item on her own

Don't underestimate the entertainment value of everyday stuff you already have in your house. Small babies love washing machines, for example. Stick her in front of yours in her bouncy chair and she'll be mesmerised by the spinning clothes, the sloshing water, and the humming of the machine. And older babies are big fans of cardboard boxes – brilliant for sitting in, filling with toys, or pushing around the floor.

Do make sure the toys you give your baby are safe. Look for the Lion Mark on the box or label and check that it doesn't have removable or wobbly pieces that may break off and find their way into your baby's mouth. Never leave toys with long fur or toys with long strings attached anywhere near your small baby.

Baby Talk, Buddy Talk: Developing Early Language and Social Skills

Your baby probably won't be able to say many words of her own by the end of the year but she'll certainly be able to understand an awful lot of yours. She probably won't be too keen on meeting strangers but she'll certainly love the social buzz of a family gathering (as long as you're close by). In her first 12 months, your baby's laying much of the foundation for the language and social skills that will emerge in her second year – and it pays to muck in and help her out.

Coochy-coo: Why baby chat works

You can actually give your baby the gift of the gab – but you have to be prepared to get some very odd looks. You see, one of the very best ways of encouraging your baby to talk is to talk to your baby – a lot. And that means chatting away merrily to her pretty much from the moment she's born.

Experts agree that the more you talk to a baby, the greater chance she has of picking up words and learning to speak. So, right from the word go (as it were), give her a running commentary on what you're doing as you change her nappy, dress her, feed her, play with her, bath her, and wheel her about in her pram.

This constant chatter can make you sound pretty daft ('Ooh, look at the lovely trees, darling!') but it works. Even if your baby hasn't the foggiest idea what you're going on about, she's listening to the sound of your voice and responding to the warmth in your words. And as her understanding of this talking thing grows, she'll start to gurgle and coo, then babble, and, eventually, form her own words in reply.

Talking points: the first six months

When you're chatting away to your baby, try to

- ✔ **Make eye contact:** She'll learn as much from watching your facial expressions as from hearing your words.

- ✔ **Stick to the present:** Talk about what you can see, hear, and feel right now. Your baby has no concept of the past or the future.

- ✔ **Let her get a word in:** Pause at the end of a sentence and wait for her response – even non-verbal babies can be very vocal!

Talking points: 6 to 12 months

Your baby is now starting to understand certain words. To help, try to

- ✔ **Slow down:** Give her a chance to pick individual words out.

- ✔ **Repeat yourself:** Think about the words that describe the everyday things in your baby's life (nappy, drink, car) and use them – often.

- ✔ **Give instructions:** Now's the time to start saying, 'Give Mummy the toy' or 'Wave bye bye'. If she doesn't do it, always help her act out the request anyway. She'll soon catch on.

Do I know you? Becoming aware of self and others

Your baby's first year of social life falls into two neat phases: the happy-go-lucky and the really rather anxious. Both phases are entirely natural and normal but, as you've probably guessed, one is a touch trickier to handle than the other.

Until about 6 months or so, your baby's a giggly, gurgly, smiley delight and is probably happy to be left with almost any grown-up who responds to her giggles, gurgles, and smiles with loving attention. This doesn't mean that she doesn't love you; just that her short-term memory can't yet cope with the concept of missing you – like the proverbial goldfish, she kind of forgets that you're gone till you're back.

FAB OR FAD?

Baby signing

Baby signing (teaching your baby sign language, usually in a special class) is a big-time craze in the US, and it's starting to take off here. But is it all it's cracked up to be?

The idea behind baby signing is quite simple: Babies get control of their hands way before they get control of their vocal cords, so, if you teach them specific hand signals, they can have meaningful 'conversations' with you before they are actually able to speak.

Fans of baby signing talk of 10-month-olds signing that they're hungry, thirsty, or tired, and swear their babies rarely get frustrated because they can so easily make their needs and wants known. They also mention studies that show that a signing child, by the age of 7 or 8 years, will typically have an IQ 12 points higher than a non-signing child.

Cynics point out that non-signing babies make gestures, too, and if we all listened more carefully to our little darling's 'almost-words', we'd quickly understand what she was after, too. And to counter those IQ studies, they point to other research suggesting that any linguistic advantage signing children have over non-signing children disappears completely by the age of 3.

So what's a parent to think? Most experts agree on one thing at least: Baby signing won't do your baby any harm and it can be lots of fun. Go along to a class if you fancy it (find out more at www.babysigners.co.uk) or buy a book, such as Joseph Garcia's *Complete Guide To Baby Signing* (Nortlight Communications, £29.99) but don't fret if the whole idea's not for you (or your baby).

'There are countless ways to communicate with your baby and knowing a few gestures is certainly useful,' says Liz Attenborough of the National Literacy Trust's Talk to Your Baby campaign. 'But the last thing parents should feel is guilt if they don't do signing classes.'

At some point after 6 months, though (and generally before 1 year), your baby may start to get very upset when she can't see you (even if you're only in the next room). She's now ever so capable of missing you and is also beginning to get her head round the (scary) idea that she's a separate person (as opposed to being some kind of part of you). She may also become very shy or wary of strangers, often burying her head into your shoulder when some nice old lady says hello to her in the street.

This sudden social wobbliness may only last a few weeks but more often takes a while longer to pass, as she slowly learns that you always come back and she will be okay with trusted others until you do. During this time, it helps to be extra-patient with any clinginess and to build up her trust and self-reliance by

✔ **Playing peekaboo:** She thinks you're having fun with her (and you are) but you're actually teaching her about 'object permanence' – that things still exist, even if you can't see them. Which makes it (a little) less scary when you disappear in the future.

✔ **Making a photo album:** Fill a small album with pictures of you and other close relatives, so you can look at them and talk about your family together. Again, you're reinforcing the idea that people are still there, even when they're not with her. Don't forget to include a few photos of her, too.

✔ **Taking it slow with new faces:** If you're visiting a friend's house, let her sit on your lap for a while and get used to the new sights and sounds before letting your friend whisk her off for a hug.

✔ **Avoiding a change of carer:** If this just can't be helped, be prepared for the fact that your baby may need lots of reassurance and may take longer to settle into the new arrangements.

✔ **Leaving with a smile:** Whether you are off to work or out for an hour, try your best to keep your goodbyes short and sweet. Her cries for you will only intensify if you linger longer out of guilt.

It's a boy/girl thing: girls talk; boys walk

Right, let's not beat about the non-sexist bush: Boys' and girls' brains are not wired the same way at birth.

Girls come better equipped to acquire language and deal with emotion; boys come better equipped to track objects with their eyes and develop spatial awareness. Not only that, but girls and boys actually begin developing and using various parts of their brain in a very different order.

All this mean it's not too much of a mystery why the two sexes tend to reach their developmental milestones at markedly different points in their first year: Generally speaking, boys get on with the physical stuff first, while the girls concentrate on the mental and emotional.

Why does it pay to know all this? Partly so you don't panic when your best friend's little girl can say 50 words and your little boy can barely say 'Dada'. And partly so you remember sometimes to parent a little counter-intuitively and play to your child's gender weaknesses rather than strengths.

So, while it's lovely to watch your little girl's face light up as you sing songs together, it's also worth letting her have a good, long kick at the toys dangling from her playgym. And, by all means, play mock rough-and-tumble with your little baby boy but don't forget that he needs a quiet cuddle just as much – perhaps more – as a more emotionally advanced baby girl.

Six Cool Things New Mums Should Do (Eventually)

Here are some great activities to build into your baby's week. I didn't choose them because they're super-stimulating (although, actually, they all are) but because they're fun, and will become even more so as your baby enters her toddler years and wants to get into the action more. There's no need to rush, though – your baby will not suffer one iota developmentally if you don't manage any of the things on this list in her first six months – but do try to give most of them a go before her first birthday.

1. **Get singing.** All babies love music and beam with approval when they're played or sung to. From about 3 months, they respond well to action nursery rhymes, and gradually learn to anticipate the actions that are coming next. If your nursery-rhyme repertoire doesn't extend much beyond 'Twinkle Twinkle', find a baby-and-toddler singing group near you (ask at your library). Your child will enjoy the energy of a group singsong and, as she gets older, will join in and rush for an instrument to bash.

2. **Get to the library.** No, not to get a book out (although some libraries do have excellent baby book sections) but to get social. Loads of libraries organise all sorts of baby-friendly activities, from toy-sharing schemes to baby bounces and storytelling sessions. Find out what your local one has to offer.

3. **Get wet.** Buy your baby a swim nappy and head for your local pool (preferably one with a separate, warmer toddler pool). Even small babies get a kick out of floating round in your arms, and for 8- or 9-month-olds who aren't mobile but are full of beans, bouncing around in water is a fantastic way to splash off energy.

4. **Get to the playground.** As soon as your baby can sit, she can get into the swings. And whizz down the slides (first with you holding her, then with you waiting to catch her at the bottom). Go in the morning or early afternoon, when the bigger children are at nursery and school.

5. **Get bubbly.** Blowing bubbles is about the biggest fun you can have with your baby for the least amount of parental energy. Blow bubbles for her at first, so she can stare and poke and pop. Later on, help her to blow, too. Guaranteed giggles from about 3 months to, oh, 13 years.

Over-stimulating (and How to Avoid It)

A newborn baby is a very simple creature: She eats, she sleeps, she cries, she poos – and that's about it. She responds delightfully to a nice cuddle and some loving words but anything more exciting going on around her and she just zones out. Of course, as her size and capabilities grow, she starts taking more of an active interest in life but she certainly doesn't wake up one morning needing full-on, round-the-clock, multi-sense-stimulating entertainment.

I'm only telling you this because I felt I wasn't being a 'proper mum' unless I filled my growing baby's day with all sorts of amazing, brain-boosting experiences – only to wonder why he was always tired and ratty, and I was absolutely wrung out.

The truth is, you really don't have to try that hard to stimulate a baby – their little brains are set a-spinning by the most mundane of everyday things. You may think a trip to the shops is nothing to write home about but, for your little baby, it's as thrilling as a trip to Paris. To her, all the strange, new, ever-changing sights, smells, and sounds of the high street (so familiar to you that you hardly notice them) are wondrous, vibrant – and exhausting.

Overdo the trip-to-Paris-type excitement and a baby gets over-stimulated, over-tired, and overwrought. And who has to cope with the fallout? You do. If you want a happy, contented end to your baby's day, don't schedule too much exciting stuff into the beginning and the middle of it. Take no notice of the other mums dashing from one brain-boosting baby-activity class to another (they're making the same mistake I did) and restrict yourself to one stimulating 'experience' a day.

And, when you're at home, don't feel you've got to be a one-parent entertainment zone. Of course it's good to sit and play with your child and encourage her to try new things but it's important to remember to

- ✔ **Keep it short.** Never expect a small baby to pay attention to anything (including you) for longer than two minutes at a time. Even a 10-month-old will struggle to concentrate on one thing for more than five minutes. Babies just can't do it. Once you've accepted that, life becomes a whole lot less frustrating – for the both of you. And you can get on with enjoying life together – in short little bursts.

- ✔ **Forget the hothousing.** There's no point trying to 'teach' your baby anything with flashcards and the like because she simply hasn't got the brainpower to remember it for more than a day. Babies under 1 year can learn to recognise faces and spoken words, but only from about 21 months does the memory-recall area of their brain really begin to mature.

> ✔ **Don't be scared to let her be.** Every now and then, babies need to chill out, just like we do. Sometimes, they're happy just fiddling with a toy on their own or looking at the way the sunlight's dappling the leaves in the garden. Yes, they flourish and thrive on us showing them all the incredible things life has to offer – but just not all the time.

Your baby may not be able to talk, but she can definitely tell you when she's had enough. Watch her closely when you're playing with her: If she averts her gaze and won't make eye contact, now's the time to wrap up the game and move on.

On or Off? Babies and TV

Babies don't really get TV. Before the age of 6 months, the television is just a flickering light show, so they could be watching *Bob the Builder* or *Newsnight* and it wouldn't much matter. After 6 months, something sedate with nice big faces and/or jolly music will probably hold their attention for a short while but pretty much everything else will be too fast-moving to be meaningful.

So, should you let your baby watch TV or not? Well, if you find it keeps your baby happy for a couple of minutes while you have a quiet cup of tea, it's certainly not going to do her any harm.

But be mindful of the habit you may be forming for the future – for yourself as much as for her. Watching lots of TV can have some not-very-nice effects on toddlers and older kids (see Chapters 15, 18, and 24), so keep your baby's box-watching short and sweet now or you could set up a pattern that you'll both find hard to break in the years to come.

Chapter 11

Keeping Baby Healthy

In This Chapter
▶ Dealing with everyday illnesses
▶ Spotting the signs that it's serious
▶ Making the right choice about vaccinations

I hate to have to say this, but your baby's going to get ill. Not too often and not too horribly, God willing, but pretty much inevitably. And you're going to have to deal with it. Which is all rather scary when you've never been responsible for a poorly babe before. All the questions. All the worries. How high a temperature is too high? Is that rash serious? Should you call the doctor? Or are you just being hysterical?

Over time, of course, (vomit-splattered) experience will probably teach you all you need to know about childhood sicknesses. But, while you're still finding your feet as a soother of small ills, this chapter should answer your questions, relieve your worries – and help make you both feel better.

 The information in this chapter is no substitute for personal medical advice. Nor should it overrule your intuition as a parent. You know your baby better than anyone else: If you're worried about any aspect of his health, take him to see your GP.

Newborn Niggles and Teething Twinges

Right, let's start nice and calmly with the stuff that's ever so common, ever so easy to spot, and ever so simple to deal with.

Cradle cap

Cradle cap is a painless but not very pretty skin condition (seborrhoeic dermatitis, to be exact) that can affect your baby's scalp. No one's sure what causes cradle cap, but it does tend to run in families.

✔ **Spot it.** Greasy, flaky, or crusty patches of skin on your baby's scalp. Can become quite thick in places.

✔ **Sort it.** Do not pick the scales off. Loosen them instead by rubbing a little olive oil into his scalp before you put him down for the night. In the morning, gently brush the scales out, then put baby shampoo on his (dry) hair and wash it out. If the cradle cap is really severe, see your GP.

Oral thrush

Oral thrush is an infection in the mouth, caused by an overgrowth of candida, a yeast fungus that lots of us carry in our bodies. One in seven newborns gets oral thrush, probably after being exposed to *Candida* on their way through the birth canal.

✔ **Spot it:** White, creamy, or yellow patches in his mouth. (Don't confuse these with milk residues.) And, sometimes, an unwillingness to feed.

✔ **Sort it:** See your GP. Your baby may need a course of anti-fungal drops. If he's breastfeeding, you may need to put anti-fungal cream on your nipples; if he's bottlefed, you'll be advised to throw away the teats you're using and buy new ones.

Nappy rash

It's almost inevitable that your baby will get nappy rash at some point. It's just a skin irritation caused by a reaction to the chemicals in his wee (and, sometimes, in his nappy wipes, too). Nappy rash is more common during a tummy upset (the micro-organisms in his poo can increase the inflammation) and can be made worse by a *Candida* infection (see the 'Oral thrush' section, earlier in this chapter, for more on this).

✔ **Spot it:** Red, raw patches of skin on his bottom or in his groin. If there's a candida infection, almost all of his 'nappy area' will be red and you may see little spots around the edges.

✔ **Sort it:** Change nappies frequently, dry the skin round his bottom carefully, and use lots of zinc-oxide barrier cream at each change. Let your baby go nappy-free as much as your carpets – and nerves – can stand. See your GP if you suspect an infection.

Teething pains

It's anybody's guess when your baby will get his first teeth – he could be born with them; he could still be toothless at 1 – but, odds on, he'll do a pretty good job of letting you know when they're on their way!

✔ **Spot it:** Red cheeks, red gums, drooling, sore or chapped skin around his chin and mouth, fretfulness, night waking, slight fever, loss of appetite, and a general desire to gnaw down on anything and everything.

✔ **Sort it:** Try rubbing a teething gel or powder on his gums. Give him baby paracetamol if he has a fever. Let him gnaw a teething ring – or your finger. Give him lots of extra cuddles and comfort.

Teething and nappy rash do tend to go together – teething babies seem to specialise in spectacularly dirty nappies. Doctors often, er, poo-poo this connection because they don't want us dismissing a possibly worrying bout of diarrhoea as 'just teething'. For more about diarrhoea, see the section 'What to Do When Your Baby is Ill', later in this chapter.

As soon as your child's first teeth appear, you need to start brushing them with a dot of baby toothpaste on a small, soft-bristled toothbrush.

Vaccinations: What You Need to Know

Just before your baby's 8 weeks old, you'll get a letter telling you he's due for the first of what seems to be an endless succession of vaccinations. Now, of course, you don't want your baby to catch measles, polio, meningitis or any of the other horrible-sounding diseases the doctors want to vaccinate him against. But that doesn't stop you feeling rather wobbly about a stranger sticking needles in your baby's leg. To de-wobble as much as possible (no loving parent can ever de-wobble completely), you need to get your head around what these vaccinations are all about.

The vaccination programme

Between 2 months and 13 months, your baby's scheduled to have five separate sessions of injections to protect him from ten really nasty childhood diseases. Some of the vaccines need to be given in two or more doses, and others need to be followed by booster doses a few months later – it's important to give your baby all the doses at the right time or the protection offered by the vaccine may not be complete.

✔ **Five-in-one vaccine:** Immunises against diptheria, tetanus, whooping cough, Hib (Haemophilus influenzae type b bacteria), polio. Given at 2, 3, and 4 months.

✔ **Pneumococcal vaccine:** Immunised against pneumococcal disease (which can lead to septicaemia, meningitis, and pneumonia). Given at 2, 4, and 13 months.

✔ **Men C vaccine:** Immunises against meningitis C. Given at 3, 4, and 12 months.

✔ **Hib vaccine:** Immunises against Haemophilus influenzae type b bacteria, which can cause severe pneumonia, epiglottitis (severe swelling of the throat), and bacterial meningitis. Given at 12 months.

✔ **MMR vaccine:** Immunises against measles, mumps, and rubella (German measles). Given at 13 months.

Fortunately, the Department of Health sends you a letter each time a vaccination is due and then follow-up letters if you don't show up for the jab. You can also visit `www.immunisation.nhs.uk` for a look at the full vaccination schedule.

The heated debate: To jab or not to jab?

You'd have to have been walking around with your fingers in your ears for an incredibly long time not to know that there have been all sorts of scare stories about the safety of baby jabs (and of the MMR jab, in particular). So, what's a parent to do? Arm him- or herself with information, that's what.

First, get the facts straight

Here, in a nutshell, are the key arguments on either side.

Those who are all for of vaccinating your child say that it

✔ **Stops him getting life-threatening diseases:** Years ago, babies died of diseases such as polio and whooping cough. Now, that's rare – thanks to the vaccination programme.

✔ **Stops others getting them, too:** The more children have the jabs, the less likely anyone is to get these diseases – good news for those too young or too vulnerable to get immunised.

✔ **Is the least risky choice:** Even though all the vaccines are tested, no one can promise they're 100 per cent safe. But, say the experts, the risk of harmful side effects is lower than the risks presented by catching the diseases themselves.

Those who are against vaccinating say that it

✔ **Overloads your child's system:** Because the newer combined vaccines target more than one disease at a time. Experts counter by saying babies are exposed to a huge number of antigens (bacteria, viruses, toxins, and so on) every time they breathe, so their immune systems are designed to cope. Plus, modern vaccines are purer and contain significantly fewer components than they used to.

✔ **Can trigger autism**: No link has been proved between vaccines and the onset of autism.

✔ **Are full of heavy metals:** This is no longer true. The new combined vaccines do not contain thiomersal, a mercury-based compound that was present in older vaccines.

✔ **Can cause nasty side effects:** This is possible. One in 1,000 babies experiences a severe vaccine reaction, with symptoms ranging from high fever to febrile convulsions.

Second, talk to your GP

If you're unsure about vaccinating your child, voice any concerns you have to your GP. You're perfectly entitled to ask questions and seek answers. Be particularly persistent with your questioning if you're aware of any cases of autism, egg allergy (many vaccines are cultured in egg), or severe vaccine reactions in your family. In the end, though, the decision is yours and you must do whatever you feel is best for your baby.

Seven ways to boost your baby's health

Be warned: This is not a list every parent will like. Some of the things on it you'll find easy to do; others you may find you're not able (or willing) to do. But the more of them you can tick off, the healthier your baby's start in life is likely to be.

1. **Don't smoke:** Nicotine is not good for developing lungs. Exposure to tobacco smoke as a baby is linked to a higher risk of cot death, asthma, heart problems, and childhood cancers.

2. **Turn up for his check-ups:** And get his weight monitored regularly at your baby clinic.

3. **Breastfeed:** For a year (or more) if you can. But your baby will still feel the health benefits even if you only manage it for one day. For more on breastfeeding, see Chapter 7.

4. **Take him for his jabs:** Immunisations are the most effective way to protect him against life-threatening diseases. For more

on this, see 'The heated debate: To jab or not to jab'.

5. **Cuddle him:** Loving touch not only makes your baby feel nice and secure, but there's also evidence it can also boost his immune system.

6. **Wean him carefully:** Wait until 6 months, if you can; if you want to start earlier, talk to your health visitor first and then take it very gradually. For more on weaning, see Chapter 8.

7. **Encourage sleep:** No sniggering – I *know* few babies sleep all night long. But while they're sleeping, their brains are making new connections and their bodies are producing antibodies and growth hormones. So try to lay foundations for better sleep by having a bedtime routine and helping him nod off on his own (for more on this, see Chapter 9).

Making jabs less of a pain

To make the whole needle-going-in process as bearable as possible (for you as well as your baby), try these tips:

- ✔ **Take along some teething gel.** And smooth a little on your baby's leg before the needle goes in – it'll numb the skin slightly.

- ✔ **Breastfeed while it's done.** Studies show breastfeeding can be a natural painkiller. If you're not breastfeeding (or not the breastfeeder), hold your baby close and distract him by chatting to him or giving him a dummy.

- ✔ **Give him baby paracetamol afterwards.** It's quite normal for babies to get a slight temperature after a jab. But if yours spikes a fever over 38°C, take him to a doctor.

What to Do When Your Baby is Ill

Well, if you're like me, the first thing you want to do is panic! Ill babies do nothing for the parental sangfroid. But there's ill, and there's worryingly ill – and you need to be able to tell the difference between them.

Fever

Babies don't have very good thermostats. Which means your baby can get a high temperature even if he's not actually ill – maybe he's just got too many clothes on, for example. Either way, though, you need to help him get his temperature down.

How to be sure that it's a fever: Your baby's normal temperature is higher than yours, so he doesn't officially have a fever unless his temperature is over 37.7°C (100°F) in the day or 38.2°C (101°F) at night. A digital thermometer under his armpit should give you an accurate temperature but, often, you can tell if he has a fever just by kissing his brow (feels hotter than your lips) and feeling the small of his back (hot and sweaty). Other symptoms can include red cheeks and loss of appetite.

What to do about it: Open a window, take off most of his clothes, and sponge him down with a warm, wet flannel. Make sure that he has plenty of fluids and, if he's over 8 weeks, give him some baby paracetamol.

How to tell if it's serious: **What matters more than your baby's actual temperature is the way he seems. If he's responsive and easily comforted, he's probably fine. Call a doctor if**

✔ He's crying inconsolably or very weakly.

✔ He's limp and unresponsive.

✔ He's having trouble breathing.

✔ He's being sick or has diarrhoea.

✔ His lips are blue.

✔ He has a rash that doesn't fade when you press it with a glass.

✔ He's had a fit (febrile convulsion).

✔ He's under 3 months old.

✔ His temperature's been over 39°C (102.2°F) for 48 hours.

✔ He's had a fever for more than three days.

Vomiting and diarrhoea

Babies are often sick; babies often get runny nappies. But, should these rather splattery bodily evacuations start happening in combination, your baby's got a germ or a bug in his system and his body wants it out.

What to do about it: Give him plenty of fluids (if he's throwing up his milk, try cooled, boiled water). And wash your hands thoroughly every time you change his nappy.

How to tell if it's serious: Most of the time, the worst is over within 12 hours. But call a doctor if

✔ He has a fever.

✔ He's being violently sick.

✔ His vomit or poo contains blood.

✔ He's showing signs of dehydration: sunken eyes, dry mouth and tongue, drowsiness, and bone-dry nappies.

✔ He's had vomiting or diarrhoea for more than 12 hours.

Coughs and colds

There are zillions of viral infections that cause coughs and colds, and small children are more susceptible to them than adults because their immune systems are still immature. Occasionally, a cough can be a symptom of a more serious illness, such as pneumonia, croup, or bronchitis.

What to do about it: Put books under the head-end legs of his cot to help the mucus drain from his nose. Keep the air moist in his room by putting a cup of water on the radiator and plug in a decongestant vaporiser (find a suitable one for his age). If his nose is so blocked he's finding it difficult to feed, put a few saline drops in his nostrils. Be warned: Babies *hate* this and it can loosen snot rather dramatically!

How to tell if it's serious: Most colds and coughs clear up of their own accord. But call a doctor if

- He has a barking cough. This is the characteristic sound of croup.
- He has trouble breathing.
- He is very wheezy.
- He only coughs at night. This can be a sign of asthma.

Spots and rashes

There's nothing like a rash to make a parent quake with fear – and, sadly for parental nerves, babies tend to get rashes quite often. Still those quaking limbs by reminding yourself that rashes can be caused by all sorts of things, many of them quite harmless. It could be

- **A heat or sweat rash.** This will disappear when he cools down.
- **A patch of dermatitis.** Caused by something irritating his skin – a new washing powder, for example, or the chlorine in a swimming pool.
- **Eczema.** Caused by an allergy or a change in the weather. (For more on this, see the section 'Wheezing, Itching, and Scratching: Allergies, Asthma, and Eczema', later in this chapter.)
- **A non-specific viral rash.** Caused by a mild virus. Usually only lasts a day or two.
- **A more severe viral infection.** Such as chickenpox or meningitis (for more on these, see the section 'Common infectious illnesses', later in this chapter).

What to do about it: If your baby seems otherwise well and alert and is feeding normally, he is probably fine and the rash will soon fade away on its own.

How to tell if it's serious: Rashes can sometimes be a symptom of a severe infection. You need to call a doctor quickly if

- He's obviously unwell or has a fever.
- He's not feeding.

✔ He's having difficulty breathing.

✔ He seems floppy or unusually drowsy.

✔ His rash doesn't fade when pressed with a glass.

✔ His rash is very extensive or very itchy or the spots are weepy.

✔ His face, mouth, or lips are swollen.

Get a copy of _What's That Rash?_ by Prisca Middlemiss (Hamlyn, £6.99). It has colour photos of 50 of the most common childhood rashes to help you work out what your child may have.

Common infectious illnesses

Unless you plan to keep your baby in a vacuum-sealed bubble (not the most practical of arrangements), daily life is going to expose him to all sorts of germs. Some he'll fight off; others may make him quite poorly. Here's your guide to spotting – and treating – the most common baby (and toddler) illnesses.

Your baby can, of course, catch infectious illnesses that are not listed here. Never feel silly about calling your GP or NHS Direct (0845 4647) if your baby is unwell or has symptoms you don't recognise.

Chickenpox

Chickenpox, with its trademark blistery rash, is caused by a virus spread in coughs and sneezes. Once your child's had it, he's (usually) immune for life.

Spot it: Red pimples spreading from head and back to arms and legs and turning into itchy, fluid-filled blisters. Slight fever and appetite loss.

Sort it: Put a little bicarbonate of soda in his (tepid) bath. Dab calamine cream on the spots. Give baby paracetamol to relieve any fever and antihistamine medicine at night to relieve the itching. If your baby's under 6 months, seems very unwell, or develops a cough, see your GP.

Contagious for: As long as it takes for all the spots to crust over.

Conjunctivitis

Conjunctivitis is an inflammation of one or both eyelids, usually caused by a bacterial or viral infection.

Spot it: Itchy, bloodshot, sticky eyes. Sometimes crusty or oozing, too.

Sort it: Bathe with cooled boiled water, from the inside to the outside, using a different piece of cotton wool for each eye. If the discharge is yellow, see your GP; he may need antibiotic eye-drops.

Contagious for: As long as his eyes are weepy. Wash hands well and use separate flannels and towels.

Hand-foot-mouth disease

This is a scary-looking but usually relatively mild disease, caused by a virus that tends to spread in the summer and early autumn.

Spot it: Tiny blisters on hands, feet, and in mouth. Fever. Low appetite.

Sort it: Dab calamine on blisters. Give baby paracetamol for the fever. Encourage him to drink but avoid fruit juices while his mouth is sore.

Contagious for: Up to seven days.

Acute otitis media

Otitis media is a bacterial infection of the middle ear. The tubes in your baby's ears are tiny and can become easily blocked – and then infected – when he gets a cold.

Spot it: Fever (often following a cold). Persistent crying. Night-waking. Loss of appetite. Tugging at face or ears. Occasionally, discharge from one or both ears.

Sort it: See your GP; he may need antibiotics. Sponge down and give baby paracetamol for the fever. If your child gets lots of ear infections, get his hearing checked: Recurrent otitis media can lead to 'glue ear'.

Contagious for: It's not.

Roseola infantum

This is a very common viral infection – about three in every ten children under 2 catch it. Once your child has had roseola, he won't get it again.

Spot it: Up to five days of high fever, then a splotchy pink rash.

Sort it: See your GP – the roseola rash looks quite similar to a measles or rubella rash, so you need to be quite sure that this is roseola, not something else. Sponge down and give baby paracetamol to relieve the fever. Keep hydrated.

Contagious for: As long as the fever lasts.

Meningitis: The need-to-know facts

Meningitis. Just the mention of the word is enough to scare the pants off most parents. And meningitis *is* a scary disease – it attacks the brain and spinal cord with incredible speed. It is also, thankfully, a rare disease, especially now our children can be immunised against so many strains of it. But, precisely because meningitis does develop so fast, you need to be aware of the main symptoms – so that, if your baby does catch it, you can spot it and call your doctor or dial 999 as quickly as possible.

Meningitis starts off looking like a bad cold or flu. Then your baby will show some (but maybe not all) of the following symptoms:

- ✔ Pale, blotchy skin.
- ✔ Cold hands and feet.
- ✔ Drowsiness or vacant staring or being hard to rouse.
- ✔ Tense or bulging fontanelle (soft spot on the head).
- ✔ Stiff, jerky, or floppy body.
- ✔ Bluish/reddish pinprick rash, marks, or bruising that don't go white even for a few seconds when pressed under a glass. Call 999 immediately if you find this.
- ✔ Strong dislike of light.
- ✔ Fever/vomiting between feeds.
- ✔ Rapid/difficult breathing.
- ✔ A high-pitched or moaning cry.
- ✔ Loss of appetite.

Note: Older children may also complain of a severe headache, aching legs, and stomach pain.

Allergies, Asthma, and Eczema

Childhood illnesses don't just come in short, feverish bursts. Some do an altogether longer-term line in day-to-day lurking, flaring up every now and then into something rather more serious. The undisputed leaders in this field are allergies, asthma, and eczema. Here's your potted guide to each.

Allergies

An allergy is a bad reaction to a normally harmless substance. If your baby has an allergy, the first time he comes into contact with the trigger substance (or allergen), his body makes special antibodies. The next time he comes into contact with it, these antibodies combine with the allergen to release powerful chemicals that cause an allergic reaction. Allergens usually fall into one of two categories:

✔ **Environmental.** Including house-dust mites, pollen, pet hairs, medicines, insect stings, and latex.

✔ **Food-related.** Most commonly, shellfish, milk, eggs, gluten, dairy products, and nuts.

Symptoms of an allergic reaction can include

✔ Wheezing or coughing.

✔ Itchy skin or a rash.

✔ Sore or itchy eyes.

✔ Runny or blocked nose.

✔ Vomiting/diarrhoea or stomach cramps.

If you suspect your baby has an allergy, keep track of his symptoms – and their possible triggers – and ask your GP to refer him for allergy testing. Some allergies can be treated with medication but the most common way to deal with them is to avoid the allergen in the first place. Children often grow out of allergies, particularly food ones, over time.

Occasionally, a strong allergy (usually to shellfish, nuts, latex, or bee/wasp stings) can cause a very severe reaction called anaphylaxis that needs immediate emergency medical treatment. Signs of anaphylaxis include a swelling face, loss of colour, difficulty breathing, and loss of consciousness.

If anyone in your or your partner's family has a food allergy, be very cautious about introducing that food to your child – and definitely don't introduce it before he is 6 months old.

Eczema

Eczema is an inflammatory skin condition that causes a red, dry, cracked, or scaly rash – and more and more babies are getting it. Your baby is more likely to get eczema if it runs in your family, but he needs to be exposed to an environmental trigger first. Everyone's trigger (or triggers) are different, but the most common ones include soaps and detergents, dry winter air, animal fur, and dust mites. To treat eczema outbreaks

- ✔ **Stop using soap.** Wash with a soap substitute, such as aqueous cream, or use a cleansing emollient in the bathwater. And swap biological washing powder for non-bio.

- ✔ **Moisturise like mad.** With special emollients – ask your pharmacist or GP to recommend one.

- ✔ **Trim his nails.** To stop scratching. And put socks or mittens on his hands at night.

- ✔ **Keep his bedroom cool.** And his bedclothes light. Heat can make those eczema patches extra-itchy.

- ✔ **Try to identify the trigger(s).** And avoid it/them.

- ✔ **Watch for weepy or crusty patches.** These can be a sign of secondary infection; see your GP.

Many children do 'grow out' of eczema. For more about this and for other expert advice, visit www.eczema.org.

Asthma

Asthma makes you wheeze (it's a condition that tightens and inflames your airways). But, if you're a small baby, so do lots of other things, including colds and other viruses and even something called 'wheezy bronchitis'. Which means it's very hard to diagnose asthma in a child under 2. Doctors may be more inclined to think your child has asthma, rather than anything else, if

- ✔ He coughs at night, even when he hasn't got a cold.

- ✔ He has other allergies.

- ✔ You or your partner have or had asthma.

- ✔ You smoke now or smoked when you were pregnant.

Even without a firm diagnosis, doctors often prescribe medication (that usually has to be taken through a special inhaler) to relieve and prevent wheezing attacks. It's also worth noting and then avoiding anything you suspect may trigger an attack (common triggers include pets, pollen, and house-dust). For expert advice, visit www.asthma.org.uk.

If your child ever starts wheezing or having breathing difficulties, always seek medical help.

Protecting your child in the sun

Baby skin burns very quickly in bright sunlight. Ideally, a baby under 6 months should be kept out of the sun altogether. If you can't really avoid it (and, let's face it, you can't skulk indoors all summer) or you have an older baby, always remember to

✔ **Cover him up.** With a wide-brimmed or legionnaire's hat and loose-fitting clothes. If you're heading for the beach, buy a high-SPF UV-protective bodysuit.

✔ **Make some shade.** With a buggy parasol or sunshade. On the beach, a pop-up UV-pro-tective tent can be a godsend – great for napping in.

✔ **Slap on the sunscreen.** Choose a high-SPF sunblock that's specially made for babies. And re-apply it frequently.

✔ **Give him plenty to drink.** Babies can quickly get dehydrated on a hot day.

If he does get burnt, give him baby paracetamol and a cool bath and cover his skin in calamine lotion. If his skin is blistered, take him to a doctor.

Part III
All About Toddlers

"Yes, I <u>know</u> the playpen's upside down."

In this part . . .

Toddlers are little whirlwinds of activity, always on the go and nearly always determined to do it 'on my own'. This part is your guide to keeping up, and staying in control! You'll find out how to crank your food-and-sleep tactics up to toddler level, how to tackle tantrums and how (and when) to potty-train. There's a guide to the strange but vital art of 'toddler-proofing' a house, and plenty of fun ideas, too – on everything from messing about in the park to squashing around with playdough.

Chapter 12

Potty-Training

In This Chapter

▶ Knowing when to bring on the pants

▶ Losing the nappies without losing your cool

▶ Dealing with poo refusal and other surprising setbacks

*P*otty-training: Two words that strike fear deep into the heart of the most capable parent. You'd think that we'd be thrilled at the idea of a nappy-less future. But we're too busy fretting about a present filled with panics and puddles – and worse. Our toddlers may be getting into pants but we're the ones getting our knickers in a twist.

So, here to straighten you out and snap everything back neatly into place is the chapter that takes the pain out of potty-training. It'll let you know how to spot when the time is right and how to take the potty plunge with A-grade panache. It'll even help you clear up any (metaphorical) mess along the way. With these pages to hand, there's no reason to think that potty-training is pants.

Why Potty-Training's Easier Than You Think – And How We Make It Harder

Take it from one who's been there, done it, and bought the Spiderman pants a few times over: Potty-training isn't that bad. Honest. If it's done at the right time and in the right order, most toddlers get the hang of it pretty quickly. True, some are a bit slow and some are a bit stubborn (and, okay, a few are a complete nightmare) but, generally speaking, it shouldn't be that big a deal.

So why, then, do we *make* it such a big deal? Mainly because

- **It's all about poo and wee.** And, as a nation, we're all a bit weird and embarrassed when it comes to talking about, and dealing with, that.

- **It's is a big new thing.** Remember how you felt about moving on to solids? Potty-training is another new rung on the parenthood ladder – and taking that next step up can be rather scary.

- **We start at the wrong time.** It's not enough for you to be up for it; potty-training only works well if your toddler's up for it, too. For more on this, see the 'Potty Preparations' section, later in this chapter.

- **We feel pressurised by others.** Your mum had you out of nappies at 10 months? Your best friend's toddler's been dry for weeks? So what? It's potty-training, not potty-trumping. And it's not a competition.

- **We think that it's going to take weeks and weeks of parental potty-hovering.** And that's a pain when you're working/seeing friends/going to the supermarket/trying to live a normal life. The truth is, if it does take weeks, your toddler's probably not ready for pants just yet.

- **We're not consistent.** We tell them to use a potty and take away the nappies – and then we stick a nappy on them when they go in the car. We tell them it doesn't matter if they have an accident – and then we scream in horror when there's poo on the floor. What's a toddler in training to think?

- **Our worry rubs off on our kids.** And feeling nervous doesn't improve a person's bladder control one bit, does it?

Realistic Expectations

Years ago (back in the bad old days when disposable nappies didn't exist and cloth nappies weren't nearly as parent-friendly as they are now), the race to get your child in pants started almost as soon as she cleared the birth canal. Now, it's not that unusual to see children in nappies well into their third year (so much so, in fact, that many nappy manufacturers have 'redesigned' their largest sizes to accommodate bigger bottoms).

Who's right: the pants-racers or the nappy-clingers? As ever, the answer lies somewhere in between – and it all hinges on the way your toddler's little body develops. Before the age of 18 months, she really doesn't have any kind of grip over her bladder or bowels: She simply 'goes' automatically when her tummy gets full up with food. Yes, you could perch her on a potty after every meal and 'catch' everything that comes out, but that's not potty-training, that's potty-management. And your child's not learning a thing.

From about 18 months (but it can be much, much later), your toddler starts to gain some control of the muscles that open her bladder and rectum. And she also starts to recognise the sensation of 'needing to go'. (Usually about two seconds before she actually does!) Only now is proper potty-training possible – assuming both you and your toddler are really ready: See the 'Potty Preparations' section, later in this chapter.

When to try for dry days

Unless you're a glutton for mopping-the-floor punishment, don't even think about taking nappies off your toddler during the day until she's at least 18 months old. And, even if she is, bear in mind that

- ✔ **Everyone develops differently.** Just because some toddlers gain a little bladder and bowel control at 18 months, it doesn't mean yours will.
- ✔ **Potty-training's not about intelligence.** Any more than crawling, walking, and cutting her first teeth were.
- ✔ **Girls tend to be ready to train earlier than boys.**
- ✔ **The average age for dry-day success is 2 and a half.**
- ✔ **It isn't a race:** Or, if it is, it's a hare-and-tortoise one. A 2-year-old is quicker to train than an 18-month-old because, in those six months, her bladder and bowel control will have grown stronger and her ability to understand the whole idea will have got greater.
- ✔ **It's not just about sphincter control.** Your child has to be ready mentally and emotionally, too. See the 'Potty Preparations' section, later in this chapter.
- ✔ **Family history matters.** If you or your partner were late into pants, your children are very likely to be, too.

When to try for dry nights

Don't expect your little L-plate potty-tot to get through the night without a nappy for a while yet. You need to crack the day-time shift before even thinking about the night-time one. In fact, it may be years – literally – before your dry-in-the-day toddler is capable of notching up nocturnal success. Hold your nappy-scrapping horses and remind yourself that

- ✔ **Children don't 'do' dry nights before they're 3 or 4, on average.** And many boys take much longer.
- ✔ **Bed-wetting is not uncommon at age 5.** Possibly 10 per cent of school-age children are still wet at night.
- ✔ **Waiting is probably safer.** Small toddler roaming the house at night looking for the toilet? Not sure I'd be able to sleep at all.

Natural infant hygiene

There's an intrepid (if damp-legged) band of parents who can't be doing with nappies. At all. They practise Natural Infant Hygiene – a kind of potty-training programme that starts at birth.

The idea is that, if you leave your newborn's bottom bare, she'll 'tell' you, with a wriggle or a grunt, when she needs to poo or wee, so you can whisk her off to the loo or hold her over a pot. If you combine this over-the-loo-holding with a 'sssss' sound, your child will, apparently, be reliably dry by 10 to 20 months.

Potty or not? Well, Natural Infant Hygiene has many points in common with 'potting' methods mothers used generations ago (and still do in some parts of the world) to reduce the (cloth) nappy washing pile. And it can be quite successful – but it's not your baby who's being trained: It's you. And, once your child gets control of her bladder and bowel muscles, you'll still have to teach her how and where to use them properly.

Potty Preparations

What makes potty-training nice and quick? Working up to it very, very slowly. It really is all in the build-up: If you spend lots of time carefully setting the scene for the potties and pants to come, your toddler's way more likely to pull off a virtuoso performance.

The warm-up

Your first task is to get poo and wee-friendly. Swallow your embarrassment and get with the toilet talk: The more comfortable your child feels discussing – and looking at – poos and wees, the better. You want her to have nothing but positive feelings about the contents of her nappy. And about potties and toilets, too. So, from about 18 months, if not before, try to

- ✔ **Get your names straight.** Not only for 'poo' and 'wee' (or whatever you want to call them in your house) but also for the parts of the body they come from. Ask everyone who cares for your child to use the same names (to avoid confusion) and pick names that will weather any public 'Mummy-the-poo's-coming-out-of-my-xx' moments.

- ✔ **Let her look at her poo.** Don't just whisk it all out of sight when you're changing her. Once her bottom's clean, show her what's in her nappy and talk about how big/small it is. Resist all impulses to wrinkle your nose or comment on the smell: Poos are great, remember?

✔ **Notice her doing a poo.** By the age of 1, most toddlers have perfected a trademark 'poo look': Maybe yours stands stock-still, or grunts, or goes red in the face, or retreats to a quiet corner. If you catch her in the act, look interested: 'You're doing a poo!' This will help your toddler start to recognise her own body's signals.

✔ **Let her watch you on the loo.** Take her with you to the bathroom and give her a little running commentary. 'I'm going to do a wee now. I'm pulling my pants down and sitting on the loo to do my wee. There, all done! Now I'm pulling my pants up.'

✔ **Get a potty.** Even if she's nowhere near ready to use it yet (for tips on choosing potties, see the 'Got the props?' section, later in this chapter). Keep it in the bathroom and encourage her to sit on it when you go to the loo and before she has a bath (cheer any happy accidents ecstatically). Talk about what the potty's for: 'It's for doing wees and poos in.' Let her get used to it but don't let it become a dolls' bed or a Lego bucket; it's a potty, not a toy.

✔ **Invite round some potty pros.** If you know anyone with a child who's just mastered the potty, get them round for a demo. The newly-trained toddler will probably be delighted to show off her potty-filling skills, and your toddler will (hopefully) be fascinated by what she sees.

Is your child ready?

You may have to live with the lavatorial chat for a fair old while before you can move on to potty-training proper. But it pays not to push it: If you start before your toddler's ready, you'll be at it for weeks and you'll both end up feeling a failure. Hang in there till you can tick off all the following:

✔ **She is over 18 months.**

✔ **She can say 'poo' and 'wee' and knows what they are.**

✔ **She's aware of doing a poo or a wee.** And maybe tells you so.

✔ **She can follow simple instructions.** Such as 'Put your toy in the box'.

✔ **She often has a dry nappy an hour or so after you last changed her.** Or she has a dry nappy after a nap. Both are signs of increased bladder control: She no longer does little wees all the time but big wees every now and then.

✔ **She can pull down her trousers.** And tries to help you get her dressed and undressed.

✔ **She knows the parts of her body.** And can point to them when you ask.

> ✔ **She's happy to sit on her potty.** And has maybe even filled it once or twice (by accident or design).

> ✔ **She's fascinated with toilets and potties.** And maybe even pants.

It may bode better still if you can tick these boxes, too, but it's not essential:

> ✔ **She likes things in the right place.** Maybe she insists on lining up the teddies on her bed, for example. This is a sign of emerging self-reliance.

> ✔ **She doesn't like being in a dirty nappy.** Or a wet one, although this is less common in these days of super-absorbent disposables.

No matter how many ready signs you can spot, never start potty-training when your toddler is in a tantrummy phase (for more on tantrums, see Chapter 13). You really don't want her having wobblies over weeing as well.

It's quite common for one twin to be ready for potty-training before the other – which is probably something of a relief all round! Once one twin is dry by day, the other one usually follows suit fairly swiftly.

Are you ready?

In an ideal world, once you're ready, you'd pick a starting date by finding (or arranging) two or three days in a row when you've no other distractions (visitors, out-of-the-house jaunts, and so on) and both you and your toddler can really concentrate on the task in hand. A potty-training child needs almost constant attention and encouragement, to begin with. For that reason, even though it may be all systems go on the toddler front, it may be wise to stay off the potty-training starting grid until the conditions are right for you, too. And they're almost certainly *not* right if

> ✔ **You're going on holiday.** Or staying away from home.

> ✔ **You've just moved house.** Or you're just about to.

> ✔ **Your childcare arrangements are changing.** Or have just changed.

> ✔ **Your child's just been ill.** Or is now.

> ✔ **You're about to have another baby.** Or have just had one.

> ✔ **You're feeling stressed.** By work or by other family stuff.

Sometimes, though, your toddler is just *so* keen to get on with potty-training you have to follow her lead, however inconvenient the timing. This does tend to happen more with older toddlers (who suddenly 'get it') or with toddlers who already have older siblings (and are desperate to be 'big girls' too). As if to prove the point, my youngest son woke up this very morning and said, 'Me pants!' You can't ignore a cue like that, even if you have got 5,000 words to write before dinner (well, at least I can call it research).

Got the props?

There's a lot of inventive potty-training paraphernalia about, from singing potties to piddle-proof car-seat covers, and some of it may well take your fancy. But the boring basics no potty-trainer parent should be without are

- ✔ **The potty:** Obviously. Look for a nice stable one with a good comfy 'seat'. You may decide you want two (one upstairs and one down); if you do, get two identical ones – or your toddler will inevitably take a liking to one of them and refuse to wee in the other.

- ✔ **The pants:** Loads of them (ten at a bare minimum). Buy cheap ones that are a little large (easier for toddler fingers to pull down quickly) and, preferably, adorned with your child's favourite TV characters.

- ✔ **The booster step:** For your child to stand on when she washes her hands. And later, when she needs to get up onto the toilet.

- ✔ **The pull-downable clothes:** Mothball the fiddly dungarees, the woolly tights, and the crotch-popping vests; potty-trainers need loose trousers or skirts with elasticated waists.

- ✔ **The small towel:** For popping in the buggy or car seat when you're out and about. You can buy more expensive protectors, but they tend to be so absorbent, some toddlers don't really mind weeing on them – and you *want* them to mind.

- ✔ **The roll of stickers:** For making a success chart (see the section 'How to make it easy pees-y for her', later in this chapter).

- ✔ **The child toilet seat:** The hole on an adult toilet seat is often big enough for a toddler bottom to fall through. This smaller-bottom-sized insert makes moving up from potty to toilet a much less scary prospect.

Pick a method, any method

There are more methods of potty-training than you can throw a changing mat at – some good, some bad, some positively dangerous to know – but three stand out from the crowd:

- ✔ **The poo-first method:** This works on the principle that most toddlers learn to control their bowels before their bladder. So you put your toddler on the potty after every meal (and at any other times when she regularly poos) and wait. Once poos are hitting potty with regularity, you move on to tackle the wees.

✔ **The run-around-naked method:** This works on the principle that a toddler with no clothes on has a greater chance of connecting bottom to potty before it's too late. So, you help your child strip off, position the potty nearby, and wait. Once potty and bottom are connecting with regularity, you move on to the clothed approach.

✔ **The put-on-pants-and-go method:** This works on the principle that most toddlers get really excited about wearing pants and anything that makes potty-training more exciting is a definite plus. So, you put on the pants, position the potty nearby, and wait. Once poos and wees are being deposited in the potty with regularity, you pat yourself (and your child) on the back for a job well done.

I'm a put-on-pants-and-go girl myself, largely because I like the idea of getting potty-training over with as quickly as possible. The other two methods can work very well but tend to take longer (because of the two separate stages). And each of them can throw up particular problems.

The 'running-around-naked' method, for example, is clearly a rather chilly prospect in the winter. Those who favour it recommend only potty-training in the summer but, if your toddler's ready in January, that's a long time to keep her eagerness in check without putting her off completely. Also, for some boy toddlers, the sight of their unclad willy in weeing mode becomes way more fascinating than the sight of a potty: I speak as a mum who spent many an hour persuading her run-around-naked first-born not to hose down every soft furnishing in sight.

The 'poo-first' method can be a winner for the child who poos with clockwork regularity and enthusiasm, but is definitely not a good idea if your child often gets constipated, has no predictable 'pooing pattern', or tends to run off out of your sight before filling her nappy. All these things can make the idea of pooing in a potty in front of you very stressful – much more so than weeing – and stress is the last thing either of you need.

Of course, it's up to you which method you pick, but I'd wager good money that the third option is the fastest, least perilous route to success. It really does pay to be brave and get with the pants from the start.

Okay, Let's Go! Potty-Training Boot Camp, Day One

Right, potties at the ready: Time for some real action! Your first day of potty-training has arrived! Stop looking so worried at the back – I'm going to talk you through this step by nappy-free step.

First, as keen as you may be to get cracking, keep your toddler in her nappy till after breakfast: You both deserve a nice, calm start to the day and anyway, she's got no chance of making it to the potty from her highchair.

Once breakfast's over, produce her 'special' pants with a flourish and help her put them on. Leave her socks and trousers off for today. Then put the potty nearby and tell her that now she's wearing her special pants, she can do all her wees and poos on the potty. Don't go into long explanations: She's no stranger to the potty by now; keep it short, simple and, above all, upbeat. Then just get on with pottering around together as you normally would.

How to make it easy pees-y for her

Your toddler will take to potty-training much more readily if you

- ✔ **Pour on the praise.** Even when she doesn't quite make it. Obviously, every 'hit' in the potty deserves claps and cuddles but near misses deserve plenty of praise, too. 'You almost did it – well done you!'

- ✔ **Give her reminders.** Toddlers can get very absorbed in what they're doing and may need prompting to remember the potty. Say, 'Do you need a wee?' every 20 minutes or so. Keep it casual, though; don't nag.

- ✔ **Help her pull her pants down.** To begin with at least, she won't have much time between realising she needs to go and actually going. If she makes it to the potty, you can increase her strike rate by getting those pants down quickly.

- ✔ **Get the stickers out.** Every time she uses the potty, give her a sticker to put on her 'success chart' (you could go to town and make a special colour-coded chart for the wall, but a plain piece of A4 does just fine). Point to the chart regularly to show her how well she's doing.

 Everyone who's caring for your child while she potty-trains needs to go about it the same way (using the same words and reacting to accidents in the same way; for more on this, see the section 'Accidents will happen', later in this chapter) or there's a real risk that she'll end up confused and demoralised. Make time to talk these things through with your partner, childminder, or nursery keyworker before you start out.

How to make it easy pees-y for you

You'll find the whole first-day experience much less stressful if you

- ✔ **Don't expect too much.** Getting two wees in the potty on the first day is good. Any more is, frankly, brilliant.

✔ **Stay in.** Going out on the first day of potty-training is asking too much of you both. You'll get the best results if you stay put, preferably in one room, and exude an atmosphere of relaxation and calm (even if you're freaking out inside).

✔ **Don't force.** It's fine to sweep your child swiftly pottywards if you spot her clutching her crotch or straining to poo, but plonking her on the potty at a time of your choosing and holding her there till she goes isn't a good idea. She'll only tense up or downright rebel.

✔ **Keep tabs.** Note down each hit and miss on a piece of paper. Look over your scorecard at the end of the day: It's easy to think that a day has gone more badly than it actually has.

Pay attention to potty-positioning: Little girls need to sit quite far back on the potty or they'll wee over the front rim; little boys need to tuck their willies down and in, to prevent a general spray-the-room situation.

Accidents will happen

You're unlikely to make it through your first day without a puddle or two (or six) to clear up. This is quite normal and doesn't matter a bit; what does matter, though, is how you react to the puddle – and its little maker. Good puddle protocol can be the make-and-break factor in potty-training, so stand by your mop and make it your mission to

✔ **Never get cross:** This can be really tough. You may have to bite back all manner of angriness when your toddler wees in her pants two seconds after telling you she doesn't need the potty, but bite it back you must. Getting cross only achieves one of two things: undermining potty confidence or encouraging potty rebellion.

✔ **Never say 'Yuk!':** Yes, peeling off poo-filled pants is not one of life's most pleasant tasks but please don't let your toddler know that. Any hint of an idea that poos, in particular, are dirty or horrid will only make the idea of being proud to do them in the potty that bit harder.

Nappies and naps

If your toddler has a day-time nap, put her in a nappy before she nods off. It's much harder to control the impulse to wee when you're sleeping and, let's face it, she's still trying to get the hang of it when she's awake! Once potty-training's going well and she's consistently waking up from naps with a dry nappy, then you can try leaving the pants on.

✔ **Be prepared:** Have everything you need to deal with accidents (cloths, wipes, bag for soaked pants, pile of clean pants, and so on) close at hand. And get the cleaning up done calmly. Rushing around in a flap will only turn every little accident into an unnecessarily big fuss.

✔ **Be reassuring:** Your toddler may feel upset or worried or cross at herself for having had an accident. Make sure that you tell her it's all okay; maybe she'll manage it next time.

✔ **Not take it personally:** She didn't wee on your shoes on purpose, really she didn't.

✔ **Not put a nappy back on:** Give it at least a day before throwing in the towel. You may be surprised how much progress a potty-training child can make in just a few hours – even after a disastrous start.

So, how did it go?

At the end of the first day, look at your little scorecard. What you see will help you decide whether to soldier on or not:

✔ **There are no 'hits'.** This is your cue to quietly pack away the pants and potty for now. Your child obviously isn't quite as ready as you thought and carrying on will only upset you both.

✔ **There are two 'hits' or more.** Celebrate! Your toddler is doing fine and will probably do even better tomorrow.

✔ **There are more 'hits' than 'misses'.** Great! You're both doing brilliantly.

The ups and downs of pull-ups

Lots of parents swear by pull-ups (thinner nappies that pull on and off like pants). They see them as a kind of halfway house between nappies and pants, offering their child the thrill of pants-style bottom cover without the risk of nasty old puddles. On go the pull-ups when they take their toddler to the park or shops, in the car or off to playgroup or nursery: no accidents, no embarrassments, no mess. But there's a catch: Pull-ups tend to make potty-training harder.

Why? Because they're nappies – thinner and more grown-up-looking, perhaps – but still nappies in all but name. And switching between nappies and pants confuses a potty-training toddler something rotten. One minute, she's supposed to wee in a potty; the next, it's okay to wee in her pull-ups. One minute, she can tell if she's wet herself; the next, she hasn't got a clue (or it certainly doesn't feel so obvious). One minute, thinking about what her bladder's up to earns her stickers and praise; the next, nobody seems to care.

Now wash your hands

You'll have to wipe your toddler's bottom for her and help her wash and dry her hands. Combine the hand-washing with a trip to the bathroom to empty the potty (let her help you empty it into the loo, if she wants to) and stand her on the booster step to wash at the big sink. On the first day, if you don't want to keep trudging up the stairs to the bathroom (or you're nervous about what may happen on the way), have a soapy-water-filled bowl and a towel at the ready downstairs.

Of course, it's up to you – and you may feel pull-ups are your only option at times – but I truly believe that you'll save yourself a lot of money and stress if you leave them well alone.

You're Almost There: Beyond Day One

Once day one is (even slightly successfully) behind you, things should start getting easier. Over the next few days, your toddler should find she's making it to the potty more and more often, going longer and longer between potty trips, and having fewer and fewer accidents. She should also be able to cope with wearing trousers (even if she needs a hand pulling them down and up).

Her rate of progress may be ever so gradual or startlingly quick but, by the end of the first week to ten days, you should definitely feel that your toddler is essentially dry by day, bar the occasional accident. If this isn't how you feel, you may have hit an unexpected setback; for help with this, see the 'Dealing with Setbacks' section, later in this chapter.

No one expects you to stay holed up in your house while all this potty-training is happening. Read the following sections for tips on taking a tot-in-training outside, and other big steps for small wearers of pants.

Venturing outside

The idea of taking your leak-prone toddler out anywhere in public fills you with dread, doesn't it? But, like many things in potty-training world, actually doing it is never as bad as just sitting at home and angsting about it. Provided that you

  ✔ **Kit yourself out.** Don't leave the house without the potty (in a carrier bag), some wipes, several pairs of pants, a couple of changes of clothes, and a plastic bag (for any soaked/dirty clothes or potty-hitting poos). Oh, and a big confident smile!

- ✔ **Pack the towel.** For the buggy or car seat.

- ✔ **Go before you go.** Try to get your toddler to sit on the potty before you leave the house. This may work better if you take the potty up to the bathroom, put it next to the loo, and say, 'Let's both do a wee now.'

- ✔ **Start off gently.** Bear in mind your toddler's current achievements. If she can last an hour or so between wees, a 40-minute trip to the shops should be quite do-able; if she can't last 20 minutes, it's not.

- ✔ **Refuse to be embarrassed.** Stopping on the pavement (or the side of the road) and popping your toddler on the potty is better than ignoring her cries of 'Wee!' because people may stare. Let them stare. Similarly, if your toddler does have an accident, change her quickly (and modestly), rather than leaving her to sit in damp pants till you get home.

Don't be tempted to pop your toddler in a nappy when you go out. Your child will find it very confusing to be allowed to wear a nappy some times but not others – and, if she's confused, she'll take longer to potty-train. Putting up with a few accidents now and having a dry-in-the-day toddler within a couple of weeks is better than having a pristine car seat but being at the potty-training for months.

Letting her take the lead

In the first day or two of potty-training, it's important to keep asking your toddler if she needs a wee but, as time goes on and potties get filled, it's just as important to start backing off. This is because

- ✔ **She needs to rely on her own body's signals.** Or she'll never be able to stay dry without you glued to her side.

- ✔ **She may get annoyed by your nagging.** Toddlers can be particularly counter-suggestive: Ask 'Do you need a wee?' too many times in one day and you run the risk of getting an automatic 'No!' even if the real answer is 'Yes'.

- ✔ **She will like being in control.** And be motivated to prove she can do it.

Save your reminders for when your toddler seems particularly absorbed in something she's doing – this is when she's most likely to miss or ignore that 'need to go' feeling. And if you know that your child will need to go soon but don't want to nag, move the potty near her and say, 'There's your potty – for when you need it.' Then walk away (and cross your fingers).

Using the big toilet

As soon as your toddler is fairly reliably dry (maybe one or two accidents a day), you can start thinking about ditching the potty for the 'big' toilet. Do this at the pace that suits your child: Some toddlers are itching to use the loo from the start; some are distinctly less keen. Either way, it tends to work best if you

- ✔ **Gradually move the potty to the toilet.** Going from having the potty near her to making it to the toilet in the bathroom is a very big change. Some keen-as-mustard toddlers (with bathrooms close by) manage this step straightaway but most find it easier if the potty's moved closer to the bathroom in a series of stages. Once the potty's actually by the toilet and your toddler knows that she can reach it in time, she should feel more confident about using the toilet itself.

- ✔ **Make the toilet child-friendly.** With the child seat and the booster step.

- ✔ **Keep hold of her.** Toilets are high up for toddlers. She'll feel much more secure if you lift her up and gently hold her in place the first few times.

- ✔ **Don't flush till she's off.** Or the sudden noise beneath her bottom could scare her silly. Also, she may like to help you pull the handle.

Some toddlers can become quite frightened of a flushing toilet, even if you take them off before you pull the chain. In this case, leave the flushing till later or your child will come to be scared of using the toilet as well. Once your toddler's a toilet pro, try flushing when she's at the door and then, if that's okay, flushing while you hold her hand.

'I can wipe my own bottom'

Younger toddlers can be whizzes at pulling their own pants up and down and washing their own hands, but wiping their own bottoms (properly) is usually beyond them – even if they think otherwise! Most children can't really manage this well until they're at least 3, sometimes 4. Until then, you need to wipe your toddler's bottom for her – or at least stand by while she has a go and then finish things off properly afterwards.

If you have a little girl, teaching her to wipe her bottom from front to back is important (so she doesn't get poo and germs into her vagina).

'I want to stand up like Dad'

Some little boys are quite happy sitting on the loo; others can't wait to stand and deliver like their Dad and their older brothers and friends. If you have a sitter, don't pressurise him to stand before he's good and ready. To help a wannabe stander:

- ✔ **Let him stand on a step.** And maybe even lift him up under the arms, if he still can't reach.

- ✔ **Show him how high to hold his willy.** And how to shake the stray drops off afterwards.

- ✔ **Give him a target.** Little boys don't have the best aim in the world. Dropping a ping-pong-ball or cork 'target' in the toilet can often improve matters enormously.

For every little boy who doesn't fancy standing up, there's a little girl who does! If your girl starts trying to wee like Dad, it's time for a talk about body parts: Explain that girls (and mummies) don't have willies, so they need to sit down or their wee will splash everywhere.

Dealing with Setbacks

Now, I know I said that potty-training wasn't that hard, but I never said that it was always a doddle. Yes, as long as you wait till they're good and ready, most toddlers will make it from soggy nappies to (almost) always-dry pants in under a fortnight – but that's not to say that some of them won't still have the odd, er, damp patch in the weeks or months to come. And there will always be a few who, consciously or unconsciously, develop a problem that upends the whole potty-training process almost before it's started.

Poo refusal

Quite a few toddlers have a 'thing' about poo. Maybe they find pooing hard work (because they often get constipated) or maybe they prefer to do it in absolute privacy. But, whatever the 'thing', it doesn't bode well for the arrival of the potty: Either they get very anxious about performing without a nappy or they flat out refuse to go unless you put a nappy back on.

In both cases, it's wise not to push. As long as she's wearing pants the rest of the time and using the potty increasingly reliably for wees, let your toddler poo in a nappy if she wants to. Provided you don't make a big thing of it, poo refusal tends to peter out of its own accord once your child's dry by day. You may find you can help things along by

- ✔ **Increasing her fruit and water intake:** This should make her poos softer and less painful to pass, if she's prone to constipation.

- ✔ **Lining the potty with a nappy:** As a kind of let's-meet-each-other-halfway gesture.

- ✔ **Positioning extra potties in special places:** The private poo-er may just need somewhere quiet to retreat to.

Regression

Even the most distinguished little graduates of the potty-training academy will have an off-day every now and again. And, occasionally, the off-days start happening every day and, surrounded by puddles and piles of sodden underwear, you feel like you're back to square one.

What's going on? Nine times out of ten, a simple dose of toddler stress is the culprit. Starting nursery or playgroup, acquiring a baby brother or sister, moving house: all are classic triggers of a temporary return to wet pants. And the good news is, it's only temporary, so don't even think about going back to the nappies. Stay as calm and uncritical as you can, dish out all the encouragement you can muster (maybe get that sticker chart out again), and you'll be home and dry again before you know it.

If your toddler suddenly regresses but there's no obvious new stress in her life and no other change in her behaviour, she may have a urine infection. Take her to your GP for a check.

The tough nut

All toddlers have stubborn streaks, but some are just stubborn all over. Their fantastically determined nature will probably bring them all kinds of success in the future but means nothing but trouble in the potty-training present.

If your toddler's refusing to go anywhere near the potty, no matter how good her bladder and bowel control, and she's still not yet 3, leave her in nappies: Potty-training's not worth fighting about for now. If she's 3 or older, you may feel you have to bite the bullet, especially if the nursery or preschool you're planning to send her to doesn't accept children in nappies. Tough-nut-cracking tactics include:

- **Backing off:** Act as if you don't care if she uses the potty or not. This can really stump a stubborn child: If she can't rile you by refusing to go near the potty, she may try to get your attention by actually using it.

- **Deferring responsibility:** Tell her that they're her wees and her poos and it's up to her to decide when to do them in the potty. You'll help if she asks but you're certainly not going to tell her what to do.

- **Bribery:** Tell her that every time she gets a certain number of stickers on her chart, you'll give her a Smartie (or whatever). Sweetening the task may not be the most PC of strategies but, if it works (and it usually does) on your stubborn little miss, you're probably past caring.

Nappyless Nights: Worth the Wait

Night may follow day but, in terms of small, dry nether regions, there may well be a considerable pause first. It's not unusual for a 4-year-old still to need a nappy at night, even if she's been dry by day for over a year. So, unless you fancy spending your nights stripping wet sheets and wetter pyjamas, I'd be in no hurry at all to bare bottoms at bedtime.

A clear sign that the nappyless night could be on the horizon is a succession of dry nappies in the morning. If both you and your child then want to give it a go, remember to

- ✔ **Protect the bed:** You can get plastic-coated sheets to put over the mattress but my kids found they made the bed uncomfortably sweaty. Look out, instead, for the small, material-topped bed-protector pads you place over or under the bottom sheet.

- ✔ **Take her to the loo before bed:** And then again before lights out.

- ✔ **Leave a potty in the room:** Or just outside. She may not need it at night but she will when she wakes up, bursting, in the morning.

- ✔ **Stay relaxed:** As with day-time training, everything goes better if you can remain patient, positive, and reassuring when accidents happen.

And, if it all goes pear-shaped? Most children take a while to get the hang of nappyless nights (and many will have the odd relapse even then) but, if your toddler's really not getting the idea, go back to nappies for a while and try again in a few weeks. (If your child's over 4, take a look at the tips for bedwetters in Chapter 22.)

If your toddler wets the bed at night, get her to help you put the wet sheets in the laundry basket and put on clean ones. Having something to do will stop her getting upset – and showing her what to do will help you stay calm.

Chapter 13

Tantrum Tactics

. . . .

In This Chapter

▶ Understanding the stages of strop

▶ Spotting – and stopping – strops in the making

▶ Handling a meltdown without having one yourself

. . . .

*Y*our child's first tantrum is a parenting rite of passage. It's as significant as his first steps or his first words – just rather more shocking. And, obviously, this time, the correct parental response does not involve delighted squeals or dives for the digital camera.

What this situation does involve is calm action and clear thinking – two things that tend to be in short supply when a small child is flailing at your feet, screaming like a banshee. So, stock up in advance on all that's calm and clear by reading and absorbing the tantrum-taming tips in this chapter.

What Lies Beneath: The Toddler Tantrum Explained

Tantrums are a fact of toddler life. I have yet to meet a child who has made it through to his third birthday without having thrown the odd wobbly (or three) at least every few days. (And some manage *way* more than that!) But they don't do it purely to wind us up (although, on bad days, it can often feel like that); they do it because throwing tantrums is part and parcel of the normal growing-up process.

Toddlerhood's a time of intensely conflicting emotions. Your child wants to stand, literally and emotionally, on his own two feet, but he's still intensely attached to you. He wants to explore the world alone but still needs you close to keep him safe. He's determined to do things by himself but still wants you to pick up the pieces when it doesn't work out. He wants to get his own way but still needs you to show him what's allowed and what's not. With all that whirling round in his head, no wonder he loses the plot sometimes!

But he won't always lose the plot in the same way. Toddle tantrums tend to fall into one of two broad categories – and it pays to be able to recognise which is which.

The beginner-level tantrum

Usually the prerogative of the younger toddler, this kind of tantrum's all about frustration. At not being able to get the jigsaw piece in the hole. At not having the words to say what he means. At not being allowed to roll in the dirt when it looks like so much fun. The screaming and stamping tend to kick off all of a sudden, with little build-up or warning, and the strength of his own emotions often surprises your toddler as much as you. This is not the kind of tantrum to come down heavy on; you need to deal with it decisively but gently.

The intermediate-level tantrum

We're talking much more deliberate (and almost always older-toddler) behaviour now. This kind of tantrum's about testing your limits and provoking your reaction. Your child either wants to do something that he knows he shouldn't or doesn't want to do something that you think he should. And he's ready for a showdown of pretty melodramatic proportions. This is not the kind of tantrum to give in to; you need to deal with it decisively and firmly.

Reacting with a Bomb, er, Aplomb

The trouble with tantrums is, it's not only your toddler who gets in a state; confronted with (and by) an out-of-control tot, most of us parents get a bit hot under the collar, too. And, in the heat of that moment, we do and say (and shout) all the wrong things. And then everyone's out of control and nobody's happy. So how do you hold it together when your little darling turns into a little devil? Cling fast to the two key tantrum-taming states of mind.

Staying cool: Chill skills you need to know

Think about it: Your child's never going to regain his cool if you lose yours. You need to be the calming presence in the middle of his storm. Easier said than done, of course, but it certainly helps to

✔ **Count to three:** Before you do or say anything. This will give you time to react with admirable calm.

- **Remember that he's not being bad:** He's just acting his age. As you should be.

- **Know that shouting makes things worse:** And will either scare your toddler stupid or teach him to shout back louder.

- **Think of his good points:** Even while he's writhing in ugly fury on the floor, run through a mental list of all the sweet, gorgeous, funny, lovely, giggly, huggable things he does and says most of the rest of the time. It's a great way to put tantrums in perspective.

Being firm: It's what he wants (really)

You are the parent; he is the child. You are in charge – and it's your job to be. And right now you need to get the message across, firmly and clearly, that tantrums are not okay and will not get him what he's after. If that makes you feel a bit weak at the knees, take strength from the knowledge that

- **Every child needs boundaries.** They make him feel secure because it's clear what's expected of him. Yes, he'll push against them, but that doesn't mean they shouldn't be there. Far from it: It's their continued existence – and your consistency in maintaining them – that keeps his sense of security so strong. (For more on boundaries, see Chapter 2.)

- **Wavering doesn't work.** If you give in, your child will strop again and again and again. Well, it worked the last time, didn't it?

- **It won't make him love you less.** Honest.

Forget what people say about the 'terrible 2s'; when it comes to tantrums, the reality's more like the 'terrible 1-and-a-halfs-to-3s'.

Best times to tantrum? A toddlers' top ten

1. When I'm being put in the car seat
2. When I'm being put in the buggy
3. When Granny comes to visit
4. At the supermarket
5. Whenever we need to get somewhere fast
6. When my well-behaved friends come to play
7. When I have to put on or take off hats/coats/boots/shoes
8. When we have to go out
9. When we have to come home
10. Whenever anyone's on the phone

Your Anti-scream Action Plan

So much for the cool, calm, and collected theory, but how do you get it to work in practice? Here's your four-step guide to tantrum-taming perfection.

Spotting the tantrum triggers (and why you're probably one of them)

The easiest route to a strop-free life is to stop the strops happening in the first place. And the canniest way to do that is to mug up on the most common tantrum triggers – and avoid them like the plague. Your evasive-action warning bells should start ringing if

- **Your toddler's tired or hungry.** Toddlers (and adults) get cranky when food or sleep is in short supply. Life runs so much more peacefully on a daily routine that includes regular mealtimes and regular bedtimes.

- **You're doing something strange.** If you're going anywhere or doing anything out of your normal routine, talk your toddler through it first. If he has some idea of what to expect, he's less likely to kick up a fuss.

- **Your house isn't toddler-safe.** If all you ever say is, 'No! Don't touch that!', you're practically inviting rebellion.

- **Your toddler's taken on too much.** He's desperate to do things himself, but that doesn't mean he always can. You need to get good at anticipating frustration (at the puzzle piece that won't fit, at the sock that won't come off) and stepping in to help – without taking over.

- **You don't notice the good stuff.** Which could tempt him to give the bad stuff a go. Don't let your toddler think the only way to get your attention is to get ugly; if he's behaving nicely, lay on the praise.

- **You're always in a rush.** Mornings are peak tantrum time because toddlers don't understand that being late for work/school/nursery is not a good idea. Build in a little extra time for those dawdling toddler feet.

- **You're expecting the worst.** Dreading that visit to Great Aunt Prim-and-Proper's house? Don't let it show. Toddlers are quick to pick up on our tension – and tense toddlers are tantrums waiting to happen.

- **You haven't planned ahead.** Wherever you're going, always arm yourself with a tantrum-distraction plan: a snack for the traffic jam, a colouring book for the GP's surgery, a series of 'three more goes down the slide'-type warnings for park-closing time.

✔ **You're a control freak.** If you never let your toddler choose what to do/wear/eat – even just once in a while – he's almost bound to rebel. Lighten up a little; you'll both have more fun.

✔ **You're expecting too much.** He is a toddler. He doesn't do reasoned discussion. Or patient waiting. Or keeping out of your way.

Heading off the meltdown

Uh oh: Just when you thought you had all the triggers covered, you see your toddler's bottom lip start to wobble and that tell-tale pre-tantrum redness start to flood his little cheeks. Quick! You can still avert disaster if you

✔ **Distract him:** Point with huge excitement to a car in the street or a toy across the room. Suddenly 'spot' a cat in the garden. Or 'hear' the postman rattling the letterbox. Anything that will divert his attention from what's upsetting him.

✔ **Act the fool:** He won't put his shoes on? Well, you'll put them on then! Laughing at Daddy being silly is a great way to break the tension.

✔ **Drop it:** Is this an issue you need to battle over? Or are you heading for a fight over something quite trivial? This is your last chance – before the tantrum hits and you have to stand firm – to let it go.

✔ **Seem to agree:** Instead of saying, 'No biscuit! Eat your sandwich!', say, 'Yes, sandwich first, then biscuit.' Crafty, huh?

✔ **Offer closed choices:** Older toddlers love making choices – it makes them feel gloriously in control. All you have to do is make sure that both choices produce the result you're after. So, to the child who's hatching a huff about putting his trousers on, say, 'Which trousers do you want to wear? The red ones or the blue ones?'

✔ **Check he's understood you:** Toddlers sometimes throw a wobbly because they haven't a clue what you're going on about. Get down to his eye-level, hold him gently by the shoulders, and say, 'Listen to Mummy.' Then give him simple, clear instructions (not too many all at once). If he still looks stumped, say, 'Come on, let's do it together!'

Oh no! Stopping the strop

Despite your best efforts, the tantrum's landed – with a very loud bang. You now have to figure out a way to get your pint-sized ball of fury to calm down – for both your sakes. Take a deep 'I'm-in-control' breath and

✔ **Stick to your guns.** Remember, if you give in now, he'll think that tantrums get you what you want.

✔ **Talk quietly.** Partly because it'll stop you shouting, and shouting only raises everyone's temperature. Partly because it'll help you feel calm and composed. And partly because your toddler may actually stop screaming just to hear what you're saying.

✔ **Forget explanations.** No one can appreciate a logical, rational argument when they're completely hysterical. Especially a toddler.

✔ **Ignore it.** Don't talk, don't look at him. Leave the room if necessary. Nothing deflates a strop more quickly than the lack of an audience. This tactic works for both beginner and intermediate level tantrum throwers (refer to the 'What Lies Beneath: The Toddler Tantrum Explained' earlier), but don't do it too coldly with beginners.

✔ **Try a hug.** Some younger toddlers can scare themselves silly by the intensity of their outburst. In which case, you can calm them by holding them tight. I have to say, though, that this approach never worked on my own children: They needed space to writhe around in on their own.

✔ **Offer a way out.** A toddler can get 'stuck' in a tantrum – sometimes to the point where he can't even remember what he was so upset about in the first place. Help him snap out of it by distracting his attention or finding something interesting for him to do. This strategy works for beginner-level tantrums and some long-playing intermediate ones, too.

✔ **Impose consequences.** For the older toddler who's deliberately kicking up and repeatedly refusing to do as you ask, you need to make it clear that bad behaviour has consequences. Send him to sit at the bottom of the stairs and tell him he's having time out. Leave him there for a couple of minutes (no more) and then ask him if he's ready to come back and behave nicely. Please only use time out for really defiant behaviour; this tactic's not nearly so effective if you use it all the time.

All toddlers have tantrums. You're not a bad parent because yours does, too.

Calming after the storm

How you react after a tantrum's over is just as important as how you react while it's going on. Your toddler needs to know that your love for him hasn't changed – and you need to reconnect with all those good feelings you have for him when he's not being such a monster of vileness. So

✔ **Give him a hug.** And praise your child for stopping the strop.

✔ **Forgive and forget.** He's been through enough (as have you!). Don't punish him further by going on and on about it.

✔ **Find something nice to do together.** Parenting can be fun, remember!

Special Tantrums, Special Measures

No parent relishes the idea of dealing with a tantrum; we just grit our teeth and get on with it. But one sub-species of strop exists that requires such superhuman levels of tooth-gritting, it's a wonder we've any surface enamel left at all. I'm talking, of course, of the tantrum *with witnesses:* Those excruciating, earth-swallow-me-up-now moments when your child displays his absolute worst side for all to see – and, sometimes, bear the bruising brunt of.

Ssh, everyone's looking! The public strop

Staying calm when your toddler's throwing a wobbly in your own house is hard enough, but when the wobbly's being thrown on the street, in the playground, or at the supermarket, your sangfroid's set to defrost in double quick time. Before it dissolves altogether, try to

- ✔ **Be consistent.** You have to deal with this in the same way as you would at home, or your child will realise that throwing tantrums in public is amazingly effective. This is a lesson you don't want him to learn.

- ✔ **Ignore all bystanders.** If they have kids, too, they're probably full of sympathy; if they don't have kids, their opinion doesn't count.

- ✔ **Beat a retreat.** If you're somewhere where a noisy tantrum just isn't okay (a restaurant, church, swanky shop), pick your child up and leave.

How to avoid the I-want-a-sweet-at-the-checkout tantrum? Bring your toddler down from the trolley (so he's below sweet-display level) and distract him by making it his special job to help you unload stuff onto the conveyor belt.

Pushing, biting, and other nasty habits

Your toddler is, by nature, a possessive little creature, and he'd be a very unusual little creature indeed if he learned to share and take turns before at least the second half of his second year. Until then (and maybe for many weeks more), he's likely to push and pull and snatch and grab and even – eek! – bite to get what he wants. At this age, he's unlikely to be doing this with malice a forethought but, obviously, it's not the kind of behaviour you can blithely ignore. So

- ✔ **Make it clear that this isn't on.** Take your toddler aside and say firmly, 'No biting/snatching/pushing.'

- ✔ **Show concern for the hurt child.** As soon as you can. It makes it clear to your toddler that behaviour like this does not get your attention. It also shows the hurt child's parent that you're taking this seriously.

- ✔ **Leave if it continues.** If your child has clearly lost the plot, putting some space between him and the other children is best for everyone. Take him to a quiet corner and say, 'Start playing nicely or we will go home right now.' If that doesn't work, head for the door.

- ✔ **Never bite (or push) back.** It'll only teach him that adults do it, too.

- ✔ **Don't read too much into it.** Biting, especially, horrifies us parents, but to a toddler (who doesn't yet understand the nuances of aggression) it is no worse than hitting or pushing. Biting another child's hand when he's 2 does not mean he's going to turn into Hannibal Lector at 22.

Smacking (why it won't get you anywhere)

We all know that smacking a child isn't a good idea – there are umpteen studies that prove it and, in some parts of our country, it's actually against the law. But, hand on heart now, have you really never been tempted to slap your child – even once? There are some times – when we're tired, fed up, being driven to distraction – when it's all we can do not to lash out. And these are exactly the times when we need to remind ourselves that

- ✔ **Smacking doesn't work.** Yes, it stops the bad behaviour for now, but it doesn't help your child control his behaviour in the future. Children behave much better when they're motivated to please you, not to avoid making you angry.

- ✔ **Smacking sends the wrong messages.** It tells your child that hitting someone smaller than you is okay. It also teaches him to be scared of you.

- ✔ **Smacking makes you feel guilty.** After the red mist lifts, you'll feel bad about losing it. The best move is to say sorry (even if your child's too young to understand the words, he'll pick up on your emotions) and to think about how to avoid doing it again. See Chapter 28 for ideas on keeping your cool.

Chapter 14

Food and Sleep

In This Chapter

▶ Getting to know what's normal – and what's not

▶ Working through those eating worries

▶ Sorting out problem sleepers

*W*e all need to eat and we all need to sleep – and we need to do both nice and regularly. Yes, well, try telling that to a toddler! There's no end to the number of complicated little caveats and crafty little cop-outs an under-3 can come up with at mealtimes and bedtimes (and beyond). And every single one of them can drive a parent crazy.

So, this is the chapter to reunite you and your sanity (or, better still, make sure that it never goes walkies in the first place). Because you really need to keep your wits about you right now. It's important to know what's normal and what's not on the toddler food-and-sleep front. And it's wise to find out how to nip unhealthy nod-and-nosh habits in the bud. But it's most crucial of all not to get sucked into full-scale parent-toddler food-and-sleep warfare. Plates and PJs at the ready? Then let's begin!

Toddler Eating: The Need-to-Know Facts

If you thought feeding your baby got a bit stressful at times, brace yourself for bad news: Feeding a toddler ain't exactly a piece of cake either (as it were). But it's tricky for different reasons. This time, it's not so much what to give her when and how, as why on earth she isn't eating it. Toddlers are notorious for picking at, fussing over, and downright refusing to eat their food. Which is very, very frustrating if you're the grown-up who's taken the trouble to cook it.

But, actually, all this finickiness is absolutely normal at this age and stage. And we parents are only making rods for our own backs by expecting anything else.

Spare yourself no end of mealtime stress by boning up on the following toddler food facts:

✔ **She doesn't need to eat that much.** Your toddler may be way more active than she was in her baby days, but her body is not growing nearly as fast. She only needs about 1,000 calories a day now (rising to 1,300 at 3). And, if you've ever been on a 1,000-calorie-a-day diet, you'll know that's not a lot of food.

✔ **She's not a same-amount-every-day kind of girl.** Toddlers can stuff themselves silly one day and then hardly touch a crust the next. You'll only get a clear idea of her overall intake if you review it by the week, rather than the day.

✔ **She knows when she's full.** Toddlers tend to have a simpler relationship with food than many of us adults: They eat when they're hungry and stop when they're full. Even if what they're eating is really yummy and there's loads more of it on their plate.

✔ **She wants to feed herself.** And not only is that a less reliable way of transporting food from plate to mouth, it's also parent-provokingly slow. And let's not even mention the 'fun' she can have building carrot-slice towers or plopping peas in her juice.

✔ **She's forming opinions about food.** About the way it tastes and about the way it looks. And her opinions are (generally) achingly conservative: Don't expect her to be keen on trying anything new.

✔ **She's sensing that it matters to us.** And if not eating her broccoli gets her a lot of attention, maybe that's the way to go.

Good eats, good treats

Nutritionists will tell you it's vital to get your toddler to eat a balanced diet: Establish healthy eating habits early on, they say, and your child will continue to eat well and stay healthy in the years to come. And I wouldn't quibble with that. But, bearing in mind the toddler food facts in the previous section, reaching this healthy-eating nirvana with an under-3 could actually take some doing. That doesn't mean, of course, that we shouldn't give it a jolly good try.

What we should all be aiming for

To be sure of providing your child with a properly balanced diet:

✔ **Give her a wide variety of foods.** So that she becomes accustomed to different textures and tastes and gets lots of different nutrients.

✔ **Get her food groups right.** Every day, serve up

> Six servings of grains and potatoes (including pasta, rice, bread)
>
> Five servings of fruit and vegetables
>
> Two to four servings of calcium-rich food (including milk, cheese, yoghurt, and fromage frais)
>
> Two servings of protein-rich food (including red meat, chicken, fish, eggs, lentils, beans).

✔ **Limit (or ban) squash, fizzy drinks, and juice.** Because they're crammed full of sugar. Stick to milk or water.

✔ **Avoid cakes, biscuits, and sweets.** And sugary breakfast cereals. Too much sugar can lead to weight problems and tooth decay.

✔ **Keep salt out of her food.** Avoiding salt is good for her blood pressure

✔ **Offer only healthy snacks.** Such as cheese, toast, and fruit.

But back in the real world . . .

As sensible and worthy as each of the aims in the previous section are, they are quite hard to achieve at each and every meal – and nigh on impossible when your toddler's having a bad food day. So, the wised-up parent takes a slightly less rigid approach: Yes, the aims are still aims – and good ones at that – but it's rather more realistic to

✔ **Stick to the 80/20 rule:** Which is, if she's eating healthily about 80 per cent of the time, you're doing great. Don't get too uptight about the other 20 per cent.

✔ **Think frequent fuel:** Her tummy is small, so three big meals a day isn't going to suit her. Go for three small meals a day, with two or three decent snacks in between.

✔ **Look at labels:** Particularly on packets of ready-made sauces and on cereals and yoghurts that are packaged to appeal to kids. Many of them are very high in sugar and/or salt. Fine for your toddler to eat every now and again but not every day of the week.

✔ **Think in meals rather than food groups:** If breakfast is cereal with fruit and/or toast, lunch is a sandwich with a protein-rich filling, salad, and fruit, dinner is protein with potatoes/rice/pasta and veg and yoghurt, and snacks are fruit and cheese, you're definitely on the right track.

✔ **Get real about sweet stuff:** Undesirable they may be from a nutritional point of view, but they taste jolly nice. And banning sugary foods doesn't work: Take it from one who was never allowed them as a small child, discovered them at 10, and has craved them ever since! Offer biscuits, cakes, and the like in moderation and as part of a normal meal.

✔ **If she's not drinking water or milk, make it fruit juice:** At least it contains vitamins and minerals, unlike fizzy drinks. But do dilute it to at least half juice to half water.

Your toddler still needs lots of calcium: about 550 ml (1 pint) of cow's milk a day, or plenty of cheese and yoghurt.

Don't give whole nuts to toddlers (or any child under 5): They're just the right size to block small windpipes. And avoid peanuts or foods containing peanuts if anyone has a nut allergy in your family.

Never let your child run around as she eats: The food's much more likely to go down the wrong way or even choke her. Insist that meals – and snacks – are eaten at the table or, at the very least, sitting quietly on the floor.

Little porkers: The truth about tubby tots

There's always an exception to every rule – which means that not every child goes all food-fussy the moment she's hits 2. Some continue to eat with gusto right through their toddler years. And are we pleased? Are we heck! We're too busy worrying about fat tummies and weight problems and a future filled with outsize trousers.

Manners maketh matters worse?

Do you want your child to eat nicely and have good table manners? Or do you want her to think that eating's fun? Because, with a younger toddler at least, that's the choice you face. Insisting that your 18-month-old uses a knife and fork correctly or that your 2-year-old keeps her elbows off the table isn't a wise idea: She's too young to manage it and, if you keep banging on about it, you'll make mealtimes so stressful (for you both), she won't feel like eating at all.

What works better is to remind yourself that all toddlers eat messily and have the manners of a caveman. And then ever so gently

✔ **Dripfeed the Ps and Qs.** Make a point of always saying, 'Please' and 'Thank you' yourself when you're at the table, and elsewhere, particularly when you're talking to your toddler. After a while, you can say, 'What do you say?' when she asks for/gets something. She'll probably look blank, so smile and say it for her.

✔ **Show her how.** To hold a cup with two hands. To hold a spoon. To lay the table. And let her practise often, even if it gets messy.

Yes, childhood obesity is on the up – and a number of under-3s are worryingly overweight – but it's important to realise that most toddlers start their second year scoring pretty highly in the chubster department. This (entirely normal) 'baby fat' will disappear over the next couple of years, as their increasingly active little bodies become leaner and more muscular. But, if your toddler doesn't do the food-fuss thing along the way, this thinning-down process may well take longer or be more gradual than most.

So, instead of panicking about the size of your toddler's thighs right now, what you actually need to be doing is focusing on what they may be like in a few years' time. Experts agree that a child's weight at 4 is a much better indicator of future obesity problems than her weight at 1. So, use the next three years as an opportunity to push her eating and exercise habits in a seriously healthy direction. To do this, you need to

- ✔ **Watch her portion sizes.** Don't load up her plate with more than she really needs. The average toddler portion is about a quarter of an adult one. So, where you have four potatoes, for example, she has only one.

- ✔ **Keep her active.** Children who run, jump, climb, dance, and walk their little socks off every day rarely have problems with their weight.

- ✔ **Don't cut out the good fat.** No, it's not wise to fry all your child's food in lard and serve up cream cakes on the side, but it's not wise to put your toddler on an adult-type low-fat regime, either. Fat is an essential part of the toddler diet. She needs full-fat milk and yoghurt until the age of 2. After that, you can switch to semi-skimmed but she'll still need to take at least 20 per cent of her total calories from fat.

- ✔ **Sort out the snacks.** Don't offer too many (three a day, max) and don't make them too sugary.

- ✔ **Don't comfort her with food.** If she's grazed her knee, give her a big cuddle, not a big bag of crisps. Food should be linked to hunger, not emotional reward.

- ✔ **Look at your own food habits.** If you're stuffing down the biscuits, chances are your child will want to follow suit.

- ✔ **If her weight's really concerning you, see your GP.** She will tell you whether you're right to be worried or not. And, if necessary, help you work out what to do.

Food and teeth: Surprising stuff

You probably already know that sugar's bad for toddler (and adult) teeth. But are you sure that you know exactly what sort of foods tooth-rotting sugar tends to lurk in? Obviously, there are the usual suspects – sweets, sugary snacks, chocolate – but there are also a fair few

(continued)

(continued)

sneaky ones. Sugar is as a main ingredient, for example, in fizzy drinks (up to seven teaspoons a can), fruit-flavoured squash (four teaspoons a glass), and fruit yoghurt and fromage frais (up to three teaspoons a pot).

Then there's dried fruit. Seriously. Raisins, dried apples, and fruit bars do contain lots of good things, as well as sugar, but they're so sticky, they coat your child's teeth in sugary residues that increase the risk of decay. Some dentists believe raisins to be as damaging to teeth as sweets.

And it's not just sugar you need to be wary of; it's fruit acids and other acidic additives, too – because they can erode away the protective enamel surface of your child's teeth (which is already much softer than an adult's). They lurk in fruit juice, fruit squash, fizzy drinks (including sugar-free ones), and possibly even some brands of yoghurt and fromage frais. To protect your child's teeth, always try to

✔ **Have sweets in one sitting.** When it comes to tooth decay, it's not the amount of sugar your child's eating, it's the frequency with which she eats it. If you treat your child, don't spin it out: Letting her suck on raisins or boiled sweets all afternoon is asking for dental trouble.

✔ **Never brush her teeth straight after meals or snacks.** If there's acid in her mouth softening the enamel, brushing will only cause more erosion. Always wait at least half an hour before getting out the toothbrush. And don't brush more than twice a day.

✔ **Get into straws.** If your toddler drinks her (well-diluted) juice through a straw, the liquid won't come into nearly so much contact with her teeth.

✔ **End a meal with a small cube of cheese.** This can rebalance the pH levels in your toddler's mouth, neutralising the harmful effects of sugar and acids.

What We Worry About: Common Parent Complaints

Right, so it's more or less a given that your toddler's going to get picky about food (if she hasn't already). And that's fair enough, under the biological circumstances. But there are some toddlers who can't be doing with general pickiness; they like to *specialise* – either by completely refusing one particular food or by taking pickiness to almost hunger-strike extremes. And there's probably nothing that winds a parent up more.

Should your toddler develop a specialist tendency, cling fast to the knowledge that it won't last for ever. And that it's unlikely to cause much damage while it does. Cultivate a supreme indifference to the specialism in question – toddlers being the contrary little creatures that there are, any obvious sign that you're desperately keen for them to stop doing something usually results in gleeful determination to carry on even longer. And employ some (subtle) specialist tactics of your own.

She won't eat vegetables

They may be full of impressively scientific-sounding nutritional goodies, such as phytonutrients and antioxidants, but, to many toddlers, vegetables are just bitter, fibrous, and dull. To up the veg-to-mouth success rate:

- ✔ **Act cool.** It may drive you nuts to see the vegetables left untouched, but you'll only make it more of an issue if you show it. Grit your teeth and clear away her plate without comment.

- ✔ **Don't give up.** Experts believe that it can take up to ten tastings to get a child to accept a new food. So don't lose heart: Keep dishing up those greens, and she may well surprise you one day.

- ✔ **Get sneaky.** Purée up some veg and add it to pasta or meat sauces. If she can't see lumps of carrot (or whatever), she's unlikely to refuse it.

- ✔ **Keep portions small and varied.** Rather than sticking a dauntingly large lump of broccoli on her plate, serve up three tiny florets and a teaspoon-ful of peas. By giving her less and offering a choice, you up the chances of her trying at least one.

- ✔ **Don't bargain.** Saying, 'If you eat up all your veg, you can have ice cream for pudding' only reinforces the idea that veg is especially vile. By all means reward veg-eating with ice cream, if you want to, but don't make it a condition.

- ✔ **Involve her.** Older toddlers often eat more veg if they've had a part to play in its preparation. So ask her opinion: 'Sweetcorn or leeks?' And then let her help you put them in the pan or pull off the outer leaves.

Fruit is just as important as veg, nutritionally speaking – and, thankfully, it has much more toddler appeal. There's no need to fret yourself silly about veg refusal if your child knows her way round your fruit bowl.

She won't drink (cow's) milk

It's not unusual for toddlers (especially breastfed ones) to dislike or go off cow's milk, but it really isn't a nutritional emergency. At this age, your toddler needs a good daily dose of calcium to help her grow, and experts generally recommend that you meet this by serving up about 550 ml (1 pint) of milk a day (including milk used in cooking and breastmilk or formula, if she's still having either). But there's no reason why you can't meet her calcium needs with other dairy products, such as cheese, yoghurt, fromage frais, and even (milk-based) ice cream.

If your child won't eat any dairy products at all (or you think that she has an allergy to them), see your GP. She may need to take supplements.

If you're still breastfeeding, good for you! There's no reason to give up now (unless you want to), but it is important to know that breastmilk's no longer the mainstay of your child's diet. She should be getting most of the calories and nutrients she needs from solid food now. When you (and your toddler) feel ready to stop breastfeeding, read the section on weaning in Chapter 7. And, unlikely as it may sound, you'll probably find some of the tips in 'Giving up the bottle' come in very handy, too.

Giving up the bottle

Toddlers don't need bottles; they need cups. Drinking cow's milk, formula milk, or fruit juice from a bottle at this age is really bad for their teeth, especially if they take a bottle to bed at night. And, drinking loads from the bottle in the day can restrict their appetite. But you try telling a toddler that! Giving up the bottle can be a very big deal for some. To make the whole process easier:

✔ **Be sure that she's got the cup knack.** Try out beakers, spouted cups and cups with a built-in straw until you find the one she likes. Then offer it, filled with her favourite drink, at every meal and snack. Don't pressure her to drink from it; patience is all.

✔ **Make bottle-time boring.** Insist that she sits on your lap or in a certain chair to have her bottle – no playing or running around. And once she gets down, bottle-time's over.

✔ **Cut down gradually.** Over a couple of weeks. Drop the bottle she's least interested in first.

✔ **Get crafty at bedtime.** The is usually the last bottle to go. Work a cup of milk into your bedtime routine (before tooth-brushing), then simply 'forget' to offer the bottle and see what happens. If your toddler asks for it, try distracting her attention; if she asks again, offer a bottle or cup of water. Usually, if you're quite firm, that's all it takes. If your child really kicks up a fuss (this is more common with older toddlers), you may have to give in for now and resort to sneakier measures later: staying overnight at Granny's, perhaps, and 'forgetting' to pack the bottle, or maybe even ashamed bribery of the 'Give up your bottle and we'll go to the zoo' variety.

✔ **Expect crankiness.** Your child's losing a much-loved friend. Give her extra cuddles as she adjusts, particularly at those times of day when she'll miss her bottle most.

She won't eat meat

Meat often gets a thumbs-down in toddler world – usually because it's just too darn chewy. So, stoke up your child's carnivorous tendencies by making those meaty offerings smooth and small. Slab of roast beef? Chop it up into teeny-tiny pieces. Making shepherd's pie? Buy lean mince and, once you've browned it off, put it through the blender before piling the potato on top. Wish she'd like pork and chicken? Cultivate a taste for it by dishing up chipolata sausages or whizzing up some chicken, apple, onion, and breadcrumbs in a food processor and forming the mixture into tiny homemade chickenburgers. Keep the faith; she'll get there in the end.

If your toddler really won't touch any type of meat at all (or you don't want her to because you're a vegetarian), there's no need to panic about protein deficiencies. She can get all the protein she needs from cheese, eggs, lentils, and (unless she's a vegetarian) lovely, smooth-mashed fish.

She won't let me feed her

Er, well, that's because she wants to feed herself! And there's no reason not to let her. No, she won't do it as efficiently and quickly as you and, no, she won't have great spoon control at first but everyone's got to start somewhere, haven't they? Buy her some child-sized cutlery (make sure that the spoon has a biggish bowl, so she has a greater chance of scooping food onto it), pop on a large bib, spread a splash mat on the floor, and let her get on with it.

Not every meal has to be a spoon-wielding splatathon: Finger foods are still a great option. On days when you just can't face wiping down the walls again, satisfy your self-feeder with a plate of tiny sandwiches, breadsticks, slices of fruit, halved cherry tomatoes, and cubes of cheese.

Help her eat yoghurt by holding the pot for her while she dips the spoon in. Sit well back, though, or you may need a bib, too!

She won't try anything new

The words 'adventurous', 'eating', and 'toddler' rarely appear in the same sentence. But some toddlers take the phrase 'conservative taste' to whole new levels of monotony. Either they get stuck in a food groove: They just want pasta or cheese sandwiches – and nothing else. Or they happily shovel down any of a handful of food favourites but, should anything even slightly different appear on their plate, they clamp their little mouths tight shut. Tackle both by

- ✔ **Keeping at it:** Just keep offering the new food. Even if she doesn't taste it. It will soon become so familiar a sight, she may forget she's boycotting it.

- ✔ **Keeping it simple:** She may like meat sauce, she may like cheese sauce, and she may like pasta, but stick them all together in a lasagne and that's something new. And, therefore, yukky.

- ✔ **Keeping it familiar:** Never try a new veg with a new main dish. That's new-ness overload – and doomed to failure.

- ✔ **Keeping it in perspective:** If she only ever wants cheese sandwiches for lunch, is that really the end of the world? It's a nutritious choice and she actually wants to eat it: Result, in my book.

- ✔ **Issuing invitations to tea:** Dish up the new food when her toddler friends are eating with her. If they slurp it up, she may decide to follow suit. Peer pressure can be a wonderful thing!

She just won't eat

Your toddler may not be eating much – remember, she doesn't actually need to – but it's unlikely she's actually starving herself. Even if it seems that way to you. If she's hardly touching her main meals, ask yourself if

- ✔ **She's filling up on snacks:** If your toddler's nibbling and grazing throughout the day, she may well have no appetite for a bigger meal. Limit snacks to twice a day.

- ✔ **She's filling up on milk or juice:** If she's drinking more than 550 ml (1 pint) of milk a day or more than 175 ml (6 oz) of juice, that's too much. To put it another way, if your child drinks four cups of milk and three cups of juice, she's had 1350 calories – probably more than she needs all day – without eating a thing.

- ✔ **She's teething:** Toddlers quite often go off food, particularly chewy stuff (such as pasta), when their gums hurt. I could tell when all my kids were cutting molars because of their untouched plates.

- ✔ **She's eating too late:** A tired toddler loses the appetite plot. Try to serve up before the crankiness kicks in; or serve her main meal at lunch and a lighter meal towards the end of her day.

Five ways to fox fussy eaters

However strange your toddler's particular food fads are and however infuriating you find them, they'll be over with more quickly if you stick to these five golden rules:

1. Never get cross. If she's refusing a food just for the sake of it, the whole idea will lose its appeal if you don't react. If she actually dislikes it, getting cross with her will only make her dislike it even more. So, if she's obviously finished eating, remove her plate without criticism and don't offer anything else until her next mealtime.

2. Keep trying. Remember, it can take ten tastings (at least) for a toddler to accept a new food. And all toddlers' tastes change over time. Be patient.

3. Don't go to too much trouble. Nothing's more riling than seeing your child reject a meal you've spent hours preparing. Increase the calm by keeping your cooking quick and simple.

4. Keep the portions small. Don't overwhelm her already fragile appetite with big heaps of food. Remember, a toddler portion size is one-quarter the size of yours. It's more motivating for her – and more pleasant for you – if she feels able to cope with what's on her plate.

5. Make eating fun. Mealtimes should be about conversation, not confrontation. Keep the atmosphere light and jolly (however stressed you're feeling inside). Eat together as a family as often as you can. Make your toddler laugh by cutting a star in her toast or arranging her raisins like a smiley face. Or take it all outside and have a 'special' picnic in the garden.

Sleeping Patterns: What's Normal, What's Not

Let's do the bad news first, shall we? If, from birth to 1, a baby gradually starts to sleep more and more, then, from 1 to 3, a toddler gradually starts to sleep less and less. But (and this is the good news), it's only a little bit less – and, if things do go a bit pear-shaped, it's (generally) much, much easier to sort.

Over the next couple of years, your toddler's need for sleep decreases, on average, by about two hours in every 24 (see Table 14-1 for more details). But most of that decrease gets accounted for in the day-time, as she becomes more and more able to make it through to bedtime without an afternoon snooze. (Whether *you* feel able to make it through to her bedtime without her afternoon snooze is another matter, of course – see 'A word about naps'.)

Table 14-1	Your Age-by-Age Guide to Toddler Sleep	
Age	*Hours of day-time sleep*	*Hours of night-time sleep*
12 months	2.5	11.5
2 years	1.25	11.75
3 years	1	11

This chart is only a guide, not a timetable that your toddler must adhere to. Some toddlers, like some adults, do seem to need less or more sleep than most. If your toddler is getting more or less sleep than the chart indicates but seems perfectly content in every other way, then she's fine.

A word about naps

At 1, many children are still having two naps in the day, although some hardy little cherubs are already fending very well, thank you, on just the one. By 18 months or so, though, almost all toddlers will have dropped down to one nap a day – or will be signalling strongly that they need to, either by fighting sleep at naptime or bedtime or by waking super-early in the morning.

And then comes the end of naps altogether. At some point between 2 and 4 (it varies hugely from child to child), your toddler will be able to make it through the day without any sleep at all. You'll be able to tell when because you'll clock the same sleep-refusal or dawn-rising antics as before. Once she's given up her nap, it will probably take a while for your child to adjust. And while she does, she may well get a little tired and cranky at suppertime – or even doze off at the table. This is perfectly normal and will pass, although you could try bringing her bedtime forward for a while to compensate.

Now, if you're anything like I was, you won't exactly be thrilled at the prospect of parenting life without a nice toddler-free break in the day. But, actually, the prospect is far worse than the reality. Especially if you get your toddler into the idea of a daily 'quiet time': At the same day every day (generally, when her nap used to be), announce that it's 'quiet time' and sit with her on the sofa while she looks at books, watches a video, or listens to a song tape. She may only last five minutes to begin with but you'll find you can gradually extend quiet time until it provides you both with a proper break in the day.

One last little post-nap tip: If and when your toddler starts going to nursery or playgroup in the morning, you'll probably find she's exhausted when she comes home. Sometimes, it's worth temporarily re-introducing the afternoon nap at this point. Or at least not worrying too much if she dozes off on the sofa during quiet time.

What Keeps Us Awake At Night – and What To Do About It

Most toddlers are quite capable of sleeping for an unbroken 11-hour stretch at night, but that doesn't mean they always will. And, bearing in mind all the weird and wonderful physical and emotional changes of the toddler years, it's probably unfair of us to expect them to.

But – and it's a large but – there's a big difference between the annoyance of the odd interrupted night and the zombie-like horror of a real and regular sleep problem. If your toddler keeps you up at night, every night, you need to find a way to deal with it before you all collapse from exhaustion.

She still won't sleep through

First, let's be clear what we mean by not 'sleeping through'. We're not talking waking up early in the morning, and we're not talking waking up once at night and settling right back. We're talking repeated waking throughout the night, accompanied by massive amounts of parental sleep deprivation.

If this sounds like you and your toddler, you owe it to each other to get it sorted. You both need your sleep: She can't be a joyful toddler without rebooting properly at night, and you can't be a joyful parent without a good dose of zzz's under your belt.

Nine times out of ten, the reason for all this nocturnal upset is that your child has not yet learnt how to fall asleep – or get back to sleep – on her own. So, every time she wakes in the night (and we all surface briefly at regular intervals), she yells out for you. To stop this, you have to 'train' her to get herself back to sleep – and the only way to do that is to get tough. Which means you

- ✔ **Don't respond to her first cries:** Wait for between two to ten minutes (depending on the state of your nerves) before you go in.

- ✔ **Don't pick her up:** Reassure her calmly and/or pat her gently instead.

- ✔ **Leave when she's awake:** And beginning to calm down.

- ✔ **Hold your nerve:** If the yelling starts again, wait a little longer than last time before going in. (You'll find more on this in Chapter 9.)

- ✔ **Repeat the process till it works:** With unswerving determination. It won't work if you give up halfway through the first night.

Sleep-training a toddler is harder on your ears than sleep-training a baby (toddlers can yell louder), but toddlers generally get the whole idea much more quickly. It shouldn't take more than two or three days. Hang in there!

If your toddler cries all night despite your best efforts, see your GP or health visitor and ask to be referred to a children's sleep clinic. If you think that the broken nights started or worsened at around the time your toddler switched to cow's milk, it may also be worth finding out if she has an allergy to lactose.

Your toddler doesn't need breast or formula milk at night. If she's still waking for a feed, she's doing so from habit, not hunger.

She suddenly won't sleep through

If your toddler used to sleep well but now doesn't (and is clearly not ill), you need to turn detective. Sleep disruption often follows some other kind of disruption during the day. Top of your list of suspects should be:

- ✔ **A change in childcare arrangements.** Or some other big change in the family set-up or routine.
- ✔ **The arrival of a new sibling.** Go to Chapter 25 for information on how to ease your child into her role as older sibling.
- ✔ **The arrival of new teeth.** Chapter 11 can help you deal with teething pains.
- ✔ **The arrival of nightmares.** Often fuelled by something seen earlier on TV. Not common under the age of 3 but not unheard of, either. (For more on nightmares, see Chapter 18.)
- ✔ **Going away on holiday/an extended visit.** Strange cots can be unsettling. As can adjusting back to her old one when you're back home.

Once you've found the culprit, all you can do is be a patient source of comfort and reassurance (but not wide-awake-making out-of-cot activity) until the anxiety or the pain dies down. Should the broken nights continue beyond this point, you probably need to stop them becoming a habit by getting tough (see the section 'She still won't sleep through', earlier in this chapter) for a night or two.

She won't go to bed

Bedtimes and toddlers are not a natural mix: Going to bed means staying still (not a favourite toddler occupation) and being away from your parents (even less of one). So it's no wonder some of them start to resist bedtime with every ounce of their (newly discovered) muscles of independence.

Trouble is, many parents find a child kicking off at bedtime much less stressful (to begin with) than a child kicking off in the middle of the night. So they don't do much about the situation. And, before you know it, bed refusal has become a habit. If you ever want an evening to yourself again, you're going to have to

- ✔ **Get her to bed before she's too tired.** An overtired toddler is bad news on the bedtime front: Tiredness makes her fractious and a fractious child is primed for a fight. Learn to spot the signs that she's ready to drop – and remember that these include a sudden post-supper burst of energy. Hyperactive toddlers are often hyperknackered ones.

- ✔ **Review the bedtime routine.** If you're not already in the habit of quietly winding down to bedtime with a bath, a story, and a kiss goodnight, get into it now. Too predictable for words? Yes, that's the idea! You want your toddler to come to anticipate and enjoy each of the gradual stages that propel her gently but firmly into bed. Take your time, particularly with the story: Nothing lulls a child into pre-sleep drowsiness better than a much-loved voice reading a much-loved tale.

- ✔ **Bring out a comfort object.** Have a special teddy or a soft toy that gets tucked into bed with your toddler just before lights out.

- ✔ **Leave the room decisively.** Don't linger and don't rise to requests for extra cuddles/stories/tucking in.

- ✔ **Don't return for at least ten minutes.** This usually does the trick. If it doesn't, go in, pat her gently, say calmly, 'Sleep time now', and leave again. Repeat determinedly until it works.

- ✔ **Deal firmly with escapees.** If your toddler's in a bed and gets out of it after lights out, return her gently and firmly. Stay calm and look like you mean business. Repeat as often as it takes.

For really recalcitrant escapees, consider a stairgate at the bedroom door. Harsh, perhaps, but effective.

Do check the sleep chart (shown in Table 14-1) before you start any of this; your toddler could be fighting bedtime because she really doesn't need to be going to bed this early. Or she could be sleeping more than she needs to in the day-time.

She comes into our bed

This one comes in two versions: the one that needs sorting and the one that doesn't. If your toddler comes into your bed, either in the middle of the night or in the early morning, and you don't mind and – just as importantly – your partner doesn't either, then fine. But if you – or your partner – do mind, you need to act. Simply resolve between you to take her back to her own bed each and every time she appears at your bedside. The each-and-every-time bit is the important thing here, or she won't get the message properly.

If your toddler has taken to bedhopping at night, always remember to close the stairgate at the top of the stairs – in case she takes a wrong turn.

She gets up too early

This is perhaps the sleep problem parents of toddlers complain about most. And, unfortunately, it's the most difficult to solve – mainly because it seems to be a phase most toddlers go through, whether they've always been good sleepers or not. To improve the situation, try

- ✔ **Totting up how many hours of sleep she gets:** Look at the sleep chart in Table 14-1. If she's already getting more than enough sleep for her age, maybe you're putting her to bed too early? Or letting her sleep too long in the day-time?

- ✔ **Putting up blackout blinds:** Screening out dawn's light may encourage her body to keep releasing melatonin, the hormone that promotes sleep.

- ✔ **Stringing up some fairy lights:** On a timer switch. Then tell her it's only morning time when the lights come on. For this idea to work, you need to give her an early taste of success, so start off setting the timer for the time she usually wakes, then slowly move it later every day.

- ✔ **Getting a novelty clock:** Many shops and mail-order firms sell a toddler 'alarm' clock with a bunny face: You close bunny's eyes at night and tell your child she can only get up when bunny opens his eyes in the morning. Some toddlers do obey bunny's orders slavishly; others sit up all night waiting excitedly for bunny to wake up.

- ✔ **Offering rewards:** An older toddler often responds well to a star chart (especially in combination with the lights on a timer): She gets a star every time she wakes up at the right time. Or you can tell her about the 'sleep fairy' who brings rewards to good sleepers – put a trinket box by her bed for the reward to 'appear' in.

- ✔ **Having a toy box in the bedroom**: For your early riser to amuse herself with. Obviously this doesn't work in combination with the blackout blinds! Or if your toddler likes to 'share' her playing time with you.

- ✔ **Repeating, 'It's a phase.':** And wearily waiting for it to pass.

Time for a 'big' bed?

Your child cannot stay in a cot for the rest of her life. Obviously. But when do you move her into a bed? Well, you could do it early on, before she's old enough to realise that beds are easier to get out of than cots. But then she may not understand why she's being moved and get upset. Or you could wait until she's older – and maybe even wants to make the move. But then, if she's already started climbing out of her cot, there's almost no chance of her staying put in bed.

Not easy to pick a winner, is it? So be guided by practicalities instead. If you need the cot for a new baby, make the move now. Otherwise, just go for it when you're feeling ready for a new challenge. Accept that there'll be nights when your toddler finds her way to your bed – and that you'll have to deal with it by calmly returning her to her room. As with any change in routine, your child will take a while to adjust, but to help make it easier you can

✔ **Give her time to get used to the idea.** Take her with you to choose her bed. Set it up in her room and let her practise lying on it. If she seems a little hesitant about sleeping in it at night, suggest she tries it at naptime first. Or take the slats out and put the mattress on the floor, so she can have a few nights to get used to it without worrying about falling out.

✔ **Make everything safe.** Put cushions on the floor in case of night-time tumbles. Or fix a bedguard to stop her falling out. Make sure that the stairgate is closed and that the path from her bed to yours is stumble-proof and dimly lit.

✔ **Be very boring at night.** Her night-time wanderings will soon stop if her tedious parents just keep taking her back to bed without the slightest reaction to her escapology skills.

Chapter 15

Keeping Your Toddler Safe

. . . .

In This Chapter

▶ Spotting (and reducing) the hazards in your house

▶ Protecting your kids on the road

▶ Helping them play safe without reining them in

. . . .

*H*aving children does weird things to your view of the world. Suddenly, it's full of all sorts of child-endangering scary stuff – rickety steps, sharp knives, poisonous chemicals, fast cars – that you've never really noticed before. And they make you *very* nervous. As, indeed, they should. Every small child needs a parent with extra-sensitive safety antennae – to keep him out of danger until he's old enough and wise enough to do it for himself.

You probably found this a (relatively) easy task when he was tiny and stayed in one place but, now that he's big enough to rush around all over the shop, you and your antennae are going to have to work overtime. You're not going to be able to prevent every little accident (no parent can) but, with a bit of forward thinking and a few clever little devices, you can do a heck of a lot to prevent the really big ones. This chapter shows you how.

Toddlerproofing Your Home: The Hands and Knees Tour

Toddlers are little sticky beaks. They love poking their noses, heads, fingers, toes into anything and everything. Which means it's your job to make sure that the anythings and everythings in your house are either quite safe to poke into or have been moved well out of toddler reach.

Learn some basic child first-aid now (start by reading Chapter 29). If, God forbid, your toddler does hurt himself badly, you really don't want to be flapping around helplessly wondering what to do.

To toddlerproof your home, get down on the floor (hands and knees, please) and take a good look round your home from toddler-eye-level and see what potential hazards you stumble across. Don't just think about what your child can do, touch, reach, and climb now; consider what he'll be able to manage next – toddlers have an uncanny ability to develop a new skill overnight and scare the pants off you with a death-defying demonstration in the morning. Keep your eyes peeled for:

- ✓ **Plug sockets:** Those little holes are like magnets to curious fingers. Cover empty sockets with plug-in covers.

- ✓ **Blind cords and curtain tie backs:** Make sure that these are well out of reach. Dangling strings and ropes can easily get wound round necks.

- ✓ **Windows:** Could your toddler open them? Or push a chair or chest over to one and then climb up and open it? If so, fit a lock or catch that will stop him getting it open far enough to fall out. If you have sash windows, only ever open them from the top.

- ✓ **Table-top ornaments:** If they're breakable, precious (or heavy enough to cause harm when falling), put them on a high shelf or pack them away for a while.

- ✓ **Coins, watch batteries, buttons, paperclips:** Anything small enough (and shiny enough) for a toddler to swallow.

- ✓ **Trailing flexes:** Tuck them behind furniture or right down between the skirting board and the wall. And never leave your iron, blender, or kettle plugged in where little hands can get hold of the flex and pull.

- ✓ **Sharp corners at toddler-head-height:** Slip on ready-made plastic corner covers or fashion your own from cork, felt, or bubble wrap.

- ✓ **Top-heavy chests of drawers or bookshelves:** Toddlers have been killed by easy-to-topple furniture. If it has drawers at the bottom, fill them with something heavy. If not, bolt it to the wall or get rid of it.

After you check the items in the preceding list, pay particular attention to the four top toddler danger zones described in the following sections.

Twin toddlers 'exploring' together can get themselves into much more danger much more quickly than a single child. Be double-thorough on your tour.

Danger zone one: The kitchen

This is where most accidents happen: partly because it's where you and your toddler probably hang out the most; partly because it's full of all sorts of equipment that looks fun to fiddle with (but absolutely isn't). To de-hazard your kitchen as much as you can:

- **Turn in the handles of saucepans when you're cooking.** So your toddler can't reach up and pull the pan of hot stuff off the stove. And, if you can, try only to cook on the back burners.

- **Watch where you leave hot drinks.** A cup of tea can scald a toddler's thin skin even ten minutes after you made it. Push teapots, coffee jugs, and full cups right to the back of your countertop.

- **Keep the door of your washing machine closed.** And when you need to get a new one, choose a model with a child lock.

- **Put sharp knives out of reach.** As well as matches, skewers, scissors, tin openers, pizza wheels, and the like.

- **Never sit your toddler on the countertop.** Putting him within reach of kitchen tools isn't a good idea. Nor is it wise to let him think that it's okay to be up there, or he'll climb up one day on his own.

- **Keep all your cleaning stuff well out of reach.** The traditional under-the-sink cupboard is a complete parenting no-no: You don't want your toddler swallowing bleach when your back's turned.

- **Say goodbye to tablecloths.** One little toddler tug and anything sharp or hot on the table is heading his way.

- **Tie a knot in plastic bags.** When you bin them or store them to re-use. This makes it hard for your child to pull one over his head and suffocate.

- **Lose the little fridge magnets.** They may be fun, but your child could put them in his mouth and choke.

- **Use the harness on the highchair.** Even if he hates it.

- **Put cupboard locks on low cupboards with dangerous/fragile stuff inside.** Or rearrange everything and put the risky stuff up high.

Fill one low cupboard with toddler-friendly stuff (plastic basins, sieves), so he's got somewhere to poke around in while you cook. It'll make him less likely to poke around elsewhere.

Every house should have at least one smoke alarm in it. They're cheap, easy to fit, and can give you precious extra minutes to escape should you ever have a fire. Don't forget to change the battery once every 12 months.

Danger zone two: The bathroom

The trouble with bathrooms is, they've got water in them. And – brace yourself for a scary statistic – a child can drown in 2 to 3 cm of water in less than one minute. Makes you see that toilet in a whole new light, now, doesn't it? Your must-do bathroom safety tips include:

- **Keep the bathroom door closed.** And the lid on the toilet down. If your very small toddler can open the bathroom door, get a loo-seat lock, too.

- **Put all your medicines out of reach.** Preferably in a locked cupboard.

- **Keep all your lotions, potions, razors, and hairdryers on a high shelf.** Baby are very good and grabbing anything that comes within reach!

- **Turn your water temperature down.** And always test the bathwater with your elbow before you put your child in – a child's skin scalds more easily than an adult's.

    Think about getting a thermostatic mixing valve (TMV2) fitted to your hot-water tank: It costs about £100 but ensures that the water coming out of your hot taps is always a safe temperature.

- **Never leave your child alone in the bath.** Even for a second. And never leave your child alone in the bathroom when the bath's running.

- **Remove the bathroom door lock.** Or make sure that you can unscrew it from the outside – and stash a screwdriver above the door frame.

Danger zone three: The stairs

Pretty obvious, this one, really (we adults have enough trouble staying safe on the stairs ourselves). And so is the solution: stairgates. But, just in case you need a little motivation to get on with fitting them, let me tell you that 35,000 children under 4 hurt themselves falling down stairs every year. So

- **Gate the stairs at the top and bottom.** And don't forget to shut them! Especially if your toddler's no longer in a cot and could wander at night.

- **Make sure that the top gate is of the screw-to-the-wall gate variety.** The pressure-fit gates are great (and often much more convenient) but not at the top of the stairs – if your toddler pushes or falls hard against it, it may give way and let him tumble down.

- **Fix the bottom gate a few steps up.** So your child has the chance to practise going up and down a little.

Danger zone four: The garden

Yes, I know that the garden isn't strictly a room in your house, but it is one of the biggest and best playspaces your toddler has at his daily disposal, so you do need to get out there and make sure that it's hazard-free:

- **Fence off ponds and water features.** Or, better still, fill them in. And always store paddling pools upside down: 2 cm of (rain)water is enough for a toddler to drown in.

- **Lock up gardening tools.** And weedkillers, slug pellets, and fertilisers.

- **Make sure that your fences and gates are really secure.** You don't want your toddler getting out onto the road or into next door's garden pond.

- **Always mow the lawn alone.** With your toddler inside the house.

- **Keep your barbecue (and barbecue bits and pieces) out of reach.** And keep your toddler away from the barbecue when it's lit – and while it's cooling down (longer than you think).

- **Check the garden regularly for cat poo.** Some cat (and dog) poo can carry worms and bugs that could make your toddler ill.

- **Put swings and other play equipment on grass.** Or wood shavings. Not concrete or decking. And check the nuts and bolts regularly.

- **Keep garden sheds and greenhouses locked.** If you're buying a greenhouse, pick one made of safety glass.

- **Be careful what plants you put in your garden.** Some quite common garden plants have very prickly thorns or leaves; others are poisonous or have poisonous berries (for a list of toddler-toxic plants, download the Child Accident Prevention Trust's *How Safe Is Your Child In the Garden?* leaflet at www.capt.org.uk).

If you think that your child has eaten a poisonous plant, remove any bits left in his mouth, but don't try to make him sick. Ring your GP or NHS Direct (0845 4567) for advice; if you then go to A&E, take a sample of the plant with you.

What about other people's houses?

Obviously, you'll get some pretty odd looks (and probably lose a few friends) if you insist on doing a hands-and-knees hazard-spotting tour of every house your toddler's ever likely to set foot in. So, you need a few little stay-safe tricks up your sleeve when you go visiting. First and foremost, don't let your child out of your sight, especially if she's unfamiliar with the layout of the house you're in. It's frighteningly easy to get distracted by juicy gossip or polite chit-chat and, before you know it, your toddler is teetering at the top of the cellar stairs or trying to prise the lid off a bottle of drain cleaner. You can also

✔ **Move the trinkets.** If Granny hasn't already had the presence of mind to put her collection of miniature glass cats out of toddler reach, do it for her. Say, 'I hope you don't mind but I put your lovely cats up there – I'd hate for them to get broken while we're here.'

✔ **Be careful with older children's toys.** Some craft and construction toys for the over-3s are made up of (or break down into) dozens of tiny little pieces which toddlers do seem programmed to put in their mouth. Keep your toddler well away from them.

✔ **Have a secret stash.** Of plug covers and elastic bands. Then, if you're staying a night or more in a relative's house (or a hotel), you can quietly cover the empty socket by your toddler's bed or wind a band securely round the knobs of the cupboard full of cleaning stuff.

Houseproofing Your Toddler

All the hazard-spotting trouble you've taken and all the safety devices you've fitted will make a massive contribution towards keeping your toddler out of harm's way. But there are two other crucial toddler-safety rules you have stick to: Watch him like a hawk, and teach him some basic safety habits. The first rule's pretty self-explanatory (if exhausting in practice); the second may seem like a tall order with a toddler, but it's actually just a matter of endless repetition. So

✔ **Get with the vocab.** Start using (if you haven't already) words such as 'Ow!' and 'Hot!' often and in context. Touch your cup of tea, for example, draw back your hand in mock pain, and say, 'Hot!' And have a few stock phrases, such as 'Be careful!' ,'Don't touch!', and 'No, that hurts!', to wheel out every time your toddler gets too close to something danger-ous. The more you use them, the sooner the message will stick.

✔ **Be firm about no-go areas.** Remove him from them gently but firmly, using one of your danger phrases. Again, repetition is the key.

✔ **Show him how to carry things safely.** Which means not running! Start with plastic beakers with (a little) water in: Two hands. Move on to craft scissors: Blade in hand, (rounded) points down.

✔ **Make him a stair master.** Make it your mission to teach your child how to manage the stairs as soon as possible. Start by showing him how to slide down on his tummy (feet first). Once perfected, this is lots of fun! Then, when he can walk up stairs (hold his hand at first), practise walk-ing down with one of his hands in yours and one on the banisters. (If you don't have stairs in your house, go out and find some – at a friend's house, perhaps – and let your toddler have plenty of up-and-down time.)

✔ **Insist on tidy-up time.** The earlier you can instill the habit of clearing up one jigsaw/game/set of toys before getting out another, the better. It's amazing how many trips and falls are caused by toys left on the floor.

✔ **Make him sit down to eat.** Even if he's only having a snack. It's not just polite; it's less of a choking hazard.

✔ **Set a safe example.** Take care not to cut safety corners when you're doing stuff round the house – even if it takes longer to get things done. The best way to teach safe habits is to demonstrate them yourself.

Staying Safe on the Road

Roads are dangerous enough places for us – and we've (mostly) got the ability to think logically and judge speeds and distances accurately. Toddlers haven't. Which means we need to throw everything we've got into keeping them safe when they're out with us in the car and on the pavement.

Buckling up in the car

Your toddler is probably big enough to be out of a rearward-facing car seat by now (check the weight limit on the seat you've got). So, unless you've got a double-duty seat that can be turned round to face forward (see Chapter 30 for more about this), you'll need to buy a new forward-facing seat. These can be pricey, but most models should adjust to fit your child up to the age of 4.

Make it a habit before every car journey to check that

✔ **Your child is securely belted into his seat.** And you've adjusted the straps to make them snug.

✔ **The car's seatbelt is buckled in.** And no part of the buckle is resting on the frame of your child's seat. If it is, it could snap open in an accident.

It is illegal for a child under 3 to sit in the back or front of a car unless he's in a proper child seat. Never let any child sit in the front if your car has a passenger-side airbag.

The metal buckles on the child-seat straps can get red-hot in the summer sun. Pull your child's T-shirt well down over his tummy before you clip him in.

It's not just your buckling technique you need to master. Other in-car safety must-dos include:

- ✔ **Activating the back-door child locks:** Even if you think that your toddler can't reach to open the door yet. Those arms grow fast.

- ✔ **Having zero tolerance for strap shruggers:** Nearly all toddlers go through a phase of slipping their arms out of their straps. Make it harder for yours by always pulling the straps tight. If he does wriggle clear, stop the car (unless you're on the motorway, when stopping something else, such as your toddler's favourite music tape, is obviously safer) and say that you're not going on until his arms are back in. If it helps you sound more scarily strict, remember that, by law, every child under 3 must now be properly strapped into a child seat.

- ✔ **Never letting your child get out on the side nearest the road:** Pavement side only – and make sure that he knows why.

- ✔ **Not getting distracted:** However loud, whiney, hysterical, or horrid the noises from the back seat. Your job is to concentrate on the road. If you need to soothe a tantrum, deal with bad behaviour, or hand over food or drink, pull over and stop first.

Kerbside rules

It's never too early for your child to get streetwise. Toddlers need to know that walking along the pavement is not a walk in the park. And you need to know that you can get to the shops without bursting a blood vessel every time your child's toe gets within an inch of the kerb. So, to build up his road sense and reduce your street stress

- ✔ **Talk traffic.** Explain that the road is for cars and the pavement is for people. Show him the kerb and say that this is where you stop – always.

Play 'stop-go' games indoors. March/run/dance around together when you say 'Go!'; stand still when you say 'Stop!' Your aim? To get to the stage where you *know* that your child will always screech to a halt the moment you need him to.

- ✔ **Always use pedestrian crossings if you possibly can.** Teach your toddler about waiting for the cars to stop before walking over a zebra crossing; ask him to help you spot the green man at a pelican crossing.

- ✔ **Practise stopping at driveways.** Walk along hand in hand and ask him to tell you when you should stop. Once he's got the idea, go to a quiet street and do it again, this time without holding his hand.

✔ **Insist that your child holds your hand to cross the road.** Always. And, before you cross, have him help you look and listen for cars.

✔ **Keep kerbside of your child as you walk on the pavement.** Encourage him to walk next to you, holding onto your hand or the buggy, if the pavement is busy. If it's not, allow him to walk on his own – he'll enjoy the freedom – but stay close.

✔ **Never let him ride in the buggy if he's not strapped in.**

✔ **Be extra vigilant in car parks.** Drivers often can't see small children when they're reversing. And toddlers don't expect cars to go backwards.

You should still cross roads safely when you're not with your child. All adults are role models for children: If another child sees you nipping out between parked cars or crossing when the man's still red, you've just made life more difficult (and dangerous) for another parent.

Playing Safe

Most toddler accidents happen at home but, of course, that's not to say the world outside your door is blissfully hazard-free. Far from it. There's not exactly danger round every corner, but there are certain play places where you need to put those safety antennae of yours on maximum alert.

Toddlers move fast and can get into sticky situations even faster. Which means we parents of toddlers have to anticipate, supervise, and intervene our grown-up socks off. What we really need is eyes in the back of our head. But, until they invent those, these general safety tips should help.

✔ **Get there early.** Time your visits to the park, the playground, the pool, the soft-play centre for times when older children are at school or play-group. There'll be more room for your toddler to play in and less chance of him getting hurt by older ones' more 'energetic' play.

✔ **Go in a group.** It's tiring keeping a toddler safe and happy outdoors on your own. Meet up with other mums and watch your toddlers together.

✔ **Stand out from the crowd.** If you're heading out somewhere busy (a fair or a fun day, perhaps), dress your toddler in bright clothing and tie a brightly coloured balloon to your buggy. It'll make it easier to find each other if, shudder at the thought, either of you loses sight of the other.

For specific tips on keeping your child safe in at the pool or at the park, read on.

Danger! Don't lose your perspective

I met a mum once who had never (and would never) take her two girls to the playground – in case they fell over. Her girls had lovely ungrazed knees but were the most anxious, nervous children I've ever seen. Remember, there's a difference between being safety-conscious and being downright neurotic. Yes, dangers lurk in every house and every playspace but that doesn't mean everything is a potential death-trap. Getting over-anxious about every last thing your toddler's up to could turn him into the kind of child who's scared to try *anything*. And not only could that seriously destroy his fun and self-confidence, it could also delay his growth and development: Children need to be able to take chances and mess up and fall off and learn from their mistakes and try again. What we parents have to learn to do is to make things as safe as possible for our children – and then stand back and let them get on with it. Reducing risk is good parenting; avoiding risk is not. Hang on to your sense of perspective and keep your child safe, not stifled.

At the park

Today, public play spaces for kids are usually springy-soft underfoot and a pleasure for any parent to behold. That doesn't mean, however, you can take your eye completely off the toddler-safety ball. It's still wise to

- ✔ **Teach him playground protocol.** As in not throwing sand about, not walking in front of a moving swing, and never going down a slide until the child before him has got down and off.

- ✔ **Keep him close.** However much your toddler loves dodging about in and out of trees, don't let him race off out of your sight. If he does go haring off, hare after him – fast.

- ✔ **Be cautious around dogs.** Even the gentlest pooch can get spooked by an over-excitable child. Don't tug your toddler out of the way, though – you don't want to give her the idea that dogs are terrifying. Just quietly position yourself between child and canine as your various paths cross.

In the park with more than one child? Stick fast to the toddler. Even if it means leaving your baby in the pram for a few seconds. Even if it means taking your eyes off your preschooler for a minute. Of all the age groups, toddlers are the least predictable and the most accident-prone.

Never swing your child around by his arms, however much fun it seems to be. Or pull him along by his arms. Children's joints are loose; you could easily dislocate his shoulders or elbows.

At the pool

Toddlers love water. But they don't understand its dangers. Which explains why a child under 4 is 14 times more likely to drown in a swimming pool than be knocked down by a car. To keep safe at the pool

- ✔ **Stay super-vigilant.** Don't turn your back for a moment when you're near a pool. Never let your toddler run or play near the water's edge.

- ✔ **Get in with him.** Even with armbands and floats, no child under 3 is safe in a pool without an adult in beside him.

- ✔ **Give him 'swimming' lessons.** Your child's unlikely to learn to swim until he's at least 3, but splashing about the teaching pool with you and a qualified instructor will increase his water confidence and can teach him basic safety rules, such as holding onto the side. But never be lulled into thinking that this means your child's safe in the water. He's not.

Chapter 16

Playing, Learning, and Socialising

In This Chapter

▶ Boosting your child's language skills

▶ Finding great things for busy bodies – and hands – to do

▶ Understanding how your toddler plays (with you and with others)

Come on, this is no time to be taking it easy! You need to be up and ready for action. There's so much growing, talking, learning, and playing to pack in between the ages of 1 and 3, no toddler worth her salt's going to waste a second of it standing around doing nothing. So, get your parental skates on: Life's about to get busy, busy, busy.

Right now, your toddler's on the verge of walking and talking (or can maybe do a little of either already); in two years' time, she won't just be walking, she'll be running and jumping, and she won't just be talking, she'll be stringing all sorts of words together and asking endless questions. All this means your toddler's going to be making many mighty developmental leaps – some slowly but some so fast, they could catch you completely by surprise.

This chapter's all about encouraging those leaps – without getting pushy. And learning ways to help your child enjoy her new skills while she's working on the next ones. It's going to be full-on but it's going to be fun. You'll look back on these action-packed days later and smile – maybe with some relief that they're over, but also a twinge of sadness that they're past.

Word Up! Encouraging Language Skills

One of the really special thrills of parenting a toddler is hearing her babyish babbles become almost-words, then those almost-words become unmistakably 'proper' words, and then those proper words become an amazing stream of increasingly grammatical sentences (although, not so-thrillingly, nearly always starting with 'Why?').

Saying Daddy before she says Mummy – it's not personal

Your 1-year-old's been babbling away in seven shades of gibberish for months and then, suddenly, out of nowhere, comes that crystal-clear first word: 'Dada!' Yes, well, you can stop puffing out that proud paternal chest right now because it doesn't (necessarily) mean your toddler's expressing any parental preferences.

Every child's first word has two things in common: it's a simple sound and your toddler's been hearing it a lot. It's often 'Dada' or 'Mama' but is just as likely to be 'duck', 'no', 'look', or 'Hi!' And, whichever one your child picks, it's got far more to do with chance than planning. Sorry, Dad!

Of course, this doesn't all happen overnight; it's a gradual process (see Table 16-1 for more on this) that can often seem to slow down or even stop a fair few times along the way. And it doesn't happen at the same time for every child: Some say their first word before their first birthday; with others, you don't hear a recognisable peep until they're well past their second.

Please don't make any assumptions about the timing of your own child's first words: As with other areas of development, each child gets the hang of things in her own way and at her own pace – a pace dictated as much by her body as her brain. She may understand almost everything you say, for example, but just not have mastered her mouth and tongue muscles well enough yet to say anything comprehensible back to you. There's lots you can do to encourage her verbal skills, but you can't force her to talk before she's ready. So, don't get sucked into the competitive-parent thing: It really doesn't matter whether your toddler says 'duck' before or after anyone else's does.

Table 16-1	Your age-by-age guide to toddlerspeak	
Age	*Number of 'proper' words she can say*	*What she'd say with a yellow fruit in her hand*
12 months	1 or 2	'da da'
18 months	6 to 20	'Nana'
2 years	50 or more	'Rosie nana'
2.5 years	200 or more	'I eat nana'
3 years	1,000 or more	'I'm eating a banana'

This chart is only a guide. based on what the average child is saying at each age. If your child is saying more than this, you've nothing to worry about; if your child is saying less, she's probably just a late talker (there are plenty of them) and you've nothing to worry about, either. If your child is making little effort to communicate with you, though, or you're really worried about her speech, take her to see your GP.

The art of conversation

Whether your toddler's keeping shtoom for now or already shaping up to be a bit of a chatterbox, it's really important to keep talking to her yourself. She picks up her language skills from listening to you: The more you talk, the more new words she'll be able to learn – even if she's not ready to try them out just yet. (If you've ever learnt a new language, you'll remember how you're always able to understand way more than you can ever attempt to say.)

And it's not just her vocabulary you're developing by making the effort to talk to her; you're also teaching her important social skills. The earlier your child learns to communicate with others by listening and responding (even non-verbally), the more confident she'll be in people's company and the better she'll be able to express herself when she eventually does start to speak. And children who can communicate confidently are more likely to make friends and do well at school.

But it's not just a matter of any old natter; to make the most of your parent-toddler tête-à-têtes, try to

- ✔ **Label, label, label.** Give everything around you its proper name – often. So, rather than saying, 'Give me that,' say, 'Give me the spoon.' The more words your toddler hears, the more she'll learn.

- ✔ **Describe what's going on.** Give her a friendly running commentary on what you're doing as you do it. Tell her where you're going, who you're going to see, what you're noticing as you're walking along. And, at the end of the day, talk over all you've done. You may feel a bit daft chattering away on your own but you're not; your words are all getting stored away in that little head of hers for future use.

- ✔ **Stop and listen.** Don't forget to pause your running commentary every so often to give her space to reply.

- ✔ **Speak when you're spoken to.** Even if she's talking gibberish (or just pointing), she's trying to communicate. Reward her with a reply (though it may take you several guesses to work out what she's on about).

- ✔ **Ask questions.** Encourage her to talk to you by saying, 'Do you want a yoghurt?' or, 'Which book shall we read?' Or offer alternatives: 'Shall we play with the doll or the bricks?' Most toddlers leap at the chance to tell their parents what to do!

✔ **Keep it simple.** And clear. Give your child a chance to pick the individual words out.

✔ **Don't correct.** Toddlers often mispronounce or miss out bits of words but that doesn't mean they don't count. If she says 'gog' instead of 'dog' and you understand what she means, then she's doing brilliantly. Cue whoops of delight, not criticism.

✔ **Ditch the baby talk.** Your child speaks that way, not you. However much you love the fact that she calls a biscuit a 'git', don't start talking about 'gits' every time you get the digestives out. When she says, 'git', you say, 'Yes, biscuit.' If you don't, she'll have to learn 'biscuit' later – which is just more work for her.

✔ **Repeat and reinforce.** Once your child starts talking, repeat what she's just said with enthusiasm – and added extras. So, when she says, 'Up!', you say, 'Up? You want Mummy to pick you up? Okay, up you come!'

The sway of song

I've yet to meet a toddler who doesn't love songs. Especially ones that call for loads of clapping and dancing and jumping up and down. And, happily enough, singing songs is a great way to teach new words and reinforce familiar ones. So, dredge that memory for all the nursery rhymes and action songs you've ever heard and get those vocal cords humming. Don't worry if your voice isn't up to much: It's the actions, rhythm, and repetition of the words that matter, not your ability to hold a tune.

Why dogs are cats – and other mysteries

Come with me on a little journey into the weird and wonderful world of over- and under-extension. When toddlers start talking, they can go through a phase when they either get a tad too general about things or a tad too specific. Which can be very confusing for parents.

Let's cut to the linguistic chase. If, for example, your toddler's just learned that the animal in your kitchen with four legs and a tail is called 'cat', she may well then see a dog (animal with four legs and a tail) and say 'cat'. This is over-extension: She's generalising too much. Or, she may be perfectly able to say 'teddy', but she won't use the word for any cuddly-bear-shaped toy unless she's referring to *her* teddy. This is under-extension: She's being too specific.

So what do you do about it? Absolutely nothing. It's just a phase and it'll soon pass. Bear that firmly in mind when she opens the door to the postman and says, 'Daddy!', won't you?

If your repertoire's a bit limited and singing *Incey Wincey Spider* umpteen times a day is driving you up the spout as well, buy a tape. Better still, take your child along to a toddler singing group and let somebody else take the musical lead: You'll pick up a new tune or three and your toddler will get to jiggle and jangle a whole bunch of wonderfully noisy instruments.

The power of books

Reading rocks! Not just because it exposes your child to so many different types of language, rhythm, and sound but because it does so in such a lovely, calm, lap-snuggly kind of way. And, as your child gets older and her understanding increases, reading can give her a window both on the world around her now and on the world she's yet to see. To make the most of reading with your toddler, try to

- ✔ **Choose cool books.** The best toddler books have clear, bright, uncluttered pictures and a few, well chosen words. Pick books that focus on your child's world (the park, the zoo, the bath) or on things she's fascinated with (animals, diggers, princesses). Younger toddlers love books with flaps to lift or pop-ups to pull; older toddlers love stories with a simple plot and a strong rhyming text.

- ✔ **Get your timing right.** Younger toddlers, especially, can find it hard to sit still long enough to look properly at a book. If she starts squirming around, close the book and find something else to do. Books should mean fun, not battles over sitting still.

- ✔ **Give in to repeat requests.** Your child will want to read the same book over and over again – even if you don't!

- ✔ **Pause for thought.** Don't just read the text straight through. Stop to point out detail in the pictures ('Look at the crocodile's big teeth!') or ask questions ('Where's the train?').

- ✔ **Let her chip in.** Older toddlers will happily complete the rhyme for you if you stop short. Or tell you what they think is going to happen next.

- ✔ **Take time for a review.** Is the book about something your toddler's done or somewhere she's been? Jog her memory about it. Or maybe the story's about something she'd like to do? See what she thinks.

Watching TV: The good and the bad

Are you sitting comfortably? Then let the scaremongering begin! Read too many shock-horror headlines and you'll believe that letting your toddler watch even a minute of telly is damning her to a tragic future of childhood obesity, attention-deficit disorders, and inarticulate grunting.

It's true that some studies do link too much box-watching at an early age with all sorts of behavioural and developmental disadvantages. But it's also true is that most of these studies focus on kids who are allowed to watch anything they like on telly for hours on end – which is very different to turning on for Teletubbies once a day.

Most experts now agree that letting your toddler watch a little TV won't do her any harm at all. In fact – and this is the surprising bit – they think that it can help her improve her speaking skills and find out more about the world. As long as you don't overdo it. To box-watch clever:

✔ **Choose your programmes well.** Go for high-quality, age-appropriate stuff. For a child under 2 and a half, that means something slow-paced and repetitious (and dull as ditchwater to most adults). For an older toddler, look for something that actively involves her by asking her questions or getting her to sing along.

✔ **Watch the clock.** Limit a younger toddler to 30 minutes a day; an older one to under an hour.

✔ **Watch with her.** As often as you can. Or at least potter about nearby. So you can point things out and make what she's seeing a jumping-off point for conversation and play.

✔ **Favour videos and DVDs.** Repetition and familiarity make it easier for your child to learn from what she sees.

✔ **Turn it off when you're not watching.** Background telly-noise can distract your child from listening and talking to you.

Never put a TV in your toddler's bedroom. It means she'll watch it on her own (perhaps inappropriately), and choose it in preference to books and toys.

Ready, Steady, Go! Winning Play for Active Bodies

Toddlers are real little busy bees, never happier than when they're trundling about (at ever increasing speed), poking into this, nosing into that, turning things out of cupboards, and posting front-door keys into DVD players. And that's because their brains are absolutely abuzz with new nerve activity – growing and fine-tuning the motor circuits that control and co-ordinate the way they move (and poke and nose and wreak havoc on electrical goods).

Over the next two years, your toddler's going to master all sorts of new physical feats, from running and jumping to unzipping your purse and pocketing all your loose change. She's going to be working hard on her gross-motor skills (doctor-speak for developing better and more co-ordinated control of all her body's main muscles) and on her fine-motor skills (doctor-speak for getting better at using her hands and fingers more nimbly).

And she's going to find it all much easier if you're up for joining in, helping out, and making it tremendous fun. So, get on those trainers, and have a go at some of the ideas below. Just be sure that you always remember to

- ✔ **Avoid comparing her to others.** Repeat after me: Every toddler develops different skills at a different pace. So what if yours can't hold a pencil yet? She's probably working on standing on one leg instead. Do you really think, in 20 years' time, her job interviewers are going to quiz her on exactly when she was first able to draw a scribbly line on paper?

- ✔ **Understand her type.** When it comes to developing new physical skills, some toddlers are 'motor-driven' (as in 'Great! Let's try this now!') and some are 'motor-cautious' (as in 'I'd rather watch someone else have a go first'). You probably already know which type your child is. If she's motor-driven, you may well need to slow her down at times for her own safety (and your sanity); if she's motor-cautious, you may find she's grateful (in the end) for the odd gentle but encouraging nudge.

Measure and record your child's height on or around her second birthday. As a general rule, most people's final adult height is twice their height at 2.

Upwardly mobile: From toddling to trikes

Right, we're talking big movements here – the walking, running, twisting, turning, pushing, pulling, carrying, dancing, climbing, hopping, kicking, throwing, and jumping kind. And a toddler needs to do lots of them to boost her body confidence, improve her co-ordination, release (at least some of) her boundless energy, and explore more of the world around her. Trust me, if you don't find a way to give her plenty of space and freedom to move about like this, she'll become irritable, restless, and tantrum-prone – which isn't good news for either of you.

Five things to try outside

Like puppy dogs, toddlers need to go out for a good dose of fresh air and bounding around every day – or they start destroying the furniture. Good ideas for outdoor toddler fun include:

- ✔ **Trips to the playground:** By 2, most toddlers can go up and down slides on their own (endlessly) and love rushing round trying out the other equipment. Let her challenge herself: If she can't have a go at new things here, she may find more dangerous challenges elsewhere.

✔ **Nature trails:** Head for the woods or park and collect leaves, conkers, and funny-shaped stones. Run after squirrels and pigeons. Hide behind trees. Make mud pies. Play Pooh sticks. Come home filthy and worn out.

✔ **Water play:** Let her splash herself silly in a paddling pool in the garden (always under a watchful adult eye, of course) or throw water-drenched sponges or play 'spray-chase' with you and the garden hose. In less clement weather, chuck on your raincoats and wellies and seek out nice big puddles to jump in together.

✔ **Trikes, bikes, scooters, and buggies:** Get your smaller toddler a toy buggy to push around (yes, boys too). And then, later, when her legs can reach the pedals of a trike or balance on a toddler scooter, show her which foot to push when. Once she's got the knack, there'll be no stopping her! Do get her a helmet, though, and keep that bike or scooter in the garden and on the flat until she can steer and brake well.

✔ **Ball games:** Have loads of fun throwing, rolling, and kicking balls (yes, girls too). Show her how to hold her hands to catch a (large) ball: She probably won't be able to master this before she's 3 or 4 but she'll enjoy trying. If you don't have any balls (or they've all sailed over the neighbour's fence), try jumping over or 'tightrope-walking' a skipping rope laid out on the ground.

Toddlers can walk at a fair old lick if they put their minds to it but, a lot of the time, they prefer to dawdle – well, there are so many lorries to look at, people to wave to, and leaves to pick up and examine. If you've got an appointment to keep, start off extra early or put her in the buggy.

Five things to try inside

It's pelting with rain. Or it's one of those dank, dark winter afternoons when no one in their right mind would venture outside. But your child's climbing the walls with pent-up energy. What to do? Bring on the indoor action and

✔ **Blow up a balloon.** Perfect for a spot of indoor volleyball or football. Just remember to have a spare one to hand in case of unfortunate popping incidents. (Never leave her to play with balloons on her own: If she puts a popped one in her mouth, she can choke.)

✔ **Jump on the bed.** Good for the body, good for the soul. (But not so good for the bedsprings, I know.) Also a great way to combine changing the sheets with keeping a toddler amused (when the jumping's over, she can burrow through the pile of duvets and pillows).

✔ **Have a dance.** Put on a CD and boogie round the kitchen together.

✔ **Bring out the boxes.** Large cardboard boxes are brilliant for pushing around, crawling through, filling up with toys, and clambering into. They also make great houses, rockets, boats, and, in sufficient numbers, an instant indoor obstacle course.

✔ **Do the housework.** Seriously. Give your toddler a dry duster and get her polishing the woodwork. Or let her take it in turns with you to have a go with the vacuum cleaner or dustpan and brush. All my kids were dab hands with a vacuum at 2 – wish I could say the same now!

Make sure that your house is safe for your toddler to run around in. For more on toddlerproofing your home, see Chapter 15.

If you think that your toddler's gross-motor development is very slow – if she's not even close to walking at 18 months, for example – take her to your GP. It may well be nothing to worry about but it's worth checking out.

Fun at her fingertips: Little hands at work

The toddler years aren't just about finding out what amazing things big muscles can do; they're also about discovering what amazing things smaller muscles in fingers and hands can do. Right now, your child may have about as much dexterity as a baby seal but, come her third birthday, she'll be confidently and competently using her hands to build towers, take her clothes off, make collages, do jigsaws, even draw a big smiley picture of your face.

Some toddlers take to fine-finger play like a duck to water; others take longer to see the appeal in sitting down and doing fiddly stuff with their hands. It's partly to do with temperament and partly to do with the stage of brain development they're at – and nothing at all to do with intelligence. Either way, the more varied the opportunities you provide for your toddler to have fun with her hands, the better she'll get at using them.

Five constructive things to try

Talk to a child-development expert and you'll find that the fine-motor skills toddlers acquire at this stage centre on putting in, building up, and putting together. Talk to a parent who's been there before you and you'll find that, before you get to the putting in, building up, and putting together, you first have to get through the taking out, knocking down, and pulling apart! Don't be alarmed at these destructive tendencies; they'll lead to something constructive in the end. Especially if you

✔ **Let her pour.** Half-fill a plastic bowl with water, hand her a plastic jug and a couple of smaller plastic bowls, and let her scoop and pour the water from container to container. She'll get water everywhere at first, but it all mops us easily enough, doesn't it? If you really can't face the flood, fill the bowl with small pieces of pasta instead.

- ✔ **Bring out the jigsaws.** Start with the very simple wooden ones with cut-out shapes with knobs for her to lift out and slot back. Move on to card ones with just a few big pieces. Show her how to turn the pieces round to see if they fit. Talk about looking at the picture on the box for clues.

- ✔ **Get sorting.** Encourage her to sort her toys or the family washing into groups: cars here, dolls there; socks here, trousers there. Make the groups more complicated as her language skills progress: red ones here, yellow ones there. Or extend the sorting into a more complex game: Line up the cars in a traffic jam; sit the dolls round in a circle for 'tea'.

- ✔ **Start building.** Stack bricks (or taped-up shoeboxes) into towers for her to knock down and, later, reconstruct. Beg, borrow, or buy some Duplo or simple Lego for her to build into interesting shapes.

- ✔ **Let her strip off.** Encourage her to get herself undressed at bathtime. She'll find pulling her trousers or skirt down easier than pulling her jumper over her head: Show her how to take her arms out of the sleeves first. Once she can undress, let her have a go at getting herself dressed in the morning. Not when you're due anywhere anytime soon, though!

Don't worry if your toddler doesn't seem sure whether she's left- or right-handed. Her hand preferences won't emerge until she's at least 3.

Five creative things to try

Your toddler will enjoy any chance you give her to mess around with paints and paper and glue, but do be warned: Mess is the operative word here! Cover her with an apron, and the floor and the table with newspaper first. And don't expect your creative session to last long; to begin with at least, you'll spend longer setting up and clearing away than she spends actually creating her masterpiece. Good ideas for her first arty-crafty ventures include:

- ✔ **Drawing with chalks:** Well before your child can handle a pencil, she'll be able to wrap her fist around a chunky stick of chalk. Get in a supply of black paper and let her make colourful, sweeping swiggles.

- ✔ **Fingerpainting and stamping:** Cover her hands with paint and show her how to press her hands and fingers onto paper to make pretty prints. Cut reversed-out shapes in a potato, pile on the paint, and watch her stamp random patterns all over the place.

- ✔ **Playdough:** Great for squishy, squashy, sausage-rolling fun. As her hand-control improves, let her use cutters to make shapes. Older toddlers enjoy pressing stones, leaves, and keys into playdough to make patterns.

✔ **Cutting and sticking:** Give your toddler a glue stick (or paintbrush) and show her how to smear the glue onto paper. Then hand her some bits of shiny paper, pictures from magazines, tissue paper, foil, or string and let her get sticking. From about 2, she may be ready to try snipping the bits of paper herself with a pair of craft scissors.

✔ **Decorating cakes:** Ooh, the sticky, licky delights that can be had with a few fairy cakes, a bowl of icing, and a toddler in charge of picking and placing the dolly mixtures on top!

Got an extremely active toddler who's not keen on sitting down to paint and glue? Get a child-sized easel and let her get artistic standing up.

The Art of Play: With You, With Others

Playing is a toddler's job description. It's the way she develops and grows and figures stuff out. And has a jolly good time along the way. But she doesn't always need or want to play the same way – or with the same people.

As much as your toddler relishes playing with you, she's now reaching the age when she can also gain real pleasure from playing with others of her own age. She can also learn from playing on her own or from playing with you in a new and different kind of way.

Friends over? Time to parallel play

Watching two toddlers playing together is a strange thing – that's because they don't play *with* each other, they play *beside* each other. They may both be playing very happily with the same kind of toy, but they're each doing it in their own little private bubble.

Or that's how it seems. Actually, if you look a little closer, you'll find they are interacting – in a weird kind of way – by imitating each other in the way they handle and use their toys. It's the beginning of collaborative play and you can help it along nicely if you

✔ **Presort the toy box.** Toddlers are possessive little creatures and can't share and take turns properly yet. If the playdate's at your house, minimise the squabble risk by hiding away your toddler's most-prized toys and trying to put out two similar toys of each type (two lorries, two dolls, and so on).

> ✔ **Stay nearby.** You need to be close enough to intervene in any toy-grabbing battles or to stop any rough-and-tumble getting too rough and tumbly. Toddlers really don't do sharing, but if you need tips on finding a way through the 'Mine! No mine!' squabbles, see Chapter 19.

> ✔ **Change the pace.** Often. Break up periods of parallel play with snack-time (sitting together to eat) or a few minutes of adult-directed play (playing hide and seek, messing around with playdough).

> ✔ **Keep it short.** But don't be surprised if, five minutes before your toddler's little friend is due to go home, they both start playing together like life-long best mates.

In adult company? Time for reflective play

Let's take an average toddler-Dad play session: Dad says, 'Let's play trains!'; toddler gets excited and rushes to the train-set box; Dad starts pulling pieces of track out and fitting them together; toddler helps, under fatherly direction; Dad sets train on the tracks; Dad and toddler happily watch the train go round; end of session. Absolutely nothing wrong with that – except that it was Dad who called all the shots.

There is a different way to play it. And it can produce some amazing results. Instead of you deciding what to play, let your toddler decide. And then let her carry on dictating the pace. You just look on and, every now and then, reflect back to her a comment about what she's doing. As in: 'Oh, you're playing with the trains' or 'You're getting the track out' or 'You're putting the level crossing next to the bridge'. It feels very odd doing this (it certainly doesn't come naturally), but you'll find your toddler really blossoms under this particularly quiet but attentive parental spotlight. She'll feel important, encouraged, valued – and all because you sat back and let her run the show.

Going solo? Time for independent play

Toddlers have a lot to gain from playing on their own: It teaches them to be self-reliant and encourages them to use their imagination. And you have a lot to gain, too: The chance to spend time with another child, to get on with supper, even (whisper it) to put your feet up for a minute with a cup of tea.

Some (usually more outgoing) toddlers have no problem pottering away on their own for a while (provided you stay reasonably close by), but others do struggle a bit to entertain themselves. To help a reluctant solo performer

> ✔ **Stop being the court jester.** Spending every waking minute entertaining your toddler isn't your job. It's really not healthy for either of you.

✔ **Try some parallel play.** Need to write a letter? Sit your toddler next to you with her own paper and pencil and let her scribble while you scribe.

✔ **Prepare the material.** Fill a basket or a low cupboard with solo-play wonders: pots to bash with a wooden spoon, a tape machine to put a song tape into, a plastic tea set for make-believe tea parties.

✔ **Withdraw in stages.** Think of an activity your toddler really likes that she could do alone, if she wanted to. Start off by playing with her but not talking. The next time, get up in the middle, walk across the room, and then come straight back. Gradually, over a series of days, leave her for longer and longer and eventually try leaving the room momentarily. Always return with a cheery smile and say, 'Aren't you playing well!'

✔ **Keep talking.** Your toddler's happily playing on her own for a little while; that's not a licence to go off and ignore her completely. As you get on with whatever else you're doing, comment on what she's up to and admire what she's achieved.

Playtime over? Time to tidy up!

Make it a hard-and-fast rule in your house that your toddler has to tidy her toys away – into the right boxes – when she's finished playing with them. Not only will it help keep your house tidy and make walking through the living room less of a gamble with serious injury (if your bare feet have ever made contact with an errant Sticklebrick, you'll know what I mean), it will also make you feel ever so smug when other parents gasp in admiration. Oh, and if anyone dares to suggest you're being a trifle draconian, point out that tidying-up is teaching your toddler to identify objects and sort them into groups – both vital reasoning and decision-making skills that are an important precursor to reading. Which is true.

Making the most of toddler groups

Toddler groups are a godsend for anyone looking after a small child all day. These get-togethers are usually stuffed to the rafters with great toys and ride-ons and often have craft activities and singing sessions to take part in, too. Toddler groups are also great places to meet and chat to other parents or carers with a child the same age as yours.

Your toddler will probably get the most out of a group like this after she's turned 2. Before then, the sight and sound of so many small bodies rushing about may just be too overwhelming for her to handle. When you do start taking her, bear in mind that she'll probably find the whole experience completely exhausting the first few times; don't feel you have to stay for the whole session if she's clearly worn herself out, and don't plan to do much else for the rest of the day.

She – and you – will soon get into the swing of things, though, and you'll both probably find it a wonderful way to make new friends.

Part IV
All About Preschoolers

"Well, he may be clever at building things but when is he going to start using the potty?"

In this part . . .

How do you choose the right preschool? You'll find all you need to know in Chapter 20, including the signs to look for, the questions to ask and a guide to settling your child in. And there's more! This part also covers all the other aspects of parenting a preschooler, from handling strops and fussy eating to chasing away monsters from under the bed. And there's a whole chapter on clever and imaginative ways to play – either just the two of you or taking turns (yes, really!) with friends.

Chapter 17

Behaviour and Discipline

. . . .

In This Chapter

▶ Getting to grips with stubbornness, rebellion, whining, and 'poo-poo' talk

▶ Understanding key discipline do's and don'ts

▶ Teaching nice manners and great life values

. . . .

So, you made it through the terrible 2s? Brace yourself for the tricky 3s and the thorny 4s! No, it's not going to get worse, exactly; just different.

Preschoolers are enormous fun but they're no angels. (As you'll find out pretty quickly when things aren't going your child's way.) They may not go in for the full, flailing-leg toddler strop quite so much any more, but they waste no time acquiring a whole new repertoire of bad-behaviour tactics to try our patience with instead.

So, gather round for your preschooler-grade top-up dose of extra-long-lasting resilience, serenity, and fortitude. It comes with its own set of neat ideas for dealing with naughtiness, nastiness, and downright disobedience. And, because it's you, I'll throw in some very cool tips on teaching your child to behave nicely, generously, and respectfully towards others. You never know; you may turn out to have an angel after all!

Warning! Tough Times Ahead!

There's no point beating round the bush here: You're not going to make it through the preschool years without finding your child something of a parenting challenge. Not all the time, mind, but you'll have moments – maybe even a long series of moments – when his behaviour becomes so contrary and disagreeable, you'll wonder if you can find the strength, calm, and consistency to deal with it properly.

It's partly because it's all new – curtain-up time on whining, for example, as well as interrupting, name-calling, and point-blank refusals to co-operate. And partly because he can sustain acting up for so long – goodbye quick-flash toddler tantrum; hello slow-burn brat attack. So, before you plunge in and try to sort it all out, it's worth taking time to understand what on earth is going on inside his head.

Why little darlings act like little demons

The journey from 3 to 5 is quite an emotional rollercoaster ride. Your child is much less impulsive than he used to be and much more articulate. But, although he can now argue, debate, and challenge till the cows come home, he hasn't yet acquired the emotional maturity to express his feelings clearly and logically or to understand how other people may be feeling.

And then there's the independence thing. He wants to have more of it, which can make him shockingly wilful and rebellious. But the reality of actually trying to deal with stuff on his own can overwhelm him with anxiety and fear.

Your preschooler is, essentially, an emotional work in progress. And a pretty fragile one at that. So, as upsetting as it is to see him behave so dreadfully at times, try to remember that he isn't doing any of this deliberately to annoy you. He's not being malicious; he's being normal. Which means

- ✔ **He could be going through a difficult patch.** Experts have identified the age of 3-and-a-half as a particularly trying time for many parents. At this age, your child's likely to be reaching his apogee of stubbornness and inflexibility, but he's also maxing out on the uncertain, unsettled, and insecure front. It all makes for a rather combative combination.

- ✔ **He's learning to reason.** But not, alas, to be reasonable.

- ✔ **He wants to decide for himself.** Which just isn't possible all the time – let alone sensible.

- ✔ **He thinks that the world revolves around him.** And egocentrics find the concepts of waiting, sharing, and taking turns very odd indeed.

- ✔ **He's strong-willed.** But essentially powerless in an adult world. How frustrating is that?

- ✔ **He's testing limits.** To find out who he is and what he can do. And who's going to have to set – and maintain – those limits? You.

- ✔ **He's ultra-curious.** Which may mean he takes your alarm clock apart. He's not doing it to provoke you; he's doing it to see what happens.

✔ **He's overwhelmed.** He may not be a toddler any more, but he can still easily lose the plot if he's tired, hungry, scared, or frustrated.

✔ **He's picking up ideas elsewhere.** Friends are becoming an increasing influence. So, if little Johnny at preschool is always shouting, 'Poohead!' chances are your child will treat you to some copycat renditions at home.

Great expectations? Lower them now!

There is another major cause of parent-preschooler conflict: us. Now that our children have reached an age where they can manage simple tasks and obey instructions, we sometimes expect them to do more than they're actually capable of – and then we assume they're misbehaving when they aren't.

Just because your child can hang up his coat on a peg, for example, it doesn't follow that he will remember to do it every time he comes in (his memory and organisational skills may not be up to that yet). Or just because he can feed himself, it doesn't mean he won't spray peas on the floor or spill sauce down his front (his hand-eye co-ordination may not be good enough yet).

It helps to remember that, just as it's normal for your preschooler to be all over the place emotionally at times, it's also normal for him to make mistakes or be inconsistent. And, although it's your job to make it clear what kind of behaviour is okay and what's not, you don't have to make a major issue out of every single mess-up. Save your energy for the stuff that really matters.

Managing Behaviour

Understanding why your child's acting up is one thing; knowing how to deal with it is quite another. And, it has to be said, there is no magic, one-size-fits-all discipline solution. But there *are* a whole range of great tactics to work into your parenting repertoire – and a whole range of not-so-great tactics to avoid. The following sections tell you what you need to know.

Tactics that work

Here, in no particular order, are my tried-and-tested peace-restoring ploys. Some of them will work better on your child than others, and some of them work will better in certain situations than others. But do read them all: It's well worth having as many options as possible at your discipline disposal.

Redirect him

Often (and this applies to younger preschoolers especially), the problem's not what he's doing but how he's doing it. So he fancies doing some drawing? Fine. But he's standing over your open address book with felt tips poised. Not fine. Resist the urge to hit the roof. Just calmly remove the address book, give him some paper, and say, 'My address book's not for drawing on. Draw on this instead.' Major parent-preschooler clash averted.

Offer choices

Your preschooler's desperate to make his own decisions, which means he'll bridle and baulk at many of your decisions. So, instead of creating long, stressful standoffs over silly, everyday things, give him the decision-making upper hand – in a sneaky Mum-wins-either-way deal. Rather than saying, 'Put your socks on!' and getting a stroppy 'No!' in reply, say, 'Which socks do you want to wear today? The blue ones or the red ones?' Result: happy parent, happy child (with socks on).

Put on an 'Am I bovvered?' face

Sometimes, the best reaction is no reaction. Ignoring bad behaviour is amazingly effective – what's the point of acting up without an audience, after all? Be warned, though: Ignoring bad behaviour can be incredibly hard – especially if the bad behaviour in question involves your child shouting, 'I hate you, Dad!' The only way through it is to put on an act of supreme detachment. Calmly say 'Really? I *love* you,' and then carry on with whatever it is you're doing. Sometimes, imagining you're not Dad but some other sensible adult helps: This way, you're more likely to see the behaviour for what it is – attention-seeking – rather than a personal attack on you.

Be firm and calm

This one couldn't be simpler. It's all about looking – and sounding – like you mean business. When you're clear about what you want him to do and firm about the way you say it, your child will usually comply. Without you even raising your voice. So, don't stand wimpishly at the top of the stairs saying, 'Shall we have a bath then, darling?'. Go right up to him, look him in the eyes, and say, 'Time for your bath!' Cue preschooler ascending bathwards.

Help him put it into words

Preschoolers aren't very good at expressing how they feel, which means they often revert to showing you in other, more destructive ways. Next time your child starts stamping his feet, acknowledge his feelings: 'You seem really cross.' And help him to see there is another way to let you know about it. 'Next time, just tell me you're cross and I'll try to help.'

Create a diversion

An oldie but a goodie, this is just the tactic to wheel out to stop a stubborn preschooler digging in for the long-haul protest. And humour should nearly always be your weapon of choice: Sing a nursery rhyme with the wrong words ('Twinkle, twinkle, chocolate bar'); say that you're going to tell him an important secret, then scoop him up and whisper in his ear, 'You're my very special boy!' (a good way to get bolshy children into car seats, this); put his hat on your head and pull a puzzled face; have a race with him to see who can get whatever it is you want him to do done first; drop to all fours and pretend to be a cat. Oh, and when in doubt, tickle.

Get the stickers out

This is the age when the reward chart comes into its own. Say your child clamps his mouth shut the moment you want him to brush his teeth. Stick up a sheet of A4 in the bathroom and tell him that every time he brushes his teeth (or has them brushed) without fuss, he can put a gold-star sticker on the chart. And when he's got six/eight/ten stars, you'll take him to the aquarium/on a picnic/to the shop that sells Batman pyjamas. All should go tooth-sparklingly well as long as you

- ✔ **Keep it simple.** Only tackle one issue at a time. Reward charts with several columns, multiple conditions, and umpteen behaviours to 'fix' are confusing, daunting, and demoralising.

- ✔ **Keep it achievable.** Don't make the treat contingent on 50 consecutive stickers: Your child needs to be able to scent success soon.

Suggest better options

It's always possible that your preschooler doesn't actually understand what he's doing wrong. Or, even if he does, he hasn't a clue how to do it right. Help him out. If he's screeching for attention, say, 'It's not okay to scream. I'd love to hear what you've got to say but you have to talk quietly.' With an older preschooler, encourage him to work out the solution himself: 'It's not okay to yell "More!" at me. Can you think of a better way to ask me?'

Declare a time out

If your child's behaviour has escalated to a point where he's losing control, you need to take decisive action to help him get a grip again. And, at this age, a period of 'time out' can do this very effectively. Simply take him to a step or some other dull-as-ditchwater part of your house and tell him firmly that he's going to be staying there for a time out until he calms down. Then walk away. (The beauty of this tactic is that it gives you valuable time to calm down, too.) To make time out work for your child, you need to

- ✔ **Give him clear warning.** Along the lines of, 'If you do that again, we'll have to have a time out.'

- ✔ **Make sure that he knows why he's there.** When you put him in time out, tell him exactly what he's done wrong. 'I'm putting you in time out because you hit your sister. Hitting is not okay.'

- ✔ **Never leave him too long.** For a younger preschooler, a couple of minutes is about right. Older preschoolers often respond well to deciding for themselves: 'I want you to think about what you've done. When you are ready to come back and play nicely, let me know.'

- ✔ **Always follow up.** When the time out's up, clearly explain (again) what it was all about. 'I'm glad you're ready to play again. No more hitting, okay?' Then let it go.

- ✔ **Use it sparingly.** If you impose time out for everything from playing with his food to picking his nose, it will lose its impact. Remember, time out's a last-resort cool-down technique, not a punishment.

Impose consequences

Your child is old enough now to learn that if he steps over the limit, there'll be consequences. That if he keeps throwing his food on the floor, for example, his plate will be taken away. That if he doesn't put his dirty clothes in the washing basket, they won't get washed. That if he keeps throwing sand in other children's faces, he'll have to leave the playground.

The key here is to make sure that your child realises he has a choice: Stop the bad behaviour or suffer the consequences. Make sure that he understands exactly what the bad behaviour is and what the consequences will be. And then, if he chooses not to stop, calmly let (or make) them happen. It's a great way to get over the concept that we're all accountable for our own actions; children who don't face consequences for their actions can all too easily become spoiled, inconsiderate, insecure adults.

Watch your language

One of the latest buzz-phrases being bandied about by parenting experts is 'accentuate the positive'. They mean we should stop barking negative, critical commands at our children and focus instead on only using positive words of instruction. We should be telling our children what to do, not what *not* to do.

In this way, 'Stop running!' becomes 'Slow down and walk', and 'Stop shouting!' becomes 'Use your quiet voice'. It may all sound dreadfully PC but, actually, I think it's got a lot going for it. And maybe not entirely for the reasons the experts put forward. Yes, kids do respond better to positive words than negative ones, but using them also makes a difference to us parents, too.

Having to stop and think of a positive spin to put on your negative reaction gives you time to bite back the instinctive irritation in your voice – and sound award-winningly calm. And saying nice, clear, positive stuff, instead of dishing out constant criticism, makes you feel good about yourself, good about your kids, and ever so wonderfully in control. Try it and see.

Younger preschoolers can get very absorbed in play and find it very difficult to change from one activity to another. To avoid breakdowns, give them a series of clear signals that change is afoot. So, 'Five more minutes in the playground, then we're going home,' then, 'Three more minutes,' and so on.

And don't forget to notice the good stuff!

We all get so concerned with what our children are doing wrong (and how we're going to deal with it) that we can forget to notice when they're doing it right. And that means we're missing a trick – because one of the most effective way of stopping bad behaviour is praising good behaviour. You really can make the good moments last longer by acknowledging them more.

Don't underestimate the positive effect your praise can have on your child. As well as encouraging him to carry on behaving well in future, it will also boost his desire to learn, to believe in himself, and to stand on his own two feet.

The best way to praise? Make it really specific. So, rather than a vague, 'You played well with Lucy,' get in there with a more detailed, 'I really liked the way you shared your toys with Lucy today. Well done!'

Tactics that can backfire – and why

Just as important as knowing the tactics that work is knowing the tactics that don't. Otherwise, you may start off down the wrong discipline track and wind up making everything ten times worse. So, dump the following misguided strategies in your parenting wastebasket right now.

Reasoned debate

Preschoolers do debating, but they don't do reason. So there is absolutely no point getting into long discussions about the pros and cons of putting spaghetti in your hair (or whatever other mischief your child is currently up to). It doesn't matter how much detail you go into about table manners, food waste, and basic haircare, your child will still counter with 'But why?' every time you pause for breath. Save yourself stress – and shampooing time – by saying firmly, 'Because I say so.' You're the one in charge, remember?

Shouting

We all feel the urge to shout at times but doing so's really not a good idea – for lots of reasons. First, it means you're out of control and an out-of-control parent stands almost no chance of restoring a general air of peace and calm. Then, there's the fact that shouting doesn't work. Oh, it may stun your child into submission the first few times you shout, but that won't last. Shouting all the time will either turn your child into a timid little mouse (not great) or, more likely, a little ball of fury who shouts back (*definitely* not great). If you want to raise a co-operative, enthusiastic child, keep the decibels down.

None of us is perfect. We all lose the plot and shout sometimes. But shouting once in a while, when you're at the end of your tether, is very different from shouting all the time, even at the smallest thing. If you do lose it, don't beat yourself up about it. Apologise to your child and move on.

Threats you don't follow through on

There's a big difference between pointing out consequences (see the 'Impose consequences' section, earlier in this chapter) and issuing empty threats. If you tell your child that something will happen if he doesn't stop doing what he's doing, then you must be prepared to make it happen. So, saying, 'Do that again and we won't go on holiday!' isn't a good idea if you've already bought the plane tickets and booked the hotel. All it will teach your child is that you don't mean what you say – so why should he bother listening?

'Wait till your father gets home!'

The longer your child has to wait to see the consequences of his bad behaviour, the harder he'll find it to link the two together. Make sure that the consequences happen pretty darn pronto. So, no bedtime story may be a very clear and logical consequence of acting up at bathtime, but won't really cut it as a consequence of throwing breakfast cereal at one's brother.

Five patented parent wind-ups – and how not to let them get to you

There is bad behaviour and then there is *bad* behaviour – the kind of thing that makes you wonder how you and your partner's perfectly nice DNA could ever have combined to create such a maddening little monster.

The key, sanity-saving thought to hang on to here is that the things that wind you up most are almost certainly winding up the parents of every other preschooler in the country. Practically every child of this age tries out the same handful of hideous behaviours to see how effective they are at getting him what he wants. Your job is to make it very clear that they're not effective and they never get him what he wants – and then he'll give up trying.

Easy if you know how, you're thinking? Okay then, here's how:

  ✔ **Wind-up one: The manipulative tantrum.** This is the toddler tantrum taken to a whole new level. Your child has learnt – because you've given into this kind of behaviour before – that screaming at the top of his voice or bursting into floods of tears will rapidly ensure that he gets his own way. So, the moment you say no about anything, however trivial, he trots out the histrionics. He may not even be that upset; he just knows it pays to look that way. Top tactic? Ignore the dramatics and stand your ground. The tantrums will stop when they no longer get results.

✔ **Wind-up two: Whining.** Some preschoolers perfect a whining voice so grating it'd try the patience of a saint. And that's the idea: Soon, you'll become so irritated by the perpetual whinge in the background that you'll give in just for a quieter life. Top tactic? Start with diversion. If that doesn't work, either ignore the whining completely till it stops, or say, 'I can't hear you when you talk in that whiney voice. I'll listen if you talk in a nice voice.' If you choose the second option and he does change his tone, don't just say no automatically; make a show of listening carefully and considering his request.

✔ **Wind-up three: Interrupting.** You're on the phone or talking to a friend and your child's constantly pulling at your sleeve and speaking to you. He's being extremely annoying but not deliberately so: Your attention is distracted and he wants it back. Top tactic? Patient education. Show him how to touch your arm as a 'secret sign' that he wants to talk to you and say that you'll touch his hand back to tell him you know that he's waiting (the first few times he does this, give him your attention almost straightaway, so he sees how well it works). Stop your conversation frequently to praise him for being so quiet. Suggest he thinks about what he'd like to do after you've finished.

If your child often interrupts when you're on the phone, he may think that you're free when you stop talking. To help him understand that phone calls are about listening as well as speaking, let him use the phone every now and then (when Granny calls, for example).

✔ **Wind-up four: 'Poo-poo' talk.** Preschoolers inevitably hear other preschoolers using 'potty language' and speaking in silly voices and then they try some of it out at home to see what they can get away with. Initially at least, talking this way is more about trying to assert their independence ('Look what I know!') than trying to be rude (they may not even know that it is). Top tactic? Don't overreact. If you do, your child will learn that these words have parent-shock value and he can use them again to get your attention. Either ignore it completely or, if your child is name-calling a sibling or friend, explain that it's not a nice word to call someone and ask him to say sorry. Then create a fascinating diversion.

✔ **Wind-up five: Defiance.** You ask your child to tidy up his toys and he shouts, 'No!' It's enough to make any parent see red. Top tactic? Keep your cool. Don't argue, plead, or bargain. Let him know that you understand that he doesn't want to do it but that it still needs to be done. Then take him by the hand and say, 'Come on, let's do it together!'

Teaching Please, Thank You, and Other Good Manners

We don't just want our kids to be well-behaved, we want them to be polite, too. Not just because it would give us a smug-parent glow (although that's always nice) but also because having good manners helps your child mix well with other people (big and small) and teaches him respect for their feelings.

Trouble is, learning to mind all those Ps and Qs can take a very long time (they shouldn't be called Ps and Qs, really; there are so many of them, you need the whole alphabet). So the sooner – and the simpler – you start on manners, the better. Skip the finer points of napkin-folding for now and try to

- **Believe in magic words.** Tell your child that 'Please' and 'Thank you' are magic words that make people smile and want to be nice to you. Demonstrate how to use them in context. If he forgets (and he will, frequently), say, 'What's the magic word?' and look delighted when he gets the right answer.

- **Explain obvious stuff.** Like why chewing with his mouth open is horrible for others to watch. Or why talking with his mouth full makes him impossible to understand. When there's a reason for a rule, it's easier to remember it.

- **Practise meeting and greeting.** He may be able to say 'Hello' but it's no good if he just stares at the floor and mumbles it. Teach him to look people in the eye and smile as he says it.

- **Introduce him to Big Voice/Little Voice.** He needs to know that there are some places where it's okay to be loud and others where it's not. When you're off somewhere, tell him if it's a Big Voice or a Little Voice place. You'll probably need to remind him when you get there, too!

- **Ask him to say, 'Sorry'.** Even if you suspect he isn't really. And even if it was a genuine accident. He may not be old enough to feel contrite about his every misdeed, but he is old enough to learn that there is a social protocol about these things. (For tips on encouraging empathy and making amends, see 'Instilling Values', later in this chapter.)

- **Don't expect too much.** Particularly at mealtimes. With so many table manners to remember, it'll take him a while to get them all down pat. Most children don't even get close until they're about 6.

- **Praise like crazy.** When he does mind his manners. Or indeed when your partner does in front of him. Say something like, 'Because you said please so nicely, Mummy, *of course* I'll make you a cup of tea.' Your flappy-eared preschooler will lap it all up.

It's no good expecting good manners from your child if you're a bit lacking in that department yourself. This is the time for all parents to go into exemplary please-thank-you overdrive.

Instilling Values: Five to Teach Your Child by the Age of 5

I know, I know, I've just spent the best part of a chapter telling you that your preschooler isn't up to anything too complex on the emotional front, and now I'm talking life principles! But what I'm getting at here is the idea that, if you create the right home environment, your child can start absorbing the essence of key values long before he can articulate the concepts behind them.

And because all five of the values below lie at the core of successful socialising, cultivating them in your preschooler means you're giving him a leg-up to a friend-filled future – as well as starting to teach him some of the most important lessons he'll ever learn about life.

- ✔ **Justice:** This is all about encouraging your child to put things right when he's done something wrong. It's about more than saying sorry (although that little word's also important; see 'Teaching Please, Thank You, and Other Good Manners', earlier in this chapter); it's about *showing* that he's sorry. So, if your child squashes his friend's playdough creation, he should apologise – and then you can help him make amends by rolling out some more playdough for his friend to start over with.

- ✔ **Honesty:** Kids don't get deceitful before the age of 6. Until then, they're quite transparent in their dishonesty: They may fib to dodge the blame but they do it very badly. And this is your window of opportunity: Get the message over now that telling the truth gets more reward than hiding it, and you'll be told fewer porkies in the future. So, when your child fibs, help him fess up: 'I don't think that's true. Why don't you tell me what really happened?' And when he does, praise his honesty and make a big point of reducing the severity of the consequence you were going to impose for the original misbehaviour.

- ✔ **Self-esteem:** So he wants to make a rocket out of cereal packets? Show faith in your child's ideas and abilities, even if you know that he's going to need a helping hand. The child who's willing to try, who knows he won't be judged if he fails, is the child with the confidence to handle most of the challenges life throws at him.

- ✔ **Empathy:** Under-5s find it hard to put themselves in other people's shoes, but that doesn't mean they can't start to learn the value of being considerate. Use opportunities, such as lending a friend a book or giving an elderly neighbour a hand with her shopping, to talk to your child about being helpful and kind, and how being nice to people makes people be nice to you back. Help him link actions and feelings by talking about things that make you sad or happy. If your child does or says something unkind, ask him how he would feel if someone did or said that to him. See if he can come up with ways he could have acted differently. One day, he'll amaze you with his thoughtfulness.

✔ **Love:** Nice and simple, this one. The more you fill your child's house with smiles, loving words, and affectionate gestures – towards him and towards other key people in his life – the freer he'll feel to express his love to others. And that, perhaps, is the most valuable life lesson of all.

Chapter 18

Food Fights and Sleep Frights

In This Chapter

▶ Playing it cool when eating gets faddy

▶ Making food fun

▶ Chasing off monsters and other sleep-stealers

*Y*ou can lead a preschooler to bed and table, but you can't make her sleep and eat. It's not that she's not up to it physically: She's perfectly capable of managing both on her own quite nicely, thank you. It's just that her mind keeps getting in the way – and making it all so much more difficult.

And what's to blame? Nasty thoughts. Either popping up in her dreams or directed at what's on her plate. Cue your brand-new role as nasty-thought de-programmer and happy-thought re-adjuster. Don't worry: It's not nearly as hard as it sounds. And this chapter will make it even easier.

The Picky Eaters' Club

You've probably already been introduced to the weird and whimsical world of faddy eating – many toddlers are only too delighted to give you an extended tour (see Chapter 14). But preschoolers can, alas, do faddy *with attitude*. Combine a wilful preschooler personality with an increasing repertoire of 'Yuk!'-related words and it doesn't bode well for stress-free mealtimes. Unless, of course, there's a sort-it-all strategy you prepared a little earlier.

Getting the nutritional facts straight

Over the next two or three years, your preschooler's appearance will probably change quite dramatically. And that's because she's losing her 'baby fat' – the trademark big tummy and chubby thighs of infancy and toddlerhood. But – and this is important – there's a big difference between changing and growing. And she's still only growing relatively slowly. Which means her calorie needs may not be as big as you think.

Preschoolers only need about 1,200 to 1,800 calories a day, depending on their age and activity levels. That total's a little more than a toddler but fewer than the average adult. And at least partly explains why we think that preschoolers are such picky eaters – we're judging them by our needs, not theirs.

You also need to know that

- ✔ **She needs good amounts of fat and protein.** Preschoolers don't just need a different number of calories to adults; they need them in different forms. Your child may be eating less than you but she needs proportionately more fat and more protein in her diet than you do.

- ✔ **She needs variety and balance in her diet.** Every day, aim for six servings of grains and potatoes (including cereal, pasta, rice, and bread), five servings of fruit and vegetables, two to three servings of calcium-rich products (including milk, cheese, yoghurt), and two servings of protein-rich food (including red meat, chicken, fish, eggs, lentils, beans).

- ✔ **Her appetite varies.** Depending on whether she's cold or hot, well or ill, full of beans or worn out, in a good mood or a bad one. Try not to fret.

- ✔ **She needs (healthy) snacks.** Her tummy is still too small for her to be able to eat enough on three meals a day.

- ✔ **Hunger can affect her behaviour.** You can eat when you're peckish; she has to wait for your say-so. Watch for the signs (sudden grumpiness or tearfulness for no apparent reason) and offer a blood-sugar-boosting snack, such as a banana or a piece of cheese.

- ✔ **Her tastes are expanding.** Which means she may be willing to try food she's refused in the past. But don't bet on it!

- ✔ **She's open to influence.** Your eating habits are no longer the only ones she notices. She's now picking up ideas and opinions from her friends, from TV ads, and maybe even from food packaging.

Look after her teeth by restricting fizzy drinks and making sure that she brushes properly twice a day. For more tooth-protection tips, see Chapter 14.

Eat up! Feeding fads that drive you mad

Now you know how it's all supposed to be, let's move on to tackling how it all too often actually is. Preschoolers, I'm sorry to say, do an exasperatingly effective line in parent-baiting food fads. Here's a rundown of the most common – and most annoying – ones, with tips on how to counter them with admirable composure (even if you're silently screaming inside).

The hunger striker

She picks at her food like a bird. You can't remember the last time she ate everything on her plate. And, some days, she hardly eats a thing. You're at your wits' end and worried that she's not eating enough to stay healthy.

Parent ploy? Pretend not to notice. And certainly don't say anything out loud. Either your child's not very hungry (and there can be umpteen different reasons for that), or she's starting to see not eating as a very effective way to get your attention. Making this into a big issue is going to backfire, either way. Take reassurance from studies showing that, at this age, most poor eaters do, in fact, take in enough of the nutrients they need to stay healthy. And few preschoolers will stage a proper, all-out hunger strike for more than a couple of days. Make it easier for her to eat more by stressing out less.

Try putting a lot less food on her plate. It may make mealtimes seem less daunting for her. For other subtle ways to encourage poor eaters, see the section 'Ten ace appetite-boosting ideas', later in this chapter.

Don't forget that if your child's eating a good lunch at playgroup or preschool, she may well not want much at supper.

The creature of habit

All she wants for lunch is Marmite sandwiches. All she wants for dinner is pasta and cheese. Or maybe, on a very adventurous day, pasta and butter and cheese. Any food stuff that doesn't feature on her meagre list of favourites is greeted with howls of protest and a face so sour it would embarrass a lemon.

Parent ploy? Meet her halfway. Remember that your preschooler likes structure and familiarity. She's also dead keen to assert her independence. And that's what's behind all this. So, serve up her favourites (you know that she'll eat them, after all) with a spoonful/slice of something else on the side. Encourage her to take a 'no thank you' bite of the 'yuk stuff' – and pile on the praise if she does.

Determined to dish up something new? Invite some of her friends round for tea. If she sees her friends tucking in, she may well be tempted to follow suit.

The green grosser

She eats well enough – as long as the stuff on her plate isn't green and good for her. Forget five a day; you're lucky if you score five fruit-or-veg portions a week.

Parent ploy? Don't give up. A child can take up to ten tastings to accept a food – and, if my kids are anything to go by, considerably more if it's a member of the cabbage family. Keep serving up the veg with each meal and encouraging her to take a 'no thank you bite' (it may turn into a whole mouthful one day). Fruit, being sweeter, is generally less of a problem, but you can certainly up her intake by serving it with ice cream or in smoothies. For other ways to make fruit-and-veg more appealing, see 'Ten ace appetite-boosting ideas', later in this chapter.

The hamster

She's not eating much. You beg/cajole/order her to eat another mouthful. She does and you rejoice. But then a large bulge appears in her cheeks. She's stowed the offending morsels there until she gets the chance to spit them out.

Parent ploy? Stop the begging/cajoling/ordering thing. The fact that your child's already playing games with you over food is proof enough that this tactic is not working. And things will only get worse if you carry on. Just grit those teeth and, however little she eats, take her plate away without comment.

The squish-and-poker

You give her a sandwich and she peels off the top layer of bread and prods and sniffs the filling. You give her peas or cherry tomatoes and she squishes them into the plate with the back of her spoon. One by one.

Parent ploy? Ignore it. She's not doing anything any other preschooler wouldn't do – children this age are an inquisitive lot, and squishing, prodding, and poking food is all part of the package. In fact, it's exactly this kind of curiosity that can help her get up the nerve to taste and enjoy a whole range of new foods.

The crusts-off queen

She'll eat toast but only with the crusts off. She'll drink milk but only from the pink cup. She'll eat spaghetti with tomato sauce but only if the spaghetti and the sauce aren't actually touching each other.

Parent ploy? Take a deep breath! And tolerate her little idiosyncrasies as much as you can (obviously, if the pink cup's in the dishwasher, she'll have to have the green one). This kind of behaviour is normal at her age and is usually fairly short-lived. But do teach her how to make her requests politely: 'Please can you cut the crusts off?' gets the bread knife out but 'No crusts!' certainly doesn't.

The dawdler

She takes half an hour to eat a tiny pot of fromage frais. She pushes her food around the plate with her fork for ages before it gets anywhere near her mouth. Frankly, if you need to get anywhere after lunch, you have to dish it up at breakfast-time.

Parent ploy? Bring the curtain down. By having some kind of time limit on meals: 20 minutes is probably more than long enough. But do try to figure out what's behind the dawdling: Some preschoolers are just plain slow eaters; some find it hard to feed themselves when they're tired; others only start the go-slow when they've eaten enough to take the edge of their hunger and have lost interest. For everyone but the naturally slow eaters, you can usually speed meals up very effectively by having a 'beat-the-egg-timer' race.

Try not to get cross if your preschooler suddenly rejects one of her favourite foods because 'Sally at playgroup says it's yuk'. Yes, it's annoying that her friend's putting her off, but it can work the other way round, too. Who knows, she may come home from tea at Sally's one day and tell you, 'We had liver and courgettes, Dad, and it was really yummy!'

Food mistakes even good parents make

We all want our kids to eat well and grow up with healthy food habits. But that's not always easy. Because it's not just about choosing and cooking the right food, it's also about instilling the right kind of attitude towards food. And many of us adults haven't sorted that one out for ourselves yet. So, as well as understanding the food do's, try to get to grips with these don'ts:

- ✔ **Don't give her adult portions.** They're too big for her. A preschooler portion is one-half to three-quarters the size of an adult portion.

- ✔ **Don't force/coax/bargain/plead.** Every time you feel the urge to coax another runner bean into her mouth, remind yourself that studies show the more children are forced to eat a certain food, the less likely they are to eat it next time. Either she eats the bean or she doesn't. End of story.

- ✔ **Don't overdo the snacks.** Snacks are small, (preferably) healthy, and a way of keeping her energy levels stoked up between meals. They're not a chance for her to cram in a zillion sugary calories to make up for not eating her breakfast/lunch/supper.

- ✔ **Don't forget to lead by example.** If she only ever sees you eating crisps, she's hardly likely to ask for an apple, is she? And don't talk about your weight worries, either. She's picky enough without you implanting the idea that eating can make you unhappy with your body.

- ✔ **Don't overdo the juice.** Even the healthiest 100 per cent fruit juices can damage her teeth and kill her appetite, if you give her more than 150 ml a day. Limit juice to meals, and offer milk or water the rest of the time.

- ✔ **Don't make her clean her plate.** Because it's important that she's allowed to respond to her body's 'I'm full' signal. Psychologists have found that people who were made to finish their meals as children are more likely to be overweight as adults.

✔ **Don't use food as a reward.** Eating should be a response to hunger, not to good behaviour or emotional upset.

✔ **Don't ban 'bad' foods.** Which adults most crave junk food, sweets, cakes, and chocolate? Yup, the ones who weren't allowed to eat them when they were little.

✔ **Don't eat in front of the TV.** A TV supper is okay for a treat once in a while but mealtimes should really be sociable events – a time for talking and tasting, not box-watching. There's also increasing evidence that routinely eating in front of the telly can raise a child's risk of obesity.

✔ **Don't worry too much.** Your child really doesn't have to be a model of nutritional perfection. If she eats healthily 80 per cent of the time, you're doing very well indeed.

Ten ace appetite-boosting ideas

You've probably had your fill of food fads and food fights by now. So, here comes the bit where you make food fun! The more your child associates food with having a good time, the more likely she is to tuck in with gusto. It's not exactly rocket science, but it does call for a little creative thinking. So, switch that brain into resourceful mode and

✔ **Take her shopping.** If she's helped buy the food, she'll feel proud and excited about it. Don't panic: You don't have to hit the supermarket with her if she's still a child of the tantrum-throwing-in-the-trolley variety. Pop out with her to the local shops instead. Ask her to help you sort out the shopping list: She can check the fridge ('Have we got enough milk?') while you write, or she can make a list of her own with drawings instead of words. Then let her hold the list and be 'in charge' of reminding you what to get.

✔ **Get her gardening.** It's amazing how many children get turned on to fruit and veg when they've had a hand in growing it. We've been a tomato-loving family ever since the summer we stuck a few tomato plants in a growbag on our patio – the kids took it in turns to water them and squealed when they spotted a tomato that was red enough to pick. If you haven't got a garden, take your child to a pick-your-own and spend an hour or two collecting (and gobbling) juicy fresh strawberries from the fields.

✔ **Let her cook.** She'll be keen to taste anything she's had a hand in making. A 3-year-old can break eggs, spoon in sugar or flour, tear up lettuce leaves, and wash vegetables. Older preschoolers can make their own sandwiches, as long as you slice the bread first.

✔ **Keep her active.** Nothing makes you more ravenous than running your parents ragged round the park all day.

✔ **Make her the menu-planner.** Draw up a big list of meals she (quite) likes and let her choose which ones she's going to have on which days. Stick the finished plan up on the wall for all to see.

✔ **Talk about what different foods can do for her.** But skip the nutritional lingo and keep the explanation nice and simple. Tell her how bread, pasta, and potatoes give her bounce, how fruit and veg can stop her getting ill, how meat and fish make her strong, how milk, cheese, and yoghurt help her bones and teeth grow.

✔ **Eat with her.** Often. Not only will she see you tucking into the same food as her, she'll also come to associate mealtimes with social fun.

✔ **Dish up on time.** Don't let tiredness ruin her desire to eat.

✔ **Let her serve herself.** She'll love tipping her own cereal into her bowl and pouring on the milk (put it in a small jug first). Or sprinkling her own helping of parmesan over her spaghetti bolognaise. When you're eating together as a family or have some of her friends over, do a 'pick and mix' meal: Put bowls of chopped ham, tuna, grated cheese, cooked veg pieces, cherry tomatoes on the table, give everyone a plate of pasta and let them choose and serve their own toppings.

✔ **Get silly.** Use biscuit cutters to make toast teddies or trains. Flatten her mashed potato and draw a ketchup face on it. Make a banana penguin: Peel back the skin in three moves, then put the bit of skin with the stalk on it (the beak) back in place (the other two bits are the flippers) and waddle it along the table towards her.

But what if she's a big eater?

It's possible that you never have to deal with faddy eating. Your preschooler may have a great appetite and gobble up everything you put on her plate. Which is highly gratifying, of course. But – especially if your child is not on the skinny-minny side – this may just leave you worrying about her weight.

Are you right to worry? Well, to be honest, it's hard to say. Preschoolers come in different shapes and sizes, and being bigger than average doesn't necessarily mean being unhealthier than average. And then there's the way preschoolers grow: They don't do it gradually; they do it in spurts, often suddenly widening out before, equally suddenly, shooting up. Add to that the huge variation in the time it takes preschoolers to lose their sticky-out-tum 'baby fat', and you can see why even paediatric dieticians find it hard to tell the healthy big from the porky big at this stage. (For this reason, most child-obesity weight charts don't even start till age 5.)

So, even if your food-loving preschooler is on the comfortably padded side, there may well be nothing to worry about. And it's certainly not a good idea to put her on a diet just in case. What you can do instead is take a few simple steps to lower her risk of being overweight when she starts school. To do this:

- ✓ **Watch her portions.** Remember that a preschooler serving is only one-half to three-quarters the size of an adult one. Try letting her serve herself: Studies of 4-year-olds suggest that children who fill their own plates take and eat roughly the right amount of food for their age but, when an adult gives them a bigger portion, they eat significantly more.

- ✓ **Talk to her about 'feeling full'.** Children (and adults) who stop eating when they feel full are less likely to become overweight. Most preschoolers instinctively recognise the 'full' feeling and stop, but some, especially those who've always been encouraged to clean their plate, simply ignore it. If you suspect your child does this, explain about eating until her tummy feels 'comfy'. Tell her this feeling sometimes comes just after you've had enough, so it's always worth waiting and counting to ten before asking for seconds.

- ✓ **Keep her active.** Good eaters are less likely to get porky if they're good exercisers, too.

- ✓ **Get savvy with snacks.** Don't offer too many (three a day max) and make sure that they're not all of the cakes and biscuits variety.

Sleep and Not-So-Sweet Dreams

By now, your child should have got the hang of the whole stay-in-bed-and-sleep-till-it's-morning thing. But don't count on all that delicious unbroken parental slumber just yet! A few nasty little surprises are lurking in the night-time shadows, and you're going to have to deal with them first.

What's normal, what's not

Before we get on to the stuff that can disrupt your child's sleep, it helps to know what to expect her sleep to be like on days when nothing comes along to disrupt it. Preschoolers generally need about 11 to 11.5 hours' sleep a night (see Table 18-1). Some 3-year-olds may still need a regular or occasional nap in the day but by 4, almost all preschoolers will be bowling through the day without stopping for a snooze (for more on giving up the day-time nap, see Chapter 14).

These changes in sleep needs are small but, if you're not in the know, you may not adjust and that can lead to your child

- ✔ **Waking too early:** If she hasn't given up her day-time nap, she definitely needs to now. If she has, are you putting her to bed a little too early? Remember, she probably only needs 11 hours' sleep, so if her bedtime's 6.30 p.m., she's going to be up and raring to go at 5.30 a.m.

- ✔ **Not getting enough sleep:** Before, it didn't really matter if your child went to bed at 8.30 p.m. because she could sleep till 7.30 or 8 a.m. and get all the shut-eye she needed. But now that she needs to be up and out of the house early enough to get to playgroup or preschool, her usual bedtime may be too late – and that will make her grumpy and difficult during the day. Bring lights-out forward five or ten minutes a day until she's able to get the 11 hours or so she needs.

Table 18-1	Your Age-by-Age Guide to Preschooler Sleep	
Age	*Hours of Day-Time Sleep*	*Hours of Night-Time Sleep*
3 years	1 or 0	11 to 11.5
4 years	0	11.5
5 years	0	11

Adapted with thanks from Solving Children's Sleep Problems *by Lyn Quine (Beckett Karlson, £12.99).*

This chart is only a guide, not a timetable that your preschooler must adhere to. Some preschoolers, like some adults, do seem to need less or more sleep than most. If your child is getting more or less sleep than the chart indicates but seems perfectly content in every other way, then she's fine.

What keeps her up – and how to get her back down

Three to 5 is the peak age for having bad dreams and being scared sleepless by thoughts of monsters lurking in the dark. It's also the peak age for inventing a million-and-one reasons why your parents shouldn't put the light out just yet. Here's your step-by-step guide to getting her to the land of Nod in either case.

Stalling before lights out

Delaying tactics of the bedtime kind usually happen for one of two reasons: either your child's worried about something, or she just prefers chatting away to you to hitting the hay. Spotting which is the current reason in question is usually pretty easy.

If she's just chatty, be kind but firm. Make it clear that if she wants to have a chat, that's fine, but it may mean you have less time for her bedtime stories. Have a cast-iron just-before-lights-out ritual: end of story, tuck in teddy, kiss her and teddy, lights out, for example. And be ready for a killer question – 'Why is the sky blue, Mummy?' – just as you reach for the switch. Respond with a calm, 'Gosh, that's a great question. Let's talk about it in the morning when we've lots more time.' And then leg it.

If she's scared, try the tips in the next section.

Fear of the dark and stuff that goes bump in the night

Fears of monsters, robbers, ghosts, and the dark are a normal part of growing up. Sometimes, they're sparked off by something your child's seen on TV, heard from a friend, or read in a book; sometimes, they're a manifestation of other anxieties – about changes happening at home, perhaps – that surface when the day-time bustle is over and the house is quiet. Either way, try to

- ✔ **Take her fears seriously.** Don't tell her she's being silly. She needs someone to listen to her, not laugh at her.

- ✔ **Dampen, not fuel, her fears.** There's a fine line between taking her fears seriously and making them worse. Don't cross it. If she thinks that there are monsters under her bed, for example, don't pretend to shoo them away. Tell her monsters only exist in books and films, so you know that they're not under her bed, but you'll have a look just to reassure her.

- ✔ **Give her some light.** If the dark's spooking her out, leave her door open and the landing light on. Or put a night-light in her room. You could even get creative and give her a torch with a cut-out smiley face taped over it, so she can project smiles onto the ceiling if she gets scared in the night. (Warning: This idea can backfire with excitable boys – they'll be waving their torches around all night long!)

- ✔ **Wind down slowly to bedtime.** Make the final half-hour before you start your bedtime routine a calm time to enjoy each other's company – no noisy games or exciting videos. At bedtime, pick a lovely, gentle story.

- ✔ **Reassure her.** If she calls out when you leave her room, put on your best calm voice and say something like, 'It's okay. We'll keep you safe while you're sleeping.'

- ✔ **Take her back to bed.** If she gets out in the night, comfort her as much as you like – even stay with her till she falls asleep again – but do it in her room. If you let her come downstairs or sleep in your bed, it just makes it harder for her to think of her room as a safe place.

Children of this age often develop night fears (or nightmares) when they start preschool or playgroup, or acquire a new sibling. Don't read too much into it.

If the night waking goes on for a long time, she may not really be scared any more; she's just got used to the attention it brings. You may have to be firmer in the night: Go in and reassure her that she's safe but leave fairly quickly.

Nightmares

Nightmares are just as normal as night fears and are usually caused by the same sort of anxieties. They tend to start at some point between 3 and 6 and often come in little phases. If your child wakes up in a fright

- ✔ **Comfort her straightaway.** Stay calm, put your arms around her, and talk to her quietly. Let her tell you about her dream if she wants to but don't press her for details if she doesn't offer them.

- ✔ **Settle her back down quickly.** Say, 'The dream's gone now; it's all okay.' And pat or stroke her gently till she settles for sleep.

- ✔ **Turn her pillow over.** To turn the nightmare away.

- ✔ **Talk to her about it the next day.** If she wants to. She'll probably be able to remember what it was about. Reassure her that you'll keep her safe from harm.

- ✔ **Try the wind-down to bedtime routine the next night.** See the earlier section, 'Fear of the dark and stuff that goes bump in the night'.

Night terrors

Night terrors are a bit of a preschooler speciality. They're not common but, if your child's going to have night terrors at all, she's probably going to have them at this age. They are very different from nightmares and can be quite shocking to witness. Your child may sob or scream, sit bolt upright or thrash around, but, although her eyes are open, she is not fully awake and won't know who you are. It's hard to do nothing while your child looks so terrified but it really is best to

- ✔ **Let it run its course.** Don't try to wake or comfort her – you run the risk of making things much worse. If she does wake, she'll be confused and disorientated: Now's the time to hug and reassure her.

- ✔ **When she relaxes, step in.** And calm her back to sleep. She should go back to sleep easily.

- ✔ **Don't mention it the next day.** She won't remember it.

- ✔ **See your GP if her night terrors are extremely frequent.** Very rarely, night terrors turn out, in fact, to be nocturnal epilepsy – it's worth getting it checked out.

Waking to a wet bed

When (or if) your preschooler is out of nappies at night (for more on how and when to do this, see Chapter 12), you'll almost certainly have the odd (or even not-so-odd) wet bed to contend with after the lights are out. (Now you know why they're called the wee small hours!)

The younger your child is, the more likely you are to be stripping sheets at midnight: One in three 4-year-olds wets her bed regularly, compared to one in six 5-year-olds. If you're going through a bad (damp) patch, it may help to consider the following:

- ✔ **Is the path to the loo (or potty) sufficiently lit?** A child who is scared of the dark may wet the bed in preference to having to brave a shadowy corridor.

- ✔ **Does your child have a urinary tract infection (UTI)?** An infection can make it hard for her to keep control of her bladder, but, if she has one, she'll probably be having trouble staying dry in the day, too. UTIs are more common in girls than boys; see your GP if you're worried.

- ✔ **Is your child really ready for this?** Episodes of bedwetting are usually short-lived; if your child is under 4 and has been wetting the bed every night for a while, it may be worth putting her back into nappies and trying again in a couple of months' time.

Getting dry by night is not a race. And it's got nothing to do with your child's intelligence. Your child may have an IQ to rival Einstein's, but she's still not going to be able to stay dry at night till her body's physically capable of it. And that can happen at any time between 2 and 7.

Chapter 19

Playing, Learning, and Socialising

. . . .

In This Chapter

▶ Feeding minds and firing imaginations

▶ Keeping growing bodies busy

▶ Smoothing the path for sharing and making friends

. . . .

The preschool years are jolly good fun. Your child is full of curiosity, energy, and enthusiasm for life. Now he's done all the really dramatic developmental stuff (first steps, first words), he's concentrating on lots of little improvements and fine-tuning – and each small progression delights him more than the last.

Because he's talking and thinking more, he's starting to make up stories, share simple jokes, and ask ever more complicated questions. And because he's walking and running with ease, he's leaping at any chance he gets to rush about all over the place and explore. He's still fairly full-on, of course, but no longer in that leg-clingy, can't-take-your-eyes-off-him-for-a-moment toddler way. His focus is opening out, engaging him more in the world outside his family as he starts to develop friendships with other children of his age.

So where do you come in? Well, what your preschooler needs from you right now is patience and a positive attitude: The patience to indulge his curiosity, answer his questions, and encourage his enthusiasms; and the positive attitude to help him forge friendships and seek new outlets for his boundless energy. And just how do you do that? Read on.

Mind Games and Make-Believe

From the age of 3, your child is able to think more flexibly. He's no longer happy just to learn what something is called; he also wants to know what it's for and how it works. He's increasingly able to remember what happened yesterday and relate it to what's happening today and what may happen tomorrow. And, best of all, he's starting to use his imagination to play in all sorts of fun and fascinating new ways.

Imaginary powers

Time to brush up those acting skills! Your child is about to become a master of make-believe, and he's got you marked down for many a guest appearance – not to mention a fair bit of stage management, too.

'Let's pretend!'

Toddlers aren't averse to a spot of pretend play (talking to dolls, barking like a dog), but preschoolers really get into it. And take it to a whole new level. They invent or re-enact complex storylines, take on characters, and lose themselves in an increasingly rich and detailed imaginary world of their own.

And it's all astonishingly good for them – so good, in fact, that many experts believe that the more your preschooler pretend-plays, the better he'll become at creative thinking, problem-solving, and making friends. And that's because:

- ✔ **It lets him try out different roles.** By playing at being Mum, Dad, the doctor, the astronaut, he's 'becoming' an adult and the one in charge.

- ✔ **It allows him to express and explore emotions.** By practising a sad face, a scary face, or whatever. And pretend play's a safe way to act out his fears or anxieties. Or voice feelings he knows are unacceptable in real life – such as wanting to send his brother to prison.

- ✔ **It enhances his pre-literacy skills.** Teachers will tell you that the ability to tell/retell a story with structure and detail is a bridge to early reading.

- ✔ **It helps him empathise.** If he pretends to be someone else, he's a step closer to understanding how that person feels.

- ✔ **It gives him confidence.** To see beyond what he already knows and have the courage to explore it.

Your preschooler probably doesn't need much encouraging to launch himself into the land of make-believe, but to help him enjoy it even more, you can

- ✔ **Fill a dressing-up box.** But not necessarily with loads of fancy bought costumes. He can have fun with your old cast-offs, charity-shop finds, even fabric remnants – my sons wrap these round their shoulders, fix them with a clothes peg, and, voilà, a superhero cape!

- ✔ **Provide some props.** Think tea sets, doctor's kits, cash registers and pretend money, toy building tools or cooking utensils, swimming goggles, hats and purses, torches, junk mail.

- ✔ **Start him off.** A younger preschooler may need a little help to get going. Show him how to line up chairs to make a bus or train. Or how to make a tent with a blanket. Sometimes, all it takes to spark his imagination is simply asking him who he'd like to pretend to be.

✔ **Follow, but don't lead.** Join in the fun but let him direct the show. Remember, it's his make-believe world, not yours. At pretend tea parties, for example, he should always be 'mother'.

Making things up

There's a small downside to all this wonderful pretending stuff: A blurring of the line between fantasy and reality. All preschoolers exaggerate and make things up – that's quite normal – but you may have to step in if your child's penchant for story-telling is taking a detour into untruthfulness. You need to establish now (before he's old enough to see the potential advantages of lying) that honesty is a quality you value very highly. So

✔ **Don't accuse him.** There's no need to get heavy – he's not being deceitful. Just quietly say, 'I don't think a monster scribbled on your bedroom wall, did it?'

✔ **Invite him to revise his story.** 'Tell me what really happened.' And then, when he does, tell him how much you appreciate his honesty.

Not telling the truth at this age is just imagination running riot, rather than deliberate deception. Even if he does insist that the monster scribbled on the wall, you *know* that it's not the truth and, after telling him you know as much, you can leave it at that.

Having an imaginary friend is very common at this age. And, no, it's not a sign of madness! Quite the reverse, in fact – experts believe that inventing an imaginary friend is a sign of an empathetic and sociable nature.

It's a boy/girl thing: The car/doll divide

Your child is realising that there are boys and then there are girls. And he's curious about the differences – especially now that the obviously anatomical ones are no longer concealed in nappies. Turn a blind eye to the inevitable mutual pants inspections – it's normal (and short-lived) preschooler behaviour.

You may also find your child starts to gravitate towards a stereotypically gender-specific style of play (dolls' tea parties for the girls, superhero battles for boys). You could argue for hours about whether this is the result of innate gender differences (girls like quiet play, boys like rushing about) or peer pressure (stick a Spiderman-crazy girl in a preschool and watch her head straight for the dolls the other girls are playing with), but the key point to remember is that both styles of play are perfectly normal and perfectly acceptable.

This is especially important for the 'superhero-battler' sort of child because playfighting with toys is often frowned upon by adults who fear it'll turn children unpleasantly aggressive. Playfighting is not at all the same as proper fighting (which clearly needs stopping quick) and, left to his (or her) own instinctive devices, a battler often collaborates and co-operates with other battlers just as smoothly and imaginatively as a member of the tea-party set.

Curiouser and curiouser

Your preschooler's brain is abuzz with questions – about everything he sees around him. And you're the one he's going to turn to for answers.

Why, why, why?

Why is water wet? Where does the sun go at night? How are rocks made? Why is the sky blue? Hmmm. They never told you you'd need degrees in chemistry, astronomy, and geo-physics when you became a parent, did they?

Preschoolers can – and often do – ask you mind-bogglingly difficult questions all day long and, as baffling (and irritating) as this can be, questioning's actually a great sign – of an active intelligence and an open, enquiring mind. And that's something any parent would want to encourage. So, as you scrabble around for suitable answers, remember to

- ✔ **Look excited by challenging questions.** Even if it's the 999th of the day and you're fed up to the back teeth of them. A friend of mine has a Brilliant Question notebook, in which she makes great show of writing down her daughter's more metaphysical probings. This makes her daughter feel very special and gives my friend more time to think up an appropriate answer to such teasers as, 'Can God see me when I wee?'

- ✔ **Not be afraid to admit you don't know.** Not knowing's nothing to be ashamed of. In fact, by admitting it, you can actually teach your child that not knowing something is the beginning of finding out. Get yourself a children's encylopaedia and look the answer up together.

- ✔ **Be prepared for the follow-up.** 'Where does the sun go at night?' 'To a country called Australia.' 'Why does it go there?' 'Because it's their turn to have sunlight.' 'Why is it their turn?' And so it goes on.

- ✔ **Be ready for public embarrassment.** When your preschooler chooses the supermarket queue as the best moment to ask, 'Why does that lady have a moustache, Daddy?' or 'How will the new baby come out of your tummy, Mummy?' have a few stock phrases up your sleeve to use in reply. Such as, 'Does she? Ooh, look at that huge lorry!' or 'That's a great question. Let's talk about it properly at home.'

- ✔ **Spot the questions that don't need answers.** Younger preschoolers can get stuck in a 'Why? Why? Why?' groove, often as a stalling or attention-seeking tactic. This is the time to respond, 'Because it just is!'

Working things out

You don't always have to be the fount of all knowledge; your inquisitive little preschooler will love finding and working things out for himself. So

- ✔ **Let him link cause and effect.** Give him different colours of paint and ask him what happens when they're mixed. Give him a bowl of water, a pebble, a feather, a spoon, a cork: Which ones sink, which ones float?

- ✔ **Help him improve his grasp of time.** Talk about yesterday, today, and tomorrow. Help him count down the days to future events: 'Three more sleeps till we go to Granny's.' Encourage him to use the past tense: 'Tell me what you did today.'

- ✔ **Ask leading questions.** Such as 'How did you know that jigsaw piece fitted there?' or 'What do you think will happen if we take the bottom brick out of your tower?'

- ✔ **Play memory games.** Put three or four objects on the table, then cover them with a tea towel and see if he can remember them all.

- ✔ **Stoke his enthusiasms.** So, if he likes animals, for example, visit the zoo/the aquarium/a farm/a pet shop, read books about different species and habitats, and get him out in the garden with a magnifying glass or pair of binoculars.

'Where do babies come from, Mummy?'

Yup, this is the age when *those* sort of questions start – so it's wise to have some kind of answering action plan at the ready. Obviously, it's best to tell the truth (tales about storks and gooseberry bushes will only confuse him and, ultimately, undermine his confidence in anything else you tell him). But keep your answer simple and age-appropriate.

You could talk about Mummy's egg and Daddy's seeds (what's a few mixed metaphors between you and your child?) and about a special baby-making cuddle. A preschooler really doesn't need any more detail than that.

If you always respond honestly and straightforwardly whenever the subject of sex comes up, your child will grow up thinking it's natural and normal and he's always known about it – and then no shame or embarrassment will exist on either side.

A word about TV

Some parents see nothing wrong with having the telly on all the time; some parents regard it as the instrument of the devil. Who's right? As so often with these things, the truth lies somewhere in the middle. Your preschooler can learn a lot of interesting, stimulating stuff from TV. But if he's sitting in front of it for too much of his day, he's missing out on an awful lot of other interesting, stimulating, *real-life* stuff. So

✔ **Limit TV to an hour a day.** Or less. Watching's not compulsory, after all!

✔ **Turn on for specific, age-appropriate programmes.** Or make use of the many excellent DVDs aimed at preschoolers. And then turn off.

✔ **Don't feel guilty for using TV as chill-out time.** Sitting passively in front of the telly at some point in the day is not a bad thing for an otherwise all-singing, all-dancing preschooler. He could probably do with a short period of rest and calm – and I'm sure that you could, too!

✔ **Be mindful of his 'fear factor'.** Some preschoolers wouldn't bat an eyelid at the baby clownfish's mum being gobbled up at the start of *Finding Nemo;* others would have to be carried screaming from the room. There is a huge variation in what children find scary at this age, and you should always pick DVDs to suit your child's fear threshold, not his friends'. Preview anything he hasn't watched before – and then watch it with him the first time, so you're there to reassure him that everything's going to turn out okay in the end.

Look Who's Talking! Language Skills

Your child's language skills are really taking off now. His vocabulary is expanding all the time and, over the next couple of years, he'll move from simply communicating his basic needs to being able to tell complicated stories and ask thoughtful questions.

His pronunciation and grasp of grammar will also improve quite dramatically. By the time he's 4, people outside your family will be able to understand what he's saying quite clearly, although your child may sometimes stutter over his words when he's upset or excited.

Reading really comes into its own now (check your library for some of the hundreds of wonderful books for this age group). He'll love hearing you read longer, more detailed stories, especially if you put on silly voices for each of the different characters.

He may also pretend that he can read himself – either by holding a much-loved book and spouting the words off by heart or by sitting with a book and mumbling to himself as he scans the pictures. This is pre-reading and may mean he's ready to learn some letters, but it's not your cue to get in there and teach him to read properly; at this age, you'll probably both end up frustrated. For more helpful ways to help your child prepare for school, see Chapter 20.

Let's Get Physical! Revving Up Those Motor Skills

Your preschooler's going to be developing all sorts of new physical skills over the next two or three years. But they won't be of the 'camcorder moment' variety. We're talking the small but constant refinement of skills he already has, not the sudden huge leaps of ability he made in his baby-and-toddler years.

That's not to say that there's nothing to celebrate or that there's not much you can do to help him out. The more opportunity you give him to practise – and the more encouragement you give him as he does so – the more physically accomplished and self-confident your child will become.

Active bodies

Right, let's take a look at that gross-motor skill checklist, shall we? Walk? Tick. Run? Tick. Then it's on to all that hopping, skipping, tip-toeing, standing-on-one-leg, going backwards stuff. And to manage all those, your preschooler's going to be working on his strength, co-ordination, and balance – which really translates as bounding around a heck of a lot. Good preschooler-friendly ideas for said bounding-around include:

- **Softplay centres:** Indoor adventure playgrounds wrapped up in bouncy padding, so that preschoolers can run, climb, slide, swing, explore – and fall off – without hurting themselves. Time your visits carefully, though: They can get very busy.

- **The park/playground:** An oldie but still a goodie. Big open spaces are just the thing for scampering around in. Have races. Go on scavenger hunts. Take a kite – there are some fab easy-to-fly ones about now.

- **Walking on walls:** The short, wide ones, obviously. Brilliant for improving balance, if not so brilliant for getting anywhere fast. If yours is a wall-less world, chalk a line on the pavement to 'tightrope-walk'.

- **Ball play:** Play bounce catch: At 3, most preschoolers can throw over-arm and can sometimes catch a ball with their arms held straight out; by 5, they're using their hands to catch (not always successfully). Improve aim and accuracy by playing skittles (with soft-drinks cans).

- **'Proper classes':** Your child may love the idea of dance classes or foot-ball practice but, then again, he may not. To up your chances of success, pick a class where the emphasis is on short bursts of movement and lots of fun; avoid classes that require long periods of calm concentration or expect children to obey complicated rules.

- ✔ **Paddling pools:** To fill up with a hose and splash himself silly in. Or to dip sponges in for throwing at targets (watch out: This could be you!).

- ✔ **Traditional games:** Such as hopscotch, treasure hunts, obstacle courses, hide-and-seek, bean-bag racing (bean bags on heads), musical statues.

- ✔ **Trikes and bikes:** The 3-year-old leg should be just about long enough to pedal a trike (or a bike with stabilisers) but, be warned, steering's a bit much for the 3-year-old brain. By 5, your child should be a whizz on three wheels (or four) and may even be ready to try two. However many wheels are underneath him, though, always make sure that there's a helmet on top.

Preschoolers don't do stamina. They tend to rush around everywhere at top speed and then suddenly run out of steam. Alternate periods of active play with periods of quieter play (for quiet-play ideas, see the next section).

Don't compare your preschooler's abilities with another's. Remember that every child develops different skills at a different pace.

Busy fingers

Your preschooler is getting quite nimble with his hands. His fingers are still awkwardly chubby, but he's got good control of them. And now that his attention span is increasing (up to at least 15 minutes at a time by 4), he's able to do a lot more for himself – from washing his own hands to creating all sorts of arty-crafty masterpieces. To give him lots of hands-on fun:

- ✔ **Do jigsaws.** He's ready for proper cardboard ones now, with 20 or more pieces. Show him how to use the picture on the box to work out where the pieces go, and how the pieces with straight sides go round the edge.

- ✔ **Draw.** At first, just let him scribble away. Then you can introduce him to the idea of 'proper' drawing by showing him how to make dots, draw a line, a cross, and a circle, and colour in. By 5, he'll probably be able to draw a person with a face, legs, and arms (but not all in proportion) and his colouring in will be more precise but still straying outside the lines.

- ✔ **'Write' his name.** When he's confident holding and using a pencil, make the outline of his name in little dots and get him to practise joining up all the dots to spell his name. Let him 'sign' cards in this way.

- ✔ **Thread.** Preschool fingers love threading beads onto string. Buy a special set of threading beads or go DIY with a bootlace and rigatoni pasta.

- ✔ **Paint and stick.** Let him use lots of paint colours and show him how to dip his brush in water before changing from one to the next. Ask him what he's painting and what colours he needs. The sticking (with PVA glue or a glue stick) is all about collages: The bigger and more crammed with stuck-on bits, the better. Pin his finished works up on the wall or use them as birthday cards or even wrapping paper.

✔ **Cook.** He can break the eggs and stir in the flour when you're making cakes. He can grate cheese and peel carrots (with an easy-grip peeler). He can even help make his own sandwiches.

✔ **Use scissors.** Starting with random snipping at 3 and progressing to cutting almost-straight lines at 5. (You can buy special children's scissors for left-handers.)

✔ **Dress himself.** He should be able to manage this by 4, except for doing up buttons and zips. To start with, he'll be painfully slow, of course, and you'll probably be itching to step in and take over. But, unless he's actually getting frustrated, it's important to give him the time to do things on his own – it does wonders for his self-esteem. If you need to speed him up (or he's deliberately dawdling), try racing him: 'Who do you think can get their socks on first: You or me?'

By 4, your preschooler will probably be showing a preference for using one hand over the other. If it's the left hand, that's fine. Don't try to make him change to the right. You'll only confuse him and dent his confidence.

Fine day, bored kids? Give them each a pair of blunt-tipped scissors and send them out into the garden to 'cut' the grass.

Fun with Friends

This is the age when your child really begins to understand the meaning of friendship and how to interact properly with others of his age. He'll gradually move from parallel play (the side-by-side play so beloved of toddlers) to co-operative play (taking turns, throwing a ball back and forth, group games).

To begin with, he may form – and change – friendships quickly, and it may be a while before he's enough of a social animal to share nicely. But, by the end of his preschool years, he'll be so into the friendship thing, he'll be gagging to go round and play at other people's houses – maybe even without you in tow.

Mine! All mine! Oh, okay, your turn

Put out the flags! At long, long last, your child is realising that sharing is cool – or at least worth trying. Don't go getting over-exited, mind: It's not going to turn all peace, love, and understanding overnight. It's probably going to be more like a slow, gradual slackening in the shoving-and-snatching department. To help speed the process up, though, you can

- ✔ **Encourage his awareness of others' feelings.** By saying things such as, 'Daddy feels sad – let's give him a hug.' Or pointing out people's expressions in picture books: 'Thomas looks very cross, doesn't he?'

- ✔ **Demonstrate sharing in action.** Dole out an uneven number of strawberries/grapes between you, starting with you. 'One for me, one for you . . . one for me and, oh, they're finished. Tell you what – I'll share this last one with you.'

- ✔ **Praise any sharing you spot.** Massively. Whether it's your child doing it or not. And praise descriptively – so not just, 'Well done, Jack!' but 'You're sharing that Batmobile really nicely with Jill, Jack!'

- ✔ **Have a special shelf for his special toys.** And then make it a rule that everything else is for sharing.

- ✔ **Watch what you say.** 'Take turns' is often a better choice of words than 'share'. Some children who've 'shared' food before automatically assume sharing means cutting in half. And no way are they going to let that happen to their favourite toy.

- ✔ **Practise taking turns.** By playing simple board games. And by using a kitchen timer to signal the beginning/end of turn-taking play sessions.

- ✔ **Teach him how to ask.** Make sure that your child knows that, if he wants to play with something that someone else has, he must always ask, rather than grab. And, in your house at least, when someone asks nicely, the grown-ups will always find a way for him to have a turn – even if he may have to wait a little while first.

It's playtime!

You may (or may not) have been having other children over to play for ages now but, odds are, they're your friends' kids and you're the one doing the inviting. When your child starts going to preschool or playgroup, though, he'll start making new friends and will want to do some inviting of his own. Welcome to the world of preschool playdates! Here's how to make them fun for everyone (including you).

The home fixture

The main stress-saving rule here is: Don't be too ambitious. The success of the playdate doesn't depend on your game-leading/organic wholemeal biscuit-baking/collage-material-supplying abilities. Honest. So take a chill pill and

✔ **Keep it small.** Don't invite more than one friend round at a time – unless you actually enjoy tearing your own hair out.

✔ **Keep it short.** An hour or two at most. Any more and they'll get cranky.

✔ **Respect the other parent's wishes.** She may be happy for her child to come on his own; she may feel she should come along, too.

✔ **Help them connect.** Have a game or a craft activity ready, so they've got something to get into straightaway. After the preschooler ice has broken, you can back off and let them decide what to do next.

✔ **Schedule a snack.** Every fixture needs a half-time break.

✔ **Stay close.** But don't breathe down their necks.

✔ **Intervene firmly.** If you have to. If the guest child is misbehaving, say 'I can't let you do that, John' or 'We don't do that in this house, John'. And then distract them both with a new activity.

✔ **Smooth the way for goodbyes.** Give the guest child a few minutes' warning that the playdate's nearly over. Doing so helps ward off the 'time to go now' meltdown on your doorstep.

'Magic painting' is a playdate winner. Give them a paintbrush and a pot of water each and let them go outside to 'paint' the garden toys and furniture.

The away fixture

Your preschooler will probably be desperately keen to go and play at his friends' houses. If he's never been to a particular house before, though, he's likely to want you to come with him the first time (or two). After that, try staying with him for fifteen minutes or so and then leaving. Some preschoolers (and, it has to be said, some parents) take longer to adjust to the idea of going to a playdate on their own than others. But making a big issue of it is pointless – they all get there in the end.

Your child may happily go to playdates on his own, but birthday parties are a different kettle of fish. The crowd of kids, the frenetic atmosphere, the unfamiliar location, the strange entertainer: Any (or all) of these could completely unnerve him. Be prepared to stay with him for as long as it takes.

Chapter 20

Heading to Preschool

In This Chapter

▶ Making the right preschool choice

▶ Settling your child in happily

▶ Looking ahead to primary school

*P*reschools come in all shapes and sizes, but they all have the same end goal: To help get your child ready for primary school. And have a fine, fun time along the way.

If your child already goes to a nursery that takes children up to the age of 5, she's not in for that much of a change. But if she's always spent her days with you (or another carer), she's going to have some adjusting to do.

Luckily, this is exactly the age at which most children really get into the idea of making friends and playing in a group, so it's probably not going to be nearly as bad as you think. Especially if you smooth the path for her with some of the preschool – and primary-school – preparation tips in this chapter.

Choosing the Best Preschool for You Both

Okay, first we need to define terms because, very confusingly, only a handful of the places that provide preschool education actually call themselves a 'preschool'. You'll probably actually be choosing between:

- ✔ **A school nursery:** Based, as the name suggests, in a primary school. Takes children from age 3 or 4. Offers half or whole-day sessions, five days a week. Free but competition for places is often high.

- ✔ **A community nursery:** Often takes children from age 2. Offers half or whole-day sessions, five days a week. Some may have part-time places. Most charge a fee. The operating committee may be parent-run.

✔ **A workplace nursery:** Based (no prizes for guessing) at your place of work. Often takes children from infancy. Some are more flexible about hours/days than others. Fee-paying but often subsidised by employers.

✔ **a private nursery:** May take children from infancy (although some only start at age 2 or 3). Tends to be more flexible – offering long days (up to 6 p.m.) or short days, full-time or part-time. Some private nurseries are very 'hothousey' (aiming to get children into private school); some follow a particular educational method (Montessori, Steiner). Fees can be stomach-churningly high (but not always).

✔ **A playgroup:** Takes children from age 3 (and, occasionally, 2). Offers half-day sessions, five days a week. Often free and, usually, parent-run.

From the age of 3, all children are entitled to free, part-time preschool education. Any bill you are sent from your child's preschool should show clearly how this sum has been deducted from the fees you owe.

What matters most?

Obviously, your choice is restricted by what's available in your area, which ones you stand a chance of getting a place at, how much you're able to pay (if anything), and how many hours/days a week would best suit you and your child. Before you make any decisions, though

✔ **Talk to other parents.** Especially ones with children already at the preschools you're considering. Ask them what they like – and what their child likes – about the preschool they've chosen. Their answers can be very revealing.

✔ **Look at Ofsted reports.** Every preschool is regularly inspected and you can read these findings at www.ofsted.gov.uk. Do bear in mind, though, that, if the last inspection was a while ago, things may have changed quite considerably since (for better or worse).

✔ **Consider the practicalities.** Think distance: It may be a lovely mornings-only playgroup but, if the venue's half an hour's walk away, you'll hardly be home before you need to start the journey back. And think commitment: If parents are expected to help out at sessions or raise funds, will you be willing/able to pull your weight?

✔ **Check out as many as you can.** Sometimes, the most oversubscribed, most raved-about preschool in the area just doesn't do it for you; sometimes, the shabby, unprepossessing little preschool down the road turns out to be absolutely wonderful. But you'll never know if you don't make the effort to look around. (For more on how to do this properly, see the sections 'What to look for' and 'Ten questions not to leave without asking', later in this chapter.)

A long waiting list is not necessarily a sign of a great preschool. Or of a great preschool for *your child*. Don't follow fashion; follow your gut instincts.

What to look for

Some preschools have got the prospective-parent tour down to a fine art; others are more, er, challenged in the meet-greet-and-dazzle-you department. But what really matters is not the style and patter of your tour guide but the sights and sounds around you. Keep your eyes peeled for

- **Bright, clean, safe play areas:** They don't have to be vast and they certainly don't have to be beautifully fitted out, but they should be dirt-free, uncluttered, and child-friendly.

- **Happy, purposeful kids:** It should be obvious that the children are enjoying what they're doing. And are interacting positively with the staff as they do so (showing them their paintings, for example).

- **Happy staff:** Do the carers look as if they like their job? Or have they all got that supermarket-checkout-girl look?

- **A welcoming feel:** Do the staff smile at you when you come in? Do they smile at your child? Do the children have named pegs for their coats and named trays for their artwork/letters home? Is there a picture board naming all the staff? Are the loos child-friendly?

- **Artwork on display:** Good preschools are proud of their children's work and know the boost it gives the kids to see it up on the wall.

- **A good variety of toys:** Including, perhaps, dressing-up stuff, toy cookers and playhouses, ride-on toys, puzzles, dolls, and a book corner.

- **A relaxed atmosphere:** It really shouldn't feel as though the children are learning in a forced, formal way. Everything should be play-centred.

- **Some outside space:** Not essential for everyone, of course – but important if you have a very bouncy, active child.

Researching all the options is tiring but worth it: If you're happy with your choice of preschool, you'll transmit that confidence to your child.

Ten questions not to leave without asking

'Is there anything you'd like to ask?' I don't know about you, but that's a phrase guaranteed to turn my mind completely blank. To stop this happening to you on your preschool tour, make a note of the following questions and keep them in your pocket to prompt your blank mind back into a suitably conscious and articulate state. Listen carefully to the answers you get: They could radically alter your impression of the preschool you're looking at.

- ✔ **How long have most of your staff been working here?** A rapid staff turnover is not a good sign. A good preschool should have at least some staff who have been there for years.

- ✔ **What is the ratio of staff to children over the age of 3?** One to eight is the answer you're looking for. And it's worth asking what sort of qualifications the staff have, too.

- ✔ **Do you have a daily routine?** Most preschoolers feel more at home when there's some sort of recognisable structure to their day. This question also allows you to find out how long each activity lasts for: Children this age have short attention spans.

- ✔ **How do you discipline?** Obviously, you want to hear that they'd do pretty much what you'd do.

- ✔ **Does my child need to be potty-trained?** Or, if not, how do they handle potty-training?

- ✔ **How do you keep in touch with parents?** Will your child have a special 'keyworker' assigned to her? Will you be given a daily report? A weekly newsletter? Monthly meetings? Do you have to make an appointment to speak to staff?

- ✔ **Can I stay for a little while and watch?** A good preschool would have no problem with this.

- ✔ **What sort of food do the children eat?** You may have strong ideas about what your child should or should not be offered, or you may be concerned about allergies.

- ✔ **Do you take the children on outings?** And, if so, do you seek parents' permission every time? Or just ask them to sign a blanket letter of permission? You may feel it's important to know exactly where your child is at all times.

- ✔ **Can I come back with my child for a trial session?** Because then you can ask the most important question of all – to your child: 'Do you like playing here?'

Getting Ready for the First Day

So, you've found – and secured a place at – a nursery or playgroup you like. Great! But don't you go thinking this preschool thing's all done and dusted just yet. Your next task is to make sure that your child's first few days at preschool are happy, positive, and stress-free.

Preparing your child

Don't make the mistake of thinking that talking too much about going to preschool will unsettle and frighten your child. In fact, the more you prepare her for what she'll experience at preschool, the more quickly she's likely to settle in. Children (and adults) always feel more secure when they know what's happening and what to expect. So

- ✔ **Talk her through it.** Explain, in an upbeat way, what her preschool day will be like. Include as many details as you can and be ready for questions. Make it sound fun, but don't insist that she's going to love it or she may not feel she can voice her worries. Find a book about starting preschool and read it together.

- ✔ **Boost her social confidence.** If your child's not used to the company of other children, now's the time to work on this. Take her to your local parent-and-toddler group (even if it's your idea of living hell) or a singing class – anywhere where she can adjust to the idea of being surrounded by, and playing with, a group of children her age.

- ✔ **Get her used to having time away from you.** She may already separate easily from you because she's used to other people taking care of her. But, if that's not the case, it's worth asking a friend or a relative to help you out. Start by leaving her for a very short time (half an hour at the most) and gradually work up to longer periods away from you.

- ✔ **Walk past it.** As often as possible, so her preschool-to-be becomes a familiar sight. If it's been a while since you looked round, phone to ask if you can come in again with your child for an hour or two.

Settling in and saying goodbye

Don't plan on doing much else during your child's first week at preschool – she's going to need you close at hand. Most places operate some kind of settling-in process, which involves you staying with your child for a while (maybe all her first session), then leaving for short periods, gradually extending the time you're away until she's happy to stay for the whole session without you. How quickly your child settles largely depends on her personality, but you can make it a lot easier for her if you

- ✔ **Don't rush.** Allow plenty of time to get ready and get yourselves out of the house in the morning. You both need to arrive at preschool feeling perky and positive.

- ✔ **Hold your nerve.** Your feelings are crucial: Your child will pick up on them. Let her see you looking confident, cheerful, and relaxed.

✔ **Have a goodbye ritual.** Always say goodbye to her in the same way: with a hug or a kiss and a form of words that tells her clearly – and truthfully – when you'll be back. So, not 'Daddy's just going to move the car' but, 'Daddy will see you at snack time'.

✔ **Leave quickly.** Don't linger or hesitate. Give her a big smile and go. And then blub in the car park if you need to.

✔ **Don't expect too much.** Some preschoolers wave their parents off without a second thought; others sob and cling for all they're worth. If yours is a clinger, ask her keyworker for advice: She may feel you need to take the settling-in more slowly; she may be able to reassure you that your child stops crying the instant the door closes behind you. And, remember, every child is different – but they all get there in the end.

Tears are not a sign that your child hates her preschool. They're a sign of a secure parent-child attachment – something to feel proud of, actually!

If your child is still unsettled after a month of preschool – and, by 'unsettled', I mean she seems truly miserable when you drop her off, rather than simply sad to see you go – it's just possible that the preschool you've chosen is simply not for her. Discuss your concerns with the staff and, if you don't feel reassured or things don't change markedly for the better, remove your child and start looking for somewhere else.

And when she comes home

You're not going to like this, but forewarned is forearmed: Your child will probably be a bit of a nightmare for a while. However much she enjoys her preschool sessions, she's going to find them exhausting – and, because a tired preschooler usually means a fractious preschooler, it's wise to be prepared for some less-than-angelic behaviour at home. If your child's already given up her day-time nap, try reinstating it for a while. Or at least have a 'quiet time' after preschool, so she can recharge her batteries.

Anticipate a relapse. Even happily settled preschoolers often have a (short-lived) tearful patch after a couple of weeks. This can also happen when there are changes at home, such as the arrival of a new sibling.

Thinking Ahead to Big School

No rest for the wicked! Right slap bang in the middle of all this preschool malarkey, the spectre of primary-school admission rears its ugly head. To find the right primary school for your child, you pretty much go through the same process as you did to find the right preschool – only, this time, you don't get to make the final decision. Your local education authority does that for you, based on a list of preferences you send in. Which means it's worth taking the time to draw up your list wisely.

Making the right choice

Legally, your child doesn't have to start school till the term after her fifth birthday but, in practice, most primary schools admit children in the autumn term of the school year that they turn 5. So, you'll probably have to get your child's completed application form in to the local education authority in the school year that she turns 4 (make sure that you find out exactly what the closing date is).

Remember, this is the school year (September to August) we're talking about, not the real year (January to December). So, if your child's 5 on 31 August 2010 (28 February 2010 in Scotland), she'll start school in the autumn of 2009 but, if she's 5 on 1 September 2010 (1 March 2010 in Scotland), she'll start school in the autumn of 2010. (Just to confuse things even further, some English and Welsh schools do allow summer-borns to start in the spring term, but that doesn't affect the application-form deadline.)

Four steps to narrow your choices

Once you've figured out when that form needs to be in, you know how long you've got to pick your preferred schools. And, to help narrow down your choices, you need a four-step plan:

- ✓ **Step 1: Do your homework.** Get hold of your local education authority's list of primary schools. Ring up the schools within a reasonable radius of your home (the closer you are to a school, the more chance your child has of getting in). Ask for a copy of their prospectus and their special admissions criteria (if any). Look up each school's most recent SATs (final-year exam) results (www.dfes.gov.uk/performancetables) and Ofsted report (www.ofsted.gov.uk).

- ✓ **Step 2: Get real.** Take a critical look at your preferences so far. Are they really within manageable walking/driving distance? Are they all over-subscribed? Do any of them have special admission criteria (proof of church attendance, for example)? Have you ruled out your nearest school just on the published results? Maybe it's worth taking another look – the exam marks of one year group aren't everything.

- ✓ **Step 3: Go visiting.** Look round as many schools as you can (you'll probably have to make an appointment) and get a feel for their different atmospheres. Are you made to feel welcome? Are there good displays of the children's work? Do you warm to the Reception (or P1, if you're in Scotland) teacher? Does her class look bright and well organised, with space inside and out?

✓ **Step 4: Check out the kids.** Often, you'll be assigned a pupil to take you on the school tour. Use this opportunity to find out more about the school. Ask her what she likes about it, what the school rules are, what her favourite subject is, and what activities she likes doing best.

It's a boy/girl thing: Gender-based questions to ask

Boys and girls react in very distinct and separate ways to the formality of early learning. And, though a school cannot be all things to all children, it's definitely worth finding out whether the ones you like recognise how differently boys and girls learn.

So, if you've got a boy, ask:

✓ **How much are the children allowed to run around?** How many breaks are built into the day? At this age, boys can find sitting still very hard.

✓ **How much importance is based on reading and language development in the first year?** Boys tend to develop these skills more slowly than girls.

✓ **Will my child have access to non-fiction books?** Boys respond better to factual stories than fictional ones.

✓ **Are there any male teachers in the school?** Male role models are hard to find in some primary schools.

And, if you've got a girl, ask:

✓ **How much encouragement is there to take part in team sports?** Girls naturally prefer games that involve taking turns, but some element of rough-and-tumble can be a good thing.

✓ **How do you, as a female teacher, see your position as a role model for the girls?** It's not uncommon for girls to fall in love with their teacher!

✓ **Is there much emphasis on problem-solving in maths and science sessions?** Girls tend to be slower than boys in developing this skill.

And, whatever you've got, ask:

✓ **How do you deal with the differences between boys and girls at this stage?** Teachers should know that it's never too early to teach both sexes the importance of respecting the other.

What your child needs to know before she starts – and what she doesn't

You've got the place, you've got the uniform, but has your child got what it takes to start school? Should she be able to count to ten? Or 100? Is reciting the ABC enough, or should she really be starting to read?

The truth is, there's an enormous range of ability in every Reception (or P1) class – as you'd expect when some of the children are probably almost an entire year older than others. Teachers are trained to build on what each child knows and to compensate for what she doesn't.

If your child can already read and write, that's great, but it won't be expected. And you certainly shouldn't push your child to get to grips with either, if she doesn't enjoy it. Reading has nothing to do with intelligence and is more about the ability to de-code and concentrate. And writing is almost impossible to master until a child's developed the fine-motor skills needed for forming letters. If you want to try a bit of pre-school coaching, always be led by your child – let her think that learning is fun, not a struggle.

There are some things your child *does* need to know, though: Simple, practical skills that will help her cope much more easily with school life. The school will probably send you a list of these in the summer term before your child starts. They usually include being able to

- ✔ **Go to the toilet on her own and wipe her own bottom.**
- ✔ **Hang up her own coat. And do up the zip, if it has one.**
- ✔ **Blow her own nose.**
- ✔ **Respond to her name.** And, better still, be able to recognise it when she sees it written down.
- ✔ **Use a knife and fork.**
- ✔ **Tidy up after herself.**

If your child is keen to write or learn her letters, do make an effort to find out how they teach this at her school – it's almost certainly changed since you were 4! If you teach her a different way, she'll only have to 'unlearn' everything and start again from scratch.

What if we don't get the place we want?

It's horrible to get a letter telling you your child doesn't have a place at your first-choice school. In the throes of your upset and disappointment, you imagine your child is now doomed to an educational future of struggle and failure. But there's absolutely no reason why that should be the case. Before you move halfway across the country or throw all your money at the private sector (both of which are options, of course), consider:

- ✔ **Lodging an appeal:** Your chances are not high but, if you put forward a clear argument, based on the school's admissions criteria and your child's specific educational needs, you will be listened to.

- ✔ **Staying on the waiting list:** Places do come up between now and the start of the autumn term. And, even if they don't, places often come up at other times of the year, as families move out of the area.

- ✔ **Giving the other school a go:** It may not be nearly as grim as you imagine.

Part V
All About Schoolies

"That was a super game and
the best team won."

In this part . . .

*T*he day your child starts school is a bit of a watershed in every parent's life. And this is the part to steady your nerves. In it, you'll find practical tips for preparing your child (and yourself!) for the first day, the first year, and beyond. There's a special chapter on fostering school-age friendships and boosting your child's self-image, and some no-holds-barred advice on keeping him fit, safe and healthy. Look out, too, for the sanity-saving tips on teaching your child about responsibility, choices and self-control.

Chapter 21

Starting School

. . . .

In This Chapter

▶ Getting your child off to a positive start

▶ Being prepared for some strange new challenges

▶ Building a good relationship with your child's teacher

. . . .

Scared? Nervous? Worried? Stressed? And goodness knows what your
child's thinking. Starting school is a big thing – for you, as well as your
child. But there's absolutely no reason why it should be a *bad* big thing.
Especially if you've taken the time to suss out the stuff you really need to
know. Which, by strange but handy coincidence, is exactly where this chapter comes in.

School's Cool: Creating the Right Attitude

You want your child to like the idea of going to school. And the only way he's
going to do that is if you like the idea, too (or at least seem to). So don't
ignore what's coming up in September: The weeks from now until then are
your opportunity to paint a positive picture of school life and show your
child you're confident that he'll fit in just fine.

If you haven't already applied for a school place, do it now! Phone your local
education authority for details and read the advice in Chapter 20.

The more you know about something, the less scary it seems. So do all you
can to help your child understand as much as possible about his school life
to come: What will happen when he first gets there, where he'll be expected
to go, how he'll be expected to behave, and what he'll be expected to do. The

more familiar he is with the pattern of the school day, the easier he'll find it to settle in. So it'll help to

- **Get him used to the building.** Walk/drive past it often, pointing out the playground, the hall, his classroom (if you know where it is). Visit the school – towards the end of the summer, many schools organise special 'taster' sessions for new starters; if yours doesn't, ring up and ask if you can bring your child in.

- **Read reassuring books.** Such as the superbly nerve-settling *Starting School* by Janet and Allan Ahlberg (Penguin, £4.99).

- **Meet some classmates.** Maybe your child already knows some of the other boys and girls who'll be in his class. If so, that's great. If not, take the phone numbers of some of the other parents at the school's parent-orientation meeting and arrange for the kids to meet up in the park for a little get-to-know-you session.

- **Talk him through the school day.** Your school should already have sent you a simple outline (if not, ask for one). Tell your child his teacher's name is Mrs X and that she'll always start the day by taking the register (explain what this is). Describe what happens at assembly, at playtime, at circle time, at lunchtime (and what the dinner ladies do).

- **Get him to try his uniform on.** (If the school has one.) So it's not yet another strange new thing to deal with on his first day. The same goes for his PE kit: Make sure that he can put it on and take it off on his own.

- **Explain the hands-up rule.** How that's what you do when you want to answer a question. And how shouting out the answer isn't allowed.

- **Work on his practical skills.** Make sure that he's able to hang his coat up, wipe his bottom, blow his nose. For more on this, see Chapter 20.

- **Sound positive but realistic.** Don't oversell school as a fun factory. There's no reason why he shouldn't find it fun, of course, but going to school is not the same as going to Legoland.

Don't forget that the weather in September can be quite warm – consider buying one summer-uniform outfit now (it'll probably be in the sales, so that's a bonus). And don't buy too much winter stuff: Many children have a *huge* growth spurt in their first school year.

If your twins are going to be in separate classes (most schools do have a policy of splitting twins up), limber them up for the split by arranging them each a few solo sessions at preschool or solo playdates with friends.

No one expects your child to be able to read before he starts school. If he can, great. But pushing a child to read before he's ready can be very counter-productive. If he likes sharing books with you, can recognise his own name, and knows that there are words on street signs and food packets, he's doing absolutely fine for his age.

Taking the First Year (Reception, P1) in Your Stride

You'd think that your child's first year at school would be called Year One. But you'd be wrong. In England and Wales, it's called Reception, and, in Scotland it's called P1. And it's not just the terminology that could throw you: There are a fair few other facts of first-year life that a parent may find surprising or a child may find tricky. Here's how to be starting-school-savvy from Day One.

The first day

So, the big day finally dawns. How are you going to handle the emotionally charged journey from house to classroom door? By remembering to

- ✔ **Give yourself plenty of time.** You really don't want to be yelling at your child to hurry up and brush his teeth on this day of all days.

  Allow a little extra time in the morning to take that all-important first-day-at-school photo!

- ✔ **Think positive.** You've done all the preparatory work – it's all going to be fine. Remember, your feelings guide your child's feelings.

- ✔ **Find your child's coat peg.** And point out where the toilets are.

- ✔ **Introduce yourself to the teacher.** In the calmest, friendliest voice you can muster. And then introduce your child.

- ✔ **Leave decisively.** The teacher will tell you when the moment's come. Let your child know exactly when you're picking him up (some schools start with half-days for the youngest children), give him a big smile, and then go. Reserve all sobbing and wailing for the street outside.

And at the end of the day

- ✔ **Be early.** So he doesn't have to scan the playground anxiously, looking for your face.

- ✔ **Come equipped.** With a blood-sugar-boosting drink and a snack. First days are very energy-sapping.

- ✔ **Don't press for information.** He may be too tired to give you a blow-by-blow account of his day. Just let him chill out and be quiet for a while. You'll get the details when he's ready.

If you have identical twins, help the teachers out by creating a point of difference between them: Different styles of shoe, maybe, or different-coloured bands in their hair.

Ten little things that'll make a big difference

It's not just your child who has a lot of new stuff to get used to; you do, too! It can be quite a challenge for both of you to adjust the rhythm of family life to accommodate the demands of the school-day routine – and to keep track of all the special events, extra activities, and meetings that are happening at school. The key to keeping on top of it all? Here are ten tiny (but crucial) tips:

1. **Do proper bed and breakfast.** Your child needs a bedtime that allows him enough sleep and a breakfast that gives him enough energy to be properly on form for school in the mornings. For more on this, see Chapter 22.

2. **Put nametapes on everything.** Shoes, pants, lunchboxes, hairbands – the lot. You wouldn't believe what a 5-year-old can mislay on a daily basis!

3. **Go through your child's school bag every evening.** Looking for school notices, newsletters, and notes from the teacher. There's nothing worse than discovering the note about Dress-Up-As-A-Dinosaur Day on the morning of the day itself!

4. **Get a calendar or noticeboard.** Or both. It's the only way to keep track of school events, term dates, special assemblies, party invites.

5. **Walk to school.** If you possibly can. Walking's a great way for your child to burn off his restless early-morning energy and it gives both of you a chance to chat before you begin your separate days. If you have to drive, why not park a little distance from the school and walk the rest of the way?

6. **Get all the school stuff ready the night before.** The last thing you want to be doing in the morning is running around looking for his reading book.

7. **Be a volunteer.** Offer to go into school to help with reading or to be a helper on a school trip. You'll get a fascinating insight into the class dynamics.

8. **Teach your child hat etiquette.** Tell him to put his hat (and gloves) in his coat pocket when he gets to school. Hats left on pegs get forgotten or fall off. And, trust me, you can get mighty weary of hat-buying in a few short weeks.

9. **Get to know the other parents.** Because some of them could become valued friends over the next seven (or more) years. And also because they may hear things your child's forgotten to tell you.

10. **Dress before breakfast.** Make it a rule that no one eats breakfast in their pyjamas. Children wake up hungry and hunger's a powerful getting-dressed motivator – much more effective than, 'Come on, we're going to be late for school!'

Strange faces, tricky places

No sitting in ranks at desks; the first year at school is all about learning through play, and because playing's what your child's been doing at preschool for a fair old while, things should all seem reassuringly familiar. There are, however, a few other aspects of big-school life that may take more getting used to.

Playtimes and lunchtimes

Hanging out in a classroom with 29 other children the same age as you is one thing; venturing out into a heaving throng of older children is quite another. Which means, at first, that your child may find lunchtimes and playtimes the most daunting part of his day. Good schools deal with this by briefing the dinner ladies to keep an eye on their youngest charges and having 'clubs' or 'quiet areas' for the littler ones to retreat to when the playground hubbub gets too much. If this isn't happening in your school or your child's still anxious about lunch/playtime after the first few weeks, have a word with his teacher.

It takes time to settle into school, just as it would take you a while to feel comfortable in a new job. Give it at least two months for your child to get used to it all.

Reading and writing

Every day, your child has a 'literacy hour' (although he may not know it's called that and it may not be called that at all in Scotland), during which the teacher uses a system called *phonics* to help him and his classmates sound out and copy the letter combinations that make up words. This is the beginning of reading and writing. And it's important to know that

- ✔ **Speed isn't everything.** Some children 'get' reading straightaway (they may even have started reading before they started school); some progress slowly and steadily; others find it all rather more of a struggle. But it's certainly not always the 'brainy' kids who read quickly and the 'thick' ones who don't: Reading is more about decoding than intelligence. And the slow-starters soon catch up: In a couple of years' time, you'll probably be hard pressed to spot those who struggled at the start.

- ✔ **Writing is a physical skill.** Even if your child knows exactly what he wants to write, he can't do it properly if he hasn't got enough control of his fingers and hands yet. And that's an age-and-gene thing, not a brain thing. Typically, the younger boys in a class will find it harder to write (at first) than the older girls.

It's a boy/girl thing: The great gender divide

You probably already noticed it happening in preschool but it's in this first year of school that it really seems to get set in stone: Girls play with girls; boys play with boys. A hardy few do cross over the gender divide from time to time but they're definitely in the minority and often have to put up with 'Eew, you like Barbie/Bionicles!' type jibes for their troubles. You can't do anything about it, so don't bother trying. Just resign yourself to single-sex playdates from now on.

Homework

Yes, homework starts this young! But there shouldn't be much of it – maybe a few minutes' reading every day and some writing or simple maths once a week. Most teachers would agree, though, that, at this age, homework's not really about learning anything extra but about establishing a regular habit of working outside the classroom. To reinforce this habit nicely

- ✔ **Set a time for it.** If 'homework time' is always 5 p.m. (or whatever), your child's far more likely to settle down to do it without fuss. Pick a time that suits him best: Maybe he's the get-it-over-with-straightaway type or maybe he needs an after-school chill-out first.

- ✔ **Choose the right place.** You can read with him on the sofa but, for written work, he needs to sit properly at a table.

- ✔ **Cheer him on.** Sit next to him and encourage him as he works. If he gets stuck, help him out. Helping's not cheating; it's demonstrating that you think that his schoolwork is important and worth doing.

- ✔ **Don't stress about it.** It doesn't matter if his homework's not perfect or if he doesn't finish it. It just matters that he has a go.

Making friends

Of course, it's entirely possible that your child will buddy up with another child on their very first day at school and that they'll remain the best of friends from there on in. But, much more likely, your child will take a while to get to know his classmates and to bond with anyone in particular. To ease the friendship thing along a little

- ✔ **Name names.** Ask your child who he sits next to on the carpet, at lunch, at storytime. Show an interest in any other children he talks about. Gradually, you'll build up a picture of the personalities in his class.

- ✔ **Have playdates.** Give everyone a few weeks to settle into school, then invite some of your child's classmates to tea. Keep these playdates small (one child at a time) and short (the school day's exhausting enough).

- ✔ **Model friendliness.** Let your child see you meet and greet his classmates' parents in the playground. If you're always smiley, friendly, and chatty, he's much more likely to be, too.

Take the 'I didn't play with anyone' comments with a good pinch of salt. Children often only remember the last activity they did or the only time they played alone. If you probe further, you'll find he also had a laugh over lunch with A and B, and played catch at break with X and Y.

Bouncy boys and summer-borns

There are two groups of children who have the hardest time settling into school: boys and summer-borns (or turn-of-the-year-borns, in Scotland). It's not their fault; it's just how it is. And it pays to be ready if your child falls into either group (or both).

Let's take the boys first. Generally speaking, their problem is sitting still. At this age, boys experience intermittent surges of the male hormone testosterone which make them desperate to rush around and, frankly, not all that keen on precision-based skills such as cutting, colouring, and writing. Good teachers are aware of this and will adjust school tasks accordingly but you can also help your child out at home. Encourage his fine-motor skills in a boy-friendly way by letting him draw on big pieces of paper with big pens and letting him work on the floor, rather than a table. Keep these sessions short to start with (so he doesn't get distracted) and gradually lengthen them to help his concentration span improve.

With summer-borns, it's all about realistic expectations. If your child's birthday falls in July (or January, in Scotland), for example, there'll be children in his class a good ten months older than him – and, when you're 4, ten months is nearly a quarter of your life. That's a lot of life and learning experience your child hasn't yet had the chance to have. So, don't expect him to find this first year of school easy: He may struggle with reading and writing and also with the social side of things. Over the years, the age gap will matter less and less and there's no reason why he shouldn't catch up (or even overtake) everybody else. But what's crucial now is that he doesn't start to believe that he's not as bright as his classmates. Bolster his self-esteem by praising him for the stuff he's really good at, valuing his opinions, and showing your belief in his ability to learn.

Things that may take you by surprise: Part one

You can prepare your child meticulously, you can read every last scrap of information the school sends you, you can even memorise the curriculum, but things will still happen during your child's first year at school that you really didn't see coming. Unless, of course, some nice book-writing person's thought to tip you the wink.

✔ **The sudden blip:** It's not uncommon for your child to trot happily to school for a couple of weeks and then, just when you're congratulating yourself on a transition well done, throw a wobbly and not want to go any more. This is all about the novelty of school wearing off and the realisation that this is a permanent change kicking in. Be kind but firm (no skipping school) and the blip won't last long.

✔ **Teacher worship:** Your child's teacher is now a central figure in his life and, often as not, the object of his unstinting adoration. Be prepared for, 'But Mrs X says' or even, 'I love Mrs X.' And use it to your advantage: 'Come on – we don't want to be late for Mrs X, do we?'

✔ **'What did you do today?' 'Nothing':** Most children are tired, grumpy, and monosyllabic at the end of the school day. Give yours a drink and a snack and then ask specific questions: 'Who did you play with at break?', 'Did you have PE?', 'What was the best thing you did today?' If your child's still reluctant to talk (and this isn't unusual), don't nag. A better way to find out more is to invite a classmate to tea and listen to their conversation on the way home – always *very* revealing!

✔ **Sibling shock:** You're probably so focused on settling your oldest child into school, you haven't thought about how all this may affect his younger sibling(s). Some siblings barely register the change but others, particularly if they're now having to go to preschool on their own, may feel all-at-sea for a while. Be understanding.

✔ **'I'm a camel and you're making the costume':** Most schools put on some kind of nativity play/Christmas show at the end of the first term and parents are usually expected to come up with the costumes. Which is fine if your child is a shepherd (tea towel on head) but rather more tricky if he's a chicken! Don't get too stressed about it: No one's expecting a haute-couture creation (although you can bet at least one parent will achieve just that; see the next bullet point, 'Competitive parents'). Keep it simple (your child has to be able to get into it, after all). And then brace yourself for the Easter bonnets/World Book Day outfits to come!

✔ **Competitive parents:** There are always a handful (and they *are* a handful!) of these in each year group. You can spot them by the way they crane their necks to see if your child's reading book is on a higher level than their child's. Don't let them wind you up: They're not doing it to lord it over you; they're doing it because they're so desperate for their child to do well, they've forgotten all about the usual social niceties. Rise above it.

✔ **Bad behaviour at home:** Starting school is exhausting. Which means your child's not going to be in the most upbeat and sunny of moods when he gets home. In fact, he's probably going to be a bit of a pain for a while, especially if you're expecting him to be polite to visitors or take part in some after-school activity. I'd recommend not banking on doing anything much after school for the first couple of months at least – you'll probably regret it if you do.

The Lowdown on Moving on Up: From Infants to Juniors

After the Reception (P1) year, your child's progression through primary school is 'packaged' in different ways, according to where you live. If you're in Scotland, he'll move seamlessly on and up over the next six years from P2 to P7. In England and Wales, either he'll have two more years in Infants and then four years in Juniors (either in the same school or in a separate Junior school). Or he'll have three more years in First school and five more years in a separate Middle school.

It's all a bit confusing, especially if you happen to move from one area to another. But more important than understanding the vagaries of our various education systems is being there for your child as he works up to – and then makes – the transition from the 'small' primary years to the 'big' ones.

Schools in England and Wales all follow the National Curriculum, while Scottish schools have their own separate curriculum guidelines. But, wherever your child's school is, you'll find his teachers place the greatest emphasis on the core subjects of English (and Welsh, in Welsh-speaking schools), Maths, and Science. So, bearing in mind that not every school does everything exactly the same way (especially in Scotland), here's a quick look at what you may expect your child to be learning about those subjects when.

The 'small' years (Years 1 and 2)

Between Year 1 (P2) and Year 2 (P3), your child's school day gradually becomes less and less play-based and more and more focused on longer spells of concentrated learning.

- ✔ **What he's doing at school:** Taking part in 'show and tell' sessions to improve talking and listening skills, listening to stories, reading simple books – to his teacher or in a group, forming letters, spelling simple words, learning about full stops and capital letters, counting up to 100, recognising coins and money, using a ruler, measuring liquids, examining insects and plants, recognising and sorting different materials.

- ✔ **How you can help at home:** Read him stories, encourage him to 'sound out' words and read to you, share your 'news' around the dinner table, help him develop his hand control with craft activities or Lego sessions, play board games with dice, let him 'pay' for things in shops, cook together (chemistry in action!), and visit child-friendly museums.

If you live in England, your child will have SATs (a combination of tests and teacher assessments) in all the core subjects at the end of Year 2. Please don't let yourself – or your child – get worried about them: They don't count for anything 'official' as far as your child's concerned and they should be conducted in a very low-key way.

The 'big' years (Years 3 and 4)

In Years 3 and 4 (P4 and 5), your child's attention span is much greater and he's expected to produce a lot more written work. He has probably progressed enough with his reading to be able to read 'non-picture' books on his own. (Year 5/P6 and up are for children beyond the ages covered in this book. If you want to find out more about the curriculum in later primary-school years, visit www.parentcentre.gov.uk or parentzonescotland.gov.uk.)

 ✔ **What's he's doing at school:** Reading independently – and to his teacher and in a group, writing fluently with proper punctuation, working on grammar, having spelling tests, counting up to 1,000, learning times tables and simple fractions, telling the time, doing double-digit sums in his head, and conducting simple science experiments.

 ✔ **How to help at home:** Continue to read him stories, encourage him to read to you, get him books from the library, encourage him to take phone messages and write letters to relatives, test him on his spellings, ask him what the time is, give him pocket money to save or spend, and visit child-friendly museums.

Some children do find the transition from Year 2 to 3 (P3 to 4) harder to handle than others, especially if it involves a change of school. Don't worry if your child seems unsettled for a while: It should soon pass.

Towards the end of Year 4 (P5), do some research on the secondary schools in your area. It's good to have a realistic idea of what your options are as secondary transfer approaches.

Things that may take you by surprise: Part two

Now that you – and your child – are no longer the 'newbies' in the playground, you'll probably both feel a lot more confident about school life. But that's not to say that there may not be one or two things that pop up to puzzle, perplex, or genuinely worry you in the years ahead.

Teasing and bullying

Saying horrid things, falling out, and even the odd bit of pushing and pulling are a nasty but normal part of school life. And it's important to teach your child to shout, 'No, I don't like that!' when others step over the mark. But when another child is consistently dominating yours, either physically or verbally, and making him miserable, it's bullying. And it needs sorting fast.

If you think that your child is being bullied (either because he's told you about it or because his behaviour has suddenly changed and he's very reluctant to go to school), you need to

- ✔ **See his class teacher and the head teacher.** All schools should have an established policy for dealing with bullying, so it's not up to you to sort it out (much as you may be itching to). If nothing is done or the bullying doesn't stop, follow up with a formal letter of complaint to the head, detailing some of the bullying incidents, and asking what action is going to be taken to keep your child safe.

- ✔ **Give him lots of support and reassurance.** Explain that this isn't his fault – it's the bully who has problems, not him. Insist that he tells a teacher every time the bully is mean to him: Asking for help is the right thing to do and doesn't mean he's weak. You can both find great advice at Bullying Online (www.bullyingonline.co.uk).

Never assume that your child won't be a bully. Most kids bully other kids at some time: Even the most angelic child can have a bad day. Teachers usually nip occasional bullying like this quite smartly in the bud. But, should you be told your child is becoming a persistent bully, you need to take it seriously. Find out the facts, talk to your child, and work with the teacher to sort it out. You can also download helpful advice at www.kidscape.org.uk/parents.

'Secret' streaming

You'll probably find that, as your child moves up the school, he's assigned certain tables to sit on for different subjects. You're rarely told what the significance of all table-swapping is, but it's doesn't take a genius (or even a competitive parent) five minutes to work out that it's all about streaming. So, if your child's a Hexagon for reading and a Triangle for Maths, for example, it probably means he's ace with books, but not all that hot with numbers. What really matters here, of course, is not which table your child's on for what but what you both feel about it. So

- ✔ **Watch what you say.** Don't get over-excited or over-neurotic about your child's 'place' in the class. It means very little in the early school years and 'places' often shift about quite fluidly from term to term. Stay calm and cool – or your child may pick up on your worries.

✔ **Watch what he says.** Children do work out what the tables are all about amazingly quickly. And some of them can let it affect their confidence in their abilities. If your child ever tells you he's rubbish at Maths/ reading/ whatever, you need to explain to him that, sometimes, different people are good at different things. And that some people take longer to understand things at first but end up just as good as everyone else. For more on this, see the tips on 'Nurturing a Sense of Self' in Chapter 24.

Weirdly nice school reports

School reports today are very different to the ones you probably got as a child: They're all full of jargon and they're all supremely positive. And, while it's good to see the back of those sarcastic one-liners teachers of yesteryear used to specialise in, it does mean you can get an over-optimistic impression of your child's attitude and achievements. To give you an idea of how this happens, here are some typical 'nicey, nicey' teacher comments with their (possible) 'straight from the hip' translation:

✔ **'Always participates in class debates':** Could mean 'Won't stop talking'.

✔ **'Shows himself to be knowledgeable':** Could mean 'Shows off'.

✔ **'A perfectionist':** Could mean 'Works very slowly'.

✔ **'Is gaining confidence':** Could mean 'Extremely shy'.

✔ **'Independent and self-sufficient':** Could mean 'Won't do as he's told'.

✔ **'A well-behaved and consistent member of class':** Could mean 'I can't remember who this child is'.

Seriously, though, it does pay to follow up the reports you get with specific, precise questions at parents' evenings: Just because the report says, 'X has done fractions', for example, it doesn't always follow that X *understands* fractions. (For other advice about questions to ask your child's teacher, see the section 'Listen and learn at parents' evenings', later in this chapter.)

The Secrets of Good Parent-Teacher Communication

It's important to get on well with your child's teacher : She is, after all, the person who has the biggest grasp of – and the most influence over – your child's progress at school. And building a good parent-teacher rapport is a definite art, both on a day-to-day basis and at the termly parents' evenings.

Be the kind of parent teachers appreciate

Teachers will tell you that parents usually fall into one of two camps: the 'invisibles' and the 'in-yer-faces'. As you can imagine, neither camp is particularly appreciated. What you need to do, then, is position yourself nice and visibly but extremely pleasantly between both camps by remembering to

- ✔ **Smile.** And say hello when you pass any of the teachers in the corridor. You'd be amazed how many parents don't do this.

- ✔ **Reply quickly to notes.** About permission for school trips and so on.

- ✔ **Keep her informed.** Of any stuff that's happening at home that may affect your child's behaviour in class.

- ✔ **Be appreciative.** Comment on the classroom displays you like or pass on any nice remarks your child has made about school (except the 'I love Mrs X' ones, perhaps!).

- ✔ **Fill in the contact book.** Or reading record book (or whatever else it's called). It's a good way for the teacher to see how often you read with your child and what may (or may not) be concerning you.

- ✔ **Volunteer to help out.** With reading or school trips.

- ✔ **Be on time.** To drop off and pick up. And make sure that your child has all the stuff he needs for school each day.

- ✔ **Not hassle her in the playground.** Especially in the mornings when she's busy trying to get everyone into the classroom. If you want a word and she doesn't have a set time when she's available to parents, send her a note asking when you could see her.

Listen and learn at parents' evening

You wait all term for the chance to ask the teacher all sorts of searching questions about your child's educational progress and then your mind turns to mush the minute you sit down in front of her. Actually, this may not be such a bad thing: You see, parents' evening is as much for the teacher to talk to you as it is for you to grill her. Start by giving the teacher time to tell you about your child – she could well have some interesting or surprising observations to make. Then, ask her some of the following key questions:

- ✔ **Is my child happy and settled?** Has he made friends?

- ✔ **Do you have any concerns about his behaviour?**

✔ Is he keeping up with the reading, writing, and Maths levels expected for his age?

✔ Does he join in class discussions and answer questions?

✔ Does he have any particular strengths or weaknesses?

✔ Can you suggest specific ways I can help him at home?

Chapter 22

Eating, Sleeping, and Staying Healthy

In This Chapter

▶ Instilling a healthy attitude to food

▶ Encouraging good sleep habits

▶ Keeping tabs on growing bodies

*1*t's been five long years coming, but things are finally easing up on the eat-your-food-and-go-to-sleep front. Whisper it quietly, but mealtimes and bedtimes could actually start to become quite civilised affairs, featuring your child eating without fuss (shock!) and going to sleep without protest (gasp!).

Your job now (after you've finished patting yourself on the back) is to encourage your child to see that eating right and sleeping well isn't just a good parent-pleasing tactic but a great healthy-lifestyle decision, too. In this chapter, you'll find lots of tips to help you send out the right kind of messages about food and sleep, and keep a small body fit and safe.

Smart Food Tactics for Smart Kids

Your child will probably have a bit of a growth spurt during her first year or two of school, which generally means her appetite improves enormously. As a rough guide (please don't get your calorie-counter out), an active 5- or 6-year-old needs to chomp through about 1,800 calories a day, rising to 2,000 for a 7- to 9-year-old – about the same as a not-very-active adult woman.

Good choices, bad choices

It's as important now as it was when your child was younger to try to make sure that her diet is varied, healthy, and balanced. Trouble is, although she may be more willing to eat, she's also more aware of many of the less-than-healthy food choices pushed by advertisers and favoured by other children at school.

What to do? Well, you can't pretend that junk food doesn't exist or that your child wouldn't choose it over some hardcore-healthy, lentil-weaving alternative. But you can introduce the idea that some foods – and some eating habits – are better for her body than others. And smart people try to make sure that they eat more of the better stuff than the rest. To do this:

- **Talk about what different foods do.** Both in general terms: Healthy food helps keep you fit and well, with bright eyes and shiny hair. And more specifically: Starchy foods, such as pasta and potatoes, give you energy; protein-rich foods, such as meat, eggs, and fish, help your body grow; dairy foods, such as milk and cheese, build your bones and teeth; fruit and vegetables can help stop you getting ill; 'good' fats, found in nuts, seeds, and oily fish, boost your brain power and eyesight. And foods containing lots of sugar and/or 'bad' fats (cakes and sweets) taste nice but aren't good for your body or teeth if you eat too much of them.

- **Don't ban 'bad' foods.** She'll only secretly covet them above all others. Just make them an occasional (and pleasurable) part of your normal diet.

- **Try not to reward with food.** It only makes eating fill an emotional need, rather than a physical one.

- **Look at labels.** Give your older schoolchild two boxes of cereal or two pots of yoghurt and help her work out which is the healthiest choice of the pair. Tell her that the higher up on the ingredients list a certain thing comes, the more of it there is in the product. Show her how to read the nutritional information table, looking for sugar, saturated fat, and salt (sodium) content. And explain about packaging and how manufacturers often specifically design it to grab children's attention.

- **Explain the 80/20 rule.** Which is: If you eat healthily 80 per cent of the time, you can eat whatever you like the other 20 per cent of the time.

- **Have five-a-day races.** Pin a chart on the wall for every member of the family to tick each time he or she eats some fruit or vegetables. Who's going to be first to get their five ticks for the day?

- **Bring on the breakfast.** The old wife who said this meal's the most important of the day wasn't telling tales. Especially as far as schoolkids are concerned. Your child needs a good breakfast (preferably some combination of porridge, wholewheat cereal, yoghurt, toast, and fruit) to maintain her concentration throughout morning lessons.

Your child will be starving at the end of the school day. Lunchtime in schools is usually just after midday, making it a long stretch from then until supper. Always rustle her up an energy-boosting post-school snack.

Tackling weighty issues

The older children get, the more conscious they become of their looks. And this can lead to two sticky food-related situations: your chubby child being teased for being 'fat' (to get some idea if she really is, see Table 22-1) or your perfectly normal-sized child becoming convinced she is fat. In either case, what your child needs from you is a serious boost to her self-worth (of which more in Chapter 24) and a reassuringly sensible attitude towards food and weight. Which means you need to

- ✔ **Watch what you say.** Never make comments about your child's weight. And never let your child hear you talk about your own weight worries or dieting plans. Studies show parents with a negative body image or eating issues often pass on these attitudes to their child. This kind of copycat behaviour is especially common between mothers and daughters.

- ✔ **Know your fat facts.** In relation to kids of this age. Which are that there's a close correlation between the amount of TV a child watches and the amount of extra weight she's likely to be carrying. And that overweight children tend to down a lot of their unnecessary daily calories away from the table: snacking in the car or in front of the telly.

- ✔ **Get your portions right.** At this age, a portion of pasta or rice should be about the size of your child's palm and a portion of meat or fish the size of a deck of cards. Studies suggest that children who are allowed to serve themselves generally get their portion sizes spot on.

- ✔ **Keep her active.** It's hard to have a weight problem if you exercise regularly. As a rule of thumb, 6 to 9-year-olds need an hour of moderately intense activity (hide and seek, ball games, swimming, walking, cycling) over the course of every day.

- ✔ **Tweak your food choices in a healthier direction.** Ditch the biscuit snacks for grapes, popcorn, low-fat yoghurt, or rice cakes with sliced banana. Replace sugary breakfast cereal with a wholewheat alternative. Swap squash for water with a 'grown-up' twist of lime or lemon.

- ✔ **Slow meals down.** Encourage your child to chew and taste, rather than stuff and go. And talk to her about the 'full' feeling our tummies get when we've eaten enough for now.

- ✔ **Don't put your child on a diet.** She may not need to go on one and, even if she does, an adult diet plan's not appropriate. If you're worried about her weight (to see if you should be, see Table 22-1), visit your GP.

Table 22-1	Is My Child Unhealthily Overweight?				
	Increased health risk		High health risk		
	Waist measurement		Waist measurement		
Age	Boys	Girls	Boys	Girls	
5	55.6 cm	55.4 cm	57.0 cm	57.2 cm	
6	57.1 cm	57.0 cm	58.7 cm	58.9 cm	
7	58.8 cm	58.7 cm	60.7 cm	60.8 cm	
8	60.9 cm	60.4 cm	62.9 cm	62.7 cm	
9	63.2 cm	62.0 cm	65.4 cm	64.5 cm	

Adapted from McCarthy, HD, 2001. European Journal of Clinical Nutrition

School lunch or lunch box?

Most parents like the idea of their child having a nice hot meal in the middle of the school day and, thankfully, many local education authorities are now making a big effort to improve the kind of food their school kitchens serve up. The quality does vary from one place to another, though, so, if you're thinking of going for the school meals option, do find out what's on the menu first (go in and ask) or, better still, sample the meals – many schools do hold tasting sessions for parents.

If you decide to go for the lunch box instead, bear in mind that it's not automatically the healthier option. In fact, according to recent surveys, barely a quarter of packed lunches even meet the nutritional standards laid down for school meals! To pack your child a healthy lunch (without getting up at dawn to bake your own granary rolls), try to

✔ **Be sparing with butter and mayo in the sandwiches.** And be generous with the bread. Good low-fat fillings include tuna, ham, turkey, mozzarella, or sliced banana.

✔ **Always include fruit and, preferably, some veg.** Try carrot sticks, cherry tomatoes, easy-peel clementines, grapes, raisins, or 'fruit skewers' (chunks of fruit threaded on a straw).

✔ **Think popcorn, breadsticks, or dried fruit, instead of crisps.** And scones, currant buns, or fruit loaf instead of shop-bought cakes, chocolate, or biscuits.

✔ **Avoid fizzy drinks.** In favour of fruit juice, flavoured milk, water, or yoghurt drinks.

Oh, and don't pack too much: Those dinner ladies don't give them long to get it down.

Want to try this? Widening tastes

Now that you've made it through the faddy-eating years (or are at least starting to see light at the end of the fusspot tunnel), you can afford to vary things a little on the menu front and coax your child to taste and try different sorts of food. To encourage rather more of an adventurous attitude to eating:

- ✔ **Get her cooking.** She's much more likely to try something new if she's had a hand in preparing it. A 5-year-old should be more than capable of making a sandwich. By 9, she should be able to follow an easy recipe and cook a cake or make a pasta supper all by herself.

- ✔ **Let her experiment.** Kids love concocting their own mixtures for a fruit salad or smoothie. Or choosing their own (bizarre) toppings for a pizza.

- ✔ **Give her a trowel.** And get her out in the garden. Researchers say that kids who spend just 30 minutes a week planting, watering, or weeding vegetables are much more likely to eat them. Good grow-your-own choices include tomatoes, runner beans, potatoes, lettuce, and pumpkins.

- ✔ **Make her your menu-planner.** Sit down with her on a Sunday and plan your meals for the week. Look in the fridge and cupboards to see what you've got to play with and what you'll need to buy; talk about which vegetables and fruits come with each season, and all the different ways you can cook and serve them. Buy a cookbook full of great pictures and get her to choose one meal a week that she's never tried before. Don't force her to eat it if she doesn't like it, but pile on the praise if she does.

- ✔ **Eat together.** All children eat – and behave – better when sitting down to a family meal at a properly set table.

- ✔ **Eat out.** Your child's at just the right age to get a thrill from eating in a restaurant: Old enough to cope with the wait for food but still young enough to think being out with your parents is cool. Unpretentious French and Italian restaurants are your best bet but, if you really want to give her something to talk about at school, try Chinese, Indian, Turkish, or, coolest of all, a sushi bar.

Time for Bed! Sleep for Schoolies

Your child now needs about eleven hours of sleep a night, dropping to ten by the time she's 9 (see Table 22-2). This means she'll be spending rather less time under her duvet than she used to, so you have to adjust to the fact that

✔ **She's going to be up later.** You can no longer count on adult-only time starting promptly at 7 p.m. Unless, that is, you actually fancy being woken at 5.30 a.m. by a lively 7-year-old.

✔ **She mustn't be up too late.** Or she won't be in good enough shape for school. Studies show a definite link between not getting enough sleep at this age and poor achievement at school.

Use Table 22-2 to help you work out a suitable bedtime for your child – and then stick to it.

Table 22-2	Your Age-By-Age Guide to Schoolchild Sleep
Age	*Hours of night-time sleep*
5	11
6	10.75
7	10.5
8	10.25
9	10

Adapted with thanks from Solving Children's Sleep Problems by Lyn Quine (Beckett Karlson, £12.99).

This chart is only a guide – not a timetable that your school-age child must adhere to. Some children, like some adults, do seem to need less or more sleep than most. If your child is getting more or less sleep than the chart indicates but seems perfectly content in every other way, then she's fine.

Into bed

Take it from me: Children of this age are *never* tired – or so they say! And every other child in their class goes to bed *much* later than they have to. Don't let this stop you being firm about bedtime. Ignore grumpy protests about your unfair treatment (grumpiness is a classic sign of tiredness, by the way) and

✔ **Explain your reasons.** Tell her she needs sleep even if she doesn't think she's sleepy. It's vital for her body (which grows and rests while she sleeps) and for her brain (which needs to recharge for the next day).

✔ **Don't tell her friends when her bedtime is.** Or she may lose face. Even if they're all exaggerating their own bedtimes (which they probably are).

✔ **Have a wind-down ritual.** Of the good old bath, bed, story variety. Once your child sets down this path, bed is the inevitable end stop.

✔ **Anticipate last-minute requests.** It's amazing how often impending bedtime makes a child suddenly remember her homework or realise she's incredibly hungry. Make sure that homework is done, snacks are eaten, and all is quietening and slowing down before the bath water is run.

✔ **Ban TV from the bedroom.** Not only will it stop her getting to sleep, it could mean she's watching all sorts of unsuitable stuff. The 9 p.m. watershed's there for a reason.

✔ **Let her read.** Your child's not too old for a story from you, but she is old enough for 'reading time' of her own when you're done. Once she's in bed, leave her for a while to read (or look at) a book or listen to a story tape before coming back to give her a kiss and turn the lights out. It's a great way to help her relax before she settles down for the night.

Be especially firm about bedtimes at the beginning and end of term: At the beginning because you need to get back into the swing of the school routine, and at the end because she'll be exhausted (even if she won't admit it).

Out of bed

Those ghastly babyhood scream-all-nighters may be a (not so dim and) distant memory but there are still a few things that can still get your child out of bed when she should be in it. Top of the list are:

✔ **'I can't sleep.'** Some children get quite upset about this. Reassure her that it happens to everyone occasionally. Tell her to relax by tightening and then letting go all her body parts in turn, from her toes to her head. Prevent it happening in future by winding down gently to bed and by letting her read in bed before lights out (see the preceding section).

✔ **'I'm scared.'** Fear of the dark is still common at this age. Leave her bedroom door open and the landing light on. Or fix her up a nightlight.

✔ **'I've had a bad dream.'** Schoolchildren often have nightmares and some of them may get night terrors. Don't make too much of either; settle her back down as calmly and quickly as possible. For more detailed advice on dealing with bad dreams, see Chapter 18.

✔ **'I'm awake. Why aren't you?'** Some children are just early risers – no matter what time you put them to bed. If yours is, she needs to know when 'proper' getting-up time is – give her a clock or set an alarm. Then leave a book and a drink out, so she has something to do while she's waiting. You could allow her to watch (suitable) TV, but be careful that this doesn't motivate her to get up early on purpose!

Wet beds

Bedwetting at this age isn't that unusual – but nobody talks about it! Experts reckon that 15 per cent of children under 7 and about 5 per cent of children under 10 wet the bed. Bedwetting often runs in families – most kids who wet the bed have at least one relative who did as a child, too. And it's way more common among boys than girls. In most cases, the problem goes away on its own. As long as you remain positive and supportive – getting cross about wet beds (annoying as they are) is very counter-productive.

If your child is still wetting the bed after the age of 7, see your GP; he may recommend drug treatment or using special alarms that will wake her the moment she starts to wee in her sleep.

If your child suddenly starts wetting the bed after having been dry at night for six months or more, it's also a good idea to see your GP. Regressive bedwetting can often be a response to stress (school worries, for example, or the arrival of a new sibling) but, occasionally, it can be a sign of diabetes, a bladder infection, a bladder-function problem, or chronic constipation.

Keeping Your Older Child Healthy

Over the past five years, you're probably become a master at dealing with tummy bugs and mopping feverish brows (if not, you can mug up on such delights in Chapter 11). But now you need to get to grips with the hot health topics of this age and stage.

Wobbling teeth

Your child is starting to lose her milk teeth and the tooth fairy will be making many a flying night visit to your house (bear this in mind when establishing the going rate for teeth). As her permanent teeth come through, you need to

- ✔ **Take her to the dentist regularly.** Even if there's nothing wrong with her teeth, it's wise to get her used to going up and down in the dentist's chair and having someone poking around in her mouth.

- ✔ **Switch to fluoride toothpaste.** Like you use. Children's toothpaste is generally only suitable for milk teeth.

- ✔ **Make sure that she's brushing properly.** She probably won't let you do it for her any more, so teach her how to do it correctly. Use an egg timer to remind her how long to brush for (two minutes). If she's a very reluctant brusher, ask your dentist if she can use an electric toothbrush.

- ✔ **Remember that wobbly teeth make eating painful.** Don't be surprised if your child doesn't want to eat apples or anything too crunchy.

Accidents will happen

Active kids fall over or bash into things with tedious regularity. Never be without ample supplies of plasters and antiseptic wipes. And read, learn, and inwardly digest the three following tips:

✔ **Cleaning a cut?** Give your child an apple to bite into as your hand approaches the wound.

✔ **Removing a splinter?** If it's sticking out, cover it with sticky tape and pull it off. If it's

deeper, prise it out with a sterilised needle. While you're prising, distract your child with the apple-biting trick or get her to sing you a song.

✔ **Taking a plaster off?** Do it underwater in the bath. It hurts a lot less.

For more serious accidents, see Chapter 29: 'Ten First-Aid Must-Knows'.

If one twin is losing milk teeth faster than the other, avoid tooth-fairy jealousy by making sure that money's left under both pillows every time.

Keep tabs on your child's sight, too. Checks with an optometrist are free – and especially important if either you or your partner has poor sight.

Growing up and puberty

No, don't panic! The joys of puberty are probably some way off: The average age for the start of the whole long process is 10 for a girl and 11-and-a-half for a boy. But some children do start earlier than this. So be prepared and

✔ **Get talking about periods.** Yes, even if you have a boy. Girls need to know what to expect; boys need to know that periods are natural and normal. The easiest way to do this? Don't hide your own tampons or sanitary towels away and answer questions as and when they come up.

✔ **Anticipate moods.** And body hair. These are often the first two signs that those pubertal hormones have been unleashed.

✔ **Prepare her (or him) well.** For the physical changes that lie ahead. Puberty's much more scary when you only half-know the facts. Visit www.lifebytes.gov.uk for child-friendly explanations.

✔ **Give her (or him) privacy.** Children often become very self-conscious about their bodies as they start to change. Don't make fun of her for shutting the bathroom door and don't expect her to have baths with her siblings.

✔ **Buy lots of soap.** Sweatiness and smelly armpits are another early sign. And need counteracting with daily washing.

✔ **Be frank about sex.** But don't overdo the detail. Just answer each question honestly and calmly and wait to see if she has a follow-up.

Bringing home more than homework

Deep breath now: There are going to be times when your child will be itching to come home from school. Quite literally. Several species of creepy-crawly specialise in hanging out on school-age bodies, and your child will be lucky to make it through primary school without playing unwilling host to at least one of them. So, be on the lookout for:

✔ **An itchy head:** Culprit? Headlice. These brown, sesame-seed-sized insects hang out in human hair, suck blood from the scalp, and lay their sticky little eggs on the hair shafts. The eggs then hatch out into more headlice, leaving the egg cases (nits) behind. Your child's caught them by putting her head close to the head of a classmate who's already got them (the lice can't jump or fly, but they can crawl). You can buy chemical lotions to kill the lice, but they don't always work (some headlice now seem to be resistant). Your best bet is to wet the hair, put on loads of conditioner, and comb through it carefully with a headlice comb (most chemists sell them) until you've removed all the lice. You'll need to repeat the process in four days' time in case you left behind any eggs and they've since hatched out. Conditioning and combing is a big hassle – which you'll doubtless repeat many times in the years to come – but it's is the only way to beat the lice.

✔ **An itchy bottom:** Culprit? Threadworms (or pinworms). These little worms make a home in your child's intestines and wriggle out of her bottom at night to lay their eggs. You can often see them in your child's poo – they look like little white cotton threads. Your child's caught them by touching a (microscopic) egg (probably on another child's hand) and then putting her fingers in her mouth. You get rid of them by taking an anti-threadworm pill (treat the whole family), boil-washing pants and bedding, trimming your child's nails, and training her to wash her hands extra thoroughly before she eats.

✔ **Itchy skin:** Culprit? Scabies or impetigo. Scabies are tiny, spidery parasites that burrow into your child's skin and make itchy, red bumps. Impetigo is a bacterial infection that causes an itchy, blistery rash, often on the face. Both spread incredibly easily from child to child and need medical treatment; see your GP and keep your child off school.

Keeping Your Older Child Safe

Your child's old enough now not to poke her fingers into plug sockets or fall down the toilet but, as she becomes increasingly independent, there are other dangerous situations she could find herself in. Hopefully, she never will, but it's no use pretending the possibility doesn't exist. To protect your child as much as you can, you need to help her to protect herself. By

- ✔ **Making sure that she knows her phone number.** And full address. She also needs to know how to use a phone and call 999. Pin a list of other important numbers – Granny, a neighbour, the police station – on the noticeboard, so she can find them in a crisis.

- ✔ **Teaching her to check who's at the front door before opening it.** And to never open it to someone she doesn't know without your say-so.

- ✔ **Sharpening her road sense.** Ask her to choose a good place to cross and to tell you when she thinks that it's safe to go over. But don't let her cross busy roads on her own till she's at least 8 – she may think that she's more than capable before then but, actually, she really won't be able to judge a car's speed and distance accurately enough.

- ✔ **Explaining what to do if she gets lost.** Which is to head back to your agreed meeting place (always agree one at the entrance to a fair, a museum, a big shop). And then ask either a member of staff (someone in uniform) or a mum with children for help.

- ✔ **Telling her about 'stranger danger'.** But you don't need to go into great detail. Just explain that if anyone tries to pull her into a car or take her somewhere she doesn't want to go, she should yell as loudly as she can, kick and squirm, and run away. Tell her to trust her instincts and avoid anyone who says or does anything that makes her feel uneasy.

Dress your child in bright clothes whenever you're going anywhere busy. And write your mobile phone number on her hand or arm. Should you get separated, you've far more chance of spotting her in a crowd. And she's at least got some way of contacting you.

Chapter 23

Behaviour and Responsibility

In This Chapter

▶ Fine-tuning your behaviour management for school-age kids

▶ Nurturing responsibility with choices and chores

▶ Encouraging politeness and consideration of others

Child-behaviour experts often call the ages between 5 and 8 the 'easy years'. I'm not sure that I'd call them easy exactly (there are plenty of behavioural challenges a school-age child can throw at you), but they're certainly easier than the baby, toddler, and preschooler years. And that's because your child is fast developing a better grip on his emotions and an altogether more reasonable approach to life.

And if your child's changing, so should you. The way you manage his behaviour needs to keep pace with the way his emotional perspective is maturing. He still needs you to set the limits, of course, but he also needs you to be willing to listen, to compromise, and, increasingly, to allow him to make his own decisions. That's doesn't mean learning fancy new discipline techniques; it just means tweaking the ones you've already got. Use this chapter as your how-to-tweak guide – and a jumping-off point for teaching your child more about choices, responsibility, and self-control.

What to Expect: The Good and the Bad

There's quite a distinction between the emotional behaviour of a just-turned-5-year-old and the about-to-turn-9-year-old. One's still perfectly capable of throwing a strop at his parents; the other's much more likely to get upset with himself. One is only just beginning to develop a sense of himself; the other is very much his own person. The change from one to the other is very gradual – and involves far less parental firefighting than the oh-so-contrary toddler and preschooler years. But along the way, you'll see new sides to your child – some of which you'll like and some of which you won't:

> ✔ **He loves rules.** And in the early school years, he'll be very concerned that they're followed – and that rule-breakers are held to account.

- ✔ **He can lose the plot quite easily.** Especially at the end of the school day. Between the ages of 5-and-a-half and 6, in particular, he can be fine one minute, impossible the next.

- ✔ **He can be very co-operative.** He's very receptive to the idea of helping his parents out and working as a team.

- ✔ **He's less selfish.** He can share well and empathise better with others.

- ✔ **He has his own ideas and opinions.** But he can sometimes be very rude or defiant when expressing them.

- ✔ **He's able to reason.** And to be reasonable. (Usually.)

- ✔ **He likes making decisions.** And is able to learn from experience.

- ✔ **He's increasingly influenced by teachers and friends.** Which means he may bring home attitudes you don't like. And, when he's older, he may question your opinions and values.

- ✔ **He tunes you out.** From about the age of 7, he can get completely absorbed in his own thoughts. Which means he may not respond to your requests because he's lost in his own little world.

- ✔ **He's self-critical.** The older he gets, the more he'll ask of himself and the more he'll measure himself against others and find himself wanting.

Refining Your Tactics One: Encouraging Good Behaviour

Everyone prefers carrots to sticks. And your child's no exception. He's far less likely to behave badly if you make behaving well a wonderfully rewarding experience. Not to mention the boost he'll get to his self-worth from knowing you really value and appreciate his behaviour. Here, in no particular order, are the top eight good-behaviour carrots to dangle in front of a school-age child.

Spend some time alone with him

Once your child's going to school, your time with him gets squeezed – and often swallowed up completely in the post-classes, pre-supper rush. But it really pays to find five or ten minutes every day to spend alone with him. Snuggle up on the sofa, take a walk, play a game, sit with him while he has his bath but, above all, take time to listen and let him know that you're there for him. If you give regular attention like this, he won't need to seek it in other, less constructive, ways.

Set clear rules

Your child needs to know what behaviour's expected of him. If you don't make it clear what constitutes good behaviour and what constitutes bad, what chance does he have of behaving consistently well, even if he wants to? Take care, though, not to overload him with rules (this is a home you're running, not an army barracks) and make sure that the rules you do lay down are appropriate for his age (you can probably let up on that always-hold-my-hand-when-you-cross-the-road rule, for example). And, most important of all, make it clear that breaking a rule always has a consequence (see the section 'Refining Your Tactics Two: Handling Bad Behaviour', later in this chapter).

At this age, it's a good idea to involve your child in setting some of the rules (and consequences). For more on this, see the 'Hold family meetings' section, later in this chapter.

Dish out the praise

Never miss an opportunity to praise the good stuff your child does. There really is no way to overstate the power a parent's praise has to make a child feel good about himself, increase his confidence, believe that he can behave well – and want to keep doing so. And those are feelings he needs in particularly large doses at this time in his life when he's starting to compare himself with others and worry that he's not up to scratch (read more about nurturing his self-respect in Chapter 24).

Every day, aim to make more positive comments about your child than negative ones. And always try to be specific: 'I thought the way you included your baby brother in that game was really kind.' If you see your child behaving well but you're too far away to talk to him or caught up in adult conversation, give him a silent sign of your approval with a ruffle of his hair, a smile, or a big thumbs-up.

Give rewards

Rewarding good behaviour isn't bribery; it's payment for a job well done – and an incentive to continue in the same vein. Rewards give your child something to aim for and, once earned, are a tangible acknowledgement of his achievement. You can give rewards as a 'one-off bonus', whenever you see your child behaving in a way you particularly approve of or appreciate. But rewards often mean more when given as a 'performance-related bonus': After your child has worked towards them by maintaining an improvement in a certain behaviour over a set period of time (for this, you'll need a sticker chart; see Chapter 17 for details). Rewards any school-age child would appreciate include:

- ✔ **Privileges:** Either permanent ones or one-offs. Such as being able to stay up a little later, have a friend for a sleepover, watch a little extra TV, be excused a chore, or play for longer on the computer.

- ✔ **Special treats:** Such as going to the cinema, the zoo, or a football match. Or spending a sibling-free day with one parent. Or being given that shirt, those trainers, or that DVD he's coveted for months.

- ✔ **Money:** This is the option most favoured by older schoolchildren. And it combines particularly well with the working-towards-a-reward system – the clink of a coin hitting the bottom of the money jar at the end of a successful day can really spur a child to repeat that success (and clink) again tomorrow.

Seek co-operation cleverly

What's the word you use most every day? Bet you anything it's 'Don't!' And have you ever stopped to consider how morale-sapping it must be to suffer your 'Don't' barrage all day, every day? Time to be a little more inventive – and encouraging – with the way you issue instructions. You can

- ✔ **Switch to the positive.** Simply swap, 'Don't leave your coat on the floor!' for 'Hang your coat up!'

- ✔ **Describe what you see.** Which means saying, 'There are felt tips all over the table. They'll need putting away before I can serve supper', instead of, 'Don't you ever clear up after yourself?'

- ✔ **Say it in one word.** Sometimes, one word is so much kinder than a whole bunch of them. And more effective, too. So say 'Shoes!' as you come in the door, rather than 'Don't walk those horrible muddy shoes of yours all over the carpet!'

- ✔ **Write notes.** This is my all-time favourite way to issue instructions because it always works and it always makes my children smile. Instead of saying, 'Don't keep leaving your toothbrush in the sink!', stick a note by the bathroom mirror saying, 'Dear [insert name of child], Please put me back in my holder when you've finished with me or I go soggy. Love, Your Toothbrush.'

Make sure that he's heard you

If my house is anything to go by, a serious amount of 'misbehaviour' isn't really misbehaviour at all but cloth-earedness. From about the age of 7, your child develops an impressive ability to lose himself in his own little interior world and zone out all the domestic hubbub around him. So, when you've asked him to do something a zillion times and he still hasn't moved a muscle, he may genuinely have not heard you. Make sure that you've got through to him – touch him on the shoulder or use a funny code phrase, such as 'Ears up!' – *before* you make your request.

Be open to negotiation

There's nothing more frustrating than a parent who issues an automatic 'no' to your every request, without even taking time to think it over. It also weakens the power of your 'no' if you trot it out unthinkingly umpteen times a day. Your child is old enough now to present his reasons for his request, so you should be fair enough to consider them. And, sometimes, to say 'yes' (even if your first instinct is to say no). To do this, you need to

- ✔ **Listen.** Let him state his case. Ask him why he wants to do this, why it's so important to him, and how he's going to deal with the issues it may bring with it. If he wants to spend all weekend at his friend's house, for example, when is he going to do his homework?

- ✔ **Let him make bad choices.** Learning from mistakes is very effective. So, if he still wants to spend all his birthday money on chocolate, even when you've talked through other options, let him. He won't do it again!

- ✔ **Say 'yes', with conditions.** 'Yes, you can go to your friend's house but only if you do your homework before you go.'

- ✔ **Come to a compromise.** 'No, you can't go all weekend because you need to do your homework on Saturday morning but you can stay over on Saturday night if you like.'

- ✔ **Make 'no' mean 'no'.** Being open to negotiation is not the same as being worn down by repeated pleading. If you need to say 'no', say it firmly, decisively – and finally.

Hold family meetings

If you and your child are always clashing about the same thing – getting to school on time, for example, or constant fighting with his sibling – hold a family meeting to sort out a workable solution. It's a great way to change behaviour and show your child you value his opinions at the same time. Keep the meeting short and constructive and remember to

- ✔ **Brainstorm.** Point out the problem and give everyone a chance to talk and pitch in with their ideas. But be careful not to let it descend into bickering or accusations.

✔ **Don't dismiss any idea.** However silly or unworkable. Write down every suggestion that's made.

✔ **Come to an agreement.** Ask everyone to think which solution(s) would work best for all the family. And what penalties may be appropriate for not sticking to them.

✔ **Type it up.** And get everyone to sign it. Then stick it up on a wall as a reminder for all the family.

✔ **Finish on a high note.** Play a board game, watch a family film, share some ice cream. Something to get you all laughing together.

Refining Your Tactics Two: Handling Bad Behaviour

Your child's not going to behave like an angel all the time. In fact, it would be rather worrying if he did. For, however brilliant you are at bigging up behaving well, there are going to be times when your child will be just too tired, too frustrated, or too angry to keep himself in check. And that's when you need to step in and show him how to regain control – so that, eventually, he comes to realise that there are ways he can handle his feelings better himself. Here, from the gentle to the tough, are the eight best misbehaviour-managing tactics to try.

Have a code word

This needs a little forward planning. While all is nice and dandy on the behaviour front, get your child to help you choose a special word or phrase (nonsense ones are best, to avoid confusion) that you can say when he's starting to act up. Tell him that when he hears you say the code word, he should stop what he's doing, take a deep breath, and try hard to calm down.

This works particularly well when your child's playing in a group because you can give him a warning about his behaviour without making him lose face – although suddenly piping up with 'Alien bananas!' may well earn you some weird looks from his friends.

Act as cool as a cucumber

Your child's having a meltdown about something or other. What's the worst thing you can do? Have a meltdown, too. Because that's only going to turn the heat up even further. Dampen down all your urges to scream and shout and work on an Oscar-winning portrayal of icily cool parental calm. You may find it helps to make your voice deep and low, and to keep repeating what needs to be done (and why) over and over again: 'It's time for lunch. You need to come in and wash your hands – you know the rules. It's time for lunch. You need to come in and wash your hands . . .'

Acknowledge his feelings and share yours

He has to stop drawing pictures and get in the car. He doesn't want to stop and he's cross. As he stomps and sulks, he's not really looking for you to get his crayons back out and cancel the trip (he knows that's not going to happen). He just needs someone to acknowledge how he feels.

So do it – but make it clear how you feel, too. 'I know that it's frustrating for you to have to stop drawing but I need your co-operation now or we'll never get to the dentist in time.' Now he understands you – and feels you understand him – you'll decrease the tension all round.

Withdraw your attention

Okay, so nothing doing: Your child's still acting up. Bring on the patented I'm-ignoring-this-and-leaving-the-room technique (see Chapters 13 and 17). But this time, add in a little now-that-you're-older finesse: As you turn on your heels to go, say, 'I can't listen to you properly while you're shouting/whining/stamping your feet. Let me know when you're ready to talk calmly.' This gives him – and you – the chance to simmer down.

Make him take a break

Sometimes, it's clear that it's not you who should leave the room but your child. Time out is not the right card to play at this age: It may have worked for your preschooler but, by now, it's lost its edge – school-age children tend just to use the allotted time on the step (or wherever) to seethe on the injustice of life and sulkily plot revenge. What you can do instead, though, is dress time out up in less punitive clothes and call it 'taking a break'. All you need to do is

- ✔ **Explain the situation.** Say, 'I can see you're very angry. I think that you need to take a break and cool off a bit before we sort this out.' Stay calm; remember, this is not meant to be a punishment.

- ✔ **Let him choose where he goes to cool off.** It always helps to give him some feeling of control.

- ✔ **Let him decide when he comes back.** Then you'll know that he's really ready to talk.

Offer a choice: Way out or consequence?

When your child's being very confrontational, and none of the options above are working, give him one last chance to escape facing the consequences of his misbehaviour. Offer him a simple choice: Stop doing whatever it is he's doing or X/Y/Z will happen. Give him a count of three to decide. It really is his choice.

And what should X/Y/Z be? If it isn't obvious (because he's breaking a rule that already has established consequences), it needs to be something that relates as directly as possible to his misbehaviour. So, if he's throwing his chess set across the room, you may decide to take away the chess set for the rest of the day. When you're deciding on the consequence, remember to

- ✔ **Make it fair.** You may be hopping mad that he took a biscuit from the tin without asking you but giving him a six-month biscuit ban is probably rather over the top, as consequences go.

- ✔ **Make it separate.** Don't link it to any reward system you've got in place. The stars on the chart or money in the jar that you awarded him for good behaviour shouldn't be subtracted for bad.

- ✔ **Make it do-able.** So, if he doesn't get dressed for school on time, he goes to school in his pyjamas: Good, logical consequence – but are you really prepared to carry it out? Don't say it if you're not.

If the cause of all the aggro is a sibling quarrel, an alternative way out can be to offer both children a set time to come up with a solution they're both happy with. Step in quick, though, if it starts getting out of hand again.

Smacking is never a good consequence: It sends all sorts of wrong messages and it doesn't work. (For more on this, see Chapter 13.)

Impose consequences

This is where you have to be the bad guy. But you do *have* to be. Because he's chosen this option (you did give him a way out, remember?) and if you don't *always* follow through and impose the consequences, he'll choose the consequence option again – because he may get away with it again. And you really don't want to repeat this process too often. So

- ✔ **Do it quick.** Don't faff around or wait for Daddy to get home; get on with it. If the consequence doesn't happen immediately, it loses impact.

- ✔ **Do it calmly.** You may be angry. You may be sad. Don't show it.

- ✔ **Don't waver.** Even if he pleads, begs, or blubs. You have to follow through or he'll never take you seriously again.

The five patented parent wind-ups – and how not to let them get to you

You'll find there are some particularly parent-provoking misbehaviours that your child now seems to specialise in. It's not personal, it's just what all children of this age do. And it will pass, just like the toddler tantrums did. But, until then, you need some strategies for dealing with them nice and swiftly – before they do your head in. So, here they are:

✔ **Wind-up one: Backchat.** There's something about the cheeky, smart-aleck comment that really grates on the parental nerves – particularly if it's accompanied by a 'get you!' rolling of the eyes. Top tactic? Don't rise to the bait. Ignore it and keep your focus on what you want your child to do, not what he's saying. If he's being incredibly rude, calmly say how you feel: 'I do not like your tone of voice. I'll listen to your objections when you decide to talk politely.'

✔ **Wind-up two: Lying.** It's always a great shock when your child tells his first deliberate whopper. But all children do it at some point, either to cover up a mistake or to avoid your disapproval. Top tactic? Offer him a chance to come clean: 'I don't think that's true, is it?' Then make sure that his honesty pays off – thank him and then forgive his mistake or at least lighten its consequence. And explain to him what he loses by covering up the truth: Your trust, which means you can't give him the extra independence he craves.

✔ **Wind-up three:** 'But everyone's got one except me.' To listen to him, you'd think that he was the most deprived child in the kingdom – he's absolutely, definitely, positively the only child in his class without a Playstation, a new Man United football strip, a custom-carved, gold-plated pirate's castle in the garden. And you're just being a mean, mean parent by not getting him one. Top tactic? Rest easy in the knowledge that he's not the *only* one in such a state of deprivation (children of this age do love to exaggerate). And ask him to explain *why* he needs this particular thing: If he comes up with a good set of reasons (other than 'I just do!'), tell him he can put it on his Christmas list. If, however, it's something you just can't afford, be honest. Suggest instead that, if he starts saving up for it and doing extra chores, you may be able to help him out a little. There's no better way to teach a child that many things in life need to be worked for.

✔ **Wind-up four: Losing it when he loses.** It's perfectly natural to want to win – and incredibly difficult to learn how to lose with grace. So don't be at all surprised if your child bursts into tears when he doesn't win. Top tactic? Play loads of board games at home and give him lots of practice at losing. It gets easier to take the more it happens. And model losing yourself, making sure that you draw attention to the fun of playing, whoever wins. Say, 'Well played – I really enjoyed that!'

✔ **Wind-up five: 'It's not fair!'** This is the flipside to the young schoolchild's obsession with equality and rules: At times he'll feel he's got a raw deal. Top tactic? Acknowledge his feelings and then point out the reasons for your action: 'Your brother stays up till 8.30 p.m. because he's 9; when you're 9, you'll get to stay up till then, too.' If you suspect your child's using endless repetition of 'It's not fair!' to get you to change your mind, use a killer phrase such as 'I love you too much to argue about this', and leave the room.

Forgive and forget

This is, frankly, the most important step of all. Your child doesn't want to be at war with you; you don't want to be at war with him. You may want to go over what happened and ask him what he should have done differently. But make it snappy and don't bear grudges. Give him a hug and move on. (After all, often, your child needs your love most when he's behaving at his worst.)

Done Your Chores? Fostering a Sense of Responsibility

You get into the habit of doing everything for your child but, actually, he's now of an age to do quite a lot for you (for suggestions, see Table 23-1). And that's a good thing – not just because his taking on chores lightens your domestic workload (hurrah!) but also because it boosts his self-esteem to be seen as a useful and co-operative member of the family who can be trusted with real responsibilities. So

- ✓ **Show him what to do.** He may have a vague idea of how to make a bed, but he won't understand exactly what you're after unless you take him through it, step by step.

- ✓ **Don't redo it.** So, the duvet's crumpled and the pillow's wonky? Resist the urge to put it right. What matters most is that he did it, so praise him for that. You can work on his smoothing-over technique another day.

- ✓ **Make a chores ticklist.** Daily chores probably don't need one but weekly chores will – or they get forgotten. It's also a great visual reminder of the effort he's putting in – and a prompt to show your appreciation.

- ✓ **Set a good example.** Which means no grumbling from either parent about the chores you have to do. And a fair division of labour between the two of you, please!

- ✓ **Think about rewards.** You may want to link chores to pocket money (do your chores; get your pocket money), but mull over this first. What if your child turns round and says, 'I'm not bothered about the pocket money, so I'm not doing the chores'? Perhaps you'd rather expect certain chores to be done without reward as part of the family effort to keep the house running smoothly, and save the reward for times when he does extra chores or puts in an extra-special effort.

Table 23-1	Your age-by-age chore chart
Age	*Suitable chores*
5 to 6	Clear up toys, feed pet, make bed, empty wastebaskets, empty dishwasher, set table, clear table, help dust (with socks on hands), help vacuum, empty linen basket and take dirty clothes to the washing machine
6 to 8	All the above, plus: Sweep floor, tidy bedroom, sort laundry, water flowers, get out breakfast things, load dishwasher, wash up pots and pans
8 to 9	All the above, plus: Change own sheets, put on washing machine, hang up/peg out washing, put away clean clothes, dust and vacuum properly

Plugging Away at Good Manners

It can be a long uphill struggle to teach your child good manners. (And no wonder, with so many Ps and Qs to mind.) But it really is worth persevering because a well-mannered, considerate child is popular with his teachers and his classmates and wins smiles, rather than scowls, from waiters, bus drivers, and cranky old ladies in the street. All of which makes you rather proud and your life infinitely less stressful.

Hopefully, your child's got a grasp of the politeness basics (see Chapter 17), so now you can polish them up nicely and add a few more sparkly accomplishments to the set. Sit up nice and straight, then, and

- ✔ **Work on those table manners.** Make sure that your child knows how to hold and use his knife. Teach him how to ask for the ketchup and for permission to get down from the table. Show him how to break a roll, scoop up peas with a fork, peel an orange, and butter his bread.

- ✔ **Insist on 'magic words'.** By now, all you should need to do if either please or thank you is forgotten is give him your 'and what do you say?' look. If the right word's not forthcoming, don't give him what he asked for until it is.

- ✔ **Teach him little courtesies.** Such as stopping to let other people pass on crowded pavements or through shop doors. And covering his mouth with his hand when he sneezes, coughs, or yawns. And saying 'Excuse me' if he needs to attract your attention when you're talking to someone else. And make sure that he always puts his rubbish in the bin.

✔ **Get him into the thank-you habit.** Explain that people who take the trouble to buy him presents deserve – and really appreciate – a proper thank you, preferably in letter or email form. Show him how to order his words: Dear X, Thank you very much for Y. It is [insert suitable adjective] and I can't wait to [do whatever you do with it]. Love, Z. Teach him, too, a form of words for saying thank you for a playdate or outing: 'Thank you for having me. I really enjoyed supper/watching the film/playing on the trampoline.'

Make manners more fun by having quizzes. What do you do if you think that you're going to burp? What are napkins for? What do you say to someone who gives you something you've already got? Expect interesting answers!

Chapter 24

Friends, Self, and the World Beyond

In This Chapter

▶ Learning how to deal with school-age friendships

▶ Raising a confident, caring child

▶ Helping your child to cope in a scary, grown-up world

*W*hat do most other parenting books do at this point? Stop. Honestly. It's as if, between preschooler and teenager, there's this great big developmental desert. Now, granted, there aren't as many 'firsts' to tick off over the next four years as there have been in the past five, but that doesn't mean there aren't a whole lot of changes going on for your child. Or a whole lot of stuff you can do to help her deal well with these changes – and, ultimately, even bigger changes to come.

You see, over the next four years, your child will slowly start to turn out from her family (her main influence right now) towards her friends (her main influence in her tweens and teens). And what she needs you to do is boost her confidence and self-worth, so that she develops a firm enough belief in herself to form good friendships and hold fast to the values you've taught her.

And, the more effort you make to understand, bolster, and support her now – when she's still eager to copy you and please you – the stronger your relationship will be later, as she stands on the brink of adolescence. This chapter gives you the skills *you* need to give your child the self-possession *she* needs to strike out confidently on her own.

Fostering Friendships

Up till now, you've probably 'chosen' most of your child's friends for her – by encouraging her to play with your friends' children – but now she's at school, she's going to be choosing friends of her own, many of whom you've never met before and a few of whom (whisper it) you may not much like. Now, tempting as it may be to step in and steer your child forcibly towards the classmates you'd prefer her to be friends with, don't. Wise parents focus on helping their child manage her own friendships, rather than managing them for her.

Making friends: The need-to-know facts

The first thing you need to get your head round is that children of this age don't make friends in quite the same way we do. In fact:

- ✔ **It can all seem quite random.** Your child may be 'best friends' with one child one day, then with someone completely different the next. Don't take any of this too seriously, especially in the early school years – your child probably hasn't worked out what a 'best friend' actually is yet.

- ✔ **Boys and girls do it differently.** Mostly. Boys tend to form biggish groups of four, five, or six friends; girls tend to stick to pairs or trios.

- ✔ **It's not about popularity.** Your child may have umpteen friends; she may have just one. And either is fine, as long as she's happy about it.

- ✔ **It's all very fluid.** Up until the age of 9, friendships tend to group and regroup many times.

- ✔ **She may not socialise like you.** Just because you're the life and soul, it doesn't mean your child will be (or wants to be). And vice versa.

- ✔ **It's not all about school.** Your child may find it easier to make friends outside school, particularly if she has an after-school sport or hobby she's passionate about.

Friendship smoothers and fixers

Now, while trying to manipulate your child's choice of mates is a big no-no, there's nothing wrong with giving her a helping hand in the old friendship business. After all, this buddying-up thing can be tricky to master and some children simply don't have as much natural flair for it as others. So, try to

- ✔ **Welcome all your child's friends.** And have them round to your house. Even the ones you don't much like. Don't, whatever you do, ban a child from coming round – it'll only make her seem a trillion times more interesting. Let the friendship run its course – if the child's really as unpleasant as you think, your child will cotton on soon enough.

- ✔ **Refine your child's social skills.** Tell her about the importance of eye contact and a friendly smile. Drop hints about what to say in the play-ground: 'That game looks good – can I join in?' But remind her not to pressure others: She should take 'No!' as an answer and find someone else to ask. If the school allows it, encourage your child to take in a simple toy that could act as a draw or a talking point at breaktime.

✔ **Don't get too involved.** If your child comes home and says that X is not her friend any more, don't leap in with, 'Well, I never liked X anyway.' Ask what happened and then say something non-committal, such as, 'That sounds upsetting. I hope X is in a better mood tomorrow.' That way, you avoid a whole lot of back-pedalling when your child comes home the next day and tells you X is her friend again.

✔ **Don't get prickly about party invites.** There's no point getting huffy or panicky if your child's not invited to every single birthday party. It's not personal; it's practical: Few parents have the financial or emotional wherewithal to entertain a whole class of 30 children all afternoon.

✔ **Teach your child how to put her point across.** Tell her that getting on well with your classmates isn't about doing what they say all the time. Getting on is about saying what you think but being prepared to listen to other points of view. And, often, trying to work out a compromise.

✔ **Help her deal with spats.** If she's really fallen out with a friend, 'reflect' her feelings back to her. 'I can see it makes you sad that Y won't play with you. I would feel sad, too.' You're not rubbing it in, you're making it easier for her to articulate her feelings and move on.

✔ **Chat to other parents.** You're modelling the art of friendly conversation to your child and also creating opportunities to arrange playdates.

✔ **Boost her confidence.** She'll find it easier to make friends if she feels good about herself. For more on this, see the section 'Nurturing a Sense of Self', later in this chapter.

✔ **Give her other opportunities.** If school isn't a friend-fest for her, she may have more success at football or art club.

✔ **Scale your expectations to fit her character.** There's a difference between not having many friends because you're really shy and not having many friends because you actually like your own company. The shy child may appreciate you helping her make friends; the loner child may not.

If your child's going through a tricky time with a close friend, arrange for them to do something specific together – going bowling, for example, or seeing a film. This often repairs a friendship more quickly than a less structured playdate.

If you think that your child is being bullied at school, you need to act. Make an appointment to see her class teacher. For more on this, see Chapter 21.

Nurturing a Sense of Self

A preschool child is innately self-confident – she doesn't compare herself with others and, however much she messes up, it never occurs to her to think that she's failed. By about 6 or 7, though, things have changed. All that natural optimism is ebbing away and she's starting to measure herself against others – particularly in the classroom – and see her efforts in a much less positive light. Time for you to step in and show her that, while she can't expect to be brilliant at everything, she can make the most of being herself.

Boosting self-respect

Having high self-esteem is good for a child, but having a healthy self-respect is even better. Why? Because high self-esteem is all about thinking that you're fantastic at everything (and, let's face it, few children really are), while a healthy self-worth is about knowing your strong points but understanding your limitations. And accepting – and liking – yourself just as you are. To help your child build her self-respect

- ✔ **Love her unconditionally.** Whatever her talents, whatever her failings.

- ✔ **Show faith in her abilities.** When she wants to try something new, let her get on with it. Don't hover over her, offering to help.

- ✔ **Shore up her self-image.** Encourage her to feel good about herself and her body but never comment directly – approvingly or disapprovingly – about her weight. This is particularly important for girls.

- ✔ **Let her take responsibility.** For remembering to give her homework in, for example. Even if she thinks that she isn't quite ready.

- ✔ **Save your biggest approval for genuine effort and achievement.** Rather than blindly praising every single thing she does. And be specific with your comments: 'That was hard and you really worked for it: Well done!'

- ✔ **Find time to watch.** Turn up for the school plays, assemblies, dance performances, and football matches. Yes, you may be freezing cold or bored witless, but she'll thrive in the warmth of your watchful eye.

- ✔ **Help her persevere.** Show her how to break dauntingly big tasks down into more manageable steps. Applaud her efforts to see things through.

- ✔ **Make it safe to make mistakes.** Try not to criticise; help her to see what she can learn for next time, instead. Be honest about your own mistakes.

- ✔ **Accept her insecurities.** If she says that she's rubbish at maths, don't tell her she's not. Tell her that different people find different subjects easier than others and everyone progresses at a different pace. What matters most is that she keeps improving and trying her best. Help her do this by setting realistic goals (ask her teacher for suggestions) and giving her loads of positive feedback when she achieves them.

- ✔ **Watch what you say.** Both about her to others (children this age have very 'flappy' ears) and about yourself (constant self-criticism is a habit that's easily copied).

If you do blurt out something pointlessly negative, always apologise: 'I'm sorry – that was an unkind thing to say.' And give her a cuddle.

Accepting your child for who she is

Your child may not be as brainy, as sporty, as popular, as musical as you hoped she might be. But you need to stop wishing she was – right now. If you don't, those 'if only' thoughts of yours will filter through into your words and actions, and your child will pick up on them and think that she's not good enough. Instead, seek out the things that make her special (even if they don't particularly float your boat) and invest some real attention in her interests, her friends, her world.

Giving her space

It's all part and parcel of this growing-towards-independence thing for your child to want to have a little time and space to herself. Don't be surprised (or hurt) if she disappears up to her bedroom or doesn't want to give you chapter and verse about her day at school. Respect her need for some aspects of her life to belong to her alone – she's not rejecting you, she's just growing up.

It's a boy/girl thing: Different ways to praise

Praise is one of the most powerful tools any parent can use to boost and motivate their child (as mentioned in Chapters 13, 17, 23, and elsewhere). But did you know that boys and girls respond differently to different types of praise – particularly as they get older and adopt more stereotypically gender-based attitudes to life and learning? To help you get your 'well done's right, here's your guide to praising the sex-specific way:

For a boy:

✓ **Don't gush.** Boys, especially older ones, cringe at over-enthusiastic praise, particularly in public. Keep your praise moderate, measured, and private.

✓ **Focus on his follow-through.** Boys are inclined to lose heart and concentration more easily than girls. They often need encouragement and help to stay on track.

✓ **Reward planning and organisational skills.** Boys, so full of energy, often prefer to act first and think later!

For a girl:

- ✔ **Focus on her self-belief.** A girl often views success as a fluke, not the result of their own effort or skill. Make sure that she knows exactly what she did right, so she can trust her talent.

- ✔ **Encourage self-appraisal.** Girls love to please but, by seeking your approval before all else, they can lose their ability to judge things for themselves.

- ✔ **Reward attempts to try something new.** Girls can be less inclined to take risks, especially with schoolwork. Remind her that making mistakes is a step closer to mastering something.

And, remember that, whether you're talking to boys or girls, praise is never proper praise if it has a sting in its tail. Don't taint your praise with 'if-only-you-did-this-every-day'-type criticism.

Letting her be bored

She's got enough books, games, gizmos, and gadgets to keep her amused for a month of Sundays but what does she do? Follow you round, saying, 'I'm bored!' Infuriating though it is, this is pretty normal behaviour for a 5 to 8-year-old – and is mostly a reaction to the sudden arrival of untimetabled downtime after school and, especially, in the holidays. But don't see it as your task to be her on-call boredom-buster. Being bored is actually not that bad for her: It gives her crucial time to fall back on her own devices and realise she can be the architect of her own happiness – which is a pretty good life lesson to learn. Of course, she may still need the odd prod in the right direction, so

- ✔ **Suggest a chore.** It's amazing how fast she'll find something else to do!

- ✔ **Make an 'I'm bored' jar.** Write down lots of ideas (anything from 'Write a letter to Granny' to 'Make a den in the sitting room') on separate slips of paper and put them all in an empty jar. When your child says she's bored, she can take a slip from the pot – and then do what it says.

- ✔ **Promise to play later.** Explain that you have to finish what you're doing but you'll come and find her when you have. When you do come, you'll probably find she's happily absorbed in her own thing.

Doing stuff after school

It's easy for your child to define herself and her abilities entirely by her success and popularity (or otherwise) at school. After all, that's where she spends most of her time now. But that needn't – and shouldn't – be the whole story. Why should your child's opinion of herself depend solely on her social and academic standing among a random selection of 29 of her peers? Give her a chance to test other waters by taking her to some after-school activities – she'll almost certainly have fun, may well find something she really enjoys, and could discover something she's actually very good at. And learning a new skill can only boost her sense of self-worth. Bear in mind that

- ✔ **It's best to not zone in on one thing.** Try out lots of different activities, if you can – although, obviously, not all at once.

- ✔ **She does have a say in this.** You may think that judo's great, but she may hate the idea. Don't force her to do anything she doesn't want to. And never pick activities just because you wish you'd done them as a child.

- ✔ **Sports, dance, and swimming are always a good bet.** If only for the opportunity to burn off some energy after a day at school.

- ✔ **Brownies or Cubs could be a big hit.** Even if you shudder at the memories of your own days with Brown Owl. Your child may well get the chance to try out activities you haven't thought of – or would never otherwise have been able to afford.

- ✔ **Music lessons need approaching with careful thought.** Many instruments are really only suitable for much older children (the trumpet, for example, needs a firm set of second teeth). And the piano, often seen as the starter instrument of choice, actually requires such precise hand-eye co-ordination that progress can be dispiritingly slow. Take advice before starting any instrument, have a taster session, and be ready to drop it if it's not a hit. You can always try again later.

- ✔ **It's silly to overdo it.** Some parents do tend to regard after-school activities as a competitive sport: 'Mine does more than yours.' Don't get sucked in. Your child also needs time to play in a free and unstructured way and to chill at home doing nothing much at all.

'Oh, the things they say!'

By now, your child's vocabulary is pretty extensive and she's capable of making up (the most long-winded and, often, quite plot-less) stories and having long and complicated conversations with you. Unfortunately, on occasions, what she's got to say to you is not at all what you'd like to hear. Prepare for your ears to be assaulted by:

- ✔ **'Urgh, no! Don't kiss me!'** Usually said at the school gates, just as the bell rings. Sadly, the time is fast approaching when your child (especially if he's a boy) becomes hideously embarrassed by any public sign of your affection (although she'll probably still be keen for cuddles at home). Don't worry, it'll only get worse: Soon, it won't just be your kisses that are embarrassing but your clothes, your hair, your car, your taste in music . . .

- ✔ **'*@!*^!*'** This is also the age when she discovers swear words. Be careful to react very calmly to such outbursts – the more shocked you look, the more entertaining she may find it to try that word out again. What you do need to do, though, is check that she realises it *is* a swear word: Sometimes, things can be overheard in the playground and repeated quite innocently – and that could get her into a lot of trouble at school. Point out that many people (including you, in some – or all – cases) would be very upset and offended if they heard her using that word. And then change the subject.

✔ **Endless knock-knock jokes.** And other wearyingly laboured attempts at humour. You'll find it all very sweet – at first – that she can now 'get' puns and wordplay, but the sweetness does rather wear off when you're being told the same joke for the 99th time that day.

Nine things to have done by age 9

1. **Made a simple meal.** For you. Even it it's just cheese-on-toast or a sandwich. Breakfast in bed may be dicey, though – those stairs, you know.

2. **Learnt to swim.** Preferably at least a length of the pool.

3. **Loaded and put on the washing machine.** Without turning anything pink.

4. **Done the washing up.** And dried up and put everything away.

5. **Changed and made her own bed.** Without getting tangled up in the duvet cover.

6. **Run an errand to the shops.** Although, depending on where you live and how many roads she must cross, you may have to go with her and hover by the door.

7. **Sorted her own stuff out for school.** Okay, so she'll forget her PE kit but it's still progress.

8. **Tried rollerskating or ice-skating.** And had the bruises to prove it!

9. **Slept in a tent.** On a campsite with you. Or in the garden with her friends.

Nurturing Values and Respect for Others

It's not just having self-respect that matters; it's having respect for other people and other things, such as property, moral codes, and authority. And the only way your child's going to have any of that is if you put your teacher's hat on.

Don't duck this one: The values you teach your child will have a tremendous impact both on her behaviour now and also on the type of adult she will become. And this really is your window of opportunity – she's old enough to understand what you're trying to teach her, but young enough still to value your judgement over that of her friends. So

✔ **Encourage her to help others.** Especially those less fortunate than herself. Ask her to help you sort old clothes and toys out for the charity shop. Get her to pick out little treats for children in poor or war-torn countries and pack them in a shoebox for schemes such as Operation Christmas Child (www.samaritanspurse.org) or Mustard Seed Relief Mission's Love in a Box (www.msrm.org). Encourage her to support charity fundraising events – the annual *Blue Peter* fundraising appeal is a great one to start with.

✔ **Set her chores.** So she understands how much work is involved in keeping house. And why taking on her share is important. For more on this, see Chapter 23.

✔ **Have the right attitude yourself.** Show respect for her teachers – address them politely and never criticise them in front of her. Get on with your neighbours. Show compassion for friends who are ill or having a hard time. Cross the road on zebra crossings, hand money back if you've been given too much change, park in the right spots and always buy a ticket.

✔ **Read books about other cultures.** And other countries. Explain that, no matter how different people look, how differently they speak, how different their customs, we're all the same as each other underneath.

✔ **Help develop her conscience.** Share your moral/religious values with her. Tell stories that teach the importance of showing tolerance and compassion, and standing up for what you believe to be right. Talk about the complicated decisions we all have to make – and how the choices we make can affect others as well as ourselves.

✔ **Explain why things matter.** Why bouncing on Granny's sofa will annoy her, why dropping sweet wrappers on the pavement is wrong, why shouting in the library will annoy people, why breaking other people's stuff will upset them. Ask her to put herself in their shoes: What would she think and feel if that happened to her?

✔ **Help her empathise.** If she's upset someone without realising, don't be too critical. Use her mistake as a learning experience. Explain the effects of what she's done – and ask her what she could have done instead.

Don't expect too much! She's just a child and these are values many adults struggle to live up to. What matters is that she knows what these values are – and can keep them as her guiding principles while she grows and matures.

The rites of passage

I did say that there weren't many 'firsts' in the school years, but these will definitely stick in your mind:

✔ **The first time on two wheels:** Find a gentle grassy slope. Position your child on her bike at the top, show her how to stop by putting down her feet, and then let her freewheel down. Next, get her to freewheel down with her feet on the pedals. When she can do that, tell her to pedal as she comes down. And she's done it!

✔ **The first payout:** Time to start paying out pocket money (check out the going rate first). And let her discover whether she's a natural splurger or a natural saver.

✔ **The first sleepover:** It's probably wisest to start with her sleeping over at a friend's on her own; a big sleepover party may be too much first time round. For sleepovers at your place, limit the sugar intake and suggest everyone watches a DVD in the evening in their sleeping bags – this usually spreads a little calm.

Understanding Big People's Upheavals and Small People's Feelings

Your child is starting to become much more aware of what's going on in the world around her. And she's realising that life's not all nice, cuddly, apple-pie stuff. Don't try to shield her from the unpleasant side of life – at this age, learning about it in the safe and loving environment of your home is better than picking up scary scraps from elsewhere.

Death

It's hard to know what to tell your child when someone she knows and loves has died – you're probably having a hard enough time dealing with it yourself. From about the age of 6 (sometimes, earlier), your child can understand the finality of death, so the wisest course is to keep things simple, factual, and honest. Try to

✔ **Be open about your feelings.** It's okay for her to see you cry. Or to tell her you feel sad. Seeing you being upset will help her feel more comfortable about sharing her own feelings.

✔ **Explain what's going to happen.** Share your spiritual beliefs about death and the meaning of the mourning rituals you are going to observe. Talk about the funeral, who's going to be there, and what they'll be doing.

✔ **Find out how she feels about going to the funeral.** If she really doesn't want to go, that's fine. But do find another way to help her mark the death – maybe by lighting a candle at the graveside.

✔ **Give her a photo.** And help your child remember special moments she shared with the person who's died.

✔ **Be prepared for some surprising questions.** Such as, 'Now Granny's dead, can we have her dog?' or 'So, what was wrong with Uncle X's heart exactly?' She's not being insensitive or disrespectful, she's just curious about things.

✔ **Expect her to show grief quite differently.** A child doesn't often grieve like an adult. Rather than weeping and wailing, she's likely to act up, behave babyishly, have stomach-aches, or want to talk endlessly about the person who's died. This kind of behaviour can continue for much longer than you'd expect; if it worries you, contact the Child Bereavement Trust at www.childbereavement.org.uk.

Divorce

There's no easy way to tell your child her parents are getting divorced, but you'll help her to deal with it better if you

✔ **Tell her together.** Then let her talk with each of you separately. Answer her questions honestly – Mummy and Daddy don't feel the same way about each other any more – but don't supply too much detail.

✔ **Reassure her that she's still loved.** By you both. And that you'll always be her mum and dad.

✔ **Tell her it's not her fault.** Most children assume it is.

✔ **Expect a reaction.** Either now or later. And with each parent at different stages. The most common reactions are anger or becoming withdrawn.

✔ **Go slowly with new partners.** Let your child adjust to this change before you impose the next.

Bombs and bad news

There are times when the world seems battered by an endless succession of natural disasters and terrorist attacks. And, as a parent, it's natural to want to protect your child from finding out about these things that can only frighten and worry her. In fact, though, she's reached an age when she's going to be hearing about them anyway – at school, on the radio, from newspaper headlines – and she needs you to help her put them into some kind of perspective. So

✔ **Answer her questions honestly.** Although you may feel you don't need to go into all that much detail.

✔ **Find age-appropriate sources of information.** Watching 'adult' news film of a disaster, especially when it's replayed again and again, has been shown to increase children's fears. Children's news programmes, such as the BBC's *Newsround,* usually deal very sensitively with these issues.

✔ **Reassure her of the risks.** Point out that these things have been happening since the dawn of history – neither natural disasters nor acts of terrorism are anything new. And that the chances of her being caught up in either are very small indeed. Tell her that life can never be made absolutely safe, but there are many people working to keep all of us as safe as possible. And that there's no point worrying so much about what may happen that you stop enjoying what's happening now.

The truth about TV and computer games

Given half the chance, most over-5s would spend their every waking hour glued to a screen, watching TV or playing computer games. And that, obviously, would not be a good idea. But nor would banning TV or computers completely – because your child can get a lot out of them:

✔ **They're a useful learning tool.** Most schools use TV programmes and computer games in lessons. And experts have shown that playing the right kind of computer games can improve a child's strategic and logical thinking.

✔ **They're a great relaxation aid.** After a long school day. As long as they're not your child's only way of chilling out.

✔ **They give her a social boost.** Children like sharing cultural references from TV or films. Or talking about moves in popular games.

So far, so good. But – and there's always a *but* as far as TV and computers are concerned – it's important to make sure that all the googly-eyed, geeky stuff isn't messing with her head or stopping her engaging with all the other great stuff life has to offer. So

✔ **Keep it age-appropriate.** That means picking specific TV programmes and only buying DVDs or games with the right age limit on them.

✔ **Impose a time limit.** Short bursts of TV watching or game-playing are much healthier than long obsessive afternoons in front of the screen.

✔ **Keep hardware out of bedrooms.** Have them watching or playing where you can see what they're up to – and where they can't switch on when they're meant to be sleeping.

✔ **Be savvy about the Internet.** It may be a great homework resource but your child needs to know that not everything on it is true – and not everyone is who they say they are. Block out the worst cyberstuff with filters or lockout software and make sure that your child knows never to give out any identifying details online.

Part VI
All About Siblings

"Now look for the house with the balloons
outside — that's where the party is."

In this part . . .

*P*arenting doesn't get better or worse when you have
another child; it just gets different, which is the
reason for this part all about siblings. There's a chapter
full of tips on preparing your first child for the arrival of
the second (and dealing with the inevitable jealousies that
follow). There's a chapter full of tactics for squashing sibling squabbles. And there's a chapter full of clever ways to
solve to the seemingly-impossible problem of how to give
every one of your children all the attention they need.

Chapter 25

The New Arrival

. . . .

In This Chapter

▶ Preparing your first child for the new baby

▶ Dealing with jealousy (and other, weirder reactions)

▶ Making sense of your own jumbled feelings

. . . .

*S*o, you're finally getting to grips with this having-a-child thing and now what do you go and do? Have another one! Of course, bumping up the headcount in your family is always a cause for celebration, but, while the bump's cooking, there are bound to be times when you start wondering what on earth you're letting yourself in for.

And that's what this chapter is all about. It's your guide to making the mental adjustment from having one child to having two (and, trust me, it is quite some adjustment!). It's your aid to easing your first-born gently through the sometimes bewildering, sometimes bumpy beginnings of being a sibling. And, above all, it's your source of all sorts of clever little tricks that make adding in an extra turn out to be twice as nice, rather than double the trouble.

Don't Mind the Gap!

Heading for two children under two? Suddenly pregnant again after a long, long gap? Don't listen to the voices of doom. Whether it's thirteen months, thirteen years, or anything in between, every age gap between siblings has its special joys – and, okay, some special challenges:

   ✔ **The classic 'two-year gap' can be tricky.** Your toddler doesn't yet know how to share toys, let alone your attention. Of course, it doesn't neces-sarily follow that you're going to have loads of tantrums and trouble, but it's wise to be prepared for some.

   ✔ **Having children close together can pay off later.** Caring for two (or more) tinies is very hard work but, if you can spare a weary eye to look past today's piles of nappies, toys, and dirty washing to the years ahead, you'll see that you're raising a clutch of children near enough in age to enjoy doing the same kind of thing: Something that parents of more widely-spaced kids can only dream of as they drag bored toddlers round museums and bored pre-teens to the playground.

✔ **Getting a sibling puts noses out of joint.** However old the nose and the child it belongs to. Your first-born isn't being 'babyish' if he feels resentful for a while; he's being normal.

There really is no such thing as the perfect gap or the perfect number of children (or, indeed, the perfect family). Which is just as well because few of us have lives that are organised enough or ovaries that are obedient enough to plan the production of our progeny like a military campaign.

Setting the Scene

Few children like surprises. Even fewer like sudden change. So it's not the best move to turn up one day with a little bundle in your arms and exclaim, 'Say hello to your baby brother!' As a parent, you've got nine months to get used to the idea of having another baby; your first child deserves some serious time to get used to the idea, too.

Preparing Child One for Child Two

Exactly how you help your child get his head round the facts of this new life-to-come obviously depends on his age and his level of understanding. Toddlers and preschoolers need help grasping the whole Mummy-has-a-baby-in-her-tummy thing; for older children, it's less about biology and more about emotions. You should find some, if not all, of the following suggestions useful (they run roughly in age order, starting with the toddler tips first):

✔ **Read him books about new babies.** Avoid the cringey, 'everything turns out just rosy' ones. Look for books that are funny but real – that introduce ideas such as Mummy going into hospital to have the baby, the baby crying and needing cuddles, and Mummy and Daddy being very tired. Painting an honest picture of the future is always the best policy.

✔ **Show him the scans.** Understanding that there's a baby in Mummy's tummy is so much easier when he can actually see a 'photo' of it. Older children will enjoy taking the photo into school for 'show and tell'.

✔ **Point out other babies.** Everywhere you go. It helps to embed the idea that lots of other children have baby brothers and sisters, too.

Spotting other babies is a good opportunity to rein in expectations: Some children think that they'll be acquiring an instant playmate. Help yours see that newborns don't do much but sleep, cry, and eat.

✔ **Be prepared for probing questions.** Such as 'Who put the baby in Mummy's tummy, Daddy?' and 'How will the baby come out, Mummy?' Be honest and straightforward about the facts of life but don't supply more detail than you're asked for: 3-year-olds, for example, don't need to know about sperm counts and dilated cervixes just yet.

✔ **Get him involved.** Make it all seem more real by asking him to help with the preparations for the baby's arrival. Would he like to make a picture for the baby's room? Can he help you sort out the babyclothes? What would he put on the shortlist for the baby's name? (This really isn't one for toddlers: You really don't want to get cornered into writing 'Tinky Winky' on the birth certificate!)

✔ **Let him voice his feelings and fears.** In the face of your obvious (and understandable) joy about the baby, it can be difficult for your child to tell you how scared or worried or angry he's feeling about it all. If you don't give him a chance to let those feelings out, they'll just come out in other (badly behaved) ways. Show him you understand how he feels ('Some children worry their dad won't have so much time to play with them when the baby's born') and give him time to reply. Then offer the reassurance he's after ('If you ever feel like that, come and tell me and I'll make time to play').

✔ **Be wary of over-excitement.** Some older children get really fired up by the idea of having a baby brother or sister, and count down the weeks to the birth in adorably eager anticipation. Which is lovely – but can result in a rather bumpy reality check when the baby is born. So, temper his excitement – just a little – by explaining that life with a newborn isn't all cuteness and light; it can, in fact, make everyone in the family feel pretty tired and touchy for a while.

Expecting a baby with a new partner? A new baby in a stepfamily can be a very positive thing: Proof to the brother-to-be that this new family set-up of his is a reassuringly permanent thing. But an older child may worry that, because the baby's parents live together (unlike his), it will be loved more than he is. If he's your child, tell him that you will love this baby just as much as you love him – no more, no less. If he's not your biological child, tell him you may love the baby differently but that won't change the way you love him – and there isn't one kind of love that's better than another one.

Thinking about the practicalities

Of course, it's not just your child you need to get ready for change; it's also your house and routine. You'll save yourself no end of last-minute scrabbling around after (or, in one instance, during!) the birth, if you

✔ **Sort out a sitter.** Make childcare plans for the day (or night) of the baby's birth. Because these things are so unpredictable, you may have to line up several friends or relatives, but do make sure that your child is really comfortable in the company of every person on your list.

✔ **Move the furniture.** Will the baby need the cot your first child's still in? Sort out the move to a 'big boy's bed' several months before the baby arrives. (For help with this, see Chapter 14.) Don't give the impression that your first child's being booted out to make room for the baby (even if he is, really).

✔ **Bed down your routine:** Thinking of starting your first child at nursery or playgroup? Or changing the childcare set-up in some other way? Get everything up and running well before the baby's due. Your child will experience enough upheaval in his life as it is, without you suddenly imposing big new changes in his daily routine.

If your child's already at school (or due to start), don't forget to tell his teacher that he's about to become a big brother. You can then work together to manage any emotional fallout.

✔ **Think about your wheels.** If your child's under 2, you'll probably need a double buggy for a while: You'll have to choose between a tandem (one seat in front of the other – heavy to manoeuvre up and down city pavements) and a side-by-side (make sure that it's narrow enough to get through your front door and, if it is, that the seats are wide enough for your toddler). If your child's a little older but not yet up to walking everywhere, get one of those back-of-the pushchair attachments for the small-and-weary-of-leg to stand or sit on. Much cheaper than a double buggy – and way more fun.

Hello, Baby! Making Introductions

First impressions matter. They say that people form a firm opinion of you within fifteen seconds of meeting you for the first time. I'm sure that it's not that different for children. So, it's really worth prepping the scene a little before you introduce your child to his brand new baby brother or sister. Use these simple tricks to get things off on the right footing:

✔ **Keep your arms free.** Try not to be holding the baby when your older child comes to see you after the birth. You need to be able to give him your full attention and a big cuddle – just as you've always done before.

✔ **Let your child 'discover' the baby.** Restrain the urge to scoop up your newborn for your child to marvel at. Keep your focus on your first-born and wait for him to spot the baby by himself. This is a technique to repeat when you come home from hospital: Don't come through the front door till the baby's fallen asleep (the car ride home usually does the trick for you), then leave the baby in a car seat by the door while you say a big hello to your first-born. Spend time chatting with him until he asks where the baby is or (more likely) the baby stirs and you say, 'Come on, let's fetch the baby together, shall we?'

✔ **Have the baby give him a present.** I can still remember the thrill of looking into my new sister's cot and finding a tube of Fruit Pastilles with my name on them. Suddenly, baby sisters were rather nice!

✔ **Help visitors to be tactful.** There's nothing worse than standing by while the people who used to fuss over you are fussing over someone else. Pre-warn visitors that your child's feeling a little fragile and, if the goo-goo talk still gets too gushy, divert the conversation away from the baby for a while.

Give your child the task of opening any gifts people bring and always try to take him, not the baby, with you to answer the door – that way, he'll at least get some attention to himself to begin with.

Reactions To Be Ready For

Okay, so the first sibling encounter's over; let newly expanded family life begin! You don't need me to tell you that it's going to take a while for everyone to get used to the changes – and there are going to be times when one or another (or even all) of you feels put out, fed up, or downright cheesed off. What may take you by surprise, however, is the strange kinds of behaviour these negative feelings may inspire in your child – and you.

What your child may do

Some children come right out and say it: 'Can you send the baby back now, Mummy?' Others take a less direct approach and demonstrate their general dissatisfaction with the new turn of events by acting in all sorts of strange and challenging new ways. This is annoying but perfectly normal and mostly short-lived. Be prepared for any of the reactions below and don't be surprised if your child works his way through a fair few of them before he's done.

Going backwards

Some children react to the new baby's arrival by going all babyish themselves: The chatty pre-schooler reverts to baby talk; the potty-trained toddler starts wetting his pants; the weaned-off-the-bottle/breast tot starts whining for a 'bot-bot'/scrabbling at Mummy's bra for milk. It's terribly tiresome but it's not serious; it's just a physical demonstration of your child's desire to remind you that he's still your baby, even if you've seen fit to go and acquire another one. Hang in there till it passes (and it will) by:

✔ **Being tolerant:** Don't be too hard on his babyishness (even if you really could do without it right now). Turning it into a big issue will only make it last longer. Don't comment on the baby talk or the wet pants (just seethe silently inside); offer a bottle or a breast if it doesn't bother you, or distract your child with some other treat ('special' juice, perhaps) if it does. And repeat to yourself constantly: 'This, too, will pass.'

✔ **Doubling the cuddles:** Give him lots of physical reassurance that he's still precious and special to you.

✔ **Gently pointing out the upsides of not being a baby:** Like eating ice cream, playing with toys, going on the swings. Lucky old him; his poor little baby sister's not nearly big enough to do all that, is she?

Hitting and poking the baby

Your child is naturally curious about this strange new person in his house and will want to get close enough to touch and pat and stroke. Sadly, junior co-ordination being what it is, the best-intentioned patting and stroking by any child under 4 (and some much older than that) can end up more like slapping and poking. And then all hell breaks loose: Baby screams, parents yell, and child gets well and truly told off. Which can then make your child cross enough to want to hurt the baby properly – and so the battering escalates. Stop this behaviour before it starts by

✔ **Staying calm:** Babies are tougher than you think. Grit your teeth and resist the impulse to restrain your older child's clumsy prods. The last thing you want is a child who thinks that the quickest way to get Daddy's attention is to poke his sister in the eye.

✔ **Showing him a safe place to pat:** Explain that babies like pats on the tummy, not the head.

✔ **Staying close:** It's one thing to keep your cool when your older child's hand is hovering over your baby's face; it's quite another to turn your back and let him do some serious harm. Always stand nearby and keep watch out of the corner of your eye.

Never leave your older child alone with the baby. Even the most loving and gentle child can injure a baby with an over-enthusiastic cuddle. It's not fair on either of them to leave them together, even for a moment.

Being extra naughty

No sooner have you brought the baby home than your hitherto beautifully behaved first-born goes on a wildchild rampage, breaking his toys, throwing his food, and refusing to do anything you say. It's not clever, it's not pretty, and it's your first taste of sibling rivalry in all its heated glory. Jealous of the time you're spending with the baby (time that used to be his alone), your older child is demanding your attention in the most dramatic way he can. If truth be told, you'll never get rid of the rivalry completely, but you can turn down the heat – and put a lid on the naughtiness – by

✔ **Letting the little things go:** Now's not the time to get heavy about his eating with his fingers or leaving his toys all over the floor. Save your energy for dealing with the naughtiness that really matters – and turn a blind eye to the rest for a while.

✔ **Creating a special you-and-him time:** Set aside a certain part of every day to give him the attention he's craving. You don't have to do much – read a book, have a chat, play a board game – to reinforce the special bond you had before the baby came.

Being weirdly angelic

This reaction is almost exclusively adopted by older-than-toddler girls. There you were expecting jealous tantrums and months of sulking, and here is your older child behaving like Mother Teresa: patience, tolerance, and helpfulness personified. While, of course, it is entirely possible that your child has taken to his new role as older sibling like a duck to water, it is also worth considering that he may be bottling up his feelings of resentment towards the baby. Heap on the praise for the good behaviour you're seeing now, but keep your own expectations in perspective by

✔ **Not expecting it to last:** He may be fine with the baby now but that may change when the novelty wears off, or later, when his little sibling's old enough to snatch his toys or break his stuff. Try to be just as tolerant of a late reaction as you would have been of an early one.

✔ **Encouraging him to talk:** Show him it's safe to voice his feelings about the baby, perhaps by admitting some of your own ('It's not much fun when the baby's crying a lot, is it?'). Tell him that being annoyed or sad about the baby sometimes is okay; it won't make you love him less.

Your older child's not being difficult on purpose – although it can seem like it when you're tired enough just coping with the baby. This really is a time to cut everyone some slack.

The sibling doll

It's become quite the thing among some childcare experts to recommend that you give your older child a doll as soon as he gets a sibling. Not a doll to dress and feed and push in a toy pram (although that's certainly not banned) but a doll to vent resentful feelings on. The theory is that it's a great way to take out all that newly minted sibling fury without harming the actual newly minted sibling in question: 'Don't hit your sister, darling. Show me how you're feeling with your doll.'

Some younger children do take to this idea with gusto, pummelling and thrashing their doll to within an inch of its stuffed existence. And maybe doing so does help them release all their negative feelings quite wonderfully. But you do have to ask yourself if you really want to watch, let alone encourage, your child bashing the living daylights out of a something that looks really rather like your own baby. Squeamish souls may prefer to ditch the doll and offer up some human-feature-free playdough instead.

How you may feel

It's not just your child who may react strangely to the arrival of your second-born; you may well have to deal with some pretty weird feelings of your own. If you're not prepared for these reactions, they can confuse and unsettle you mightily. So, take a tip from me and get ready for the possibility of any of the following.

Disliking your first-born

Next to your tiny, defenceless little newborn, your first-born is now this clumsy, noisy, messy giant. Every time you start to do anything with the baby, there he is, in your way and in your face. And let's not even get started on the atrocious way he's been behaving lately. You never dreamed it could come to this, but you're not having very kind thoughts about your older child.

Scary though these feelings are to admit (even to yourself), they're actually very, very normal: Your postnatal hormones are programming you to protect and nurture your new baby above all else, and anything – or anyone – that gets in the way of you doing that is going to upset you quite a lot. These feelings towards your first-born will pass as your hormones return to normal but, in the meantime, it helps to

- ✔ **Take time out from the baby.** As long as his tummy's full and his nappy's dry, your baby will be just fine in a Moses basket or someone else's arms for a while. Use this time to concentrate on your other child: Your less-than-kind feelings will probably evaporate after you spend some one-to-one time with him and re-establish your old connection.

- ✔ **Go for a walk as a threesome.** With the baby tucked up in his pram, you can talk to your older child without distraction. And there's nothing like fresh air to blow away negative emotions.

If you find you're feeling negative, numb, empty, and low pretty much all the time, you may have postnatal depression. It's nothing to be ashamed of – postnatal depression is a proper illness that affects second-time mums (and, occasionally, dads) as well as first-timers – but it's important to get help and treatment from your GP.

Feeling sorry for your first-born

You may think this is the alternative to disliking your first-born but, actually, it's more of an addition: You can quite easily feel both emotions at once. That's because it's not your hormones in the driving seat this time but your brain – and it's filled with images of your child's world suddenly turned upside down. He's probably not nearly as bewildered as you're imagining but, in any case, the outcome is best for you both if you

- ✔ **Don't pretend nothing's changed.** Running yourself ragged trying to do everything absolutely the same way as you did it before (or even better)

is only going to exhaust you now you've a baby in tow, too. Yes, your older child needs and deserves stimulation and structure in his day but he's also adjusting to change and could probably do with taking life at a slower pace for a while.

✔ **Focus on what he's gaining.** For all the downsides you're busy imagining, there are plenty of upsides to getting a sibling, too. Trust me, it won't be that long till they're a demon double act, plotting ever more fiendish ways to gang up on you!

Feeling even more knackered than last time round

Thankfully, you now know one end of a newborn from the other, so you don't feel all-at-sea in the land of latching on, winding, and wiping small bottoms. But last time you had a newborn, you could take life sleepy-slowly, dozing when your baby napped in the day to catch up on the rest you missed out on at night. Fat chance of any of that now! With an older child on the loose, a daytime snooze is, well, the stuff of your dreams. To ease the fatigue:

✔ **Have a 'quiet time' every day.** If your older child's still having an after-noon nap, use that time to do nothing but sit quietly with your newborn and rest. If naptime's a no-go, set aside an hour or so every day when you sit on the sofa with your older child and don't do much. You can look at books, listen to songs or a story tape, watch a DVD – anything that allows you both to snuggle up close and relax.

✔ **Give people a wake-up call.** Even the nicest friends and relatives tend to think that, now it's your second time round, you won't really need their help. Put them right – as tactfully as you can – and nudge them to give you a little break now and then.

Being shocked that they're different

Your first baby was up all hours for months; your second sleeps through within weeks. Your first breastfed like an angel; your second doesn't know your nipple from his elbow. How could two beings made from the same cocktail of genes turn out to be so different in so many ways? Of course, if we were thinking rationally, it shouldn't really surprise us that our children don't turn out to be carbon copies of each other, but rational thinking's often in short supply in the days immediately following childbirth. Rein in your astonishment by trying hard to

✔ **Celebrate their differences.** It may be easier for you to deal with in the first weeks, but it really would be boring in the long run if your children were all the same. Part of the delight of parenthood is watching your children carve out different characters from their shared family stock.

✔ **Be flexible.** Just because a certain way of doing things worked for your first-born, doesn't mean it will for your second. You may have to take a different approach this time around.

Five Ideas to Keep Your Head above Water

It can be tough learning to divide your attention between two children when you've only ever had to focus it on one before. Some days, you can feel so torn apart by their conflicting needs, you wonder if you'll ever pull yourself together as a parent again. You will, of course, but, in those deep, dark, despairing days when your new togetherness seems a whole world away, stoke up the hope with this five-point plan:

- **Lower your standards.** Parental perfection may be attainable when you've only one child (though I never came close), but it's not even worth thinking about when you've just brought home another. It's not the end of the world if your first-born watches TV for 45 minutes or you serve up fishfingers five nights on the trot. Cut corners and reclaim some energy: You can't be the parent you want to be when you're stressed.

- **Sort the logistics.** If both children are hungry, who are you going to feed first? Is it wise to keep the nappies in the bedroom if it means you'll be leaving a toddler alone downstairs every time the baby needs a change? Try to anticipate the aspects of your daily life that could get tricky now there's more bodies involved – and search for a stress-free solution.

- **Box clever.** Don't push your older child to 'love' the new baby; instead gently involve him in the baby's life by asking his opinion. When the baby cries, say, 'What do you think he's crying for? Shall we give him some milk?' And don't forget to 'spot' little signs that the baby loves him back: 'Look how he wiggles his legs when you smile at him!'

- **Stick to your routine.** With everything else that's going on, both you and your first-born will function better in your familiar daily rhythm.

- **Favour your first-born.** If anyone offers to help, press the (baby-filled) pram into their hands and point gratefully at the park. Although you'll instinctively want to keep your baby close, what he needs right now is pretty basic and doesn't necessarily all have to be provided by you. But what your first-born needs right now is more complicated and can only be provided by you. Every moment of undivided attention you can rustle up for him is worth its weight in gold.

Chapter 26

Squabble Solutions

. . . .

In This Chapter

▶ Understanding sibling scraps (and why they can be a good thing)

▶ Knowing when to break it up and when to leave them to it

▶ Sowing the seeds of peace

. . . .

*Y*ou know that lovely picture you have in your head? The one where you and your partner are watching your children frolic together in the garden, the sun dappling their linked arms and happy faces, their laughter tinkling through the warm summer air? Forget it right now.

Honestly, there's no point torturing yourself: All this living-together-in-perfect-harmony stuff may have worked out for Mr and Mrs von Trapp but it just ain't reality for the rest of us. Your kids will grow to love each other, they may even grow to like each other, but they will never grow tired of squabbling, bickering, and winding each other up.

Of course, that doesn't mean you should just sit back and let it all kick off. There are things you can do to defuse the inevitable sibling-to-sibling tension, and tactics you can employ to stop silly squabbles escalating into fully-blown punch-ups. And this is the chapter to find them in.

Born to Fight: Why Squabbling's Normal

Argue, snipe, tease, bicker, bully, snatch, push, pinch, shove, thump, fight: They're all part of every normal sibling's job description. And, actual violence aside, that's how it should be. Like puppies, little humans in the same litter need to have regular scraps with each other to toughen themselves up for the hustle and tussle of grown-up life. When your siblings squabble, they are learning to stand their own ground and sort out their own problems – a life skill that's far better honed early, in the safety of your home, than found wanting later in some isolated corner of the secondary-school playground.

The younger your children are, and the closer in age, the more frequent and the more physical their squabbles are likely to be. But don't go thinking peace will break out when primary school – or even puberty – beckons. Sibling spats can still be relied upon to spark off in the teenage years and, as some of us adults know only too well, often simmer on well beyond that.

Now, I'm guessing you don't fancy living in a permanent sibling war zone any more than I do. I'm sure that you even harbour hopes of your children playing together nicely some of the time. So you need to sort out some strategies for keeping a lid on things. And not just for your sake, either: The way you handle the whole sibling-squabble question can have a massive impact on the way your children rub along together in the future. React to their spats inappropriately, inconsistently, or unfairly and you could be stoking up even more of a rivalry between them; react calmly, consistently, and fairly and you stand a much greater chance of spreading peace, love, and even (shock!) proper sibling harmony.

Diversionary Tactics

The first item on your Project Sibling Harmony agenda is finding ways to stop the squabbles happening in the first place. It's frankly impossible to turn your house into a spat-free zone, but you'll certainly cut right down the squabble quota if you

- ✔ **Set clear limits.** It's never too early to have house rules. No hitting. No kicking. No pushing. No biting. No throwing things at each other. No name-calling. No taking each other's stuff without permission ('No, mine! Fights over property rights'). Having rules won't stop the squabbles happening, but it may stop them getting out-of-hand. And even if it doesn't, having rules makes sure that each little squabbler knows exactly where she stands – and what the consequences will be.

- ✔ **Keep 'em busy.** A bored child is a child spoiling for trouble. If nothing much else is going on, what better way to liven things up than snatch your brother's toy or make your sister cry? Find something diverting for idle hands to do – before they find something much more unpleasant all by themselves.

- ✔ **Pay (individual) attention.** You know those old war films where the goodies are stuck in no-man's land and one of them decides to create a diversion to draw the enemy fire? It's kind of like that with kids (except, hopefully, we parents aren't really the enemy): They create squabbles just to draw a bit of attention their way. I'm willing to bet you'll have far fewer sibling-on-sibling meltdowns to deal with if you can find it in you to give each of your children a little one-to-one time at least every other day. Don't worry: It doesn't have to be some kind of marathon of quality-time togetherness – just a ten-minute chat with your first-born on the way back from school or a tickle and a cuddle with the toddler while older brother watches TV. You'll be amazed what a difference it makes.

Siblings tend to squabble less when they all feel secure in your love and special in your eyes. For ways to make each one feel special, see Chapter 27.

Oi, Referee! Knowing When and How to Get Involved

Despite your best diversions, there'll be times when your kids just go to it, shouting and stamping for all their worth. And, if only to lower the decibel count, you'll want to rush in and sort it all out. Hold your horses: You are their parent, not their referee, and you need to fight cleverer than they do.

When to stay out of it

For common-or-garden sibling spats (silly bickering, arguments over whose turn it is to do what or who's got more of what), the most potent weapon in your squabble-squashing armoury is (apparent) lack of interest. Ignore the squabblers completely. If they stage a fight right under your nose and you really can't pretend you haven't noticed, walk away. Or send them into another room to work out their differences. Nothing dampens the fires of a sibling feud more quickly than the lack of an audience.

Designate a special 'squabbling spot' where bickering children have to go – and stay till they've bickered themselves out. A friend of mine made her spot at the bottom of the garden: It's very telling how quickly her kids' squabbles get resolved on cold, dark winter afternoons!

When to step in – and how

While the minor spats are best ignored, some squabble situations do require a modicum of parental input – and a fair few require quite a lot. Maybe one teary-eyed child has come to find you and complained of hideous sibling tortures, maybe you've overheard some completely unacceptable teasing or name-calling, or maybe the bickering's escalated to brawling and there's a real danger of blood on the carpet.

Whatever the particular scenario that calls for your intervention, always try to step in with the same peace-promoting game plan in mind:

- ✔ **Stay calm.** It's damn hard, but it's your job. Your kids are never going to get their emotions back in control if you can't do it, too.

- ✔ **Describe what you see.** 'I see two angry children and one toy digger.' It sounds such a stupid thing to do, but stating the obvious really does work – on two levels: First, it tells both your children clearly that you know that they're angry and you understand why; second, it gives you valuable time to assess the situation before wading in.

- ✔ **Stop acts of violence or hurtful name-calling.** State the relevant house rule firmly: 'No swearing/hitting.' And send both children to separate rooms to cool down, if necessary.

- ✔ **Listen to each child.** But don't get sidetracked into a long analysis of who did what to whom. You're unlikely to get to the truth, anyway.

- ✔ **Don't take sides.** Instinctively you may want to blame the older, stronger child, particularly if she seems to have come off the better from the fight, but you don't know the whole story. Your younger child may be sobbing on the floor with a red welt on her arm, but she may have been winding up her brother something rotten in the hope he'd hit her and get punished. Stay neutral at all costs.

- ✔ **State the problem and make them solve it.** 'You were playing with the digger and now you want to play with it, too. I'm sure that you can work out a deal you're both happy with. I'll leave you to talk about it for a few minutes but, if you need my help, let me know.'

- ✔ **Leave them to it.** How long you give them to sort it out and how much prompting you give to help them along the way ('You may want to . . .') obviously depends on their age, stage, and prevailing mood. But you'll probably be surprised how much even quite little children can manage on their own. Given the belief by you that they can work it out, most kids will rise to the occasion.

- ✔ **Take charge quickly if it kicks off again.** Send them off separately to cool down, if you need to. Otherwise, impose your own (reasonably fair) solution for now and have done with it.

If your older children have a really tough problem they honestly can't solve, involve yourself in the peace talks. Get them together round a table and allow each one to sound off in turn (no interrupting from the other). Write down the complaints and then summarise them out loud. Then suggest all three of you come up with solutions. Write these down – even the silly ones. Look at your list together and try to agree on a solution (or compromise) you can all live with. Formalise your agreement by signing the paper or shaking hands.

There's a big difference between perfectly normal sibling squabbles and really persistent, vindictive behaviour from one sibling to another. The latter is, thankfully, pretty rare among the under-9s but, if you come up against it, seek help; dealing with this problem on your own is very hard.

'No, mine!' Fights over property rights

Your child has lots of dolls to play with. But isn't it funny how the doll she wants most is always the one in her sister's hand? It doesn't matter that it's only got one eye, that its clothes are all torn, and that it's long been gathering dust at the bottom of the toy box, that doll is suddenly the most covetable doll in the whole world. And, boy, will she let you know about it!

It doesn't take you many 'Mine!', 'No, mine!' screaming-and-snatching sessions to realise this kind of sibling squabble has an intensity all of its own. And presents a parental conundrum all of its own: Even if you manage to persuade your over-possessive progeny to let you adjudicate between them, how on earth are you supposed to remember each and every time which child is the original owner of the toy in dispute? Spare your eardrums and salve your conscience by

- ✔ **Giving each child a place for precious stuff:** Anything on or in this shelf/cupboard/box is their private property and not to be taken by anyone else without permission. Everything else in the house is for everyone to play with and must be shared.

- ✔ **Acknowledging that sharing is hard:** But not allowing grabbing or hoarding all the same. So, to the child who's trying to snatch, say, 'You want to play with the doll? Well, I know that it's hard to wait but snatching's not allowed. Let's tell your sister you'd like it next.' And, to the child in possession, say 'Your sister would like to play with the doll, too. Can she play with it after you?' Then give the would-be snatcher loads of attention as you look together for another toy for her to play with while she waits.

- ✔ **Timing turns:** Use a kitchen timer to mark the end of one child's turn with the toy and the beginning of the second child's turn; smaller children, in particular, seem to find it easier to hand over at the bell than at the parental command.

Fixing It So They Squabble Less

You can't wave a magic wand and make squabbling disappear in a puff of smoke (nor should you really want to: Remember, it does serve a useful purpose quite a lot of the time). But you can do a few simple things to create a much more positive atmosphere in your house. To spread a little more goodwill among your siblingkind, make it your mission to

- **Give praise where praise is due.** When our kids play together nicely, we tend not to notice. Make it your business to notice – and notice loudly. Showering positive attention on kind, generous, co-operative sibling interaction is the best way of encouraging it to happen again.

- **Give them space.** Older children, especially, do like to retreat from the general family hubbub every now and then, and read or listen to music on their own. This is not (necessarily) a sign that they're sulking or feeling resentful, so don't let it faze you.

- **Never discuss one child in front of the other.** Or compare them openly with each other. It's a sure way to stoke sibling rivalry to new heights.

- **Encourage small children to play on their own.** If they're dependent on you as the only 'play leader', they'll be vying for your attention all the time. Learning to amuse yourself is an important life skill – and a child who can manage it, even only for a few minutes, is developing the kind of self-reliance that will stand her in good stead at school (not to mention the workplace). Some children do find this more difficult than others; for more about encouraging independent play, see Chapter 16.

- **Teach them to agree to disagree.** One of the best lessons any child can learn is that having a different opinion to someone else is okay, but fighting about it is not okay. Sometimes, the only way forward is for both of you to compromise – if you each give a little, you can both end up happy.

- **Create a team spirit.** Eat supper together, play board games together, watch *Doctor Who* (or whatever) together. When one child is struggling to do something, encourage help from her sibling ('Ask Tom to help you – he's good at that'). Give them tasks or chores to complete as a team. Even better, have a race to see if they can finish their team task faster than you can finish a similar task on your own. Co-operation rocks when you can beat Mum!

- **Stop squabbling yourself.** Show your children there are respectful ways to disagree and resolve conflict with your partner, your mother, your neighbour, your friends. If you want better behaviour from your kids, be prepared to lead by example.

Let your children overhear you talking to your partner or another adult about the good times they have together or a particular act of kindness or generosity from one sibling to another. Not only does this give you another chance to praise them for their nice behaviour, it also reinforces the idea that they are siblings who get along well.

'But it's not fair!'

Siblings have ultra-sensitive injustice antennae. They can pick up on an unfair (as they see it) parental decision from several miles away – and complain about it with award-winningly wearying persistence. So is the only answer to burst your parental guts to be scrupulously fair at all times? It's a worthy idea but I doubt it's really possible. You can, of course, go to great pains to dole out the biscuits or raisins in equal measure, but you can't portion out your attention like an apple pie. There will almost certainly be times, when, for one reason or another, one child will need more of your time and attention than the other. (For more about how to deal with this, see Chapter 27.) And then there are other times when being 'unfair' is actually important: Over bedtimes and pocket money and other privileges that change according to age. Listen to and acknowledge the inevitable complaints about unfairness, but try not to get drawn into debates – you won't win.

Chapter 27

Loving Them All the Same

● ●

In This Chapter

▶ Giving each child the attention she needs

▶ Trying not to pigeonhole your kids

▶ Understanding how birth order can influence their behaviour – and yours

● ●

*W*hen you only have one child, it doesn't seem possible that you could ever love another child so much. Then you have another child and realise that, of course, it is possible. But not quite in the same way. Once one becomes two (or three or four), your time and attention must be spread around; never will you be able to focus all your loving energy on one child so intensely again.

And then, as your children develop their own unique traits and take on life, your feelings towards them ebb and flow. As fiercely as you love each and every one of them, you realise that some of your kids are easier to deal with than others – and even, occasionally (whisper it), you actually prefer dealing with some of them than others.

This chapter is all about understanding the different claims our children can make on our patience and attention and time, and the different ways we tend to label them according to their personalities and roles within the family. More importantly, it's also about reconciling all these things with the overwhelming need we have to parent our kids consistently, lovingly, and equally. And, actually, that's not nearly as daunting as it sounds.

Am I Your Favourite, Mummy?

'Do you love him more than me?' My eldest looked up at me expectantly. 'Of course not!' I said. 'I love you all the same.' He looked a little disappointed at that, but I thought I'd handled things quite well, really. Until I went on a brilliant parenting course and found out better. My son wasn't after a love ranking. He didn't really want me to tell him I loved him as much as (or more than) his brothers. He wanted me to tell him I loved him for himself.

What should I have said? Something like: 'Each of you is special to me but you're my only Ben, and no one else thinks like you, smiles like you, cuddles me like you. I'm so glad you're my son.' Touchy-feely nonsense? Don't knock it till you've tried it – I can guarantee it makes a child light up inside.

Making each child feel special

Of course, you don't have to wait until they ask you to spell it out; you can let each of your children know that they're special every day, in a variety of ways:

- **Give them time alone with you.** Don't stress yourself out trying to schedule this formally into your day, and don't even think about trying to ensure that each child gets exactly the same number of minutes with you. Just make the most of any one-to-one opportunities that come your way. Ask one of them to help you chop the veg, chill out with another when the toddler's gone to bed – a few minutes of your undivided attention is all it takes to make a child feel valued and significant.

- **Be all ears.** Listen carefully to what each child tells you – and show him you're trying to understand his feelings. Say, 'And did that make you feel sad?' or 'I'm guessing that made you angry – am I right?' A child who feels understood feels accepted and valued for who he is.

- **Stay in touch.** Literally. A hug, a kiss, an arm round the shoulder can often say far more than words. And is much less easy to misinterpret. If an older child resists cuddles, don't force them on him; find other ways to stay physically close, such as sitting next to him when you watch TV or playing rough-and-tumble games in the garden.

- **Notice the good things, however small.** Maybe one child was kind to another. Or polite to Aunty Sue. Or remembered to hang up his coat. Try to find something to praise each of your children for every day.

- **Re-create your enthusiasm.** The novelty of a child of yours learning to crawl/count/swim inevitably wears a bit thin the second, third, fourth time round. Never let it show. Your youngest child deserves just as many whoops of delight as his older siblings got before him.

- **Trim the photo album.** We all take a zillion more pictures of our first-born than we do of our other children. (Oh, for the days when we had that kind of time!) Avoid hurt feelings and have a ruthless edit.

When one child needs more attention

In an ideal world, each of our children gets a precisely fair share of our time and attention. In the real world, we soon realise that we can't portion ourselves out between them with anything like that kind of accuracy. There are times when one child genuinely needs more of our attention than the others. But, whether it's a temporary thing (a child needing help learning to read, say) or a permanent one (a child with time-consuming special needs), you can help your other kids feel less resentful by

- ✔ **Explaining what's happening and why:** Studies show that children who believe that their parents are giving one child preferential treatment for a good, sensible reason are more likely to be understanding.

- ✔ **Making it clear that you value spending time with them, too:** And giving an indication when that may next be. So, to the sibling of the learner reader, for example, you can say, 'I know that I'm spending a lot of time with your brother right now but, as soon as I'm done, I'd love to hear all about your day.' For the sibling of the child with special needs, it may be better to decide with him on a specific time every day when just the two of you can be together.

Good parenting's not about dividing your love and attention absolutely equally between your children; it's about loving them all uniquely – and trying to respond to each according to his need.

What if you really do have a favourite?

Well, you won't be alone, that's for sure. Preferring one child over your others is many parents' biggest guilty secret. Perhaps that child reminds you of you. Perhaps he shares your passion for a particular sport or hobby. Perhaps he has a particular look or attitude that melts your heart. Whatever it is, you probably can't help it – but you can help what you do about it.

And you do need to do something – for all your children's sake. Studies suggest that playing favourites can actually harm your favoured child as much as the others. It's obvious that unfavoured children can end up feeling second-best; what's not so well known is that the favourite himself also suffers, often feeling anxious, depressed, and guilty at receiving better treatment than his siblings. And let's not even mention the impact of lifelong sibling resentment.

So what do you do? Acknowledge your secret feelings – to yourself and, if you're brave enough, to your partner or another trusted adult. And that's the hardest part over. For now that you've been honest about how you really feel, the path is clear for you to find ways to work harder at the relationships you have with your (currently) less favoured children. To do that, you can

✔ **Take an interest in their interests.** You may hate watching *Match of the Day* or messing about with glitter glue and scrunched-up tissue paper but, if it's your 'unfavoured' child's idea of a heaven, get down on the sofa or craft table with him and give it a go. He'll swell with pleasure at your show of interest and, you never know, you may even enjoy it!

✔ **Find a regular chore to do together.** Whether it's stripping the beds, buying the newspaper or walking the dog. Having a task to complete together makes you co-operate and communicate – and build a special new connection with each other.

He's Sporty, She's Clever: Not Letting Those Labels Stick

Brothers and sisters can turn out so different. And it's nice to single them out for their different gifts, skills, and attitudes. But please don't go too far. It's way too easy to stick your kids into neat little pigeonholes (she's brainy, he's athletic) that never allow them to stretch their wings in other directions. Or to let certain aspects of their body or character (he's clumsy, she's pretty) come to define how you see them – and how they see themselves.

Beware of labels that limit

We like giving our kids labels – it's our way of showing them we've sussed out what they're each good at and what we're proud of each of them for: 'Frank's very funny and John's very calm.' But the trouble with labels is that, doled out often enough, they can become little straitjackets, casting each child into a specific role within the family that can limit him for life. Maybe Frank doesn't always want to play the clown and maybe John would relish the chance to go crazy once in a while. By all means, let your kids know when they do stuff that pleases you but

✔ **Realise that labels can put a child under pressure.** If you're the 'good one', you've got a lot to live up to every day.

✔ **Understand that labelling one child can reverse-label another.** As in, 'Dad thinks that my brother's the "sensible one", so that must make me the "silly one". Right then . . .'

✔ **Don't let one child stake sole claim to a label.** So, your oldest is an ace tennis player? That's great, but it doesn't mean your other kids shouldn't get the chance to play tennis, too – if they want to. Even if they fluff every shot, it doesn't mean they won't find tennis fun. Make it clear that there's room in your family for more than one tennis player (or footballer, ballet dancer, musician, whatever).

Give a dog a bad name . . .

Some of the labels we give our kids aren't nearly as nice as others. And negative labels ('he's selfish', 'she's forgetful, 'he's untidy', 'she's shy') are the most limiting of all. True, there may be an aspect of a child's personality you don't like, but constantly reminding him of it is not going to do much to help him change. Instead, try to

✔ **Stop him getting stuck in that role.** By reminding him he can choose to act differently. 'You're quite capable of sharing with your brother.'

✔ **Help him see himself differently.** 'I see you've got your PE kit with you today. That's well remembered!'

✔ **Make it clear what you expect of him.** 'Your toys are all over the floor. I expect you to put them away when you've finished playing with them.'

✔ **Demonstrate what you'd like to see.** 'Gosh, there are a lot of people I don't know here today. Well, if I smile and say hello, I'm sure that they'll say hello right back.'

✔ **Avoid comparisons.** The 'Why can't you be more like your brother?' ones. And the 'Look at your brother: He's so good at . . .' ones. They only make the other child feel doubly wretched.

Born To Be Different? The Truth About Birth Order

'He's a perfectionist, like all first-borns.'

'He's the classic middle child: forever got a chip on his shoulder.'

'He's so easygoing – well, your youngest always is.'

To hear some parents talk, you'd think that their children's personalities are shaped simply by the order in which they were born. But, you know, they wouldn't be far wrong. Many experts now agree that a child's position in the sibling hierarchy can have a hugely predictable effect on his personality. And not only that: They also think that birth order routinely affects the way we parent each child. Take a look at Table 27-1 to see how.

But just because birth order can influence the way a child behaves – and the way we behave towards him – it doesn't follow that things have to stay that way. Especially if there are elements of that behaviour we don't like. With a few clever, compensatory nudges, we can steer children away from their birth-order stereotype. With a little more insight, we can modify our own assumptions and expectations. And, with a generous sprinkling of understanding, we can find ways to compensate each child for the downsides of his particular position in the family pecking order.

Table 27-1	Birth Order: How It Affects Our Children – And Us	
Place in birth order	*They tend to be*	*We tend to be*
Oldest	Determined, motivated, rule-keeping, high-achieving, born to lead	Strict, over-anxious, ambitious for them to perform well
Middle (any child who is neither oldest nor youngest)	Diplomatic, sociable, competitive, attention-seeking, peacemaking	More relaxed, less attentive
Youngest	Outgoing, charming, creative, risk-taking	Slow to let them stand on their own two feet

'I never get to muck about': Understanding your oldest child

A first-born gets it good because: We get to have him all to ourselves for a while; he tends to have bags of confidence and self-esteem.

A first-born gets it tough because: We're stricter with him and expect him to do well academically; he is so eager to please us, he often feels he must do everything right.

To help make things even better for him, try to

- **Keep reminding yourself how old he is.** Or isn't. We do sometimes expect too much of our oldest child too soon. Let him act his age.

- **Take your foot off the pedal.** Bear in mind that he's likely to be very motivated to work hard at school anyway. You may not need to push him as hard as you think.

- **Remember he's not always to blame.** He may be the oldest but he's not responsible for everything. And he doesn't always know better.

- **Give him age-related privileges.** Such as later bedtimes and more pocket money.

- **Prevent him being the family bossyboots.** His siblings shouldn't always have to play his game or follow his lead. And he shouldn't always be in control of the TV remote.

- **Give him some adult attention.** Your other children were born into a world of children; he was born into a world of adults. And he'll always blossom in adult company.

'No one ever listens to me!': Understanding your middle child (ren)

A middle child gets it good because: We've loosened up a lot and are more relaxed about parenting; he tends to find it easy to make (and keep) friends.

A middle child gets it tough because: We may take longer to notice his needs; he feels life is unfair on him – he doesn't get privileges like his older brother but he can't get away with things like his younger sister.

To help make things even better for him, try to

- **See naughtiness as a wake-up call.** Middle children will often do the most mischievous things to win their parents' attention away from their siblings. Maybe you need to make more time for him?

- **Be open to change.** Sometimes, what worked for your oldest child won't work at all for your next one.

- **Enjoy his 'win-some, lose-some' attitude.** While your first-born will be devastated at any kind of failure, from losing a football match to flunking a test, your middle child will probably be able to handle disappointment with great aplomb.

- ✔ **Make sure that your memory doesn't play tricks.** Forgetting when your oldest learnt to read/ride a bike/use the potty is easy. Your middle one's already in his older brother's shadow; don't make it worse by pushing him to do new things too soon.

- ✔ **Remind him of the benefits of being in the middle.** 'You've got an older brother *and* a younger brother – that's the best of both worlds. No one else in this family is as lucky as that!' (If you have more than one 'middle' child, you will, of course, have to amend this statement appropriately: 'You've got an older brother *and* two younger brothers – no one else in this family is as lucky as that!')

'No one takes me seriously': Understanding your youngest child

A last-born gets it good because: We've learnt to let a child develop at his own pace; he tends to be extrovert, funny, and charming.

A last-born gets it tough because: We've seen it all before and are harder to impress; he has to fit into his siblings' routines and he is always the 'baby'.

To help make things even better for him, try to

- ✔ **Not believe all you hear:** The youngest sibling often becomes very talented at shifting the blame onto everyone but himself!

- ✔ **Stick to the old rules:** You may no longer mind that your youngest gets down in the middle of a meal or watches TV before school but, if your older children weren't allowed to do it, neither should your youngest – or you'll create a whole load of sibling resentment.

- ✔ **Give him responsibility:** As soon as he's up to it, let him fetch the post, lay the table, empty the dishwasher – even if his older siblings can do it faster and better.

- ✔ **Steel yourself to do the rounds again:** You may be sick to the gills with the playground, the toy library, the toddler group, and the singing sessions but, for your youngest, they're all a fun and fascinating novelty. He deserves to benefit from the pleasures and developmental stimulus they can give him. Grit your teeth and thank the Lord that you'll never have to do it again!

When families break up and parents form new relationships, stepchildren can shake-up the birth order and cause long-held behaviour patterns to shift. This may not be the disaster you're predicting; for some children, it can actually be a welcome relief. For more on raising a 'blended' family, see Chapter 3.

But I've only got one child

Only children are supremely lucky in ever so many ways. They tend to have all the confidence of a first-born without any of the anxiety or resentment that comes with having to share their parents with a sibling. And, blessed with a less chaotic family environment and, therefore, more consistent discipline, they quickly learn to take responsibility for their actions. Only children tend to be articulate, organised, clever in school, and not afraid to take decisions or defend their own opinions. Without other children in the house, onlies grow up fast, often becoming noticeably more mature than their (many-siblinged) peers. However, there are certain downsides to being an only child – and to being the parent of an only child – and it pays to be aware that

- ✔ **He may feel ill-at-ease with children of the same age.** His more 'grown-up' attitude can make it harder to form friendships and mix well at school. Make it your mission, from really early on, to seek out and spend time with families whose kids are the same age.

- ✔ **He needs to practise how to share.** As all siblings know, it's not a skill that comes easy!

- ✔ **He may be very self-critical.** Onlies are perfectionists and sometimes need protecting from their own harsh self-judgement when things don't go quite right.

- ✔ **We tend to burden him with all our expectations.** Which only adds to the pressure he's already heaping on himself. Try to let your child be himself, not what you want him to be.

- ✔ **We can over-indulge and over-protect him.** Too much parental devotion can be stifling. Sometimes, less really is more.

Part VII
The Part of Tens

"O.K., that's settled then — I read you a story, you show me how to operate the video."

In this part . . .

*L*ike every Dummies book, *Parenting For Dummies* contains a set of little chapters full of rather useful facts – a mini compendium if you like, of the more vital stuff we parents need to know. So, eyes down for your lists of baby-kit must-haves, first-aid tips and fail-safe ways to keep your cool.

Chapter 28

Ten Ways to Keep Your Cool

In This Chapter

▶ Getting your message across – without shouting

▶ Staying calm when the kids are winding you up

▶ Relocating your sense of humour

*I*t doesn't matter whether they're 2, 12, or 22, your kids can press your 'angry' buttons like nobody else. Sometimes they don't know that they're doing it; sometimes they *absolutely* do. Either way, they have an uncanny ability to turn you from the rather lovely person you really are into a snappy, shouty monster of a parent.

If you've been finding lately that more steam's coming out of your ears than Thomas the Tank Engine, this chapter can help you keep a firmer lid on things. Every one of the ten stay-cool suggestions below has stopped me from losing the parental plot at one time or another – and, if they worked for me, I'm sure that they'll do the same for you. Of course, I'm not promising that you'll sail through the rest of your parental life on a cloud of calm, peace, and serenity, but you never know.

Find your deep voice

The more irritated you get, the higher and screechier your voice gets. But (even more irritatingly) high and screechy just doesn't cut it on the authority front. A clear, firm, deep voice is so much more effective – and makes you feel a million times more in control. Try it: Speak low and slow and, for maximum effect, right up close to the miscreant in question.

Count to ten

This is my personal favourite because it works for my kids, too. If it's time to go to school, but I find, to my complete frustration, that, yet again, I'm the only person with a coat on, I'll say, 'Right, I'm going to count to ten and, when I get to ten, I expect everyone to be standing on the doormat, ready to go to school. One, two, three . . .' By the time I get to nine, I've let off a whole heap of steam and my (coat-wearing) kids are jostling each other on the doormat, proud as punch to have beaten the countdown.

Ignore the small stuff

Is it really such an issue that little Johnny wants to wear his Spiderman pyjamas all day? Or that Rosie won't eat that last carrot? Of course you don't want your kids to get away with murder, but some things really aren't worth getting all that het up about. Don't burst your blood vessels over unimportant battles; save your big guns for the stuff that really matters.

Respect the clock

When time is short, you can bet your life your temper is, too. Nothing is more annoying than trying to get somewhere in a rush when you've kids in tow. It's almost as if the phrase 'Hurry up!' automatically makes children go slower. The only way out of this is to give yourself at least twice as much time as you think you need. Only then can you handle every 'I left my PE kit behind'/'I need a wee'/'No buggy – me walk!' kiddie stalling tactic with patience and calm – and still get where you want on time.

Give yourself time out

On the verge? Leave the room. Yell at the hall wall. Bash a cushion. Stamp your feet. Jump up and down. As long as the kids are safe (and can't get at the kitchen knives, for example), they'll survive without you for the five minutes it takes to vent your spleen on something that isn't them. Return with a saintly smile when calm descends.

Explain what you expect

This is another temper-prevention (rather than temper-cure) trick. And it's especially handy when your progeny are going to be on public display. It's all about anticipating the kind of problems that will test your patience when you're out and about, and laying down clear ground rules beforehand. So, you say, 'Okay, we're going into this toy shop to buy a present for Lucy. We're not buying anything for you today but, if you see anything you like, let me know and we'll put it on your birthday wish list.' Or, 'We're going to a cafe for lunch. I want you to sit nicely and use your knife and fork. If you do, we'll have ice cream for pudding. If you choose not to, we'll just come home. It's up to you.'

Remember how old they are (or not)

Your 2-year-old's tipped juice on the carpet; your 5-year-old's forgotten to bring home his homework again. Yes, it's infuriating, but it's what kids that age do. I had a friend at school whose mum was always yelling, 'Stop behaving like a child!' Er, hello? All of us need to give our expectations a little reality check once in a while.

Say how you feel

It's okay to feel angry, and it's okay to tell your kids you're feeling angry – much better to do that, in fact, than silently let your anger build until you really explode. Not only is this scary for your kids, it's confusing, too. Dad didn't mind the last three times I threw that toy across the room, they think, so why is he yelling the house down this time? It's better for everyone's mental health to make it clear straightaway exactly what's upsetting you and why: 'When you throw your toys like that, it makes me cross because you could break them.' Anger let out slowly is always more constructive.

Say yes (sneakily)

Can't handle another tantrum? Get clever with your words. Say your child's whining for biscuits but you don't want him to spoil his appetite for the supper that's almost ready. Instead of saying, 'No, no biscuits!' and provoking the kind of reaction that makes your blood boil, say, 'Yes, you can have a biscuit after you've had your fishfingers.' Amazing how handy that word Yes is in a crisis!

See the funny side

When my oldest was 3, he decided to play ghosts. So he sneaked off with the nappy cream (the really thick, white, gloopy stuff) and covered his 2-year-old brother in it from head to toe. When they came, giggling and gunky, into the kitchen to show us, I exploded with rage – and my husband exploded with laughter. While I couldn't see past the sticky white patches on the carpet, he could see the funny family story in the making – and he even took the photos to prove it. And, you know, his attitude was so much better: Yes, kids do stupid, messy, silly things and, yes, it's usually us left doing the clearing up, but that doesn't mean we have to have a sense-of-humour bypass. Our carpet's never quite recovered (and let's not even talk about how long it takes to get gloop out of a small boy's hair), but I'm glad I was made to see the funny side first. We still laugh about it now (but that nappy cream's kept well out of their reach).

If you do lose your cool with your kids, say sorry. It's what you'd expect from them, after all. And don't feel too bad: It's good for kids to see that parents can't always be perfect. Once you've apologised, though, move on. Staying angry won't help anyone.

Chapter 29

Ten First-Aid Must-Knows

In This Chapter

▶ Coping with big emergencies and little accidents

▶ Being prepared for the worst (even if it never happens)

*Y*ou probably don't want to think about your child getting hurt. But it does pay to grit your teeth and do it – there's nothing worse than not knowing what to do when your child's in pain and really needs you. This chapter takes you through the most common accidents kids have – some of them routine, some of them scary – and the first-aid skills you need to deal with them properly. I want you to read, learn, and absorb them all but, in truth, this is the only set of tips in the book I hope you never get to work your way right through.

One of the most important things you can do now you're a parent is take a first-aid course. And not just any old first-aid course – you need to do one specifically for babies and children (first-aid for adults is different in several key areas). You'll find out what to do if your child stops breathing: Simple, step-by-step techniques that really can make the difference between life and death. Both the Red Cross (www.redcross.org.uk/firstaid) and St John's Ambulance (www.sja.org.uk) run excellent courses.

Get yourself a first-aid box. Fill it with plasters, sterile dressings (of different sizes), antiseptic wipes, bandages, safety pins, a thermometer, and disposable gloves. Or buy a ready-filled fist-aid kit from your pharmacist or at www.redcross.org.uk/firstaidproducts.

She's had a bump

Trips, falls, grazes, cuts, scratches, bashes, lumps, and bumps: They're all part and parcel of a normal, active childhood. As is the wailing that follows five seconds after impact. You can stop most post-bash tears in their tracks with the judicious application of any (or all) of the following: a sympathetic rub, a 'special' plaster, and an ice pack. You can buy dinky, child-sized icepacks to keep in the freezer, or you can improvise with a pack of frozen peas, wrapped in a tea towel.

Clean any grazes and cuts (be warned: Small cuts to the head and lips can bleed *a lot*) with an antiseptic wipe before putting the plaster on (plasters 'work' better if they're extra large and covered in cartoon animals, by the way). If her bump was on the head, keep a close eye on her for the next 24 hours – any vomiting, drowsiness, or loss of co-ordination could be a sign of concussion and needs treating by a doctor. And be ready for the appearance of the most monumental egg-shaped lump (scary but quite normal).

She's got a huge cut

Wash it out with warm water so you can see how deep the cut goes. If the cut's bleeding a lot, hold the injured arm or leg up above the level of your child's heart, and apply pressure with a clean paper towel. If the cut's more than 0.5 centimetres deep, if it has gaping edges, if it has something stuck in it (never try to dig it out yourself), or if the bleeding doesn't stop within ten minutes, go to hospital.

She's been scalded

Kids burn much more easily than adults because their skin is so much thinner. If your child is scalded, act fast (don't mess about removing clothes; the slower you act, the deeper and more painful the burn will be). Hold the scalded area under cold running water and keep it there, however much your child screams, for at least ten minutes – it takes at least this long to stop the 'cooking' effect on young skin.

Then, if the burn is larger than a 50 p piece (or seems very deep), cover it with clingfilm or a freezer bag (yes, really) and get down to A&E. If it's smaller burn, cover it with a sterile dressing and check it daily for signs of infection (if you see any, go to your GP). Do not pop any blisters, put cream on the burn, or wrap it in cotton wool or bandages – the fluff from the material can stick to blistered skin and is agony to remove.

She's got such a high fever

Children, and particularly babies, quite often run a fever – over 38°C (100°F)– and, in most cases, you can quickly bring it down with baby or child paracetamol (follow the dosage instructions on the bottle), plenty of cool fluids, and some sponging down with lukewarm water.

But, if your baby has a fever and is under 3 months, you need to see a doctor straightaway. If she's over 6 months, seek medical help if she also has sickness or diarrhoea, has a febrile convulsion (see 'She's having a fit', below), is pulling at her ear, or if she's had the fever for more than two days. Call an ambulance if she has a rash that doesn't fade when you press it with a glass, if she's having trouble breathing, if her lips are blue, if she's crying weakly, or if she's limp and unresponsive.

If your child is over a year old, call an ambulance if her temperature rises above 39°C (102°F) and she is breathing very rapidly, is abnormally drowsy, has a severe headache or neck pain, has a dislike of bright light, has a rash that doesn't fade when pressed with a glass, or has refused to drink for more than six hours.

If your child is unconscious and not breathing, say so the instant your 999 call gets through. The ambulance service prioritises help for patients who are not breathing – and every second counts.

She's having a fit

Small children sometimes have a 'fit' when they have a high fever. Doctors call it a *febrile convulsion* and, frightening as it looks, it's usually over within five minutes and rarely has long-term repercussions. (If she is still convulsing after five minutes, though, call an ambulance.) Resist the urge to restrain your child's arms and legs; just move her to a soft surface and wait for the convulsion to pass. Once it has, give her a reassuring cuddle, then sponge her down with lukewarm water and give her some child/infant paracetamol (follow the dosage guidelines on the bottle) to help get her temperature down. Call your doctor later for advice on what to do if it happens again.

She's swallowed poison

She may vomit after swallowing poison – and there's nothing you can do about that – but don't *make* her vomit: Something that's caused her damage on the way down could cause more damage on the way up. And don't allow her to drink, either: Some dangerous chemicals are absorbed into the body even more quickly when they're diluted. Stay calm (hard, I know) and try to find out what she's swallowed and how much. Collect up any vomit (nasty but necessary), leftover pills, or packaging (to help the doctors work out how to treat her), and get to hospital fast.

She's choking

Don't shake her or turn her upside down. And don't poke around in her mouth unless you're absolutely positive you can scoop out what's stuck – or you could push it in farther. Instead, bend her forwards (or, if she's a baby, lie her face down along your forearm) and give her five firm blows between the shoulder blades. Ask her to cough, too, if she can.

If this doesn't work, you need to start some chest thrusts. Stand behind her, put your arms around her, and place one fist between her navel and breastbone. Place your other hand on top and pull firmly in and up five times. (For a baby, turn her over onto her back, and use two fingers to push firmly in and up five times on her breastbone.)

Repeat this cycle of shoulder blows and chest thrusts three times. If nothing's worked by then, call an ambulance and repeat the cycle until help comes.

She's been bitten or stung

If it's an animal bite, wash it carefully with soap and warm water and, if it's deep enough to have caused bleeding, see a doctor. If it's a wasp or bee sting, don't try to pull it out with a tweezer or, worse, your fingernails – you could actually squeeze more venom in. Instead, scrape off as much as you can with the back of a knife. In either case, expect a little localised swelling: Treat it with an icepack and then cover it with a sterile dressing. If your child starts wheezing or her lips swell after a sting, she could be having a serious allergic reaction: Call an ambulance.

She's got a nosebleed

A bit of a tricky one, this, because you've got two problems to deal with at once: Stopping the blood and calming your child (the sudden sight of blood can terrify a small child). Because you can't do the first without having done the second, start with a cuddle and lots of reassurance that everything's going to be okay. Then sit her down and firmly pinch the soft part of her nose (just above the nostrils) to make the bleeding stop. Keep her head level, don't tilt it back.

She's just not right

Trust your instincts and take her to a doctor or a hospital – even if other people think that you're over-reacting. You know your child best, so it stands to reason that you'll probably be the first to spot that something's seriously up. Explain clearly what's concerning you and why it's abnormal for your child. Okay, so it may be nothing to worry about after all, but no one's going to blame you for checking it out. And, if there is something wrong, you can get the treatment you need fast.

Chapter 30

Ten Things You Need For Your Baby (And Ten Things You Don't)

In This Chapter

▶ Kitting yourself out without breaking the bank

▶ Realising good parenting's not about great gadgets

▶ Working out which stuff is right for you

*T*ime for a little confession: I was once the undisputed Pregnant Shopping Champion of Britain. When I was expecting my first child, I single-handedly swept baby shop shelves of every last piece of kit on display. It got to the point where there was so much baby equipment piled up in our house, I thought the only way we'd be able to find room for the baby was if my husband moved into the B&B across the road.

This is not only a (shameful) confession; it's a cautionary tale. Not long after my baby was born, two things became blindingly obvious: I had the most monstrous credit-card bill, and I didn't need even half the stuff I'd bought. To save you from a similar, wallet-emptying fate, I've put together this no-guff guide to the baby stuff you actually need. Believe me, this chapter will save you lots of cash – and loads of house space.

The pregnancy magazines and the shopping advisers may tell you otherwise, but there isn't actually that much baby kit you'd be completely lost without. As long as you've got somewhere for your baby to sleep, a few things to dress her in, and somewhere to stow her when you're on the move or your arms are full, you're sorted. Anything else, however cuddly or cute, is, frankly, surplus to requirements/a bit of a luxury. Of course, you're free to buy as much as you like, but your ready-for-baby shopping list really needs only include the items listed in this chapter.

Shopping on a tight budget

If your budget is really tight, you can trim the list down even further. You can quite easily do without the Moses basket, for example, and put your baby to sleep in the cot (or travel cot) from the start. Or, if you do get a Moses basket, you won't be needing a travel cot for a while (or perhaps at all, if you don't stay away much). You obviously don't need a car seat if you haven't got a car and, if you do, you can ditch the bouncy seat and use the car seat in the house, too.

Above all else, don't buy in a panic: The shops will still be open after the birth! And don't be too proud to scout around for second-hand or hand-me-down cots, travel cots, seats, and prams – you'll be surprised at what good condition a lot of them are in.

The Moses basket

It looks a bit like a half-finished picnic hamper, but a Moses basket makes a great first bed for your baby: Snug enough to make her feel secure; light enough (even with her in it) for you to tote round the house with you. Make sure that the wicker frame is nice and sturdy, the mattress is a good fit, and the carrying handles won't cut into your hands when the basket's fully loaded. You'll need a couple of fitted sheets and either a baby sleeping bag (see Chapter 9) or a topsheet and a cellular blanket to go with it. Don't spend a fortune on a basket with all sorts of frilly extras, though – your baby will grow out of it in a few short months.

Never carry your baby downstairs in her Moses basket – it's very tricky to do one-handed without tilting the basket dangerously. And, without a spare hand to steady yourself, you could trip. Also, if your Moses basket comes with a stand (that raises your baby up to a less back-breaking height), stop using it the moment your baby shows any signs of being able to wriggle or roll over. You don't want her rocking the basket off the stand onto the floor.

The cot (and bedding)

There are cots, and then there are cotbeds. And choosing which one you want is your first challenge. Cotbeds are more expensive but, because they convert into a junior bed, they last at least a couple of years longer. Remember, though, that if you're planning to have more than one child, the second baby will need the cot at some point, so you'll have to get a bed then anyway. Whatever cot you choose, make sure that you ask yourself:

- ✔ **Is it sturdy and solid?**

- ✔ **Are the bars no more than 6.5 centimetres apart?** So little heads and arms can't poke through and then get stuck.

- ✔ **Do you want one with a dropside?** This is more expensive but kinder on your back. If you go for a dropside, make sure that you can operate it one-handed – or you'll get in a right muddle when your baby's in your arms.

- ✔ **Do you want a bedside cot?** Some (pricier) cots have a dropside that drops (or flips over) completely, so, if you push the cot right up to your bed, you can pick up your baby in the night without getting up yourself.

- ✔ **Do you want one with an adjustable base?** Makes bending down to retrieve your baby a less spine-wrenching manoeuvre. Worth it if the cot doesn't have a dropside.

- ✔ **Is the mattress included?** And, if so, is it nice and firm?

- ✔ **What's your bedding policy?** Baby sleeping bag or sheets and blanket? (For more on this, see Chapter 9.) Whichever you plump for, two of each is ample for now.

The changing mat and bag

Forget the luxury changing mats with leather hanging handles, plush padding, and embroidered towelling covers; you're choosing something your baby's going to poo and wee all over, and you need to think large, practical, and wipe-clean. It's worth getting a smaller, fold-up mat, too, for keeping in your changing bag when you're out.

And the only thing that matters about your changing bag is its size. Hand-tooled designer job or grotty old rucksack, it needs to be big enough to hold your phone and wallet and all your other bits and pieces, as well as a changing mat, nappy cream, wipes, nappy sacks, nappies, a change of baby clothes, and bottles (if you're using them). You will not be using the words 'compact' and 'bag' in the same sentence for a good few years yet.

The nappies

Now, don't go overboard here. If you're planning to use disposable nappies rather than reusable ones (for more on how to choose which is right for you, see Chapter 6), one small pack of newborn nappies is more than enough. Don't go buying those hugely-discounted super-large bring-it-home-on-a-forklift bumper packs just yet: You may find the brand you've chosen just doesn't fit your baby quite right, and, even if everything's admirably snug in the bottom department, your baby will zoom up through the first few nappy sizes amazingly quickly.

Restraint is even more in order if you're a reusable kind of parent (as it were): Don't shell out on one of those £200 birth-to-potty nappy kits unless you're absolutely sure that you've found the right cloth nappy for you. And, to be honest, you can't really be sure about that till you've put your baby's bottom in it and put it through the wash a fair few times. Find a 'real-nappy adviser' near you (call 0845 850 0606 or visit `www.wen.org.uk/nappies/contacts.htm`) and ask for a few different samples to try before you buy. You may not have enough nappies to manage without the odd disposable for a couple of weeks, but it'll be worth it in the long run.

The travel cot

Off to visit Granny? Just chuck the Moses basket in the car. But what if Granny's in Australia or your baby's got too big for his basket? This is where the travel cot comes into its own. Just make sure that you've got your head round the two main options:

- ✔ **The big, bulky one:** A sturdy, foldaway bed that'll last for years. Some come with wheels and/or attachable changing tables, and many will double as playpens, too. Can be tricky to put up and murder to carry.

- ✔ **The small, compact one:** A lightweight, pop-up tent-like bed that squashes into a tiny bag. Great for multi-destination trips but not always the most comfortable sleeping arrangement for a tiny one.

Some parents save money by using their (big, bulky) travel cot as their baby's home cot, too. If you like that idea, get one with a decent mattress.

The car seat

The single most important thing about choosing a car seat is finding one that fits properly in your car. You may well find that some seats, however good their quality, are either too big for your car or simply cannot be made secure enough. Don't be tempted to make do with something that's nearly right: Even 0.5 centimetres on the length of a seatbelt buckle can make the difference between a seat that's safe and a seat that's not. All this may mean you have to settle for the one seat that's done out in snot-green, swirly patterns but, really, what's a little bit of yukky material next to your baby's safety?

Before you even get to peruse the snot-green patterns in the shops, though, you need to decide what sort of car seat you're after. You have two choices:

- ✔ **The basic infant carrier:** A rearward-facing car seat that fits your baby for 9 to 12 months. It has a carrying handle and you can bring it out of the car and use it as a seat in the house, if you like. Some fix straight onto your car's back seat with the seat belt; others slot into a separate fixing unit that stays in your car. A few will even slot onto a 'travel system' base unit to make a pushchair (for more on this, see 'The wheels' section, later in this chapter).

- ✔ **The double-duty seat:** A pricier car seat that can be used rearward-facing for the first nine months or so, and then turned round to face forwards. It will therefore fit your baby until he's 4 (or, sometimes, even 6) years old. It has no carrying handle and doesn't come out of the car.

When you've made your choice, bear in mind that

- ✔ **Side-impact protection is important.** Most cars involved in accidents are hit side on.

- ✔ **Weight matters.** Car seats are, confusingly, categorised into Groups 0, 0+, 1, and 2, according to the maximum weight they can carry and, even more confusingly, some seats span several groups. Check carefully that the seat you're getting is suitable for your child.

- ✔ **Treat a second-hand seat with caution.** If you know the previous owners well and they can assure you that it's not damaged, fine. Do check, though, that it meets the current safety standards.

Never put an infant car seat on a front passenger seat that has an airbag fitted. If the airbag's activated in an accident, it could kill your baby.

The wheels

Please let me save you from pushchair hell (trust me, I've been there and you won't like it!). Baby wheels now come in so many different models and makes, it's very tricky to spot the right one for you. Choose wisely and your first pushchair could be your last; choose unwisely and you could end up (like me) with a costly pile of abandoned pram parts littering your hall.

Okay, first things first: Don't let a nursery-store sales adviser get within an inch of you before you're clear what the various pushchair permutations are:

- ✔ **The pram:** A chassis (frame on wheels) with (usually) a separate seat unit (so you can have it facing out or in) and, sometimes, a separate carrycot. Almost always well-built, well-padded, rather bulky, and very expensive.

- ✔ **The buggy:** A light, manoeuvrable pushchair with a fixed seat unit (facing out). Not very luxurious but easy to fold and easy on the wallet.

- ✔ **The travel system:** A buggy or pram chassis (with separate seat unit) to which you can fix a car seat (facing in), for a smooth transfer from one set of wheels to another. Can work out cheaper than buying a car seat and pushchair separately.

Not sure which one to go for? I have to tell you that most first-time parents plump for the pram – looks more sturdy, comfy, and 'proper' somehow – only to dump it for a buggy three months later when they've finally had enough of juggling seat units, clogging up pavements, and wasting 25 minutes a day trying to fold the darn thing up and put it in the car boot. Of course, if you've lots of money and/or you'll be using the pram again for a whole succession of further babies, this may not worry you. If it does, get a really good buggy now and save yourself the grief.

Whichever type of pushchair you go for, though, you'll find lots of different makes to choose between. Don't splash your cash without asking:

- ✔ **Does the seat go completely flat?** Comes as standard in all prams but not in all buggies (even ones advertised as 'from birth') – and newborns need to be flat out for the first couple of months at least.

- ✔ **Three wheels or four?** Three-wheelers look sporty (some are even built for taking on sporty jogs and hikes) but can be heavy, hard to fold, and, if the front wheel's fixed, hard to get round corners on city streets. Four-wheelers aren't so stable on country lanes and rougher terrain but are generally a better choice for zipping round town.

- ✔ **Do I really want pneumatic tyres?** They make for a lovely smooth ride but they do get punctures.

- ✔ **Do I want to be able to see my baby as I push?** She'd certainly rather see your face than anyone else's. But she's unlikely to get the option if you choose a buggy.

- ✔ **Does it fit in my car?** And, if it does, is there room for anything else?

- ✔ **How easy is it to fold and carry?** Important to know if you're going to be travelling by bus or if there are stairs up to your front door.

✔ **Where will I keep it?** Is there space in your hall to keep it upright or are you going to have to fold and unfold it all the time? If it has separate parts, where will you store them?

✔ **Are the handles right?** Do you prefer two handles or one? Are they high enough or will you have to stoop as you push? Are they adjustable if your partner is a lot taller or smaller than you?

✔ **Is the shopping basket big enough?** Some pushchairs have tiny baskets – no good if you're going to be shopping on foot most days.

✔ **Will I still be using it in a year's time?** It may be just the job for a newborn, but is it suitable for life with a toddler? Ask for honest opinions from friends who already have babies.

✔ **Do I really need all these extras?** Rain cover, definitely. Foot muffs, pram snugs, parasols, sun shades, bumper bars, coffee-cup carriers, maybe not.

The baby seat

You'll love this because it gives you a chance to do things two-handed every now and then; and she'll love it because she can kick her arms and legs about and see more than just the ceiling. Skip over all the padded, musical, multi-position, baby-armchair seats and go straight for a simple, fabric-stretched-over-a-metal-frame one. Why? Because it's light, cheap, easy to dismantle and reassemble if you're going on a trip, and, when milky disaster strikes, you just whip off the fabric and stuff it in the washing machine. But most of all because this is the type of seat your baby will soon be able to make jiggle and bounce (gently) all by herself – and, boy, will that make her chuckle!

The sling

Most babies love being snuggled up close to you in a sling but not all parents love wearing them. Don't even think of buying one if your back is (or ever has been) a bit on the dodgy side. If you're up for the idea, ask yourself:

✔ **Are you a buckles-and-clips sort of person?** Or would you prefer a tie-up sling? Or even a simple stretchy one-piece hammocky job? Try on all the different sorts before you decide.

✔ **How easy is it to do up?** Will you be able to get your baby in safely on your own?

✔ **Is it Dad-friendly?** Some slings are clearly made for Mum-size frames; if Dad's going to be slinging it, too, find a make with straps that stretch to accommodate a manly pair of shoulders.

The clothes

Yes, your heart melts at the sight of all those teensy-weensy babygros and teensier, weensier baby socks in the shops but, before you grab the lot and head for the till, be warned: They'll be melting your friends' and relatives' hearts, too. So, as soon as your baby's born (maybe even before), you'll be swamped with their gifts of teensy-weensy babygros and teensier, weensier baby socks (and hats and jackets and bootees). My advice? Buy three or four newborn babygros (with feet, so you don't need socks), one hat, and something nice and warm to go on top, if it's wintertime. Then buy the same for a 3-to-6-month-old (those first 12 weeks pass in a blurry flash). And then hold your nerve and wait to see what cute little outfits get showered on you after the birth. You can always buy more (if you actually need to) later.

Ten Don't-needs (Whatever the Ads Say)

I'm not going to list all my un-needed baby buys (it would take far too long and be far too embarrassing) but here, to amuse, bemuse, and protect you from bank-balance-draining folly, is a rundown of the ten items you can most safely leave out of your antenatal shopping trolley:

- ✔ **The A-list pram:** Even if you do opt for the traditional pram over the more modern buggy, don't let the latest copy of *Hello!* be your guide to what make to pick. If you do, not only will you be paying for the most expensive pram in the shop (the celebs get them for free, by the way), you'll also be paying for it in other, more annoying ways later. For as soon as your baby's born and you put pram to pavement, you'll see that every other new parent in the neighbourhood is pushing the same set of wheels as you – which rather blunts your cutting-edge style and makes finding the right pram after mother-and-toddler group a bit of a nightmare. And don't forget that, should you have another baby in a year or so, what you'll be wheeling out then will be frankly passé on the celeb pram circuit. No, forget the pram that Gwyneth chose, and get something reliably, anonymously neutral.

- ✔ **The baby bath:** There really is no need to get a special bit of moulded plastic with pictures of baby ducks; for the few short weeks before your baby (and you) are ready to take to the big bath, you can wash her perfectly well in the sink (cover the taps with a towel) or in a common-or-garden washing-up bowl.

- ✔ **The cradle:** It may be a shiny thing of beauty next to a flimsy-looking Moses basket, but you can't carry it round the house with you (so it's up to the bedroom every time your baby has a snooze) and the hard wooden sides are not much appreciated by babies who wriggle in their sleep. And where are you going to put it when your baby's grown out of it?

✔ **The state-of-the-art baby monitor:** A bit controversial this one, I know, but, think about it: Unless you live in a 25-room mansion (and your baby's in her own separate wing), do you honestly think that you won't hear your child when she cries? If having some technical reassurance that your listening skills are up to scratch really will make you feel better, get a cheap, basic monitor but I suggest you don't waste your money on a digital, two-way, nightlight-sporting, lullaby-playing, sound-and-vision monstrosity.

✔ **Designer baby clothes:** It's gorgeous, it's stylish – and it's dry-clean-only cashmere. Er, maybe save the fancy threads for the projectile-vomit-free years?

✔ **Co-ordinating everything:** Repeat aloud daily: No one judges your ability to be a good parent by how well the fabric of your changing bag matches the fabric on your pram muff.

✔ **The electric swing:** It sounds so delightful in theory – a little seat for your baby that swings her to and fro and plays her lovely tunes. Cut to everyday reality: A little seat with a huge room-cluttering frame that swings your baby to and fro and makes a dreadful, drive-you-mad plinky, plonky racket. Delightful? I think not.

✔ **The changing station:** No pregnancy-magazine dream nursery is complete without a changing station nestling in a corner next to the matching mini wardrobe, but don't let this vision of equipment perfection fool you one bit. A changing station is, essentially, a rather over-priced platform to put your changing mat on – the idea being that changing nappies is easier if your baby's higher up. But, as soon as your baby can wiggle her body about (and that can happen at 8 weeks), she can wiggle off a rather over-priced platform and do herself a nasty injury. Stay safe (and platform-free) by putting the changing mat in the middle of your bed or, better still, changing him on the floor from the start.

✔ **The 'hygienic' nappy-disposal unit:** Here's the sales pitch – why sully yourself stuffing dirty nappies into nappy bags when you can pop them in this handy unit and it'll bag them up for you and store them tidily away until it's full enough for you to empty it into an outside dustbin? Well, call me stupid, but I reckon you'll probably be sullied already from wiping off the bottom that dirtied the nappy. And why on earth would you want to have umpteen smelly nappies, however tidily stored away, festering for days in a plastic box in your house? Yuk.

✔ **Loads of toys:** Newborns don't do toys (for more on this, see Chapter 10). And, anyway, I'll lay bets that any relatives who don't bring you teensy-weensy babygros will bring you cuddly rabbits and six-foot teddies instead.

Index

• A •

acceptance, 308–309
accident
  first-aid tips, 353–356
  potty-training process, 156–157, 159
  safe play, 199
  schoolchildren, 289
activity mat, 122
acute otitis media, 140
advertising, 282
advice
  from mother-in-law, 31
  from other parents, 30–31
  worthless, 42
affection
  favoured siblings, 338
  preschooler's values, 230
  reaction to baby sibling, 324
  schoolchild's embarrassment, 311
  tantrum response, 170
  time with partner, 29
after-school activities, 310–311
after-school care, 52
aggression, 171–172, 332
Ahlberg, Allan and Janet (*Starting School*),
  268
airbag, 361
allergy
  milk, 180
  overview, 142
  solid foods, 94, 101
almond oil, 109
anaphylaxis, 142
anger
  follow-through with discipline, 23
  potty-training accident, 156

preparation for baby sibling, 321
preschooler's behaviour, 226–227
preschooler's eating habits, 235
reaction to baby sibling, 324–325
schoolchild's behaviour, 298–299
schoolchild's friendship challenges, 307
tantrum response, 166–167, 172
tips for keeping cool, 349–352
toddler's eating habits, 179, 183
animal bite, 356
apology, 228, 352
arguing
  baby stage, 73
  parental teamwork, 28
  sibling squabbles, 329–335
artwork, 47, 257
Association of Breastfeeding Mothers, 79
asthma, 143
attachment parenting, 67
attention, of parent
  boundary enforcement, 24
  favoured sibling, 338, 339
  needy sibling, 339
  oldest child, 343
  reaction to baby sibling, 325
  rude language, 227
  schoolchild's behaviour, 299
  sibling squabbles, 330–331
  tantrum triggers, 168
attention span, child's, 128
attitude
  importance, 35
  mantras for parenting challenges, 40–42
  only children, 345
  parent's response after sibling's birth,
    326–327
  schoolchild's values, 313
  schoolchild's view of school, 267–268

au pair, 52
autism, 134

• *B* •

baby
  activity choices, 127
  appropriate toys, 121–123, 365
  boundary setting, 18
  burping tips, 91–92
  clinginess, 63–64
  cough and cold, 137–138
  crying, 61–63
  diarrhoea, 137
  dummies, 64–66
  fatigue of parents, 64
  fever, 136–137, 354–355
  holding guidelines, 66–67
  language development, 123–127
  large-muscle movement, 117–121
  monitor, 365
  nappy tips, 67–69
  necessary items, 357–365
  newborn appearance, 61
  newborn illnesses, 131–133
  outings, 70–71
  overstimulation, 128–129
  parents' duties, 59–60
  parents' needs, 71–74
  reflux, 83–84
  routine, 70
  seat, 363
  sign language, 124–125
  social development, 125–126
  talk, 205
  television watching, 129
  vaccinations, 133–136
  vomiting, 137
baby, feeding. *See also* bottlefeeding;
    breastfeeding
  allergies, 104
  burping tips, 91–92

colic, 63
  newborn hunger, 64
  nighttime feedings, 110, 113
  outings, 71
  overview, 75
  routines, 70
  solid foods, 93–101
  winding, 89
baby sibling. *See* sibling
baby, sleeping
  baby's own room, 112–113
  baby's routine, 70
  bedtime ritual, 108–109
  benefits of sleep, 136
  biological clock, 106–107
  crying, 113–116
  dummies, 65
  family bed, 105–106
  normal pattern, 103–104
  overview, 103
  potty-training expectations, 149
  safety, 104–106
  self-calming baby, 111–113
Baby stage, of development, 10, 12
baby, weaning
  baby-led, 100
  health concerns, 136
  process, 87–88
babyish behaviour, 323–324
baby-led weaning, 100
backchat, 301
balance, 249
ball, 122, 210, 249
balloon, 210
banana, 99
bath
  bedtime ritual, 108
  needed baby items, 364
  safety, 194
battery, 192
beaker, 96
bed, toddler, 189

bedding
  baby safety, 105
  needed baby items, 358–359
  potty-training, 163
bedtime
  baby's ritual, 108–111
  bottle-quitting tips, 180
  crying, 113–116
  potty-training, 163
  preschooler's sleep pattern, 239–242
  schoolchild's ritual, 286–287
  toddler sleep problems, 187–188
bedwetting
  potty-training expectations, 149
  preschooler's sleep problems, 241–242
  schoolchild's sleep problems, 288
bee sting, 356
behaviour. *See also specific types*
  birth order, 341–345
  boundary enforcement, 20–24
  boundary-setting guidelines, 18–19
  childminder selection, 50
  child's reaction to baby sibling, 323–325
  day nursery selection, 48
  nanny selection, 51
  parenting style, 19–20
  preschoolers, 219–227, 232
  Reception/P1 surprises, 274
  sanity-saving mantras, 40–42
  schoolchildren, 293–302
  sibling labels, 340–341
  tantrum types, 166
bib, 96
bike
  preschooler activities, 250
  schoolchild's rite of passage, 313–314
  toddler activities, 210
birthday party, 253, 307
biting, 171–172
blackout lining, 110
blame, 332, 343
blanket, 105

blended family
  baby siblings, 321
  favoured siblings, 344
  tips for success, 33–34
blender, 96
blister, 139, 140
body
  hair, 289
  image, 283
body temperature
  baby's fever, 136–137
  first-aid for fever, 354–355
body weight
  baby's, 82, 90, 94
  loss, 76
  preschoolers, 237–238
  schoolchildren, 283–284
  toddlers, 176–177
bombing, 315–316
books
  attitude toward school, 268
  baby toys, 122
  insufficient content in parenting
    resources, 1
  primary school selection, 262
  sibling preparations, 320
  toddler language development, 206–207
booster seat, 96
booster step, 153, 161
boredom
  baby's biological clock, 107
  bottle-quitting tips, 180
  boundary breaking, 23–24
  schoolchild's sense of self, 310
  sibling squabbles, 330
  toddler's sleep pattern, 189
bossy behaviour, 343
bottlefeeding. *See also* feeding baby
  advantages, 88–89
  baby's refusal of bottle, 90–91
  overview, 88
  safety, 89

bottlefeeding *(continued)*
  supplementary bottles, 84–85, 88
  toddler's eating habits, 180–181
  weight charts, 90
  working parents, 85, 87
bouncy chair, 96
boundaries. *See also* discipline
  blended families, 33
  enforcement, 20–24
  guidelines for setting, 18–19
  management of schoolchild's
    behaviour, 295
  overview, 17
  parenting style, 19–20
  rationale, 18
  sibling squabbles, 330
  youngest child, 344
bowl, 96
box play, 211
boys
  friendship choices, 306
  gender differences in Reception/P1, 271
  language development, 126–127
  nappy changes, 68
  newborn clinginess, 63–64
  potty-training expectations, 149
  potty-training process, 156, 160–161
  primary school selection, 262
  Reception/P1 challenges, 273
  schoolchild's sense of self, 309
brainstorming ideas, 297
breadstick, 285
breakfast, 270, 282
breast
  cancer, 76
  newborn's, 61
  pump, 85–86, 87
breastfeeding. *See also* feeding baby
  advantages, 76
  arrival of milk, 81
  baby's refusal of bottle, 90–91
  breast pumps, 85–86

challenges, 76–77
dummies argument, 65
myths, 77–78
oral thrush, 132
overview, 75–76
process, 79–80
public feedings, 86
reasons for quitting, 81–83
return to work, 55
solid food supplements, 95
supplementary bottles, 84–85
tips for success, 78–79
toddler's milk drinking, 180
vaccinations, 135
weaning tips, 87–88
breathing problems, 101, 143
bricks and blocks, 122, 212
brother. *See* sibling
Brownies (children's group), 311
brushing teeth, 178, 232, 288
bubble blowing, 127
buggy, 362
building block, 122, 212
bullying, 277
burn, 354
burping baby, 91–92
butter, 285
button, 192

• C •

cake decorating, 213
calamine, 139, 140
calcium, 175, 176, 232
calendar, 270
calm demeanor
  involvement in sibling squabbles, 332
  preschooler's behaviour, 222
  reaction to baby sibling, 324
  schoolchild's behaviour, 299
  tantrum response, 166–167
  tips for keeping cool, 349–352

calorie requirements, 174, 232
camping, 312
car seat, 360–361
car travel, 63, 362
caretaking tasks, 27
cat, 207
catching skill, 249
cause and effect, 247
certification, 51
chalk, 212
changing equipment, 359, 365
charity, 313
check-up, 135
cheeky comment, 301
cheese, 178
chickenpox, 139
Child Accident Prevention Trust (*How
    Safe Is Your Child In the Garden?*), 195
Child Bereavement Trust (Web site), 315
childcare. *See also specific types*
    baby sibling, 321–322
    baby's social development, 126
    benefits, 56
    older kids, 52
    options, 43–47, 52
    overview, 43
    parent's guilt, 55–56
    potty-training preparations, 152
    potty-training process, 155
    tips for working with carers, 54
    transition tips, 53
    working routine, 55
childminder
    benefits and drawbacks, 44–45
    care for older kids, 52
    selection, 49–50
childproofing tips, 121, 194
choices, giving children
    after-school activities, 311
    preparation for baby sibling, 321
    preschooler's behaviour, 222, 223
    schoolchild's consequences, 300

schoolchild's friends, 305–306
    tantrum tactics, 169
choking
    first-aid tips, 355–356
    solid foods, 99
    toddler's food, 176, 197
chores
    blended family, 33
    chores after birth, 60
    favoured sibling, 340
    importance, 37
    marriage during baby stage, 73
    nanny selection, 51
    support for single parent, 33
    teamwork, 27
    toddler play, 211, 215
    working parent, 55
    youngest child, 344
chores, schoolchild's
    boredom, 310
    responsibility, 302–303, 312
    values, 313
Christmas show, 274
cleaning supplies, 193
clinginess, 63–64
clock, 110, 188
cloth nappy, 67–68, 360
clothes
    attitude toward school, 268
    bedtime, 107
    breastfeeding tips, 86
    fine-motor development, 212
    needed baby items, 364, 365
    outings with baby, 71
    play safety, 199
    potty-training preparations, 150, 153, 154
    preschooler's skills, 251
    schoolchild's safety, 291
    sibling squabbles, 333
    tips for Reception/P1, 270
clutter, 27
code word, 298

coin, 192
cold illness, 137–138
colic, 62–63, 78
colostrum, 81
communication
  baby's language development, 123–124
  involvement in sibling squabbles, 332
  marriage during baby stage, 74
  parental teamwork, 28
  parent-carer, 54
  parent-teacher, 278–280
  play with toddler, 215
  reaction to baby sibling, 325
  schoolchildren's friendship challenges,
    307
  time with partner, 29
  tips for keeping cool, 351
community
  nursery, 255
  support, 32–33
comparing children, 38, 341
competitive parent
  parenting pitfalls, 38
  Reception/P1 surprises, 274
  unwanted advice, 30–31
Complete Guide To Baby Signing (Garcia),
  125
compromise, 297
computer game, 316
confidence
  boundary enforcement, 21
  oldest child, 342
  only child, 345
  preschool preparation, 259
  schoolchild's friendship challenges, 307
  schoolchild's sense of self, 307–312
  streaming, 278
conjunctivitis, 139–140
consequences
  aggressive behaviour, 171–172
  boundary enforcement, 22
  follow-through, 23

parental teamwork, 28
preschooler's behaviour, 224
rationale for boundaries, 18
schoolchild's behaviour, 295, 300–301
tantrum response, 170
consistency
  boundary enforcement, 20–21
  follow-through, 23
  importance, 37
  potty-training, 148
  tantrum response, 170, 171
constipation, 101, 161
contact book, 279
contraceptive, 78
controlled crying, 115
controlling parent, 169
conversation, 204–205, 307
cooking
  preschooler's eating habits, 236, 237
  preschooler's play, 251
  schoolchild's eating habits, 284
  toddler's eating habits, 179
  toddler's safety, 193
coping skills, 72
cords, blind, 192
co-sleeping, 105–106
costume, 274
cot, 358–359, 360
cough and cold, 137–138
countertop, 193
counting to ten, 349–350
cradle, 364
cradle cap, 131–132
crawling, 119–120
creative play, 212–213
criticism
  bottle-feeding opinions, 88
  only children, 345
  preschooler's behaviour, 224
  relationship with partner, 73
  schoolchild's sense of self, 308
crossing streets, 198–199, 291

crying
  bedtime, 113–116, 186
  breastfeeding tips, 79
  dummies, 64–66
  first day of preschool, 260
  newborns, 61–63
  Reception/P1 challenges, 274
  reflux, 84
  transition to childcare, 53, 54
Cry-sis helpline, 116
Cubs (children's group), 311
cuddling
  bedtime ritual, 108
  benefits, 136
  breastfeeding advantages, 76
  colicky babies, 63
  crying babies, 62
  nighttime crying, 115
cup
  baby's refusal of bottle, 91
  readiness, 101–102
  toddler's eating habits, 180
cupboard, 193
curiosity, 220, 246–247
curriculum, 275
curtains, 110, 188, 192
cuts and scrapes, 289, 353–354

• *D* •

dancing, 211, 311
dating, 29, 73
day nursery, 44, 47–49
daylight, 106
death, 314–315
debating, 225
decision making, 220, 222
decongestant vaporiser, 138
decorating cakes, 213
deep breathing, 81
defiance, 227
democratic approach, 20, 24
dentist, 288

depression, 72, 326
dermatitis, 138
developmental stage. *See also specific stages*
  overview, 10
  potty-training readiness, 148–149
  sanity-saving attitude, 41
  settled/unsettled phases, 12
diarrhoea, 101, 137
dieting, 283
digital thermometer, 136
diptheria, 133
discipline. *See also* boundaries
  preschoolers, 228–230
  tantrum response, 166–172
  toddler safety, 196–197
dislocated joint, 200
disposable nappy, 67–68
distraction
  preschooler's behaviour, 223–224
  sibling squabbles, 330–331
  tantrum tactics, 169, 170
  toddler safety, 198
divorce, 315
dog, 200, 207, 356
do-it-all parent, 39
doll, 325
door, opening, 291
drawing, 212, 250
dressing-up box, 244
dummy, 64–66

E •

easy-going parent, 20
eczema, 138, 142–143
eggs, 101
electric pump, 85
electric swing, 365
electronic communication, 29
empathy
  preschooler's behaviour, 229–230, 244
  schoolchild's values, 313

encouragement
  gender differences, 309, 310
  homework, 272
enthusiasm
  favoured sibling, 338
  preschooler's play, 247
  sanity-saving mantras, 41
environment
  allergies, 142
  crying babies, 62
  day nursery selection, 47–48
  preschool selection, 257
  primary school selection, 261–262
evangelist approach, 30
ex-partner, 32
expectations
  importance, 37
  only children, 345
  potty-training, 148–150, 155
  preschool preparation, 260
  preschooler's behaviour, 221, 228
  schoolchild's friendship challenges, 307
  schoolchild's values, 313
  sibling labels, 341
  success after birth of sibling, 328
  summer-born child in Reception/P1, 273
  tantrum triggers, 168, 169
  tips for keeping cool, 350
  toys, 39–40
explanations, lengthy, 170
expressing milk, 81, 85–86
eyes
  contact during communication, 124, 129
  health care, 289
  newborn appearance, 61

• F •

face, newborn's, 61
fairness
  boundary enforcement, 21, 22
  parenting style, 20

preschooler's values, 229
schoolchild's consequences, 300
schoolchild's feelings, 302
family
  bed, 105–106, 188
  childcare back-ups, 54
  versus couple, 27
  help after childbirth, 60
  life after baby sibling, 327
  mealtimes, 284
  meeting, 24, 297–298
  remarriage, 33–34
  support for single parent, 32
  togetherness, 27
fatigue
  life after baby sibling, 327
  marriage during baby stage, 73
  newborn stage, 64
  preschool attendance, 260
  preschooler's eating habits, 237
  relationship with partner, 26
  tantrum triggers, 168
fats, 232, 282
fear
  common worries, 14
  potty-training process, 160
  preparation for baby sibling, 321
  preschool preparation, 259
  preschooler's sleep problems, 240
  preschooler's television watching, 248
  schoolchild's sleep problems, 287
febrile convulsion, 355
feeding baby. *See also* bottlefeeding;
    breastfeeding
  allergies, 104
  burping tips, 91–92
  colic, 63
  newborn hunger, 64
  nighttime feedings, 110, 113
  outings, 71
  overview, 75
  routines, 70

solid foods, 93–101
winding, 89
feeding preschoolers, 231–238
feeding toddlers
  food choices, 174–176
  overview, 173–174
  parents' complaints, 178–183
  table manners, 176
  tooth care, 177–178
  weight gain, 176–177
fever
  baby, 136–137
  first-aid tips, 354–355
fine motor development
  preschoolers, 249–250
  toddlers, 211–213
finger foods, 98–99, 181
fingerpaint, 212–213
fire safety, 194
firm but fair parent, 20
first-aid, 192, 353–356
first-born child, 326–327
flushing toilet, 160
following through
  boundary enforcement, 22–23
  preschooler's behaviour, 226
  schoolchild's behaviour, 300
fontanelle, 61
food
  allergies, 94, 101, 142
  breastfeeding myths, 78
  choices for toddlers, 174–176
  outings with baby, 71
  picky preschoolers, 231–237
  preschool selection, 258
  preschooler's weight, 237–238
  schoolchild's habits, 281–285
  sensitivities, 69
  tips for Reception/P1, 270
  toddler-feeding facts, 174
  toddler's eating habits, 178–183

food, solid
  allergies, 101
  choices, 98–101
  feeding process, 96–98
  overview, 93
  safety, 99
  supplies, 95–96
  timing, 93–95
foremilk, 80
forgiveness, 23, 170, 301
formula feeding. *See* bottlefeeding
friendship
  among parents, 29–31
  attitude toward school, 268
  childcare, 52
  imaginary, 245
  preschooler's play, 251–253
  preschooler's poor behaviour, 221
  teasing and bullying, 277
  tips for Reception/P1, 272–273
  toddler's play, 213–216
friendship, schoolchild's
  challenges, 306–307
  child's behaviour, 294
  choices, 305–306
  rites of passage, 314
fruit
  preschooler's healthy choices, 232
  refusal to potty, 161
  schoolchild's healthy choices, 282, 285
  toddler's healthy choices, 175, 179
fruit juice
  cup training, 102
  preschooler's eating habits, 235
  toddler's food choices, 176, 182
frustration, 166, 168, 221
fundraising, 313
funeral, 314–315
furniture, 192, 322
fussy eater, 182, 183

• *G* •

games, 250

Garcia, Joseph (*Complete Guide To Baby Signing*), 125

garden, 195, 236, 284

gate, 194

genitals, 61

gift, 323

Gingerbread (Web site), 32

girls
  bottom-wiping technique, 160
  friendship choices, 306
  gender differences in Reception/P1, 271
  language development, 126–127
  nappy changes, 68
  potty-training expectations, 149
  potty-training process, 156, 161
  primary school selection, 262
  puberty, 289–290
  schoolchild's sense of self, 310

gluing, 213, 250–251

grains, 175, 232

grandparent
  advice from, 31
  childcare options, 46–47

grapeseed oil, 109

grief, 314–315

gross motor skills
  baby, 117–121
  preschoolers, 249–250
  toddlers, 209–211

growth spurt
  newborn hunger, 64
  reasons for not breastfeeding, 82–83
  settled/unsettled phases, 12
  timing of solid foods, 94

guilt
  bottlefeeding, 88
  favoured sibling, 339
  jar food, 101
  return to work, 55–56
  sanity-saving attitude, 41

smacked child, 172

time with partner, 29

• *H* •

Haemophilus influenzae type b bacteria, 133, 134

hand
  preference, 212, 251
  washing, 157

hand-foot-mouth disease, 140

head
  lice, 290
  newborn appearance, 61
  newborn illnesses, 131–132

healthy practices
  first-aid tips, 353–356
  importance, 37
  schoolchild's eating habits, 281–285
  toddler food choices, 174–176
  vaccinations, 133–136

heat rash, 138

height, 209

helmet, 210

highchair, 96, 193

hindmilk, 80

hitting, 324

hobby, 310–311

holding babies
  first year, 10
  guidelines, 66–67

homework, 272

honesty
  characteristics of good parenting, 36
  preschooler's pretend play, 245
  preschooler's values, 229
  schoolchild's misbehaviour, 301
  time with partner, 29

hot drink, 193

housework
  blended family, 33
  chores after birth, 60
  favoured sibling, 340

importance, 37
marriage during baby stage, 73
nanny selection, 51
support for single parent, 33
teamwork, 27
toddler play, 211, 215
working parent, 55
youngest child, 344
housework, schoolchild's
  boredom, 310
  responsibility, 302–303, 312
  values, 313
hover parent, 39, 345
How Safe Is Your Child In the Garden?
  (Child Accident Prevention Trust), 195
hug, 170
humour
  preschooler's eating habits, 237
  sanity-saving attitude, 40–41
  schoolchild's comments, 312
  tantrum response, 169
  tips for keeping cool, 351
hunger, 168
husband. *See* partner

• I •

ice pack, 353
ice-skating, 312
ignoring behaviour, 222, 331, 350
illness. *See also specific illnesses*
  first-aid tips, 353–356
  newborns, 131–133
  reasons for not breastfeeding, 83
  vaccinations, 133–136
imagination, 244–245
immunity, 76
impetigo, 291
incorrect sleep association, 115
independence
  potty-training process, 159
  preschooler's behaviour, 220
  schoolchild's sense of self, 309

sibling squabbles, 334
  tantrum triggers, 168
independent play, 214–215
indulged kid, 39–40
infant. *See* baby
infant carrier, 361
Infants (school), 275–278
infectious illness, 139–141
insecurity, 308
instructions, 124
Internet safety, 316
interruption, 227

• J •

jealousy, 324–325
joint dislocation, 200
joke, 312
juice
  cup training, 102
  preschooler's eating habits, 235
  toddler's food choices, 176, 182
jumping, 211
Juniors (school), 275–278
justice, 229, 301

• K •

keyworker, 48
kicking balls, 210
kids. *See specific ages*
kitchen
  safety, 193–194
  utensils, 122

• L •

La Leche League (support group), 79
label
  food, 175, 282
  objects, 205
labeling kids, 38, 340–341
lamp, 110

language development
  babies, 123–127
  dummies, 65
  potty-training preparations, 151
  preschooler's growth, 248
  preschooler's poor behaviour, 222
  reaction to baby sibling, 323–324
  tantrum triggers, 169
  toddlers, 203–208
lanugo, 61
latching on
  arrival of milk, 81
  importance, 78
  process, 79–80
  reasons for not breastfeeding, 82
laughter
  preschooler's eating habits, 237
  sanity-saving attitude, 40–41
  schoolchild's comments, 312
  tantrum response, 169
  tips for keeping cool, 351
lava lamp, 110
lawn, 195
library, 127
lifestyle change
  characteristics of good parenting, 36
  marital changes, 26
  overview, 9
  teamwork between parents, 28
listening
  baby's cries, 62
  favoured sibling, 338
  importance, 37
  involvement in sibling squabbles, 332
  parent-teacher communication,
    279–280
  school tasks, 275
  schoolchild's behaviour, 296–297
  toddler's language development, 205
literacy skills
  preschooler's development, 248
  preschooler's play, 244

Reception/P1 tips, 271–272
  school readiness, 263
lock
  car, 198
  cupboard, 193
  doors, 194
  gardening tools, 195
losing games, 302
lost child, 291
loud voice, 228
love, 230, 337–340
low-birth-weight baby, 90
lunch, 70, 271, 285
lying, 301

• *M* •

magnet, 193
manipulation, 226–227
manners
  boundary-setting guidelines, 19
  preschooler's behaviour, 228–229
  schoolchild's behaviour, 303–304
  toddler feedings, 176
manual pump, 85
marriage
  baby stage, 72–74
  blended family, 33–34
  changes to relationship, 26
  co-sleeping, 106
  divorce, 315
  teamwork, 26–28
  time with spouse, 28–29
massage, 109
mastitis, 80
materialism, 39–40
maths
  P4-P5 tasks, 276
  primary school selection, 262
  P2-P3 tasks, 275
mattress, 105, 163
maturity, 345

mayo, 285

measles, 134

meat, 181

meconium, 67

medication
  breastfeeding, 77, 81
  toddlerproofed home, 194

memory, 128–129, 247

meningitis, 133, 141

mentor, 33

menu plan, 237, 284

middle child, 342, 343–344

Middlemiss, Prisca (*What's That Rash?*), 139

milia, 61

milk
  breastfeeding supply, 81, 84
  schoolchild's healthy choices, 282
  spots, 61
  toddler's eating habits, 179–180, 182

mirror, 122

misbehaviour. *See* behaviour

mistake making, 297

mobile, 69, 122

money
  baby items, 358
  day nursery selection, 48
  lifestyle changes, 26
  marriage during baby stage, 73
  schoolchild's reward, 296
  schoolchild's rite of passage, 314

moodiness, 289–290

morning, 188–189, 239

Moses basket, 105, 358

mother-and-baby group, 70

mother-in-law, 31

motor development. *See* gross motor skills

movement
  babies, 117–121
  preschooler's eating habits, 237, 238
  preschooler's play, 249–251

toddler activity options, 209–213

toddler's weight, 177

mumps, 134

Mumsnet (Web site), 32

music lesson, 311

muslin, 71, 86, 92

Mustard Seed Relief Mission's Love in a Box (charity), 313

• N •

nagging, 159

name-calling, 332

nametape, 270

nanny
  benefits and drawbacks, 45–46
  selection, 50–52

Nannytax (tax firm), 52

nap
  baby's biological clock, 107
  baby's routine, 70
  life after birth of sibling, 327
  newborn fatigue, 64
  potty-training preparations, 151
  potty-training process, 156
  preschoolers, 238, 239
  toddler bed, 189

nappy
  changing process, 68–69
  disposal unit, 365
  potty-training accidents, 157–158, 159
  rash, 68, 69, 132
  selection, 67–68, 71
  shopping tips, 359–360

nappy bag, 71

nasal drops, 138

national insurance, 52

nativity play, 274

natural disaster, 315–316

Natural Infant Hygiene (potty-training programme), 150

nature walk, 210

neck control, 66–67, 118
negotiation, 297
newborn. *See* baby
news programme, 315
night terror, 241
night-light, 240
nightmare
  preschooler's sleep problems, 240–241
  schoolchild's sleep problems, 287
  toddler's sleep problems, 186
nipple
  confusion, 65, 84
  shield, 82
nits, 290
noise, 106–107, 228
nosebleed, 356
note writing, 296
nudity, 154, 212
nursery, 44, 47–49
nursery rhyme, 206
nuts, 101, 176

• O •

Office For Standards in Education
    (Ofsted), 44, 48
oil, massage, 109
oldest child, 342–343
online resources
  asthma help, 143
  baby massage, 109
  baby signing, 125
  bullying, 277
  charities, 313
  childminder selection, 49
  eczema help, 143
  first-aid, 353
  garden safety, 195
  grief, 315
  mother-and-baby groups, 70
  nanny selection, 50
  nappy samples, 360
  Office For Standards in Education, 44

primary school selection, 261
puberty explanations, 290
support for single parents, 32
vaccinations, 134
only child, 345
Operation Christmas Child (charity), 312
optometrist, 289
oral thrush, 132
ornament, 192
otitis media, 140
overstimulated baby, 128–129

• P •

paint
  preschooler's activities, 250, 253
  toddler's activities, 212–213
pants, 153
paperclip, 192
paracetamol, 135, 139, 140
parallel play, 213–214, 215
parasites, 290–291
parent
  benefits of parenting, 14
  characteristics of good parents, 36–37
  common pitfalls, 38–40
  comparisons, 14
  friendships among, 29–31
  goals, 13–14
  knowledge, 14–15
  role, 13
parent, competitive
  parenting pitfalls, 38
  Reception/P1 surprises, 274
  unwanted advice, 30–31
parent, working
  bottlefeeding tips, 85, 87
  breastfeeding challenges, 77
  breastfeeding options, 87
  guilt, 55–56
  housework, 55
  preschool selection, 256
  reasons for not breastfeeding, 83

parenting style
  boundaries, 19–20
  grandparents, 47
park, 200
partner
  baby stage, 72–74
  blended family, 33–34
  changes to relationship, 26
  overview, 25–26
  preschooler's consequences, 226
  support for single parents, 32
  teamwork, 26–28
  time with spouse, 28–29
party, 253, 307
patience
  colicky baby, 63
  preschooler's behaviour, 226–227
  reaction to baby sibling, 323
peanut, 176
pedaling, 210
peekaboo, 126
perfection, 35, 54, 345
period, menstrual, 289
perseverance, 308
personality, 339, 342
phone number, 291
phonics, 271
photo album, 126, 338
piano, 311
pinworms, 290–291
plants, 195
plaster, 289, 354
plastic bag, 193
play
  baby's activities, 127
  boundary enforcement, 24
  overstimulated baby, 128–129
  parents' goals, 13–14
  pottying reminders, 159
  schoolchild's boredom, 310
  tips for Reception/P1, 271, 272, 273
  toddler safety, 199–201
  toddler's choices, 208–216

play, preschooler's
  curiosity, 246–247
  fine motor development, 249–250
  friendships, 251–253
  gender-specific toys, 245–246
  gross motor skills, 249–250
  imagination, 244–245
  overview, 243
  poor behaviour, 224
playdough, 213
playground, 127, 200, 210, 249
playgroup, 256
pneumococcal vaccine, 133
poisoning, 195, 355
poking baby, 327
polio, 133
pond, 195
P1 (school), 269–274
poo refusal, 161
poo-first potty method, 153, 154
pool safety, 201
popcorn, 285
popularity, 306
portion size
  preschooler's eating habits, 233, 235
  schoolchild's weight, 283
  toddler's eating habits, 179, 183
positive comments
  attitude toward school, 268
  discipline of preschooler, 224–225
  school reports, 278
  schoolchild's cooperation, 296
potty chair, 153, 160
potty-training
  bedtime, 163
  consistency, 148
  expectations, 148–150, 155
  overview, 147–148
  preparations, 150–154
  preschoolers, 241–242
  process, 154–161
  reaction to baby sibling, 323
  setbacks, 161–162

pouring, 212
praise
  boundary enforcement, 21, 22, 24
  favoured sibling, 338
  importance, 37
  potty-training process, 155
  preschooler's behaviour, 225, 228
  preschooler's play, 252
  schoolchild's behaviour, 295, 296
  schoolchild's sense of self, 308, 309–310
  sibling squabbles, 334
pram
  adjustment to new baby, 322
  baby's sitting position, 119
  crying baby, 62
  needed baby items, 362, 364
pregnancy planning, 320
premature baby, 94
preschool
  first day, 258–260
  overview, 255
  plans for primary school, 260–264
  selection, 255–258
preschooler
  behaviour, 219–227, 232
  discipline, 228–230
  eating habits, 231–237
  potty-training, 241–242
  sleep patterns, 238–242
  television watching, 236, 247–248
  tooth care, 232
  values, 229–230
  weight, 237–238
Preschooler stage, of development, 11, 12
preschooler's play
  curiosity, 246–247
  fine motor development, 249–250
  friendships, 251–253
  gender-specific toys, 245–246
  gross motor skills, 249–250
  imagination, 244–245

overview, 243
poor behaviour, 224
present, 323
pretend play, 244–245
primary school, 260–264
privacy, 290, 316, 334
private nursery, 256
privilege, 296
problem solving, 332–333
protein
  baby food, 99
  preschooler's healthy choices, 232
  schoolchild's healthy choices, 282
  toddler's healthy choices, 175, 181
P2-P7 (school), 275–278
puberty, 289–290
public place
  embarrassing questions, 246
  feedings, 86
  tantrums, 171
pull-ups, 157–158
purées, 98, 100
pushchair, 361–363
pushing, 171–172
puzzle, 212, 250

questions
  childminder selection, 49–50
  day nursery selection, 48
  nanny selection, 51
  parent-teacher communication,
    279–280
  preparation for baby sibling, 321
  preschool selection, 257–258
  preschooler's curiosity, 246, 247
  primary school selection, 262
  Reception/P1 surprises, 274
  toddler's language development, 205

• R •

raincover, 71
rash
  allergies, 101, 142
  chickenpox, 139
  fever, 355
  nappy, 68, 69, 132
  overview, 138–139
  roseola, 140
  teething, 133
rattle, 71, 122
reading
  attitude toward school, 268
  P4-P5 tasks, 276
  preschooler's skills, 248
  P2/P3 tasks, 275
  Reception/P1 tips, 271–272
  record book, 279
  schoolchild's bedtime ritual, 287
  toddler's skills, 206–207
reasoning skill, 220, 225, 294
Reception (school), 269–274
record keeping, 55
Red Cross (first-aid resource), 353
redirection, 222
reference check
  childminder, 50
  day nursery, 49
  nanny, 51, 52
reflective play, 214
reflux, 83–84
repeated words, 124
respect, 28, 54
responsibility
  schoolchildren, 302–303, 308
  youngest child, 344
restaurant, 285
reusable nappy, 67–68
reward
  boundary enforcement, 21
  potty-training setbacks, 162

preschooler's behaviour, 223
  preschooler's eating habits, 236
  sleeping late, 189
reward, schoolchild's
  behaviour, 295–296, 300
  chores, 303
  eating habits, 282
  sense of self, 309, 310
rice, 96–97
role model
  boundary-setting guidelines, 19
  housework responsibilities, 302
  importance, 13
  potty-training preparations, 151
  preschooler's eating habits, 235
  preschooler's manners, 229
  Reception/P1 friendships, 272–273
  sibling squabbles, 334
  street safety, 199
  support for single parents, 33
  table manners, 176
  toddler safety, 197
  toddler's eating habits, 177
rollerskating, 312
rolling, 118
romance, 29, 34
rooting reflex, 78
roseola, 140
routine
  babies, 70
  breastfeeding tips, 78–79
  childminder selection, 50
  day nursery selection, 48
  importance, 37
  nanny selection, 51
  plan after baby sibling, 328
  preparation for baby sibling, 322
  preschool selection, 258
  tantrum triggers, 168
  transition to childcare, 53
rubella, 134

rude language
preschooler's behaviour, 227
schoolchild's behaviour, 301
schoolchild's comments, 311–312
rules. *See* discipline
blended families, 33
enforcement, 20–24
guidelines for setting, 18–19
management of schoolchild's
behaviour, 295
overview, 17
parenting style, 19–20
rationale, 18
sibling squabbles, 330
youngest child, 344

• S •

sadness
transition to childcare, 53, 54
weaning tips, 88
safety
bottlefeeding, 89
car seat, 361
child's reaction to baby sibling, 324
parents' fears, 14
rationale for boundaries, 18
schoolchildren, 291, 316
sleep, 104–106
solid foods, 99
tantrum triggers, 168
toys, 123
safety, toddler
bedtime, 189
childproofing tips, 191–197
feedings, 176
play, 215
St John Ambulance (first aid resource),
353
salt, 175
SATs (assessments), 276
saucepan, 193
scabies, 291
scalded child, 354

school
attitude of child, 267–268
Infants/Juniors or P2-P7, 275–278
lunches, 285
parent-teacher communication,
278–280
Reception or P1, 269–274
schoolchildren's behaviour, 293, 294
school nursery, 255
schoolchild
accidents, 289
after-school activities, 310–311
attitude toward school, 267–268
behaviour, 294–302
computer game, 316
eating habits, 281–285
friendship choices and challenges,
305–307
housework, 302–303
Infants/Juniors or P2-P7, 275–278
major life events, 314–316
manners, 303–304
must-do activities, 312
parasites, 290–291
puberty, 289–290
Reception or P1, 269–274
safety tips, 291
sense of self, 307–312
surprising comments, 311–312
television, 283, 287, 316
tooth care, 288–289
values, 312–314
Schoolchild stage, of development, 11, 12
schoolchild's friendship
challenges, 306–307
child's behaviour, 294
choices, 305–306
rites of passage, 314
schoolchild's reward
behaviour, 295–296, 300
chores, 303
eating habits, 282
sense of self, 309, 310

schoolchild's sleep pattern
  bedwetting, 288
  required hours of sleep, 286
  rituals, 286–287
  tips for Reception/P1, 270
science, 262
scissors, 251
scooter, 210
seatbelt, 197, 198
self-esteem, 229
self-respect, 308–309
sex
  co-sleeping, 106
  marriage during baby stage, 73
  preschooler's curiosity, 247
  schoolchild's knowledge, 290
shadowing year, 10–11
sharing
  only children, 345
  preschooler's play, 251–252
  sibling squabbles, 333
  toddler's play, 213–214
shed, 195
shellfish, 101
shepherding year, 11
shoes, 120, 121
shopping
  baby items, 358
  preschooler's eating habits, 236
  tantrums, 171
  working parents, 55
shouting, 167, 225–226
sibling
  age gaps, 319–320
  birth order, 341–345
  common reactions to new baby,
    323–327
  favoured child, 337–340
  introduction to baby sibling, 322–323
  labels, 340–341
  parent's feelings after sibling birth,
    326–327
  plan for success, 328

preparation for baby sibling, 320–322
  reaction to baby sibling, 323–327
  Reception/P1 surprises, 274
  schoolchild's consequences, 300
sibling squabbles
  distraction, 330–331
  overview, 329–330
  parent involvement, 331–333
  shared property, 333
SIDS (sudden infant death syndrome),
    104–105
sign language, 124–125
Simply Childcare (Web site), 50
singing, 110, 127, 206
single parent, 32–34
sister. *See* sibling
sitting, 119
skin condition. *See specific conditions*
slapping child, 172, 300
sleep
  cycles, 112
  deprivation, 64
  preschoolers, 238–242
  training, 115–116, 185–186
sleep pattern, baby's
  baby's own room, 112–113
  baby's routine, 70
  bedtime ritual, 108–109
  benefits of sleep, 136
  biological clock, 106–107
  crying, 113–116
  dummies, 65
  family bed, 105–106
  normal pattern, 103–104
  overview, 103
  potty-training expectations, 149
  safety, 104–106
  self-calming baby, 111–113
sleep pattern, schoolchild's
  bedwetting, 288
  required hours of sleep, 286
  rituals, 286–287
  tips for Reception/P1, 270

sleep pattern, toddler's
  length of sleep, 185–187
  night wakings, 185–189
  overview, 185
  refusal to go to bed, 187–188
sleeping bag, 111
sleepover, 314
slides, 127, 210
sling, 66, 119, 363
smacking child, 172, 300
smiling, 279
smoke alarm, 194
smoking, 105, 135
snacking
  preschooler's eating habits,
    232, 235, 238
  preschooler's playdate, 253
  schoolchild's eating habits, 283
  toddler's eating habits, 175, 177, 182
soap, 143, 290
social skills
  babies, 125–126
  benefits of childcare, 56
  preschoolers, 251–253
  schoolchildren, 305–307
  toddlers, 213–216
socket, 192
softplay center, 249
solid food
  allergies, 101
  choices, 98–101
  feeding process, 96–98
  overview, 93
  safety, 99
  supplies, 95–96
  timing, 93–95
sorting, 212
special needs, children with, 2, 339
splinter, 289
sports, 249, 262, 311
spouse. *See* partner

stairs, 194
stamping, 212–213
starchy food, 282
Starting School (Ahlberg), 268
steering year, 11
step-parent, 33–34, 321
sterilising supplies, 89, 96
sticker
  potty-training, 153, 155, 162
  preschooler's behaviour, 223
storing milk, 86, 87
stranger, 126, 291
straw, 178
streaming, 277–278
street safety, 198–199, 291
stress
  bedwetting, 288
  homework in Reception/P1, 272
  plan after baby sibling, 328
  potty-training setbacks, 162
  sibling labels, 340
strict parent, 19, 30
stubbornness, 162, 220
sucking, 63, 65, 78
sudden infant death syndrome (SIDS),
    104–105
sugary food
  preschooler's eating habits, 236
  schoolchild's eating habits, 282
  toddler's eating habits, 175–176, 178
summer-born child, 273
sunburn, 144
sunflower oil, 109
support, of friends, 29–31
swaddling babies, 62
swearing, 311–312
swelling, 101
swimming, 127, 201, 311
swinging, 127, 365
swings, 195
sympathy, 326–327

• T •

table manners
  boundary-setting guidelines, 19
  preschoolers, 228–229
  schoolchildren, 303
  toddlers, 176
tablecloth, 193
tantrum
  overview, 165
  preschooler's behaviour, 226–227
  proper response, 166–172
  triggers, 168–169
  types, 166
taxes, 52
teacher
  comments on school reports, 278
  communication with parents, 278–280
  introduction in Reception/P1, 269
  Reception/P1 surprises, 274
  schoolchild's behaviour, 294
team spirit, 334
teasing, 277
teeth
  bottlefeeding safety, 89
  dummies, 65
  preschoolers, 232
  schoolchildren, 288–289
  toddlers, 177–178
teething gel, 133, 135
teething pain, 132–134, 182
television
  babies, 129
  preschoolers, 236, 247–248
  schoolchildren, 283, 287, 316
  toddlers, 208
temperament, 12
temperature
  baby's room, 105
  formula, 89
  school clothes, 268
  water, 194

temperature, body
  baby's fever, 136–137
  first-aid for fever, 354–355
terrorist attack, 315–316
tetanus, 133
thank-you note, 304
thiomersal, 135
threading string, 250
threadworm, 290–291
threat, 226
throwing balls, 210
thumb sucking, 65
time
  adjustment to Reception/P1, 271
  away from colicky baby, 63
  with family, 27
  favouring siblings, 338
  homework in Reception/P1, 272
  importance, 37
  management of schoolchild's
    behaviour, 294
  marriage during baby stage, 73
  parents' needs, 72
  with partner, 28–29
  potty-training preparations, 152–153
  preschooler's curiosity, 247
  preschooler's eating habits, 234–235
  preschooler's playdate, 253
  reading, 206–207
  reasons for not breastfeeding, 82
  schoolchild's sense of self, 308
  schoolchild's television/computer
    habits, 316
  sibling squabbles over property, 333
  tantrums, 167
  tips for keeping cool, 350
  toddler's eating habits, 183
  toddler's TV watching, 208
  versus toys, 40
  weaning tips, 88
time out
  preschooler's consequences, 223–224
  schoolchild's consequences, 299
  tips for keeping cool, 350

toddler
  car safety, 197–199
  fever, 355
  home safety, 191–197
  language development, 203–208
  play options, 208–216
  safe play, 199–201
toddler, feeding
  food choices, 174–176
  overview, 173–174
  parents' complaints, 178–183
  table manners, 176
  tooth care, 177–178
  weight gain, 176–177
toddler, potty-training
  bedtime, 163
  consistency, 148
  expectations, 148–150, 155
  overview, 147–148
  preparations, 150–154
  preschoolers, 241–242
  process, 154–161
  reaction to baby sibling, 323
  setbacks, 161–162
toddler safety
  bedtime, 189
  childproofing tips, 191–197
  feedings, 176
  play, 215
Toddler stage, of development, 10–11, 12
toddler tantrum
  overview, 165
  preschooler's behaviour, 226–227
  proper response, 166–172
  triggers, 168–169
  types, 166
toddler's sleep pattern
  length of sleep, 185–187
  night wakings, 185–189
  overview, 185
  refusal to go to bed, 187–188
toilet seat, 153, 160
tongue-thrusting reflex, 94

toothpaste, 288
towel, 153, 159
toys
  baby's choices, 120–123, 365
  gender-specific, 245–246
  nappy changes, 69
  outing with baby, 71
  overload, 39–40
  overview, 121
  preschool selection, 257
  preschooler's play, 249–251, 252
  pretend play, 244–245
  safety, 123
  sibling squabbles, 333
  sleeping late, 189
  toddler playdates, 213–214
  toddlerproofed home, 196
traffic, 198
transitional object, 53
travel
  cars, 197–199
  cot, 360
  potty-training process, 158–159
  toddlerproofed homes, 195–196
treasure basket, 122
trike, 210, 250
trust, 125–126
tummy time, 118
twins
  attitude toward school, 268
  breastfeeding, 79
  first day at Reception/P1, 269
  lost teeth, 289
  potty-training, 152
  solid foods, 95
Twins and Multiple Births Association, 79

• U •

unconscious child, 355
uniform, 268
urinary tract infection (UTI), 242

• V •

vaccinations, 135–138
values
    characteristics of good parenting, 36
    friendships with other parents, 30
    preschoolers, 229–230
    schoolchildren, 312–314
vegetables
    preschooler's eating habits, 232
    schoolchild's eating habits,
        282, 284, 285
    toddler's eating habits, 175, 179
video, 208, 248
viral rash, 138
voice, 349
volunteering, 270, 279
vomiting, 137, 355

• W •

waiting list, 257, 264
walking
    baby's routine, 70
    first steps, 119–121
    tips for Reception/P1, 270
    toddler activities, 210
warning system, 22, 223
washing machine, 123, 193
water intake, 161, 176
water play, 210, 250, 253
water temperature, 194
weaning babies
    baby-led, 100
    health concerns, 136
    process, 87–88
weaning spoon, 96
Web sites
    asthma help, 143
    baby massage, 109
    baby signing, 125
    bullying, 277

charities, 313
childminder selection, 49
eczema help, 143
first-aid, 353
garden safety, 195
grief, 315
mother-and-baby groups, 70
nanny selection, 50
nappy samples, 360
Office For Standards in Education, 44
primary school selection, 261
puberty explanations, 290
support for single parents, 32
vaccinations, 134
weight, body
    baby's, 82, 90, 94
    loss, 76
    preschoolers, 237–238
    schoolchildren, 283–284
    toddlers, 176–177
weight, car seat, 361
What's That Rash? (Middlemiss), 139
wheat, 101
wheezing, 101, 142, 143
whining, 227
whooping cough, 133
wife. *See* partner
winding, 89, 91–92
window, 192
wipes, 69, 71
wiping bottoms, 160
Working Families Tax Credit, 44
working parent
    bottlefeeding tips, 85, 87
    breastfeeding challenges, 77
    breastfeeding options, 87
    guilt, 55–56
    housework, 55
    preschool selection, 256
    reasons for not breastfeeding, 83
workplace nursery, 256
wrap-around care, 52

writing, children's
    P4-P5 tasks, 276
    P2/P3 tasks, 275
    Reception/P1 tips, 271–272
    school readiness, 263
    thank-you notes, 304
writing, parent's, 296

• Y •

yoghurt, 181
youngest child, 342, 344

• Z •

zinc-oxide barrier cream, 69

FOR DUMMIES®

Do Anything. Just Add Dummies

HOME

UK editions

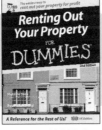

0-7645-7027-7

0-470-02921-8

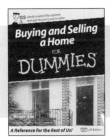

 — (DIY & Home Maintenance)

0-7645-7054-4

PERSONAL FINANCE

0-7645-7023-4

0-470-02860-2

0-7645-7039-0

BUSINESS

0-7645-7018-8

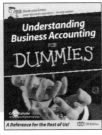

0-7645-7025-0

0-7645-7026-9

Answering Tough Interview
Questions For Dummies
(0-470-01903-4)

Arthritis For Dummies
(0-470-02582-4)

Being the Best Man
For Dummies
(0-470-02657-X)

British History
For Dummies
(0-7645-7021-8)

Building Confidence
For Dummies
(0-470-01669-8)

Buying a Property in Eastern
Europe For Dummies
(0-7645-7047-1)

Children's Health
For Dummies
(0-470-02735-5)

Cognitive Behavioural Therapy
For Dummies
(0-470-01838-0)

Cricket For Dummies
(0-470-03454-8)

CVs For Dummies
(0-7645-7017-X)

Detox For Dummies
(0-470-01908-5)

Diabetes For Dummies
(0-7645-7019-6)

Divorce For Dummies
(0-7645-7030-7)

eBay.co.uk For Dummies
(0-7645-7059-5)

European History
For Dummies
(0-7645-7060-9)

Gardening For Dummies
(0-470-01843-7)

Golf For Dummies
(0-470-01811-9)

Hypnotherapy For Dummies
(0-470-01930-1)

Irish History For Dummies
(0-7645-7040-4)

Marketing For Dummies
(0-7645-7056-0)

Neuro-linguistic Programming
For Dummies
(0-7645-7028-5)

Nutrition For Dummies
(0-7645-7058-7)

Pregnancy For Dummies
(0-7645-7042-0)

Retiring Wealthy For Dummies
(0-470-02632-4)

Rugby Union For Dummies
(0-470-03537-4)

Self Build and Renovation
For Dummies
(0-470-02586-7)

Starting a Business on
eBay.co.uk For Dummies
(0-470-02666-9)

Su Doku For Dummies
(0-470-01892-5)

The GL Diet For Dummies
(0-470-02753-3)

Thyroid For Dummies
(0-470-03172-7)

UK Law and Your Rights
For Dummies
(0-470-02796-7)

Winning on Betfair
For Dummies
(0-470-02856-4)

FOR DUMMIES®

Do Anything. Just Add Dummies

HOBBIES

Poker
0-7645-5232-5

Sewing
0-7645-6847-7

Drawing
0-7645-5476-X

Also available:

Art For Dummies
(0-7645-5104-3)

Aromatherapy For Dummies
(0-7645-5171-X)

Bridge For Dummies
(0-7645-5015-2)

Card Games For Dummies
(0-7645-9910-0)

Chess For Dummies
(0-7645-8404-9)

Improving Your Memory
For Dummies
(0-7645-5435-2)

Massage For Dummies
(0-7645-5172-8)

Meditation For Dummies
(0-471-77774-9)

Photography For Dummies
(0-7645-4116-1)

Quilting For Dummies
(0-7645-9799-X)

EDUCATION

Cooking Basics
0-7645-7206-7

The Koran
0-7645-5581-2

Anatomy & Physiology
0-7645-5422-0

Also available:

Algebra For Dummies
(0-7645-5325-9)

Algebra II For Dummies
(0-471-77581-9)

Astronomy For Dummies
(0-7645-8465-0)

Buddhism For Dummies
(0-7645-5359-3)

Calculus For Dummies
(0-7645-2498-4)

Forensics For Dummies
(0-7645-5580-4)

Islam For Dummies
(0-7645-5503-0)

Philosophy For Dummies
(0-7645-5153-1)

Religion For Dummies
(0-7645-5264-3)

Trigonometry For Dummies
(0-7645-6903-1)

PETS

Puppies
0-7645-5255-4

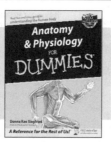

Dog Training
0-7645-8418-9

Cats
0-7645-5275-9

Also available:

Labrador Retrievers
For Dummies
(0-7645-5281-3)

Aquariums For Dummies
(0-7645-5156-6)

Birds For Dummies
(0-7645-5139-6)

Dogs For Dummies
(0-7645-5274-0)

Ferrets For Dummies
(0-7645-5259-7)

Golden Retrievers
For Dummies
(0-7645-5267-8)

Horses For Dummies
(0-7645-9797-3)

Jack Russell Terriers
For Dummies
(0-7645-5268-6)

Puppies Raising & Training
Diary For Dummies
(0-7645-0876-8)

FOR DUMMIES®

The easy way to get more done and have more fun

LANGUAGES

0-7645-5194-9

0-7645-5193-0

0-7645-5196-5

Also available:

Chinese For Dummies
(0-471-78897-X)

Chinese Phrases
For Dummies
(0-7645-8477-4)

French Phrases For Dummies
(0-7645-7202-4)

German For Dummies
(0-7645-5195-7)

Italian Phrases For Dummies
(0-7645-7203-2)

Japanese For Dummies
(0-7645-5429-8)

Latin For Dummies
(0-7645-5431-X)

Spanish Phrases
For Dummies
(0-7645-7204-0)

Spanish Verbs For Dummies
(0-471-76872-3)

Hebrew For Dummies
(0-7645-5489-1)

MUSIC AND FILM

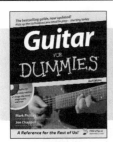

0-7645-9904-6

0-7645-2476-3

0-7645-5105-1

Also available:

Bass Guitar For Dummies
(0-7645-2487-9)

Blues For Dummies
(0-7645-5080-2)

Classical Music For Dummies
(0-7645-5009-8)

Drums For Dummies
(0-471-79411-2)

Jazz For Dummies
(0-471-76844-8)

Opera For Dummies
(0-7645-5010-1)

Rock Guitar For Dummies
(0-7645-5356-9)

Screenwriting For Dummies
(0-7645-5486-7)

Songwriting For Dummies
(0-7645-5404-2)

Singing For Dummies
(0-7645-2475-5)

HEALTH, SPORTS & FITNESS

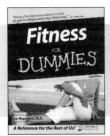

0-7645-7851-0

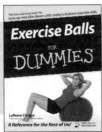

0-7645-5623-1

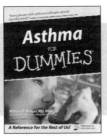

0-7645-4233-8

Also available:

Controlling Cholesterol
For Dummies
(0-7645-5440-9)

Dieting For Dummies
(0-7645-4149-8)

High Blood Pressure
For Dummies
(0-7645-5424-7)

Martial Arts For Dummies
(0-7645-5358-5)

Menopause For Dummies
(0-7645-5458-1)

Power Yoga For Dummies
(0-7645-5342-9)

Weight Training
For Dummies
(0-471-76845-6)

Yoga For Dummies
(0-7645-5117-5)

FOR DUMMIES®

Helping you expand your horizons and achieve your potential

INTERNET

The Internet FOR DUMMIES
0-7645-8996-2

Starting an Online Business FOR DUMMIES
0-7645-8334-4

Creating Web Pages FOR DUMMIES
0-7645-7327-6

Also available:

eBay.co.uk
For Dummies
(0-7645-7059-5)

Dreamweaver 8
For Dummies
(0-7645-9649-7)

Web Design
For Dummies
(0-471-78117-7)

Everyday Internet
All-in-One Desk Reference
For Dummies
(0-7645-8875-3)

Creating Web Pages
All-in-One Desk Reference
For Dummies
(0-7645-4345-8)

DIGITAL MEDIA

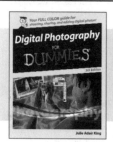

Digital Photography FOR DUMMIES
0-7645-9802-3

iPod & iTunes FOR DUMMIES
0-471-74739-4

Digital SLR Cameras & Photography FOR DUMMIES
0-7645-9803-1

Also available:

Digital Photos, Movies, &
Music GigaBook
For Dummies
(0-7645-7414-0)

Photoshop CS2
For Dummies
(0-7645-9571-7)

Podcasting
For Dummies
(0-471-74898-6)

Blogging
For Dummies
(0-471-77084-1)

Digital Photography
All-in-One Desk Reference
For Dummies
(0-7645-7328-4)

Windows XP Digital Music For
Dummies
(0-7645-7599-6)

COMPUTER BASICS

PCs FOR DUMMIES
0-7645-8958-X

Laptops FOR DUMMIES
0-7645-7555-4

Windows XP FOR DUMMIES
0-7645-7326-8

Also available:

Office XP 9 in 1
Desk Reference
For Dummies
(0-7645-0819-9)

PCs All-in-One Desk
Reference For Dummies
(0-471-77082-5)

Pocket PC For Dummies
(0-7645-1640-X)

Upgrading & Fixing PCs
For Dummies
(0-7645-1665-5)

Windows XP All-in-One Desk
Reference For Dummies
(0-7645-7463-9)

Macs For Dummies
(0-7645-5656-8)